SCHOOL OF ORIENTAL AND AFRICAN STUDIES
University of London

Please return this book on or before the last date shown

Long loans and One Week loans may be renewed up to 6 times
Short loans & CDs cannot be renewed
Fines are charges on all overdue items

E-mail: librenewals@soas.ac.uk   Phone: 020-7898 4197 (answerphone)

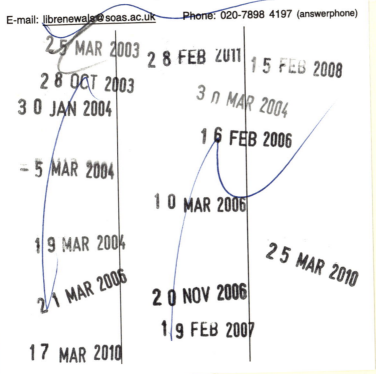

Marketizing Education and Health in Developing Countries

Marketizing Education and Health in Developing Countries

Miracle or Mirage?

Edited by

CHRISTOPHER COLCLOUGH

CLARENDON PRESS · OXFORD

1997

Oxford University Press, Great Clarendon Street, Oxford OX2 6DP
Oxford New York
Athens Auckland Bangkok Bogota Bombay
Buenos Aires Calcutta Cape Town Dar es Salaam
Delhi Florence Hong Kong Istanbul Karachi
Kuala Lumpur Madras Madrid Melbourne
Mexico City Nairobi Paris Singapore
Taipei Tokyo Toronto Warsaw
and associated companies in
Berlin Ibadan

Oxford is a trade mark of Oxford University Press

Published in the United States
by Oxford University Press Inc., New York

© *The Contributors 1997*

British Library Cataloguing in Publication Data
Data available

Library of Congress Cataloging in Publication Data
Data available

ISBN 0–19–829255–4

1 3 5 7 9 10 8 6 4 2

Typeset by BookMan Services, Ilfracombe
Printed in Great Britain
on acid-free paper by
Biddles Ltd., Guildford and King's Lynn

Preface

Governments in developing countries have, for some years, faced strong pressures to restrain public spending. National incomes often have not kept pace with population growth, causing public revenues to decline in per capita terms. Debt repayments, having grown rapidly during the 1980s, partly because of rising real interest rates on borrowed funds, have left fewer public resources available for other expenditures. Public sector deficits— initially excused as a temporary response to the oil crises and subsequent recession—have spiralled, and need to be reduced because their inflationary consequences have further undermined the prospects for a return to growth. Partly as a reaction to these developments, changes in the magnitude and composition of public expenditure have become part of the loan conditions imposed upon developing country governments by the multilateral institutions. Thus, government spending has been placed on a tighter rein, including allocations for the provision of basic services such as health and education.

Over the past two decades, however, additional arguments have been advanced which have more fundamentally questioned earlier patterns of public spending. In particular, the market place, as opposed to the bureaucracy, has been promoted by many critics as the best mechanism for organizing the production and distribution of most goods and services, including many of those that have typically remained within the purview of the state. Although such arguments have always characterized the liberal tradition in economics, they have recently been advanced with greater stridency than in the past, and have also been used to advocate the reduction of public involvement in the provision and financing of education and health services, notwithstanding the important impact these services can have upon the standards of living of the poorest members of the population.

This book, using evidence from a large number of developing countries, asks whether, and to what extent, these recent critics of the public provision and financing of health and education services are correct. It examines the arguments for market reforms in the two sectors, evaluates their effects, and draws conclusions from this experience, of benefit for policy.

Most of the chapters in the book were initially presented as papers at a Workshop on New Approaches to Financing Health and Education Systems in Developing Countries, held at the Institute of Development Studies in March 1994. The original papers were extensively revised after the Workshop, and a number of new ones were commissioned, in order to provide a more comprehensive coverage of the issues. The editor wishes to thank both the British Council and the Overseas Development Administration for pro-viding grants to cover Workshop costs, air fares for some of the participants, and some of the subsequent research costs involved in producing the book.

C.C.

Brighton
March 1996

Contents

Contents

List of Contributors

SAJITHA BASHIR   Consultant, District Primary Education Programme, New Delhi

SARA BENNETT   Economist, Health Policy Unit, Department of Public Health and Policy, London School of Hygiene and Tropical Medicine

NANCY BIRDSALL   Executive Vice President, Inter-American Bank

GERALD BLOOM   Fellow, Institute of Development Studies, Sussex

MARK BRAY   Reader in Education, University of Hong Kong

ROBIN BURGESS   Research Officer, STICERD, London School of Economics

CHRISTOPHER COLCLOUGH   Professorial Fellow, Institute of Development Studies, Sussex

ANDREW CREESE   Chief, National Health Systems and Policies, Division of Strengthening of Health Services, World Health Organisation, Geneva

ROBERT HECHT   Principal Economist, The World Bank

ELIZABETH KING   Senior Economist, The World Bank

JOSEPH KUTZIN   National Health Systems and Policies, Division of Strengthening of Health Services, World Health Organisation, Geneva

ANNE MILLS   Professor and Head, Health Policy Unit, Department of Public Health and Policy, London School of Hygiene and Tropical Medicine

CHARLES NORMAND   Professor and Head, Department of Public Health and Policy, London School of Hygiene and Tropical Medicine

J. B. G. TILAK   Professor and Head, Educational Finance Unit, National Institute of Education Planning and Administration, New Delhi

PART I

Introduction

1

Education, Health, and the Market: An Introduction

CHRISTOPHER COLCLOUGH

Many service systems—for example those providing legal, financial, business, accounting, surveying, or architectural services—are privately organized, with professional bodies regulating entry and monitoring the competence of service providers. Consumers are generally expected to pay market rates for these services, and the state typically abstains from intervention in their provision and finance, or does so only minimally. By contrast, education and health services have been, almost everywhere, provided and financed substantially by the state—including in developing countries, which are our main concern here. What accounts for these differences? Why should the costs of health and education services be more fully financed by the government than those of legal or business services? Should such differences remain entrenched in the future, or should overstretched public sectors retreat from the provision or financing of education and health services, allowing private enterprise and households to fill the gap? These questions, which have been given renewed importance by widespread moves throughout the world towards market-led economic reforms, provide the main agenda for this book.

By way of introduction, it will be useful to consider some characteristics of education and health services which are relevant to the question as to how they should best be financed. We identify some of the similarities and differences between them, as commodities, and enquire whether there are attributes which each share, and which lead to their being financed in ways that separate them from ordinary goods and services. The case for their being mainly financed by the state, which is discussed early in this chapter, reveals some of their important similarities. This is followed by a section pointing to the considerable differences between them, which are not without implica-

Samer Al-Samarrai provided helpful research assistance and comments. The chapter has also benefited from comments by Paul Bennell, Gerald Bloom, Robin Burgess, Elizabeth King, Anne Mills, and Adrian Wood. I alone am responsible for remaining shortcomings.

tions for their methods of financing. The case for and against market-led reforms is then assessed, using evidence both from the papers in this book and from the wider literature. We begin, however, with a brief overview of health and education indicators for the developing world, which provides a context for the subsequent discussion.

1.1. The Condition of Health and Education

There has been tremendous progress in improving the health and educational levels of the world's population over the past 35 years. In the early 1960s, more than 200 of every 1,000 children in developing countries died before reaching the age of 5—a rate that had halved, to just over 100, by the early 1990s (Table 1.1). Life expectancy at birth increased from around 50 to over 60 years over the same period, and infectious diseases such as smallpox, measles, and polio were either eradicated or drastically reduced.

The increased coverage of formal school systems has also been remarkable. Primary enrolments doubled in Asia between 1960 and 1992; they increased threefold in Latin America and almost fivefold in Africa over the same period (Table 1.2). The relative expansion of secondary and higher education was even faster (partly reflecting their lower base), with enrolments growing between five and tenfold in the southern continents over the three decades. In consequence, adult literacy rates were doubled in the low-income countries,

TABLE 1.1   Child mortality and life expectancy by region, 1975 and 1990

Region	Child mortality per 1,000 live births		Life expectancy at birth (years)	
	1975	1990	1975	1990
Sub-Saharan Africa	212	175	48	52
India	195	127	53	58
China	85	43	56	69
Other Asia	135	97	56	62
Latin America and the Caribbean	104	60	62	70
Middle East	174	111	52	61
Formerly socialist economies of Europe	36	22	70	72
Developed market economies	21	11	73	76
Developing countries	152	106	56	63
World	135	96	60	65

Source: World Bank (1993: 2).

TABLE 1.2   School and college enrolment by major developing country
region, 1960–1992 (millions)

Region	Year(s)	First level	Second level	Third level
Africa	1960	18.9	1.9	0.19
	1970	32.8	5.2	0.48
	1980	64.1	14.3	1.5
	1992	86.1	27.1	3.3
Annual	1960–70	5.7	10.6	9.7
growth (%)	1970–80	6.9	10.6	12.1
	1980–92	2.5	5.5	6.8
GER[a]	1991	72.5	27.9	4.6
Asia	1960	184	40.6	3.68
	1970	242.3	74.8	6.92
	1980	331.6	136	12.1
	1992	366.2	185.4	23.9
Annual	1960–70	2.8	6.3	6.5
growth (%)	1970–80	3.2	6.2	5.7
	1980–92	0.8	2.6	5.8
GER[a]	1991	104	47.2	6.9
Latin America	1960	27.6	3	0.6
and the	1970	47	7.5	1.6
Caribbean	1980	65.3	17	4.9
	1992	77.2	23.2	7.9
Annual	1960–70	5.5	9.6	10.3
growth (%)	1970–80	3.3	8.5	11.8
	1980–92	1.4	2.6	4.1
GER[a]	1991	105.8	52.4	17.5

a The gross enrolment ratio (GER) is defined as total enrolment at a given level of education expressed as a percentage of the population which, according to national regulations, is of an age to attend at that level.

Sources: 1960 and 1980: UNESCO (1990); other years: UNESCO (1994).

and the average levels of educational achievement per person were much increased.

Nevertheless, enormous problems remain. Levels of child mortality in Africa are about fifteen times greater than in the rich countries (Table 1.1). Furthermore, it can be seen that there is great variation between different developing regions, with mortality rates being about twice as high in South Asia and Africa as in Latin America. Life expectancy too varies greatly: in sub-Saharan Africa it was fully 18 years less (around 50 years) than in Latin America in the early 1990s.

As regards education, simple counts of enrolments hide the large absolute numbers of children who remain out of school. Thus, in spite of the rapid expansion achieved, the enrolment ratios shown in Table 1.2 reveal that in Africa school enrolments in 1991 were equivalent to only about three-quarters of the eligible primary age group and to less than one-third of the secondary age group. The situation was actually worse than this because the enrolment data include pupils who are older than the official school age (because of repetition and late starts). Allowing for this, we find that in Africa scarcely more than half of the children of primary school age actually attend school, compared with about 80 per cent in Asia and up to 90 per cent elsewhere in the developing world.

The evidence suggests that, in each developing region, child mortality and life expectancy at birth continued to improve throughout the period, albeit with some slowing of earlier rates of progress during the 1980s.[1] However, evidence of real decline in education during recent years is shown in Table 1.2. It can be seen that in each region the rate of growth of school enrolments was more than halved after 1980, compared with earlier years.[2] This had particularly harsh consequences for Africa, where the growth of primary enrolments fell below the rate of growth of the population as the proportion of children attending school fell sharply between 1980 and 1991.[3] Worse still, in some countries in the region, actual declines in primary enrolments were experienced over the decade. This was retrogression indeed.

The causes of these events were complex. However, of critical significance has been economic decline—particularly in sub-Saharan Africa, where the effects of recession still linger. The ability of people to stay healthy is strongly affected by their incomes, so where the latter are falling family health will also be under threat. Similarly, in the case of education, economic adversity causes returns to schooling to decline and both the direct and the opportunity costs of school attendance to become unsustainable for the poorest families. Accordingly, when incomes are falling, more children are kept out of school.

Recession, and the consequent need for governments to adjust their economic policies, also resulted in changes in the supply of education and health

---

[1] The data can be found in UN (1988) and UNICEF (1992).

[2] The only exception was the case of tertiary enrolments in Asia, which continued to grow at rates similar to those achieved in the 1970s. It should also be noted that some slowing in rates of growth of primary enrolments was inevitable in Asia and Latin America (but not in Africa) owing to their already having achieved gross enrolment ratios (GERs) of close to 100 by 1980 (see Colclough with Lewin 1993: table 1.2 and accompanying text discussion). Even in those regions, however, a reduction to levels lower than population growth rates cannot be explained in this way.

[3] Primary GERs in Africa fell from 79.3% in 1980 to 72.5% in 1991, while net ratios (i.e. adjusted for over-age children) fell from about 60% to 56% over the same period (UNESCO 1994).

services. Although in most developing countries public expenditures on health (measured both as a proportion of GDP and in real per capita terms) increased strongly over the 1980s, there were important exceptions. In Iran, Morocco, Papua New Guinea, and several countries of sub-Saharan Africa (SSA), declines in public spending on health—measured in both of the above ways—occurred (Table 1.3). Such reductions were, however, much more dramatic in the case of education. Table 1.4 shows that, although public expenditures on education as a share of GNP were usually maintained, their

TABLE 1.3   Central government health expenditures by region, 1980 and 1990

Country	1980 health expenditure as % of GDP	1990 health expenditure as % of GDP	1980 health expenditure per capita in 1987 $US	1990 health expenditure per capita in 1987 $US
Sub-Saharan Africa				
Cameroon	0.7	1.0	6.75	8.98
C.A.R.	1.1	2.6	4.65	9.84
Côte d'Ivoire	1.2	1.7	15.01	13.99
Ghana	0.8	1.7	3.28	6.55
Kenya	2.0	2.7	7.32	10.67
Malawi	1.9	2.9	3.20	3.95
Mali	0.6	2.8	1.77	6.69
Niger	0.8	3.4	3.49	10.46
Senegal	1.1	2.3	7.22	15.79
Sierra Leone	2.6	1.7	4.18	2.50
Tanzania	1.7	3.2	2.84	5.48
Togo	1.9	2.5	8.95	9.78
Zambia	2.3	2.2	7.80	5.90
AVERAGE	1.4	2.4	5.9	8.5
East Asia and the Pacific				
Indonesia	0.5	0.7	1.92	3.63
Korea	0.2	1.0[a]	4.00	41.32[a]
Malaysia	1.5	1.3	24.45	30.35
Philippines	0.6	1.0	4.09	6.36
P.N.G.	2.9	2.8	25.44	22.47
Thailand	0.8	1.1	5.57	14.29
AVERAGE	1.1	1.3	10.91	19.74
South Asia				
Bangladesh	0.6	1.4	0.91	2.56
India	0.2	1.3	0.55	4.87
Nepal	0.6	2.2	0.83	3.97
Pakistan	0.3	1.8	0.66	6.27
Sri Lanka	2.0	1.8	6.71	7.92
AVERAGE	0.7	1.7	1.94	5.12

TABLE 1.3   (*cont.*)

Country	1980 health expenditure as % of GDP	1990 health expenditure as % of GDP	1980 health expenditure per capita in 1987 $US	1990 health expenditure per capita in 1987 $US
Middle East and North Africa				
Egypt	1.2	1.0	6.57	7.34
Iran	2.3	1.5	67.95	37.85
Morocco	1.1	0.9	8.67	8.11
Tunisia	2.3	3.3	26.45	43.31
AVERAGE	1.7	1.7	27.41	24.15
Latin America and the Caribbean				
Brazil	0.8	2.8	16.58	54.68
Chile	2.1	3.4	32.55	65.06
Colombia	0.5	1.8	5.72	22.01
Dominican Republic	1.6	2.1	11.72	16.23
Ecuador	1.1	2.6	13.59	30.43
El Salvador	1.5	2.6	15.92	23.62
Mexico	0.4	1.6	7.75	28.92
Nicaragua	4.5	6.7	61.78	61.61
Paraguay	0.4	1.2	3.83	12.05
Peru	1.1	1.9	14.41	18.98
Uruguay	1.3	2.5	32.87	60.63
Venezuela	1.6	2.0	49.80	50.74
AVERAGE	1.4	2.6	22.21	37.08
High income countries	3.3	5.5	NA	NA
Low and middle-income countries	1.3	2.1	13.19	19.90

^aData shown for Korea in 1990 are in fact for 1993.

Notes and Sources: Data for health expenditures as a proportion of GDP in 1990 are taken from World Bank (1993: 210). Data on GDP per capita, for that year, in constant 1987 $US (calculated from World Bank 1995c) are used to convert health expenditure as a percentage of GDP into health expenditure per capita. Health expenditures as a proportion of GNP in 1980 are given in World Bank (1995a: 162–3). These were converted into health expenditure as a proportion of GDP by using figures on GNP and GDP from World Tables (World Bank 1995c). Health expenditures per capita for 1980 were then calculated using the same method as for 1990. The low and middle-income country totals are derived from those countries shown in the table. High-income countries did not have GDP in constant 1987 $US so data on per capita expenditure are unavailable. High income countries comprise: New Zealand, Singapore, Australia, Austria, Belgium, Canada, Denmark, Finland, France, Ireland, Israel, Italy, Netherlands, Spain, Sweden, Switzerland, UK, and USA.

TABLE 1.4 Public expenditure on education by major world region, 1980 and 1992

	Public expenditure on education as % GNP			Public expenditure on education per inhabitant ($)a		
	1980	1985	1992	1980	1985	1992
Africa excluding Arab states	5.2	4.9	5.4	42	26	28
Asia excluding Arab states	4.4	4.0	4.3	38	39	93
Arab states	4.5	5.8	5.7	111	125	114
Latin America and the Caribbean	3.9	3.9	4.4	95	71	124
All developed countries	5.4	5.3	5.3	420	441	828

a Dollar figures are in current prices.
Source: UNESCO (1994: table 2.10).

absolute value dropped sharply in real per capita terms, particularly in Africa, but also elsewhere.[4]

Governments, being major service providers and financers, have had a critical influence upon the state of education and health in developing countries, as summarized above. In view of their mixed record of success, particularly in SSA, it is timely to consider the strength of the case for helping governments to re-equip themselves as financers and providers, and to appraise alternative arguments which seek to place the responsibility for financing services more squarely upon their users than has happened in the past. It is to a consideration of these issues that we now turn.

1.2. The Case for Government Finance

The case for state financing of education and health services is based partly upon the possibility of market failure, partly upon distributive considerations, and partly upon notions of 'rights'. The likelihood of market failure arises from four particular characteristics of education and health as commodities:

1. *Externalities*. Not all the benefits of education and health services are privately captured by their direct recipients. For example, the curing of

---

[4] Table 1.4 indicates sharp declines in expenditure, measured in current prices, for Africa during the 1980s and for Latin America for the first half of that decade. This implies that dramatic cuts in the real values of such expenditures occurred. Elsewhere, nominal expenditures increased, but often less quickly than inflation. Thus, the figures shown in Table 1.4 imply that real per capita declined in expenditure for Latin America and the Arab States, as well as for Africa, over the whole period 1980–92.

contagious disease helps those who would otherwise have caught it from the carrier; increasing the educational level of females brings positive benefits to their children. Accordingly, leaving the provision of such services to the market would result in under-consumption, because people would compare only the benefits and costs to themselves of consuming these services, ignoring the impact of their own consumption on the well-being of others.

2. *Imperfections of information.* Not all the private benefits of education and health services are obvious. Thus, some consumers remain unaware of some of them. For example, the demand for immunization may not reflect the real private benefits arising, owing to people's ignorance. Equally, the impact of literacy upon individuals' health and nutrition may be greater than the demand for primary schooling would otherwise imply.

3. *Merit goods.* Education and health services can be thought of as goods with special merit (Musgrave 1958, 1987), deserving of public support to a level of supply beyond that which consumer sovereignty would imply. Thus, individuals as members of communities might accept that school attendance should be compulsory for all, even though their personal preferences for themselves, or for individuals in their own families, might differ.

4. *Public goods.* The consumption of some types of education and health service cannot be restricted easily, and cannot, therefore, be sold to consumers. For example, public health initiatives such as rodent control or insect spraying benefit everyone, and could not therefore be privately supplied and financed. Examples in education are less obvious, but would include some types of educational broadcasting, and public awareness campaigns seeking to disseminate particular messages.

Even if goods markets were perfect, capital market imperfections may still frustrate equity and efficiency goals, and provide separate reasons for requiring state financing of education and health services. Both because some of these services are wanted in and for themselves—and thus are ingredients in the notion of standard of living (Drèze and Sen 1989; 1991)—and because they have an impact upon future income, the distribution of access to them is important to society. But it is not uncommon for credit for education and health services to be unavailable to the poor—often because the lender is not prepared to take the risk of default (Burgess and Stern 1991: 49–51). For example, the market for health insurance is particularly prone to imperfections, resulting in under-coverage of the relevant populations. This is partly owing to the effects of 'moral hazard', leading some of those with insurance to over-claim, thereby increasing the costs for all. It also stems from the difficulty of providing individual risk ratings, which makes it more difficult for people with a given risk to insure themselves at reasonable cost. Accordingly, large numbers of households in developing countries would be unable to finance the health and education services they need if private financing were to predominate.

Market failure may also result from the broader economic and social context within which services are provided. For example, some economies are too small or poor to be able to provide effective markets for education and health services. Particularly at tertiary levels, demand for services may not be large enough to support more than one supplier, leading to monopoly. Thus, the market for particular health and education services may be thin, or may not even exist. Systems of remuneration and organization are also important. For example, professionals in the education and health sectors act both as advisers on the type of service required and as providers of the service. This generates a potential conflict of interest, and risks market failure under systems of private provision and finance. Furthermore, since health and education outcomes are partly produced by households, societies in which income distribution is unequal will tend also to have an unequal distribution of human capital. Greater intervention in support of the poor and the unskilled is, therefore, usually needed to compensate for unequal household capacities. In these ways, government expenditure can be used to help secure a preferred distribution of human capital in the short run, which may, in turn, bring dynamic benefits via improved growth performance.

Finally, as regards rights, the main issue raised by market-led economic reforms is the potential contradiction between adopting targets for universal access to and consumption of basic services (however defined), while at the same time charging for their supply. The idea that the introduction of charges for services, in circumstances where not everyone has access to them, is compatible with broadening such access appears odd.[5] It will be shown below (Section 1.4.1) that it is valid only under some rather restrictive, and unusual, circumstances.

1.3. Contrasting Characteristics of Health and Education Systems

Although education and health expenditures are notable for the range of social benefits which they are believed to bring, they also provide substantial private benefits. This means that, at least in principle, people would pay to use them. Whether they would be prepared to meet all or only part of the full costs of these services depends upon their perception of the magnitude of private benefits accruing and of the reliability of such benefits, and upon their family circumstances, in particular their income. There are, however, some important differences between the two sectors, which have some influence upon the ways in which they might be financed.

[5] As Stern (1989) implies, we should be uneasy about introducing charges for services which we separately believe everyone ought to use.

First, the demand for educational services is influenced partly by consumption considerations: people enjoy the process of education, and the benefits of being an educated person (e.g. the abilities to read and write), for their own sake. However, in order to become educated it is usually necessary to join the education system for a considerable number of years. People also, of course, enjoy being healthy, but this can be achieved, and maintained, for most people by only small and infrequent use of formal health services. In order to remain healthy, it is necessary to have sufficient income to sustain a healthy life and to behave sensibly, but it is not usually necessary to remain a consumer of health services on a long-term basis.

Second, there are also differences between the investment aspects of education and health services. It is widely accepted that education increases the earnings capacity of individuals via its effects upon individual productivity.[6] By contrast, although health expenditures also increase future earnings— individual productivity being a positive function of health status (World Bank 1993)—most curative interventions for acute illness merely restore earlier (pre-illness) levels of productivity, rather than adding to them: they are income-restoring, rather than income-enhancing. Thus, because of these differences in both consumption and investment attributes, the extent to which it would be practicable for people to pay for such health interventions out of their present or future income is less clear than in the case of education.[7]

It could be argued that the difference here is one of degree, rather than of kind: providing people with income-contingent loans to cover the costs of hospitalization is not too different from doing so to cover the costs of university studies, even though such a scheme would result in reduced net earnings in the case of the health loan (in comparison with pre-illness earnings), and almost always in enhanced net earnings in the case of that extended for education. Nevertheless, while the expected returns to a particular level

---

[6] The positive impact of education on earnings has been extensively documented by Psacharopoulos (1973; 1994), who finds that average earnings rise monotonically with years of education but that both social and private rates of return are highest for primary and least for tertiary education (see also Schultz 1991: table 2.1). Although most commentators take such earnings differentials to imply differences in individual productivity delivered by education, 'screening' theorists have argued that learning does not explain all the wage differences associated with schooling and work history, and some even believe that education merely sorts out those who are clever from those who are not, rather than contributing separately to productive capacity. (Useful reviews of the various types of screening theory are given in Whitehead 1981, and Weiss 1995. For recent controversy surrounding the interpretation of measured rates of return, see Bennell 1996.)

[7] Note that the impact of health and education services upon welfare and income are not symmetrical. Health interventions that restore income-generating power and a sense of well-being enhance welfare even though their impact on income may be negligible. Education, on the other hand, may be less important to the basic notion of welfare: its absence does not threaten welfare as much as would an absence of curative care, and it may be viewed by some sections of society (e.g. the poor) as marginal to their purposes. Thus, the willingness to pay for health interventions (as opposed to its practicability) may be stronger for welfare than for income reasons, and vice-versa in the case of education.

and type of education are, in principle, similar for all who undertake it, this is not true in the case of health interventions: the income-restoring benefits of a major operation, for example, vary with the income-earning capacity of the individual concerned. Thus, while private expenditures at most levels of education generate returns which, in most societies, represent a profitable investment for those from all income groups, the cost of many health interventions simply could not be financed out of future income by many of the poorest members of society. Accordingly, the default rate on loans to pay for health interventions could be expected to be greater even than the high rates presently associated with loans to finance tertiary studies (Woodhall 1987; see also Tilak, Ch. 3 below). On purely practical grounds, the possibility of such a system working seems remote.

Third, there are problems of 'agency' with both of these service systems, but they tend to be most severe in the case of education. Since most educational services are consumed before people become adults, those responsible for meeting the private costs are normally the families of recipients, rather than the direct beneficiaries. This happens less frequently in the case of health care—although here too the demand is greater among those who are dependent upon family support, i.e. the young and the elderly. Thus, comparisons of private rates of return to education and health expenditures may not adequately proxy the practicality of raising private sources of finance where there is a disjunction between those who benefit and those who are required to pay.

Turning now to costs, there are, at one level, strong similarities in the direct cost structure of health and education systems: the recurrent costs of both are determined primarily by staff salaries, and thus reflect the average skill structure of employment at each level; accordingly, primary care and schooling, which utilize people with fairly minimal levels of education and training, are usually cheap and, because the benefits are substantial (Colclough 1982; Colclough with Lewin 1993; World Bank 1993), highly cost-effective, whereas tertiary education and care are expensive because they require more highly educated staff and more complex inputs. As this book will show, there are strong parallels in the problems and policy challenges at each level that arise from these similar cost structures. On the other hand, because the period during which educational services are consumed by the average person lasts for a much longer time than is the case with health services, the direct costs of education systems usually far exceed those of health service provision. By consequence, the proportion of GNP spent upon health is usually between one-third and one-half of that spent on education.[8]

For the same reasons, the opportunity costs of educational provision also

---

[8] Public spending on health care exceeds that on education in only a small minority of countries. In 1993, these comprised Costa Rica, Panama, and the Czech Republic (World Bank 1995a: table 10).

exceed those of health systems. Participation in education stretches over many years from childhood through to maturity. Although initially the opportunity costs of participation are small, and arise mainly from the use of time that would otherwise be spent upon household tasks, such costs can still be powerful for poor families, and they account for widespread under-participation in education at primary level in the poorest countries—particularly among girls (King and Hill 1991). However, opportunity costs rise sharply at secondary level and beyond, when labour market opportunities for those with post-primary schooling become significant, and they often amount to the greater part of total educational costs at post-primary levels. By contrast, because time spent in health care is usually fairly brief, and is particularly concentrated towards the end of people's lives when labour market participation is reduced, the opportunity costs of health care, for those who receive it, are much less than those of education.

A further important difference as regards the costs of education and health services concerns the predictability of these expenditures. In the case of education, households with children are able to anticipate the timing and the magnitude of the costs of sending their children to school with close accuracy several years in advance. Although the level of schooling attained (and thus the total expenses accruing) cannot usually be predicted beforehand, there is a choice faced by individual parents—at least for years beyond the compulsory attendance age range—concerning whether or not they wish to continue to send their child to school. Such costs can be anticipated and planned for or, indeed, avoided if parents so choose. By contrast, health expenditures are unpredictable—in both incidence and magnitude. Some individuals may have little or no need to use curative services throughout their lives. Others may, with little warning, need extensive and expensive treatments, the avoidance of which may, unlike in the case of education, bring immediate and disastrous consequences for the individuals concerned.

These differences as regards predictability and risk make insurance schemes a viable option for the financing of health services, but not for the financing of education. Spreading the costs of health provision, then, is concerned partly with spreading the risks of attending to illness via some form of social insurance—financed via taxes, compulsory contributions (often from employers or employees) or voluntary arrangements. In the case of education, spreading the costs entails either charging all the people, including the presently childless, for the costs of schooling via the tax system, or raising money for schooling from charges to users, based upon ability to pay (i.e. with scholarships for the poor, subsidized by charges greater than cost to the rich—a solution that is similar to progressive taxation, except that here the childless would pay nothing for the education of others). A further alternative, widely practised at primary level, is community schooling, where villagers, or other groups, are required to provide all or some resources for the local school(s) from their own means—in cash or kind.

1.4. The Case For and Against Market Allocation: An Assessment of the Evidence

Notwithstanding the important differences between the attributes of education and health services discussed above, arguments for increasing the role of the market in their allocation typically emerge from a strikingly similar critique of the state's record in the two sectors. First, it is generally observed —or, more accurately, assumed—that, because governments in developing countries are at present fiscally constrained, enhanced resources for education and health services are not likely to be available from traditional revenue instruments.[9] Second, it is judged that resources are often misallocated, in the sense that large numbers of people have no access to education and health systems at any level, whereas some—usually the richer groups—manage to secure fairly unlimited access. Third, it is argued that publicly financed systems of health and education are often of low quality and internally inefficient, with equipment and drugs being unavailable or misused, and with high rates of absenteeism among staff. Finally, some critics point out that expecting the public sector to put things right may be unrealistic where those people upon whom governments depend for support are the richer, more articulate groups, whose interests may be threatened by a more equitable sharing of access to resources and services.

Those who advocate the introduction of charges for services and/or their private supply believe that the above problems can be mitigated. As regards the first point, it is argued that charging fees, or increasing the proportion of private sector users, could be expected to help alleviate the financial constraint facing the public sector either by increasing public revenues, or by reducing the proportion of costs that would need to be met by the state.[10] Second, the resulting improvement in the financial position of government would allow allocative efficiency to be enhanced—more resources could be concentrated on those parts of the system where social returns are greatest. Third, technical efficiency is expected to be improved by giving teachers,

---

[9] As this book will show, the set of instruments that tend to be thought of as 'traditional' in this context is unwarrantably narrow. There is much greater potential for fiscal reforms than most critics assume.

[10] User charges are, in essence, taxes that are specific to health and education. They are usually regressive. However, one important characteristic of both education and health services is that they cannot be resold—unlike, say, water, shelter, food, or some other necessary commodities. This means that, in principle, prices charged for health and education services need not be uniform, since those receiving them free of charge could not resell them to those who have to pay. It is, therefore, easier to make such charges progressive than would be the case with some other commodities. Note, however, that this is not true of the supplies needed to support such services, such as textbooks and drugs, which can be resold. Progressive charging systems can be maintained, in the case of drugs, by restricting supply on the basis of prescriptions. If people need the product for their own health, they can be assumed unlikely to sell it on. This is less easy in the case of educational supplies, where needs may be felt with less urgency.

health workers, and managers a financial stake in their enterprise, and, via the imposition of fees, increasing the likelihood that parents, pupils, and patients will demand more of their schools and health services. Accordingly, quality should rise, diversity would be promoted, and consumer choice should be enhanced, all of which should provide some counterpoint to the allocative distortions indulged by the public sector, arising from the interests by which it is controlled.[11]

These arguments have become increasingly influential over the past decade or so, as more and more governments have, from conviction or perceived necessity, cut back earlier levels of spending, and as more of them have introduced the policy reforms upon which loans from the international financial institutions (IFIs) have become increasingly conditional. This book assesses the strength of the case for this 'new orthodoxy'. It examines the lessons from countries that have shifted away from financing education and health services via standard tax instruments towards using fees, social and private insurance, community financing and/or private provision. It also examines ways of improving cost effectiveness by, among others, the devolution of administrative and financing authority to local levels, and separating the responsibilities for financing from those for service provision.

As regards its intellectual structure, the argument in the book deliberately proceeds from micro towards macro approaches. Since the 'new orthodoxy' extols the virtues of distributing education and health services according to market-determined processes, and thus is located mainly in the 'micro' sphere, the evidence for and against the existence of such benefits is first interrogated. A sufficient number of countries have introduced user charges for some implications from their experience now to be drawn. The first two papers in the book provide an assessment of this experience. These are followed by two sets of papers on private provision, and on community-based and insurance mechanisms, the latter of which aim to broaden the financing base beyond that provided by the immediate users of services. The criteria used to judge the success of these initiatives are the same for both health and education sectors, and include an assessment of their impact upon technical and allocative efficiency, equity, quality, resource generation, and consumer choice. It is shown that all of these approaches have serious limitations on at least some of the criteria used. The final two sections of the book move towards more macro issues. The papers on efficiency reforms ask whether the emphasis on market solutions has overlooked the considerable potential for making state systems of provision more efficient. Where this is the case,

---

[11] The main policy studies issued by the World Bank on health and education in the mid-1980s utilized the above arguments rather boldly (see World Bank 1986, 1987). As one would expect, more recent policy documents have finessed these ideas somewhat—partly in response to criticism that the equity costs of charges, in particular, were being ignored. Nevertheless, a shift to greater provision of education and health services by the market is still a fiercely held element of the Bank's policy advocacy (see World Bank 1993, 1995b; and Shaw and Ainsworth 1994).

opportunities for such efficiency improvements are identified. The final two papers in the book show that fiscal and organizational reforms and reforms of the polity stand out as major priorities which recent debates have largely ignored.

The remainder of this introductory chapter summarizes the more important points that emerge from later chapters, and sets them in the context of the broader debate.

1.4.1. Cost recovery

Advocates of fees for education and health services have often employed a simple demand and supply model in order to illustrate their case (Griffin 1992; Thobani 1984; Mingat and Tan 1986). Its arguments are worth setting out here, for closer inspection. The starting point is the observation that the markets for education and health services are not in equilibrium.[12] This is, first, because governments are fiscally constrained and unable to increase their supplies, and second, because there is excess demand for these services at their present prices. Accordingly, consumers as a group would be prepared to pay more than they presently do for the amount of services currently consumed. Of course, if supply were completely inelastic with respect to the price charged (as in Fig. 1.1(a)), an increase in price to market-clearing levels would have no impact upon the quantity of services available ($Q_1 = Q_2$). However, the social composition of the users of these services may change according to the characteristics of those who were prepared to pay the increased prices.

If, however, the revenues arising from higher prices were spent upon increasing the supply of the services, it is easy to see that the supply curve would have a positive slope. Here, the supply constraint could be reduced as prices rose, and more consumers would be able to use the service. If we take consumer surplus as a proxy for consumer welfare, this may still fall with the increased price, notwithstanding the increased supply of education or health services. This is illustrated in Fig. 1.1(b), where consumer surplus associated with a price of P_2 (which is given by the shaded area between it and the demand curve), is less than that associated with a price of P_1. On the other hand, consumer surplus may rise with the increased price, and for given demand is more likely to do so, the greater is the supply elasticity with respect to an increase in price. This case is illustrated in Fig. 1.1(c), where the shaded area showing consumer surplus is greater for P_2 than for P_1. This model seems to suggest, then, that in cases where education or health services are unavailable,

---

[12] It is worth recalling that, if markets were in equilibrium, a price increase—such as would be given by the introduction of an indirect tax—would result in a fall in demand for the product concerned, and a consequential fall in consumer welfare.

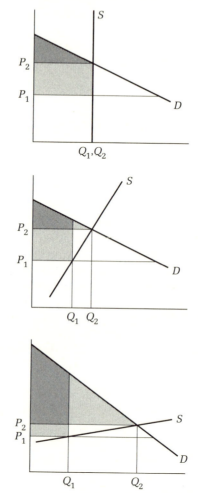

FIG. 1.1   Impact of price changes on consumer welfare in
circumstances of excess demand for health and education services
(*a*) Supply constant, consumer surplus falls
(*b*) Supply rises, consumer surplus falls
(*c*) Supply rises, consumer surplus rises

and where people would be prepared to pay (more) to secure access, the introduction of fees for service would be compatible both with enhanced coverage
of the services, and with increases in consumer welfare, as conventionally
defined.

One of the problems with this argument is that consumer surplus in the markets for education and health is not the same thing as society's welfare. There are several points to note here. First, as the price of a service increases, the composition of those who consume it will change. For example, in education, even if total enrolments rise following an increase in school places financed by the introduction of fees, some children previously enrolled are likely to drop out—to be replaced by others from families more willing to pay higher prices. Intuitively, it seems plausible that those who drop out are more likely to be from poorer households, since the price elasticity of demand for education and health is greater for them (Gertler and Glewwe 1990; Mbugwa *et al.* 1995). However, it can be shown that outcomes will depend more upon the initial mix of students enrolled than upon the relative size of the demand elasticities exhibited by particular income groups.[13] Thus, it is not possible to say, *a priori*, whether the welfare loss by the poor in response to such policies would be greater or less, than the welfare gain by the rich.

Second, the analysis is partial in a number of senses. Even if poor people chose to pay the (increased) fees, it might be that they would be reducing their consumption of other goods which we would prefer them to retain. Accordingly, the impact of these price changes upon people's participation in other markets tends to be ignored. Furthermore, the reality is not usually one of excess demand for services pertaining throughout the whole system, since not all schools and health facilities tend to be similarly affected. Thus, if a price rise were implemented nationally, those communities where the market was already in equilibrium would lose. On the other hand, since it is typically the poorer communities that are under-served, a selective introduction of fees focused upon communities where excess demand existed could result in errors of targeting.

Finally, there is a range of political economy assumptions underlying these policy recommendations which need not necessarily hold. Most important is the assumption that the increased revenues accruing from fees will in fact be spent upon increased provision of services, rather than upon other budgetary heads. The reality of the budget process in many countries suggests that this assumption is not of minor significance (Hinchliffe 1993). Furthermore, to the extent that this model is espoused by theorists in the new political economy tradition,[14] there is a risk of internal contradiction in its advocacy: if governments are constrained by interest groups requiring policy pay-offs, it is unclear how these shackles can be discarded to achieve pro-poor increases in service supply.

The above considerations raise a number of problems of principle for the general argument that increased charges can be beneficial. We need to know, however, what the experience has been with these policies thus far. Is there

13 I am indebted to Samer Al-Samarrai for a demonstration of this point.
14 For a discussion of this literature as applied to developing countries, see Findlay 1989. For a critique, see Toye 1991.

any evidence that the concerns expressed above are exaggerated? Two papers in this volume help us to address these questions.

Chapter 2 by Andrew Creese and Joseph Kutzin reviews evidence, in particular from sub-Saharan Africa, on cost recovery for health services with respect to three claimed areas of potential benefits: revenue raising, improved access and equity, and greater efficiency. The authors find that cost recovery policies have raised revenues far less effectively than was initially expected, and that net revenues are considerably lower than gross revenues because collection costs are high. As regards efficiency, it is clear from many studies that the utilization of health facilities typically drops after the imposition of charges. This negative demand response does not, however, imply a more efficient usage of facilities, since earlier utilization levels were not usually frivolous. Equally, there appears to be little evidence that differential pricing has caused a more effective utilization of primary, as opposed to tertiary, services, as some reforms had intended. The authors report limited evidence that increased revenues have, in some cases, allowed supplies of drugs and medicines to improve at the local level which has led to a better quality of service—one of the few detectable benefits of these policies in Africa.

The impact of health charges on equity appears to have been clearly negative. The reduction of demand has been concentrated among the poorest of the population, who usually need the service most. Targeting appears not to be easy, owing to the difficulties of determining who is eligible for free services. In a few cases it is reported that the improved quality of service has stimulated increased use, notwithstanding higher direct costs, but these have not been the rule. Generally, both usage and equity have deteriorated as a consequence of charges.

Chapter 3 by Jandhyala Tilak paints a similar picture of the impact of cost recovery in the case of education. The introduction of student fees at primary and secondary levels almost always elicits a negative enrolment response, and, where they are already in place, reductions in school fees often provide a highly effective means of boosting enrolments in countries where large numbers of children are out of school.[15] Although fees at tertiary level are frequently charged, they prove difficult to collect and typically recover only a small proportion of total costs. Student loans are widely used to enable the children from poorer families to participate in higher education, and to pass some of the costs of such education from the state, or households, directly to the beneficiaries. But the paper shows that default rates from loan repayments

---

[15] This was demonstrated recently in the case of Malawi, where school fees were abolished at primary level by the new democratic government in 1994. The enrolment response was massive and immediate: primary pupils increased by 58% during the course of the year. It is ironic that this should have happened in the country for which the case for introducing fees—in order to finance more school places, and achieve higher enrolments—was first made by Thobani (1984), and where fees were subsequently introduced by consequence of pressure from the World Bank. For further discussion and evidence, see Colclough 1996.

are usually very high. This, together with the high costs of administering loans schemes, and the fact that, even with low default, the pay-back period lasts over many years, means that the financial returns to the state are usually very low.

Both of these chapters suggest that user fees could be made compatible with equity and efficiency objectives only if some fairly demanding institutional reforms were in place. In the case of education, graduate or payroll taxes, whereby individual graduates or their employers pay a proportion of salary costs as a supplementary tax, seem—although they have been seldom used in the past—to offer a more efficient and equitable means of raising additional monies for education than other approaches. More generally, however, cost recovery policies are damaging to efficiency and equity, unless focused particularly upon the higher levels of the system, and supplemented by measures to protect access to these levels by the poor.

In the case of health, the evidence suggests that the revenues raised would need to be retained locally, that they would need to be translated into perceptible service improvements, and that their impact would need to be such as to *lower* the net private costs of access to effective care—for example by reducing the distance, and thus the journey time, to the nearest health facility.[16] This is a formidable list of requirements. In the light of the weak management that presently characterizes most ministries of health (particularly those in sub-Saharan Africa), there are only limited prospects, in the short term, for the introduction of such reforms in ways which would allow cost recovery policies to achieve more of the goals set by their advocates.

1.4.2. Public versus private alternatives

The main difference between policies that introduce fees for service within the public sector and those that encourage private sector growth is the aspect of compulsion. In the case of private provision, the families that end up paying fees are those that choose so to do—often in order to benefit from a better quality of service than is available within the public sector. The revenue benefits are attractive in that the public sector is relieved of the cost burden for those households using private services. The latter effectively pay twice—once via taxes and a second time via private fees. The magnitude of public resources available for education or health services remains unchanged, but

---

[16] The argument that nearby provision would make fees acceptable on account of reducing journey time has been made separately for both education and health services (Gertler and Glewwe 1990,1992; Gertler and van der Gaag 1988). These approaches have simulated the impact of user fees assuming that the willingness to pay by villagers can be proxied by, *inter alia*, the opportunity costs of journey time saved. But the partial framework within which the argument is advanced would make the implied policies vulnerable, if implemented, to unanticipated (and unanalysed) inter- and intra-sectoral changes. For a detailed critique, see Colclough 1996.

is spread among fewer consumers, thereby allowing improvement in the per capita service provided. Since the payment of fees is voluntary, consumer welfare remains higher than in the case of compulsory fees.

The quality of private education and health services is sometimes better than that provided by the state owing to the fact that private systems are better resourced. Since such qualitative differences can, in the case of education, confer elite status by affording better access to the highest qualification levels, this can be a significant cause of social differentiation and inter-generational inequality. However, it has been separately argued by those advocating private systems of health, and by supporters of private education, that such systems are more cost-effective than those provided by the public sector—that their qualitative advantage arises not because these systems are more privileged, but because they work better. This putative efficiency advantage has become part of the more general case for state withdrawal from service provision—i.e. not merely that the state should encourage the private sector so that publicly funded expenditures can be contained, but that services from the private sector should increasingly replace those provided by the state. As indicated later in this chapter, these ideas underpin the wide-spread moves to separate financing from provision, particularly in the health sector. They also inform the shift towards devolved systems of provisioning and management, which attempt to pass as much control, autonomy, and responsibility to the level of individual institutions as is compatible with system effectiveness.

Several papers in this book show that some of these judgements are premature. As regards education, the debate about the relative effectiveness of public versus private schooling dates back to a major study in the USA (Coleman *et al.* 1982) which suggested that Catholic schools in the private sector were more cost-effective than their public sector counterparts. Its findings proved controversial, owing mainly to insufficient attention having been given by its authors to the correction of selection bias (i.e. the question of whether or not all the chosen pupils could be treated as if randomly drawn from the same population, once measured differences in characteristics had been allowed for) between the samples of students in the different sets of schools. As Chapter 5 by Sajitha Bashir shows, these early studies, and most of those that followed, are vulnerable to this criticism, and cannot be taken to have established the greater cost effectiveness of private schooling.

Bashir's own study of government, aided, and unaided primary schools in the state of Tamil Nadu in India, however, uses a different methodology: the cost effectiveness of the three sectors is assessed by comparing incremental unit costs and incremental changes in predicted mean achievement scores. It shows that in Tamil Nadu private aided schools are more cost-effective, but private unaided schools are less cost-effective, than public schools at primary level. These results, therefore, contradict those of earlier, less careful, studies, in that private schools receiving the least public support are shown to be also the least cost-effective. On the other hand, they also suggest that some mix of public and private inputs, as in the state-aided sector, may provide the best combination of all.

The paper on Indonesia by Elizabeth King (Chapter 6), however, demonstrates that public and private schools often may not be as different in the ways in which they are financed as is commonly assumed. Primary schooling in Indonesia has, since 1977, been fee-free, but parents are nevertheless expected to contribute to school funds at levels determined by principals and parents. Public secondary schools have fees levied by central government. Thus, there are significant costs of attendance at public schools. Obviously, that is true also of private schools, but in addition they receive public subsidies in the form of teachers, buildings, and physical facilities. The paper shows that expenditures by households on both categories of schooling are significant in both rural and urban communities—indeed, pupils in urban public schools cost more, on average, than pupils in rural private schools. Thus, as in many other countries, public education is not free, even to the poor, with communities and families in Indonesia heavily supplementing state allocations. Furthermore, the proportion of funds received from the public sector, relative to total school expenditures, is often little different as between public and private schools. Accordingly—and this is of more general relevance to explaining the relative merits of public and private schools—if the latter have a performance advantage, this may be related more to the nature of school management than to the sources of school finance.

As is the case with education, the debate about the appropriate role for private health care is linked to the broader debate about the role of government in the economy. Advocates and critics of private health care tend to be divided primarily by their views as to whether or not health care is closely similar to other goods that are successfully provided by the market. The arguments advanced by advocates include the views (1) that the private sector is more technically efficient, owing to the effects of the profit incentive, which induces firms to minimize costs for a given level of output; (2) that its encouragement will allow the public sector to concentrate upon priority interventions—such as quasi-public goods, those with strong externalities, and those that are highly cost-effective—thereby achieving gains in allocative efficiency; (3) that it would promote equity by freeing-up public resources to meet the needs of the poor; and (4) that it would encourage consumer choice.

The review of evidence on these matters, in the paper by Sara Bennett (Chapter 4), reveals mixed results. As regards the most important argument in favour of the private sector—the promotion of efficiency—most comparisons in developing countries are between government and not-for-profit services, the latter usually emerging as being cheaper. However, as in the case of education discussed above, the comparisons are often technically weak—with insufficient standardization of case-mix, severity of illness, or quality of care. Furthermore, even if these providers tend to be more efficient, the fact that they are not profit-seeking organizations makes them an uncertain test of the pro-market case. There is considerable evidence that the private sector profits from the ignorance of patients by a tendency to over-treat illness, and to over-prescribe, and that the costs of care in the private sector are often unnecessarily high. On equity, evidence from Chile, Zimbabwe, and Thailand suggests that the growth of private care can—where politics are favourable—allow more government resources to be targeted at the poor. But, even so, it appears to have promoted growing differences in the quality of care received by different income groups. Moreover, even where the overall resources for health rise as a consequence of private sector growth, this does not always benefit the poor: private providers tend to bid up factor prices, thereby decreasing public sector purchasing power and adversely affecting standards of care in the public sector; several countries suffer from a shortage of doctors in the public sector owing to the much greater rewards available to those who practise private medicine. There is no doubt that public resources should be focused upon providing primary care and essential services for the poor. But this does not imply a need for mutually exclusive specialization by the two sectors.[17] The state should probably continue to provide some services across the full range of health care needs, with the private sector functioning as a supplement rather than as a replacement for public care.

   It is necessary to provide a framework for private health care which, on the one hand, ensures that required standards of ethics and care are met and, on the other, provides incentives for the private sector to act in ways that promote health policy objectives in an efficient fashion. These objectives are not easy to achieve. It should be recalled that claims for the greater efficiency of the private sector remain of dubious reliability. Notwithstanding that, private effectiveness may in any case prove infeasible where most consumers are poor and ill-informed, where management skills are in very short supply, and where governments are poor regulators. Thus, the tasks placed upon the state are likely to be substantial. New skills are needed in the public sector in order for fair and independent regulatory systems to be developed, and the advocacy of private sector development—where that is appropriate—is to imply a changed, rather than reduced, government role.

1.4.3. Spreading the burden

Financing arrangements that depend upon raising funds from the users of services will tend to promote patterns of access that reflect the underlying distribution of income in the country, particularly because most education

---

[17] Some have argued (e.g. World Bank 1993) that the provision of 'non-essential' health services should be left entirely to the private sector. Yet this part of the market is subject to informational problems and other sources of imperfection. Equally, the most buoyant part of the private market for health care in most countries is maternity care and treatments for sexually transmitted diseases. Where these essential services are partly met privately, it is probably in the interests of all that this should continue.

and some health services are expensive relative to most people's disposable incomes. Accordingly, the main way in which poor people can be enabled to gain access to schools and health services of good quality is by spreading the costs of these services more widely among the community. The main aims of such schemes are to achieve cross-subsidization from richer to poorer people and from non-users to users. As a consequence the number of contributors is increased, the average per capita cost is reduced, and payments are re-scheduled towards periods in life- and income-cycles when they can be more easily met. Taxation has been the most important means of achieving these objectives. However, there have been other schemes that have also been used for these purposes. Examples are provided by community schooling in the case of education, and by insurance schemes in the case of health provision.

One of the advantages that community schools are said to have over private schooling is that, since the costs of provision do not fall only on parents, poor children need not be excluded on the grounds of the inability of their families to pay fees. The poor can therefore be protected from the worst effects of market solutions. On the other hand, compared with state schooling, outcomes are likely to be regressive, since poor communities will only be able to afford more modest schools than those available to richer communities. One solution might be to require community provision only of those inputs that do not have a major impact on school quality and efficiency (i.e. to provide the costs of teachers, books, and equipment from state funds). This, in turn would imply, however, that the scope for achieving savings in public expenditures by encouraging community schools would be relatively limited.

Chapter 7 by Mark Bray demonstrates that, particularly in Africa and Asia, community schools have many different modes and sources of finance. Bray's analysis confirms that decentralizing the financing of schooling to the local level brings large inequities in provision: the quality of such schools varies widely between poorer and richer areas. In addition, community schooling raises important problems of regulation and control. Accordingly, attempts to use community schooling as the major solution to the financing problem are likely to be ill-conceived. However, if used to provide a supplement to public resources, it is more defensible, provided that public provision of a minimally acceptable quality of schooling for all is provided by the state.

As indicated earlier in this chapter, the risk and unpredictability of re-quirements for health care, unlike education expenditures, which are more predictable, imply that insurance schemes provide a viable means of spread-ing the costs of service provision. This has long been recognized. Indeed, social insurance schemes had their origin in the German industrial schemes set up during the nineteenth century. These covered industrial workers who were, typically, working for large companies. A levy on the payroll to provide health care was efficient and popular since it spread the costs of risk among the whole workforce. Such schemes were expanded, and their lessons informed both the national social insurance schemes of twentieth-century Europe and the more partial schemes for health and other social insurance set up in many developing countries (in particular those in Latin America), covering mainly workers in the formal sector.

A major problem facing such schemes in developing countries is that the proportion of the population working in formal sector employment is, typically, small.[18] However, as Charles Normand argues in Chapter 8, there is no reason why any particular system should have to be comprehensive in coverage, provided that there are means whereby those not covered can gain care elsewhere. Resources can be mobilized in a number of different ways. Examples include compulsory savings schemes (as in Singapore, where families save together, thereby pooling risk to some extent, while the ownership of the health resources remains with those who save), community financing approaches, and private insurance schemes. The latter include those that are not employer-based, insuring mainly those with high incomes, and often low health needs. Although some of the treatments financed in this way are low priority in social terms, others would have been made available, in the absence of the private sector, by the state. Thus, provided that subsidies to them can be minimized, a useful supplement to public resources can thereby be achieved.

These schemes are not universally successful, as the case of China, discussed by Gerald Bloom in Chapter 9, shows. In that country, the costs of rural health care rose substantially after the introduction of market reforms from the late 1970s onwards, partly because of higher salaries being paid to health workers and partly because of an increased use of expensive drugs, from which practitioners also profited. Government funding did not keep pace with these enhanced costs; co-operative medical schemes collapsed owing mainly to the shift to household and individual forms of production; and user charges were increased, accounting by the mid-1990s for a large share of health care financing in rural areas. Accordingly, many of the poorer rural dwellers became less able to benefit from health services than before the introduction of market reforms.

The solution advocated by the government was voluntary insurance schemes funded by both households and local government. But these have not worked, in part because people—particularly the poor—are either unable or unwilling to pay in advance for services they may not need, and in part because many local governments no longer have sufficient independent sources of revenue to be able to allocate adequate resources to health, particularly given the higher levels of unit costs that have followed the economic

---

[18] Jimenez (1987: 120) shows that social insurance in Latin America, the southern continent where such schemes have been most intensively developed, covers more than half the population in only four out of sixteen countries, and in eight of them (all being lower-income) only between 4% and 14% of the population were covered. For further discussion of the Latin American experience, see Mesa-Lago 1991.

reforms. There also seem to have been problems created by an absence of technical and planning capacities at the local level, by an inability to regulate the behaviour of those in charge of service provision, and by a general scepticism, on behalf of the population, of the state's ability to deliver a system of health care that will, in fact, be able to deal effectively with their needs.

Nevertheless, although health insurance is unlikely to offer a mechanism for universal coverage, the experience of other developing countries shows that both private and social insurance can play a useful role in supplementing other sources of revenue. Although many of the services financed by insurance will not be those that make the largest impact on the health of the nation, they make a valuable contribution. Normand, in Chapter 8, argues that the aim should be to avoid relatively low-priority services being provided at the expense of those with higher priority. He points out that the service provided to those insured must be better than that available to those outside the scheme, otherwise there is no incentive to join. However, since people who enrol release resources for those who do not, services can, in principle, be improved for both the insured and the uninsured. An interesting implication of this argument is that an aim of health financing should be to manage the inequity that exists in access to care in such ways as to minimize the problems for those worst off, but not to try to give equal access to a similar quality of care to all.

1.4.4. Improving efficiency

The urgency of the search for new means of financing health and education systems is fuelled by the more general funding problems of the public sector. However, since a penny saved is, in this context, roughly similar to a penny earned, the question arises as to whether opportunities exist for improving the efficiency of public health and education systems, and, if so, whether these are significant enough to provide the basis for complementary, or even alternative, strategies.

There is ample evidence which suggests that the technical and allocative efficiency of health and education systems in developing countries, and their levels of cost effectiveness, are low. In that connection, those people in greatest need (i.e. the poor) receive least attention, despite the cost effectiveness of such interventions; too much attention is given to tertiary and too little to primary services; input use is poor and insufficiently well accounted for.

As regards solutions, we have seen that the pursuit of greater efficiency in the delivery of health and education services is an important part of the argument for their private provision even though, as this book shows, the evidence is as yet far from sufficient for the case to be granted. There are,

however, a range of alternatives, which stop short of privatization, yet attempt to create, within the public sector, arrangements which replicate some
of the competitive characteristics of markets so as to encourage more efficient
production.

Such arrangements have developed most rapidly in the health sector,
where, as shown in Chapter 10 by Anne Mills, market-based approaches aim
to separate the responsibility for financing health care from that of providing
it on a competitive basis. This is said to increase efficiency by making
providers—usually hospitals, although any level of care could be included—
compete with each other to attract public or private funding, and to improve
consumer choice. In addition, the replacement of direct management within
the public sector by contractual relationships between purchasers and providers of the service should make the prices of particular products more plain
and increase managerial decentralization, both of which are expected to
enhance efficiency. Transaction costs will increase, but efficiency gains are
expected to outweigh these.

This kind of market approach would, in principle, allow consumers to
exercise choice among both purchasers and providers. In practice, however,
central and local governments are often the only relevant purchasers in
developing countries. Furthermore, making sound choices between different
providers requires levels of knowledge and sophistication which most people
in poor countries do not have. Consumer-led competition, therefore, is
probably viable only for rich countries—if at all.

The most common means of encouraging provider competition is by
contracting out tasks that were previously delivered centrally. This can work
well for non-clinical services, such as cleaning and catering, where there is
anecdotal evidence that savings and/or a higher quality of service have been
achieved. However, contracting out clinical services is more unusual. The fact
that, particularly in rural areas, there is usually no choice of institutional
providers seems to undermine the notion of encouraging competition. And
even if markets are, in principle, contestable, the substantial initial costs of
establishing a hospital may be large enough to deter competitors, even if
prices were attractive. Finally, there are questions about the ability of the
public sector to negotiate and manage contracts adequately. Information
systems may be weak, and governments may know less about their own cost
structures than private providers know about theirs. Badly specified contracts
can pass most risk to the purchaser, and provide few incentives for efficient
provision. Thus, it is questionable whether contracting is generally an
appropriate mode for the delivery of health services in developing countries.

In education, the opportunities for introducing market reforms, by separ-
ating purchasers and providers, are as great as in the health sector.
Contracted out school meals, transport, and other services are common.
Voucher schemes, such as that being introduced in the UK for nursery
education—whereby parents are given an amount of credit for each eligible

child, which they can spend on education at an institution of their choice—are also possible. Although it seems likely that these kinds of initiative could improve efficiency, and would be practicable in developing countries, very little evaluative evidence for their impact exists.

A similar absence of evidence hampers assessment of one of the most common bureaucratic reforms—the decentralization of planning and management. This is judged necessary to inform local managers of the resource consequences of their actions, and to give them some means of improving their performance. But the real impact of these changes upon efficiency have not been rigorously assessed. There are, however, many other ways of increasing the efficiency of public health and education systems in particular cases. These potentially embrace all aspects of public administration reform, which, as Mills shows in the case of health, may include the redesign of planning and budgeting systems, changes in staff mix towards higher proportions of sub-professional staff, the restructure of incentives in line with policy objectives, improvements in the efficiency in the supply and use of drugs, and general reforms to management style and culture. The priorities differ, but such initiatives are needed in many countries.

Chapter 11 by Christopher Colclough shows that there also remains significant potential, in the case of education, to achieve savings from the identification and careful application of suitable efficiency reforms. Those that appear to be most cost-effective include changes to teacher–pupil ratios (by increasing class size, or introducing double-shifting where possible), changes to the length of the school cycle, increases in the use of assistant teachers, and a range of other approaches. The paper illustrates the impact of these reforms in the case of South Africa, where some of them are being implemented as that country attempts to eradicate the effects of past discrimination in education. It is demonstrated that the financing of the new government's policy of ten years of free and compulsory schooling will require these reforms, and that their fiscal impact is potentially substantial.

All of these papers indicate that, in general, policy prescriptions in favour of market-type reforms in both the health and education sectors are being advanced without knowing whether or not the proposed solutions will improve on the systems they are intended to replace. Although the efficiency of provision is low in the public sector, its improvement would probably be easier to achieve than would the development of government capacity to negotiate and monitor contracts, and to regulate the private sector. Decentralization and strengthening local management capacity appear important to improving technical efficiency. These initiatives seem desirable with or without market reforms, the scope for which is likely to be limited in many countries. However, considerable opportunities to find efficiency savings exist in both sectors, and these should be retained more centrally on the reformist agenda than has been the case in recent years.

1.4.5. Fiscal and governance reforms

As indicated earlier, the starting assumption, in many recent analyses of education and health services in the South, has been that the prospects for increasing the resources available to the public sector to finance expenditure in these sectors are bleak. A consequence of this is that the set of fiscal policies available to, or in use by, developing country governments has often not been interrogated, except in a rather superficial way. The paper by Robin Burgess (Chapter 12) aims to remedy this neglect, by asking how fiscal reform can contribute to extending the coverage of basic health and education.

The facts that these sectors are large (relative to total public spending), and that required expenditures upon them increase in line with both population growth and average incomes, imply that any method for funding them must provide stable, predictable, and buoyant revenues. Accordingly, it is self-evident that the use of borrowing or of inflation-financing approaches cannot provide satisfactory fiscal solutions for funding these sectors. It is notable that during the 1990s, aid has financed the greater part of health expenditures in a number of countries of sub-Saharan Africa (e.g. Tanzania, Mozambique). However, this represents a short-term response to fiscal crisis which, for reasons of political economy, cannot be expected to last (even though support for human resources will probably remain easily the most effective use for aid in sub-Saharan Africa). Thus, as Burgess argues, taxation provides the only long-term option if basic health and education are to be publicly financed. Unlike the situation in richer countries, contributory social security schemes are not able to provide a significant source of additional funding in developing countries. Equally, direct taxes are not usually promising, both because of difficulties of levying taxes upon most of the population and because of high rates of avoidance among those who ought to pay. However, there is substantial scope in many countries to expand broadly based indirect taxation, such as value added tax. This tax has the merits of being easy to implement, of allowing progressivity with few distortions, and of being (at present) a relatively undeveloped tax instrument in many parts of the world.

Expenditure priorities are, of course, just as important as revenue raising in many countries: as pressures on total spending increase, it becomes necessary to review not just the level but also the balance of state activities. Given the importance of education and health expenditures for growth and development, broadly defined, significant improvements in social welfare seem possible through changes in the composition of public budgets, without increasing their overall size. There is clear evidence, for example, that low school enrolments at primary level are often as much a function of low commitment to the goal of universalizing provision as they are of poverty and fiscal constraints (Colclough with Lewin 1993: ch. 2).

As Burgess argues, attitudes and actions of governments need to be changed in the above ways. But 'new political economy' theorists are quick to remind us that advocacy of this kind risks naivety in assuming that a different rationality can win the day. This is because the existing disposition of state resources and public action reflects the array of interests that need to be rewarded if governments are to retain power. Nancy Birdsall and Robert Hecht illustrate these dilemmas in the context of health policy in Chapter 13. Their paper, which utilizes a 'new political economy' framework, attempts to explain why, almost everywhere, access to basic health care is unequal (which they document), with the poor having much more restricted access to simple, cost-effective services. However, the authors argue that, while tendencies towards self-interest on the part of bureaucrats, politicians, middle-class consumers, and professionals within the health sector may lead to an alliance against the poor in terms of the allocation of resources, such tendencies can be undermined in cases where the distribution of income is more equal, where economic growth is stronger, and where the voices of the poor are louder in the polity (as may be the case in democracies). This argument is illustrated by examining the cases of Costa Rica, Malaysia, and Zimbabwe, where growth, distributional, and political circumstances have been conducive to more equitable resource allocations in the health sector than has often been the case elsewhere.

1.5. Conclusion

This book shows that, while public systems of education and health services need to be reformed, approaches that seek merely to pass more of their costs on to consumers perform less well than is claimed by many of their advocates. Equity and efficiency losses are, in practice, endemic to the introduction of compulsory fees—particularly when such reforms are applied to primary and secondary schooling/care. Although privately financed schooling and health services can broaden the range of services available, and need not imply greater inequity of provision, the evidence that is often claimed to demonstrate an efficiency advantage in favour of private provision is shown, on close examination, to be inconclusive for both sectors. The cost effectiveness of both of these service systems can and should be improved, but usually this requires far more than changes in the sources and mechanisms of obtaining finance. The evidence shows that, at tertiary level, insurance schemes in the case of health, and graduate or payroll taxes in the case of education, should be used to achieve partial cost recovery from direct beneficiaries—thereby concentrating public funding more sharply on the lower levels. But the extent to which these alone are capable of providing solutions to the overall financing constraint is limited. Such reforms need to be made in the context of much more fundamental changes in fiscal policy—whereby, in most countries, a greater use of indirect taxation, supplemented by a change in spending priorities towards health and education, are required. Both old and new political theory points to the dangers of expecting these shifts to be made easily; but education and health services are such powerful ingredients in notions of broadly based welfare, that regimes which depend, in some sense, on popular legitimacy find calls to widen their scope and improve their quality difficult to resist. Thus, moves towards political liberalism help to preserve the integrity of publicly funded health and education services, whereas, by contrast, the influence of economic liberalism has helped to undermine them.

References

Ahmad, E., Drèze, J., Hills, J., and Sen, A. (eds.) (1991), *Social Security in Developing Countries*, Clarendon Press, Oxford.

Bennell, P. (1996), 'Rates of Return to Education: Does the Conventional Pattern Prevail in Sub-Saharan Africa?' *World Development*, 24/1: 183–99

Burgess, R., and Stern, N. (1991), 'Social Security in Developing Countries: What, Why, Who and How?' in Ahmad *et al.* 1991: 41–80.

Colclough, C. (1982), 'The Impact of Primary Schooling on Economic Development: A Review of the Evidence', *World Development*, 10/3: 167–86.

—— (1996), 'Education and the Market: Which Parts of the Neo-Liberal Solution are Correct?' *World Development*, 24/4: 589–610.

—— with Lewin, K. (1993), *Educating All the Children: Strategies for Primary Schooling in the South*, Clarendon Press, Oxford.

—— and Manor, J. (eds.) (1991), *States or Markets? Neo-Liberalism and the Development Policy Debate*, Clarendon Press, Oxford.

Coleman, J., Hoffer, T., and Kilgore, S. (1982), *High School Achievement: Public, Catholic and Private Schools Compared*, Basic Books, New York.

Drèze, J., and Sen, A. (1989), *Hunger and Public Action*, Clarendon Press, Oxford.

—— —— (1991), 'Public Action for Social Security: Foundations and Strategy', in Ahmad *et al.* 1991: 3–40.

Findlay, R. (1989), 'Is the New Political Economy Relevant to Developing Countries?' PPR Working Paper WPS 292, World Bank, Washington, DC.

Gertler, P., and Glewwe, P. (1990), 'The Willingness to Pay for Education in Developing Countries: Evidence from Rural Peru', *Journal of Public Economics*, 42: 251–75.

—— —— (1992), 'The Willingness of Households to Pay for Improvements in School Quality: Evidence from Ghana', World Bank Conference on Public Expenditures and the Poor: Incidence and Targeting, 17–19 June, Washington, DC (mimeo).

—— and van der Gaag, J. (1988), 'Measuring the Willingness to Pay for Social Services in Developing Countries', Living Standards Measurement Study, Working Paper no. 45, World Bank, Washington, DC.

Griffin, C. (1992), 'Welfare Gains from User Charges for Government Health Services', *Health Policy and Planning*, 7: 177–80

Hinchliffe, K. (1993), 'Neo-Liberal Prescriptions for Education Finance: Unfortunately Necessary or Inherently Desirable?' *International Journal of Educational Development*, 13/1: 183–7

Jimenez, E. (1987), *Pricing Policy in the Social Sectors: Cost Recovery for Education and Health in Developing Countries*, Johns Hopkins University Press, for the World Bank, Baltimore.

King, E., and Hill, M. A. (1991), *Women's Education in Developing Countries: Barriers, Benefits and Policies*, Johns Hopkins University Press, for the World Bank, Baltimore.

Mbugwa, J., Bloom, G. and Segall, M. (1995), 'The Impact of User Charges on Health Care Utilisation Patterns in Rural Kenya: The Case of Kibwezi in Rural Kenya', *Social Science and Medicine*, 41: 829–35.

Mesa-Lago, C. (1991), 'Social Security in Latin America and the Caribbean: A Comparative Assessment', in Ahmad *et al.* 1991: 356–94.

Mingat, A., and Tan, J. P. (1986), 'Expanding Education through User Charges: What Can Be Achieved in Malawi and Other LDCs?' *Economics of Education Review*, 5/8: 273–86.

Musgrave, R. (1958), *The Theory of Public Finance*, McGraw Hill, New York.

—— (1987), 'Merit Goods', in J. Eatwell, M. Millgate and P. Newman (eds.), *The New Palgrave: A Dictionary of Economics*, Macmillan, London: 452–3.

Psacharopoulos, G. (1973), *Returns to Education: An International Comparison*, Elsevier, San Francisco.

——(ed.) (1987), *Economics of Education: Research and Studies*, Pergamon, Oxford.

—— (1994), 'Returns to Investment in Education: A Global Update', *World Development*, 22/9: 1325–43.

Schultz, T. P. (1991), 'Returns to Women's Education', in King and Hill 1991: 51–99.

Shaw, P., and Ainsworth, M. (eds.) (1994), *Financing Health Services Through User Fees and Insurance: Lessons from Sub-Saharan Africa*, Africa Technical Department, World Bank, Washington, DC.

Stern, N. (1989), 'Comment on "Social Sector Pricing Policy Revisited", by Jimenez', *Proceedings of the World Bank Annual Conference on Development Economics, 1989* (Supplement to the *World Bank Economic Review* and *The World Bank Research Observer*): 143–7.

Thobani, M. (1984), 'Charging User Fees for Social Service: Education in Malawi', *Comparative Education Review*, 28/3: 402–23.

Toye, J. (1991), 'Is There a New Political Economy of Development?' in Colclough and Manor 1991: 321–38.

UNESCO (1990), *Trends and Projections of Enrolment, by Level of Education and Age 1960–2025*, UNESCO, Paris.

—— (1994), *Statistical Yearbook 1994*, UNESCO, Paris.

UNICEF (1992), *Statistics on Children in UNICEF-Assisted Countries*, UNICEF, New York.

United Nations (UN) (1988), *Mortality of Children under Age 5: Projections 1950–2025*, United Nations, New York.

Weiss, A. (1995), 'Human Capital vs. Signalling Explanations of Wages', *Journal of Economic Perspectives*, 9/4: 133–54.

Whitehead, A. K., (1981), 'Screening and Education: A Theoretical and Empirical Survey', *British Review of Economic Issues*, 3/8: 44–62.

Woodhall, M. (1987), 'Student Loans', in Psacharopoulos 1987: 445–50.

World Bank (1986), *Financing Education in Developing Countries: An Exploration of Policy Options*, World Bank, Washington, DC.

—— (1987), *Financing Health Services in Developing Countries*, World Bank, Washington, DC.

—— (1993), *World Development Report 1993: Investing in Health*, Oxford University Press, New York.

—— (1994), *Higher Education: The Lessons of Experience*, World Bank, Washington, DC.

—— (1995*a*), *World Development Report 1995: Workers in an Integrating World*, Oxford University Press, New York.

—— (1995*b*), *Priorities and Strategies for Education: A World Bank Review*, World Bank, Washington, DC.

—— (1995*c*), *World Tables 1995*, World Bank, Washington, DC.

PART II

Cost Recovery

2

Lessons from Cost Recovery in Health

ANDREW CREESE AND JOSEPH KUTZIN

2.1. Introduction

In the last decade, publicly financed health services in most developing countries have become increasingly dependent upon payments by patients. Severely practical reasons underpin this trend. Real public expenditures per capita in health have often fallen. This decline has been in progress since the late 1970s in many countries. The quality and quantity of publicly subsidized health services has fallen correspondingly. Utilization levels, particularly at rural health facilities, have declined. Outreach services no longer function, drugs are often unavailable, and health staff are unsupervised and sometimes unpaid for long periods of time. Rural populations have faced higher costs for health care in terms of transport and time to get to hospitals in larger towns, or by payments to private providers of treatment and medication. 'Free' care has come to mean unacceptably poor care.

Governments have been under pressure to contain budget deficits by reducing subsidies and raising revenue. In the health sector, the preference of most governments has been to raise fees for services in response to these macroeconomic pressures. Apparently, this has been judged to be easier than reallocating resources within the health sector. The latter option entails a clash of interests between health care providers (doctors, in particular) and politicians. On several occasions, however, cost recovery initiatives have resulted in strong opposition from the population.

In some countries (e.g. Ghana, Jamaica, and Zimbabwe at times during the 1980s) a tariff (sometimes more than a decade old) was already in place but was no longer enforced, because the prices charged had become outdated by inflation. Elsewhere (e.g. Kenya, Malawi, and Zambia), introducing fees has meant legislative change, but the revenue-collecting and management functions were expected, in the interim, to be carried out by existing staff. In yet other settings, government health workers had been operating unofficial fee systems for private gain prior to the formulation of a cost recovery policy.

Thus, circumstances have been favourable to the expansion of cost recovery policies. Run-down public services, the compliance of health care providers, competition from private sources of supply, and an increasing cost to the user of access to care of acceptable quality, have all made it easier for governments to implement official fee systems. External advice and conditionality have also helped to persuade governments to move in these directions. The resulting changes in policy have been dramatic. Cost recovery in health is now widely accepted by governments as an instrument of financing policy. By 1993, almost all countries in sub-Saharan Africa had some form of cost recovery scheme in place or about to be introduced.

Yet, questions of principle and practice remain. In most industrialized countries, user charges do not occupy a prominent position in contemporary reform movements. In most OECD countries, performance improvement in the health sector is seen to depend more on altering the behaviour of *providers* than that of consumers. In Canada, a vigorous debate on the principle of user charges is in progress, in which it is argued that such a system is both regressive fiscally and inefficient in its allocative effect. It is even claimed that promotion of user charges reflects a conspiracy by the well-to-do against the poor (Evans 1993).

It is thus important, given the facts of policy change in developing countries, to examine the effects of these recent changes. This paper reviews recent experience on cost recovery in relation to three claimed areas of potential benefit: revenue-raising, improved access and equity, and greater efficiency. The focus is principally on sub-Saharan Africa, though selected experiences from other parts of the world are included.

Some general lessons are already clear. Early expectations that cost recovery in the health sector might prove an important supplement to tax-based financing, raising as much as 15 to 20 per cent of total government expenditure, have not been met. A combination of relatively low fees, low ability to pay (as marked by high formal or informal exemption rates), and 'leakage' through inefficiency or embezzlement have kept national cost recovery levels in health in Africa to an average of 5 per cent or less. Equity improvements have not been achieved by any large-scale cost recovery scheme in health; indeed, there are several well-documented accounts of large and sustained drops in attendances at government health facilities from different countries. There is some evidence that some groups—the poor, those with communicable diseases or vaccine-preventable diseases—have important health needs which are not being met because of the limitations on access to care caused by the introduction or increasing of fees.

Country experience suggests that supporting conditions are needed if additional revenue is to be converted into improved access to care for the sickest and the poorest. Creating these conditions can be costly, requiring increased investments in infrastructure, in health, and in other sectors, such as rural banking. From small-scale projects there is some evidence of beneficial efficiency effects: where it has been possible to use revenue from cost recovery to improve the quality of services offered, the marginal productivity of such expenditures appears to have been high. There has been a strong tendency for well-managed cost recovery revenues to go into general quality improvement rather than to be specifically targeted to improve access for the poor. Despite this failure to target user fee revenues to the poor, limited evidence suggests that quality improvements made possible by this process can disproportionately benefit those with the least time and money available to travel to more distant facilities (Litvack and Bodart 1993). More often than not, however, studies have illustrated inefficiencies and inequities related to cost recovery.

In spite of this very unsatisfactory record thus far, cost recovery in health in poor countries is now widely accepted as an instrument of health policy. A clearer understanding of the desirable supporting conditions needed to improve efficiency and equity, relating to the setting of prices and exemptions and to the capacity for the retention and management of revenue, is emerging. These 'implementation conditions' provide one specific set of lessons from experience. But there are also more general lessons. Implementing successful cost recovery policies has proved both politically controversial and technically difficult. The health gains are far from clear. Cost recovery initiatives have to be, not an isolated policy change, but part of a broader reform package, in which the emphasis is on better value for (probably more) money. Careful publicity to explain the purpose and nature of changes, and to identify exempt groups, is necessary. Rapidly visible improvements in service quality are needed. In the decade ahead, cost recovery alone is likely to be less central to the thrust of health policy than it has been in the recent past. It is likely to be more concerned with realizing small but important efficiency gains, and to be accompanied by an array of complementary organizational changes and policy measures.

2.2. Why Cost Recovery in Health?

From the perspective of national budgetary authorities (a ministry of finance, for example), the *general* rationale for cost recovery in health, as in other sectors, is that of macroeconomic balance. In situations of chronic and growing trade and domestic budget deficits, cost recovery for publicly financed goods and services offers one route to deficit control. There are, of course, other instruments for achieving fiscal balance, on both the revenue (e.g. improve tax efficiency) and expenditure (e.g. lower public employment levels) sides, and alterations in these may be possible without changing the basic rationale for subsidized access to publicly financed goods and services. Cost recovery initiatives in health have on several occasions (e.g. Ghana and Mozambique) resulted directly from the implementation of structural adjustment lending packages, which emphasized control over public expenditure, improved productivity in public enterprises, reduction of subsidies for publicly financed goods and services, and accompanying fiscal and monetary policy changes. In these cases the health sector has been treated like any other sector, notwithstanding the well-known health-specific market failure arguments (see e.g. Arrow 1963; Barnum and Kutzin 1993; de Ferranti 1985; Griffin 1989; Jimenez 1987; World Bank 1993).

There are also well-developed sector-specific arguments for and against cost recovery in health. The case against full cost recovery through user charges is based on both efficiency and equity arguments. The efficiency arguments mainly concern the likelihood of market failure, health care being unlike most other commodities, where the presence of externalities and information asymmetries are less important (see Chapter 1). The equity arguments have to do with the distinction between need and demand; that is, a population's capacity to benefit from health care is likely to be distributed very differently from its purchasing power. Accordingly, unregulated market solutions will be both inefficient and inegalitarian. User fees can thus be seen as a tax on those unfortunate enough to become ill (Barer *et al.* 1979). High fee levels, whether determined administratively or by market forces, are thus likely to deter precisely those people who most need access to care. On the other hand, the problem facing policy-makers in severely resource-constrained countries is that, when fees are absent or are set too low, revenues are usually insufficient to enable the supply of services to meet demand. As a result, quality and efficiency are compromised, and the poor remain underserved.

The most compelling case for user charges in poor countries has been their capacity to provide a boost for the recurrent (usually non-salary) costs of health care provision, which have been most depleted by declining real public expenditure. When a country has a slender tax base, low formal employment, and poor prospects for real growth, few alternative sources of health finance may appear to be available. Poor countries also face a severe problem in health service provision because of rapid cost inflation resulting from demographic pressure and import price increases. Further, they often have patterns of resource allocation favouring relatively high-cost and low-effectiveness interventions. In poor countries, therefore, there may be potential benefits from user charges both in mobilizing additional resources and in setting price signals to encourage more efficient behaviour by purchasers and providers.

Cost recovery as an instrument of health policy in developing countries became prominent in the mid-1980s. During the early part of that decade a major revision of the World Bank's position on cost recovery in health took place as part of a growing concern with questions of financing. The Bank's 1980 Health Policy Paper was cautious about the scope for cost recovery as a source of finance:

User charges are unpopular with governments because of the high cost of their administration and widespread problems of misappropriation of cash by health workers. User charges are also criticized for discouraging the use of preventive services and early treatments of diseases. Many countries have proclaimed the right to free health care, thereby limiting opportunities to impose charges. (World Bank 1980: 19)

The financing strategies envisaged for the following decade in the 1980 paper depended primarily upon the achievement of overall economic growth and a higher share of public resources for health: 'governments will have to spend substantially more on health . . . growth in national income should be allocated for primary health care' (pp. 45–6). The importance of technical efficiency improvements was stressed, and a role was identified for 'local financing' schemes, such as revolving funds for drugs or locally operated insurance schemes; but cost recovery through user charges as a national strategy was not actively promoted.

In contrast, the 1987 statement on health care financing (Akin *et al.* 1987) identified four components of a reform agenda: user charges, insurance, decentralization, and a greater recognition of the role of the private sector. This document exercised considerable influence both on health policy in developing countries and within the operations of the World Bank and other external assistance agencies. It suggests that a carefully designed policy of user charges has the potential to increase revenues and improve efficiency and equity.

The vision was of government using fees to choke off a substantial and essentially 'frivolous' demand for free services, with a cost-related fee system encouraging people to use lower-level health facilities first. A substantial portion of the operating costs of current programmes (Akin *et al.* 1987: 26) was expected to be recovered, and the proceeds would be used to improve access for the poor by extending appropriate (and, presumably, fee-exempt) services to them.

The discussion of user charges in the 1993 *World Development Report* (World Bank 1993) reflects a further evolution of Bank thinking. On the basis of cost effectiveness analysis, the document recommends that countries provide a basic package of public health and 'essential clinical' interventions. Efficiency (market failure) arguments are used to promote public financing of both the public health services and some of the essential clinical services. Moreover, public financing of essential clinical services is also supported as an anti-poverty measure because the poor are disproportionately affected by the burden of disease. However, in countries where the cost of the basic package of essential clinical services is beyond the means of government, selective user charge and targeting mechanisms are advocated as a means of resource mobilization.

The more recent case for fees to improve equity differs from that posited by Akin *et al.* (1987). The *World Development Report* (*WDR*) suggests that charging fees can improve equity if fee revenues are used to improve service quality and thus make acceptable services available closer to where patients live. The important deterrent effects of non-fee costs (i.e. time and transport costs) are noted, and sub-national examples from four African countries are cited where fee policies actually led to increases in utilization, especially by the poor. The *WDR* suggests that if fees represent less than 1 per cent of household income they have little impact on utilization, even by the poor. Where fee levels are higher than this, exemption mechanisms are needed to ensure access for the poor.

In both the 1987 and 1993 documents, little recognition was given to the likely transaction costs and capacity requirements for operating fee collection and exemption systems, and for retaining and managing the proceeds in the interests of the poor. Sections 2.4–2.6 briefly review lessons from experience in relation to the three broad objectives set out above: raising additional money, efficiency improvements, and improving equitable access to health services for the poor. Before proceeding to that discussion, however, it is necessary to provide some background as to the context within which cost recovery policies have been implemented.

2.3. The Scale of Cost Recovery Implementation

The *context* in which official cost recovery policy has been pursued in health varies substantially among countries. In many parts of the world, from Eastern Europe to South-East Asia, charging users is a widespread unofficial practice, with 'gratitude payments' to health workers used to ensure patients' access to care of acceptable quality. In some countries (e.g. Ethiopia) user charges have been a long established practice, but one that has hitherto been poorly co-ordinated, and in which big variations in the enforcement of regulations occur. Systems of very low tariffs that remain unchanged for many years are also common (as in Ghana prior to 1985, Botswana, Jamaica, Lesotho, and Turkey). These have been seriously eroded by inflation since they were last reviewed, and their declining importance as a source of funds has often led to negligence in their collection.

In a number of countries revenues collected through health institutions revert to the central treasury (e.g. Eritrea, Ethiopia, Malawi, and Namibia). Sometimes (as in Mozambique in 1985) user charges for health care were introduced as part of a more general process of subsidy reduction in the public sector. In other cases (e.g. Kenya) such charges were introduced as a more or less isolated instrument of policy change, without accompanying organizational changes or a broader package of civil service reform. In yet others (e.g. China and Hungary), a policy of greater reliance on out-of-pocket payments in health was part of a much broader transformation of economic and financing structures, involving organizational and fiscal change in most sectors, and numerous changes in the health sector in addition to the user charge policy (see Chapter 9 below).

User charge policies for health care in Africa have sometimes contrasted sharply as between the government sector and the private not-for-profit sector (the latter comprising principally mission or non-governmental organization providers). Mission health facilities often have a reputation for being relatively low-cost providers (possibly because of elements of subsidy in the price of their inputs) of good-quality services. Some mission providers have shown themselves assiduous in operating assessments of patients' ability to pay and occasionally ingenious in devising non-monetary equivalents of fees (see e.g. the case of Namibia, presented in WHO 1994).

Cost recovery innovations over the last decade have also included important local, project or district-level schemes. The notion of community financing in health goes back well beyond the last decade, though community contributions in health and education have often consisted principally of donated money or labour for capital projects, such as primary school or dispensary building, or occasionally even larger construction projects. The growing failure of the government to maintain its own infrastructure in health in many countries (Abel-Smith and Creese 1989), together with an increasing disenchantment with the prospects for improved performance in public infrastructures, has led some communities to pursue more autonomous routes to the maintenance and development of their health care system. Zaire is a good example of self-financing in health following the declaration in 1986 that government responsibility would be limited to the payment of salaries of certain public servants. With support from external non-governmental agencies, several zones in Zaire have implemented innovative health financing arrangements, with a heavy reliance on user charges and some mediation through insurance arrangements (Shepard *et al.* 1990). Similar initiatives have been taken, often with support from external non-governmental agencies, in other countries, e.g. Mali, Senegal, and Benin. A major boost for the development of such schemes came through the UNICEF–WHO (African Region) initiative, later known as the Bamako Initiative, which focused initially on improving the supply of drugs through community-managed payment and purchasing systems.

So substantial has been the spread of these schemes that a recent review defines 'two models' of cost recovery in Africa—one seen at the national policy level, the other in local or project-based schemes (Nolan and Turbat 1995). Cost recovery policy in some form now characterizes almost all countries of sub-Saharan Africa. Of the 37 countries surveyed in 1993, 33 had cost recovery schemes in place (national, local, or both) or about to be introduced. The great majority of these cost recovery policies were implemented or had been overhauled since 1980.

An accompanying change of attitude on the part of decision-makers in the health sector in Africa is clearly detectable. At a recent consultation of senior officials from 12 African countries, ministers and vice-ministers of health firmly endorsed the role of user charges in overall health policy (WHO 1994).

In addition to the revenue-raising and efficiency arguments mentioned above, policy-makers also identified service quality improvement as a primary rationale for charging patients. Indeed, the goals of improving the efficiency and quality of health services appear to be much more widely shared than those of improving access for the poor. This may well reflect the fact that there is little health gain likely from extending people's access to non-functional services, thus making the improvement of quality a prior requirement. Other operational objectives, such as promoting community involvement, ensuring improvements in drug supply, and promoting a shift from public to private care, have also been identified (Nolan and Turbat, forthcoming) as under-pinning recent moves towards cost recovery.

Cost recovery is also widely used in the health sector in Asia (Griffin 1992). China, which relied on cost recovery for significant levels of resource mobilization even during the early development of its rural infrastructure, witnessed a major shift in its health financing patterns during the 1980s when overall economic reforms were implemented. This gave even greater prom-inence to user charges, while insurance mechanisms remained an important source of financing, although the number of persons covered by insurance was reduced. Table 2.1 shows the evolution of percentage contributions to total health expenditure by source. Korea, Thailand, Malaysia, Singapore, and Indonesia also have user charge policies in health which coexist as cost-sharing provisions with national or partial social insurance schemes. In Cent-ral and South America, cost-sharing is also often an important component of health insurance systems.

The widespread existence and rapid recent growth in experience with user charges suggests that, in spite of the administrative difficulties facing any pol-icy innovations, initiating such schemes is probably much less of a challenge for central government than implementing other financing options, such as social insurance. However, establishing or raising fees is not the same as getting the user charge system to function as a mechanism for improving efficiency; even less is it a guarantee of improvement in the equity of service provision.

TABLE 2.1   Source of health care finance
in China, 1980 and 1989 (% of total)

Source	1980	1989	% change
Government	31	20	−35
Insurance	45	44	−2
Fees (out of pocket)	24	36	+50

Source: Yu Dezhi (1992).

2.4. To What Extent has Cost Recovery Raised Revenues in Health?

\

The World Bank's 1987 statement on health care financing (Akin *et al.* 1987) suggested that greater revenues would result from increasing fees at government health facilities. The increased revenues would have the potential to sustain cost-effective basic services over the long term, which tended to be underfunded from government sources alone. More immediately, user fee revenues could finance a substantial share of the operating costs of ongoing programmes and facilities, especially basic curative care. The authors suggested that governments could recover 15–20 per cent of operating costs through user charges, even in poor countries. Similarly, in the *World Development Report* (World Bank 1993), the revenue potential of fees for an essential clinical package of services is asserted to be about '10 to 20 per cent of total government spending for health' (p. 118).

This section assembles evidence on the financial yield from cost recovery policies, principally in Africa. First, *national* cost recovery data are presented, then evidence on cost recovery based on records from individual health facilities is given. Second, cost recovery experiences from a range of *subnational* projects or programmes are presented. Finally, indications are given of cost recovery levels in health facilities operated by *non-governmental organizations.*

Table 2.2 presents estimates (from several different sources) of fee income as a percentage of Ministry of Health recurrent expenditure in a range of different countries. From this table, Ghana's experience shows how cost recovery levels after the 1985 policy change peaked in 1987 at around 12 per cent of health expenditure, falling subsequently as exemptions increased and the relative value of fee levels to expenditures changed with inflation by 1992. Mozambique's data show a similar high early yield, followed by a substantial decline. In China, on the other hand, the relative importance of user charges grew rapidly in the 1980s as public subsidies were withdrawn from health and some pre-existing insurance schemes dissolved, at a time when the economy as a whole was experiencing very rapid and continuous growth. The absolute levels of cost recovery were in fact much higher than those indicated in the table when insurance reimbursements are included.

Systematic evidence about cost recovery at individual health facilities is fragmentary and shows such wide variations as to make generalization hazardous. Table 2.3 on hospital cost recovery (adapted from Barnum and Kutzin 1993) shows big variations. The authors comment: 'in most countries revenues generated from nongovernment alternative financing sources remain a small fraction of total hospital expenditures. Surprisingly, the percentage of costs recovered does not appear to be related to the level of per capita income or the prevailing ideology of a country' (p. 254).

TABLE 2.2   Percentage of Ministry of Health recurrent expenditure recovered through fees, various years

Country	Percentage	Year
Botswana	1.3–2.8	1983
Ghana	5.2	1985
	11.8–12.1	1987
	7.8	1992
Guinea-Bissau	0.5	1988
Kenya	2.1	1993
Lesotho	5.8	1986/7
	9	1991/2
Mozambique	8	1985
	<1	1992
Swaziland	2.2	1985
	4.6	1988/9
Zimbabwe	3.5	1991/2
Côte d'Ivoire	3.1–7	1986
Mali	1.2–7	1986
Senegal	4.4–7	1986
Papua New Guinea	3	1987
Yemen Arab Republic	3.3	1983
El Salvador	4	1990
China (excl. insurance	24	1980
reimbursements)	36	1988

Sources: Nolan and Turbat (forthcoming); WHO (1994); Vogel (1990); Barnum and Kutzin (1993); McPake (1993); Yu Dezhi (1992); Fiedler (1993); World Bank (1993).

In a number of recent studies, particularly in the context of appraising the Bamako Initiative (BI), and of drugs revolving funds, attention has been given to the level of financial sustainability from local sources. Nolan and Turbat (1995) report that Zambia has achieved 10–15 per cent cost recovery for community projects. Other sources provide the following figures for community-based financing schemes: Benin, 43–58 per cent in BI districts (UNICEF 1991*a*), Rwanda, 14–59 per cent of recurrent costs at pilot health centres (Shephard *et al.* 1993); Zaire, up to 97 per cent of non-salary operating costs in some health zones (Bitran *et al.* 1986). UNICEF (1991*a*) also reports the following cost-sharing experiences in 1988–90 in community-based schemes: Guinea, 52 per cent; Guinea Bissau, 32 per cent; Mali, 55 per cent; Senegal, 50 per cent; Uganda, 19 per cent.

Non-government sources of health care in developing countries, both religious missions and secular aid agencies, also have substantial experience

T ABLE 2.3   Cost recovery ratios—hospitals

Country and year of data	Level of hospital	(H_A/C)[a]	No. of hospitals in study
Low-income countries			
China, 1986	Central	90.1	8
	Provincial	87.9	11
	District	97.3	7
Ethiopia, 1984–5	Urban	32.1	8
	Rural	22.9	10
Indonesia, 1985–6	All public	19.9	—
Mali, 1986	Tertiary	7.5	1
	Tertiary		1
	District		1
Niger, 1986–7	Tertiary	14.8	1
Zaire, 1988	District	78.9	1
	District	66.3	1
Middle-income countries			
Bolivia, 1988	La Paz	47.5	6
	Cochabamba	51.5	4
	Santa Cruz	38.4	5
Dominican Republic, 1986	Tertiary	2.7	1
	Provincial	2.6	5
	District	1.5	3
Honduras, 1985	Tertiary	3.5	1
	Provincial	4.5	6
	District	5.3	8
Jamaica, 1986–7	All public	2.8	22
	University	7.5	1
Jordan, 1987	All MOH	13.3	—
	All RMS	22.3	—
	University	51.3	1
	All public	22.6	—
Papua New Guinea, 1985	All public	2.5	—
St Lucia, 1986–7	Central	2.4	1
Swaziland, 1988–9	MOH	4.7	4
	Mission	12.6	2
Turkey, 1987	All MOH	12.6	—
	All University	45.4	—
Zimbabwe, 1989	Central	7.3	4
	Provincial	3.1	8
	District	1.9	30

[a] Total revenues from fees and insurance (H_A) expressed as a percentage of total recurrent expenditures or revenues (C).

Source: Adapted from Barnum and Kutzin (1993).

with cost recovery. A review of different sources of evidence from Africa (Kutzin and Waters 1994) finds a range of cost recovery in non-governmental organizations of between 25 and 50 per cent of total expenditures—substantially higher than the averages for comparable government facilities. Lower costs, plus a combination of higher prices, more energetic fee collection, and greater willingness to pay, are evinced as likely explanations, though more research evidence on both the costs and quality of NGO-provided health services is necessary. Several sources report 100 per cent cost recovery for drugs in community financing settings.

All of the above figures are estimates of gross revenue. Yet the process of collecting fees itself entails costs. Little evidence exists on the administrative costs of fee collection, but a study in Papua New Guinea found that collection costs at one health centre were 90 per cent of the value of fees collected, although the average collection cost was much lower, at just over 10 per cent. The administrative costs include those of revenue collection, which comprise the purchase or printing of receipts, cash boxes, and accounting materials, related banking charges, and the value of staff time devoted to assessing patients' eligibility to pay, collecting fees and administering their banking, transfer, or use. Second, where fees are retained for local use, there are costs associated with their management. Decision-making about the use of fee income often involves the time of the local management committee. Indecision also has proved costly, as in Ghana, where inflation and bank charges rapidly reduced the purchasing power of fee revenue. Third, introducing or improving fee policy also entails training of staff, and in addition there are the costs of consultations and of publicizing the purpose and nature of the policy change. Finally, there have frequently been losses arising from the embezzlement or misuse of funds (Bennett and Banda 1994).

In many instances, the management and administrative costs of revenue collection in local or even national schemes have been funded through external assistance. This makes any assessment of success very difficult, because hidden subsidies distort cost recovery achievements by focusing only on local costs and local revenues. Anecdotal evidence exists of cost recovery projects in which the value of external inputs has exceeded local revenues by a factor of ten or even twenty. A more comprehensive approach to accounting for cost recovery is needed if the financial and capacity requirements for successful implementation are to be fully understood.

User charges have succeeded in raising additional funds for health, but the total amounts of money recovered, measured as a supplement to the national sources of finance for health care, are well below the 10 or 20 per cent anticipated in World Bank documents. If the actual capital and recurrent costs of operating cost recovery are taken into account, the net yield of the above schemes falls. Further, as a substantial and untapped additional source of finance for health in poor countries, it seems safe to say that early hopes have proved too optimistic. Nevertheless, where suitable revenue retention, banking, and management arrangements exist, there is some evidence that funds collected have been used to improve the functioning of services. Such arrangements appear to have been achieved much more frequently in the context of sub-national projects than in nationwide government reforms. Typically, retained fee income has been used for the purchase of drugs and dressings in both national and local contexts. Thus, in situations of recurrent funding crisis, where there is severe underfunding of critical inputs, the positive impact may be greater than indicated by the often small impact on aggregate revenues.

2.5. Has Cost Recovery Improved Efficiency and Quality in Health?

The World Bank's policy paper on health financing (Akin *et al.* 1987) suggested several ways of improving efficiency in the health sector by charging fees. Most of these derive from the expected effect of prices on the behaviour of potential consumers (patients). First, fees would reduce unnecessary use of services. Second, by co-ordinating prices among different levels of facilities, fee systems could encourage appropriate use of first-contact and referral facilities. Third, where fees are in place in a facility, exemptions for specific services, such as prenatal care or tuberculosis treatment, could encourage the use of these important services. It was also suggested that providers of services would be encouraged, out of concern for the new financial implications facing their patients, to limit practices such as over-prescription of drugs. Moreover, charges were expected to provide an incentive for the provision of higher quality care.

The *World Development Report* (World Bank 1993) does not make these efficiency arguments for fees. Indeed, the Bank suggests that, where possible, governments should fully fund an essential clinical package of services (as well as public health interventions). User charges for these services are suggested only for countries in which government resources would be insufficient fully to fund even a minimal package. Charging substantial fees in government facilities, especially hospitals, for services outside the package is supported, however. The (allocational) efficiency argument for this strategy is that such charges would imply a reduction in public subsidies to non-essential services, allowing a greater concentration of government funding on those that are more cost-effective.

User fees have reduced the utilization of services to some extent, particularly by the poor, as will be shown in the next section. However, there is no evidence that such utilization was unnecessary (Creese 1991). The probable reason for this is that the other costs (of time and transport) are sufficient to deter unnecessary use.

By setting different prices for different levels of health facility (i.e. having low prices at first-contact facilities, higher prices in district hospitals, and the highest prices in tertiary hospitals), the structure of fees sends signals that can affect patterns of utilization. Such systems of 'cascading' charges exist in a number of countries, including Kenya, Indonesia, Namibia, Zambia, and Zimbabwe (Barnum and Kutzin 1993; WHO 1994). Namibia goes further in encouraging proper use of the referral system by exempting referred patients from charges at higher-level institutions. Intuitively, this type of co-ordinated pricing makes sense, but the effects of such pricing policies on the use of the referral system have not been studied. The common finding of under-used health centres and overcrowded hospital outpatient departments, as found in Zambia, for example, suggests that the use of co-ordinated pricing policy is not, by itself, sufficient for improving use of the referral network. Other measures, especially those focused on improving the quality of care available at first-contact facilities, would seem to be needed as well. Industrialized countries, trying to limit unnecessary use of hospital resources, are using techniques based on shifting payment responsibility not to patients but to 'purchasers'—i.e. agencies responsible, from fixed budgets, for buying care from different providers. One way in which these purchasers economize is to require that, under most non-emergency circumstances, patients' first point of contact with the health services is in a non-hospital ambulatory setting.

The cost effectiveness of health services can be improved by measures to increase the probability that persons with communicable diseases seek treatment. The reason for this is that such treatment (e.g. for tuberculosis or sexually transmitted diseases) benefits not only the patient but also other members of the community who would have caught the disease from these patients if they had not been successfully treated. One way to encourage persons with communicable conditions to be treated is to provide such services free of charge. In many countries (e.g. Ethiopia, Ghana, Jamaica, Mali, Niger, Papua New Guinea, and Zimbabwe), no fees are charged for treatment of tuberculosis in government health facilities. Unfortunately, as with other efficiency implications of fee systems, little is known about the impact of such exemptions on treatment-seeking behaviour for tuberculosis. If fee exemptions do encourage more people with tuberculosis to seek treatment, governments should consider applying similar exemptions to other types of communicable disease. For example, all of the countries mentioned above, except Papua New Guinea, charge for treatment of sexually trans-mitted diseases (STDs). If these charges are causing persons with STDs to delay seeking care (an empirical question for which there is currently little evidence), policy-makers should consider waiving them because the social costs of not treating a case are almost certainly greater than any revenue forgone by exempting the case from payment.

There is some evidence that revenues from community financing schemes have led to improvements in both the perceived and the actual quality of available services. An evaluation of the Bamako Initiative found that in some countries the revenues generated through drug fees were used to attain concrete improvements in health services (McPake *et al.* 1993). Some indication of the importance of improving continuity in the local supply of drugs can be gained from analysing actual expenditures from fee income. In Kenya, over half of such expenditures have been for just two items—maintenance, and the purchase of emergency drugs. Where the drugs procurement, distribution, and prescribing systems are sufficiently well managed to ensure that available drugs are currently chosen in view of the local disease pattern, cost recovery facilitates an improvement in the quality of care and thus in the technical efficiency with which the health system operates.

The available evidence suggests that the existence of fees does not encourage providers to be more restrained in their supply of services but rather the reverse. The experience of China, where fees substantially finance health services, and hence where prices are high, suggests that providers will respond to price incentives differently from the manner suggested by Akin *et al.* (1987). Certain services, including drugs and some complex procedures (e.g. ultrasound, and renal dialysis) are priced in such a manner that health facilities profit by their provision. These price distortions have led to rapid increases in the 'provider-induced demand' for and supply of such procedures and services. Indeed, it is likely that price incentives led to a potentially dangerous over-use of services, as suggested by evidence that an average of 2.3 drugs was prescribed per patient contact with the health system by the late 1980s (Bumgarner 1992). This experience has implications for other countries attempting to implement measures, such as those in the Bamako Initiative, to encourage communities to self-finance drug supplies. Many studies (e.g. Mwabu *et al.* 1993; Litvack and Bodart 1993; McPake *et al.* 1992) have found that the extent to which drugs are available in a health facility has an important positive impact on the demand for services in that facility. Thus, people seem to equate the availability of drugs with a higher probability that they will receive effective treatment. The danger is that the demand for drugs will exceed what is medically necessary, yet providers will respond to financial incentives and meet this demand in order to increase revenues. The challenge facing policy-makers is to develop and implement pricing schemes for drugs that limit the incentive to over-prescribe.

China's experience suggests that prices can indeed send powerful signals that affect both the allocation and the use of health resources. However, where user charges are set at relatively low levels, as in most developing countries where widespread insurance coverage is lacking, there is no evidence that referral patterns or the use of specific services are affected in a manner significantly different from that which would obtain if the services were provided free of charge. Where fee revenues are retained and used to purchase essential non-staff recurrent inputs, such as pharmaceuticals, they can make an important contribution to the quality and availability of services.

2.6. Has Cost Recovery Improved Equity?

The evidence regarding the effect of fees on access to services is less positive. In most cases, user fees have had negative consequences for equity because income-related pricing and exemption measures have proved difficult to implement consistently and accurately. As a result, fees have posed a greater barrier to service use by poorer persons.

Econometric studies using household survey data have found that the demand for health care services is more price-elastic for poorer persons than for richer persons (see Gertler and van der Gaag 1990 for demand studies from Côte d'Ivoire and Peru). Falling clinic attendances in many countries also suggest that user charges and, in addition, declining service quality have had severely adverse effects on equity. In Ghana, for example, a national decline in attendances was observed in 1985, the year in which fees were substantially increased: from 4.5 million outpatient visits in 1984 to 1.6 million in 1985. Utilization rebounded slightly to 2.1 million visits in 1986 (Waddington and Enyimayew 1990). The authors found that in one region urban utilization fell by more than 50 per cent one year after the increase in fees; rural utilization remained 'well below' (p. 299) pre-increase levels three years later, although there was an increase in the proportion of users in the most economically active age group (15–44). These phenomena were directly attributed to the increase in fees in 1985.

Yoder (1989) reported an average decline of about one-third in outpatient attendances at government health facilities in Swaziland in the three months following a fee increase in 1984, where the object of policy had been to equalize prices charged by public and mission health facilities. One year later, the general picture remained unchanged. Attendances at mission health facilities increased by over 10 per cent in the same period. Yoder also reported big declines at government facilities in the use of services for diarrhoeal disease (more than a 40 per cent drop), sexually transmitted disease (39.6 per cent), acute respiratory infections (43.7 per cent), and infant immunizations (37.6 per cent for the first diphtheria–pertussis–tetanus shot). He concluded that up to one-third of the drop in attendance was among patients who had previously paid least, i.e. the poorest.

Studies of Kenya's fee policy, which changed in December 1989, estimate initial drops in outpatient attendances of 37 per cent overall and of over 50 per cent in some districts (WHO 1994). The percentage of patients using government dispensaries (where fees were not charged) increased by about 10 per cent in the same period. The *registration fee* was particularly unpopular; when it was replaced by an outpatient treatment fee in September 1990, attendance rose, though still to less than pre-1989 levels. Significant movement of patients away from non-government health facilities was reported after suspension of registration fees in public facilities. Demand for medical services in government health centres increased by about 41 per cent after the suspension of cost-sharing in August 1990.

A study in Lesotho (Bennett 1989) showed drops in attendance in the two districts studied of 40 and 51 per cent after a fee increase in 1988 and corresponding increases in the use of private facilities of 19 and 35 per cent, respectively. This implies that private sources of care only partially replaced public providers. The study also showed that, although visits to all government health facilities fell following the fee increase, the decrease was greatest in facilities located in the more remote mountainous areas. Moreover, in the years following the fee increase, attendance levels rose at lowland facilities at a rate that indicated they would soon regain levels similar to those that obtained prior to the increase in fees. This recovery in utilization rates was not experienced in health centres and hospitals located in the mountains. The author also found that utilization by the most vulnerable group in the population, young children (0–5 age group), was reduced most by the increase in fees.

Inequities have also been observed to stem from the ways in which some cost recovery schemes have been managed. For example, the shift in Kenya to allow health facilities to retain all of the funds collected has been greatly to the advantage of those few districts with a provincial hospital, since this is the level at which cost recovery yields most money. In general, these are not the least disadvantaged districts. This is a dramatic illustration of a trend which has also been observed in community-based cost recovery schemes. Without some mechanisms for redistributing funds from better-off areas, such policies are inherently inegalitarian across, as opposed to within, communities.

Granting exemptions is usually advocated as a means to protect poor persons from the financial barriers posed by user fees. Barnum and Kutzin (1993) found that most countries include provisions to exempt the poor from payment of fees in government hospitals. However, they also found an array of other exemptions that ran contrary to equity goals, such as exemptions for civil servants and members of the armed forces (in Ghana, Mali, Niger, St Lucia, and Yemen). A survey of patients at Niger's central government hospital in Niamey found that the income of non-exempt patients was, on average, less than the average for the entire sample of patients (Weaver *et al.* 1990). Experience to date suggests, therefore, that, at least in some countries, existing policies for fee exemption are not pro-poor.

Even where stated policies for exemption would clearly enhance equity and improve access for the poor, implementation often varies from policy intent. The basic issue regarding the enforcement of exemption policies is to identify persons too poor to pay fees and ensure that they have access to needed services while guaranteeing that the non-poor pay the designated fee. It is administratively difficult to determine a patient's income, particularly when most income is generated through subsistence farming and patients have little incentive to be truthful about their economic status. Gilson (1988) presents evidence to this effect from Swaziland and Thailand. Moreover, even if the administrative capacity were in place, the costs of implementing a strict means testing programme might be greater than the revenues that could be collected from fees, especially where fee levels are low.

The determinants of utilization are complex, and economic factors are only one consideration in people's health care-seeking behaviour. Moreover, fees charged (formally and informally) at the point of use are only one component of the total access costs facing patients. There may often be transport costs, and there are likely to be non-monetary losses to the patient and accompanying family members (e.g. loss of time in other productive activities). Distance to health facilities is, therefore, an important factor restricting access to care for large numbers of people in poor countries. Consequently, one way to improve equity is to reduce the distance between health facilities and people. Establishing outreach services and rural clinics have been important ways of improving equitable access to care in many African countries. Often these have been disproportionately hard hit by the economic deterioration of the country, as they depend critically on good supply systems for drugs and good transport systems for supervision purposes. Claims on drugs and transportation are typically made first by higher-level facilities (WHO/UNICEF 1989). As service quality has fallen at peripheral levels, people have to travel a greater distance to get the standard of care that they had previously. It is against this background that many community financing projects have sprung up. An important step to improved equity would be to restore peripheral services to their intended level of functioning and supervision, giving priority in the transfer of fee income to support such facilities.

Akin *et al.* (1987) argued that fees could improve equity by financing the extension of services to remote areas where modern care was previously inaccessible. However, there is no evidence that new facilities have been developed by these means, nor that outreach services from existing facilities have increased. On the other hand, there is limited evidence from community studies that the recycling of fee revenues into existing facilities has improved their quality of care, resulting in improved geographic access to higher-quality services for the surrounding population. The World Bank (1993) cites studies from four African countries (Benin, Cameroon, Guinea, and Sierra Leone) which suggest that the use of formal fees can lead to a reduction in the non-fee (e.g. transport and time) costs facing potential patients in accessing care of sufficient quality. In each of these studies, the poor benefited most by the introduction of fees because their ultimate effect (when combined with measures to recycle the revenues into improved quality at local facilities) was to reduce total access costs.

For example, experience from Cameroon has demonstrated that cost recovery can be managed in such a way as to improve utilization by the poor (Litvack and Bodart 1993). The project was small and had substantial external support, but its achievements draw attention to the importance of considering the non-fee costs (time and transport) of access to care, as well as monetary charges. People incurred a saving in time and transportation costs big enough to offset the cost of higher fees and adjusted their utilization pattern accordingly (see Section 2.7 below). Although the replicability of such experience remains to be demonstrated, it suggests that, in most settings and especially in rural areas, fees are probably not necessary to deter 'frivolous' use, because non-fee access costs already provide a sufficient deterrent. Because of these costs, the poor will have less access to care even where no fees are charged.

The goal of improving access for disadvantaged groups requires policies for user charges and exemptions which are consistent with ability to pay and which do not prevent access to essential services. The evidence from several studies suggests that the poor are more deterred by price (both monetary and time-related) than are the relatively well-off. Policies to exempt the poor from payment of fees are present in most countries, but these have proven difficult to implement effectively and often have features that favour some groups of non-poor persons. There is no evidence to suggest that fee revenues have been used explicitly to extend service availability to poor persons, but fee retention to improve quality in peripheral facilities has the potential to improve the availability of better-quality services to the local population. However, there are as yet very few documented cases of improved access by the poor following on from the introduction of fees for service.

2.7. Implementation Issues in Cost Recovery

Experiences over the last decade have identified a number of conditions which appear critical to the success of cost recovery as an approach to the improvement of people's health. These are presented in relation to the three main issues identified above.

2.7.1. Improving revenue-raising and resources

User charges can mobilize some additional economic support for health services provided by government. This economic support can be converted into real health resources that can lead to improved quality at the level of the health facility. This conversion is not automatic, however, and thus increasing revenues and increasing health resources are two separate effects.

In several countries (e.g. Botswana, Jamaica, Lesotho, Papua New Guinea, Turkey, and Zimbabwe) for which an act of government is needed to change fee levels, prices remained unchanged for many years. Consequently, the percentage of government health expenditures recovered through fees fell dramatically, owing to inflation. To avoid these consequences, periodic adjustment of fee levels to keep pace with inflation should be automatic. This policy is most likely to be successful if price changes are a routine administrative rather than a political act (e.g. if fee levels are tied to a price index). Furthermore, in order to reduce costs to improve cost recovery and keep financing schemes affordable, waste and inefficiency need to be minimized. With lower costs, less revenue is needed, and thus facilities can charge lower prices (Brunet-Jailly 1991; Korte *et al.* 1992). Keeping down the costs of drugs is particularly important for the financial sustainability of community financing schemes.

Although revenue-raising is the most commonly cited purpose of cost recovery, only a small number of documented cases exist where national or health facility targets for cost recovery are pre-set. More commonly, government or providers' perceptions of people's ability to pay are the basis for fee and exemption setting, with revenue levels determined as a consequence of these.

A wide range of fee-setting options exists, differentiating by service level, type of illness, and type of patient. Flat-rate registration or consultation fees, and variable charges according to the number of items prescribed, the use of diagnostic services, or length of stay are possible (WHO 1994). The unpopularity of the flat-rate registration fee in Kenya became clear when temporary gaps in drugs supply were experienced by health units. Subsequently patients were charged according to the number of items prescribed. Cameroon uses a combined system of registration fees and drug charges, with the former being fixed by central government. Drug prices are set locally, but the prices charged by medical stores are set in such a way as to subsidize costs to more remote districts, and for essential drugs, such as chloroquine. Preferred fee-setting arrangements appear to include elements of central guidance, with local discretion in their application, rather than *either* a totally centralized or devolved system (WHO 1994).

Perhaps the most important condition for user charges increasing the level of health resources is that some or all of the revenues collected should be retained for use within the collecting health facility. In some countries (e.g. Kenya, cited in WHO 1994) a change in Ministry of Finance practice on revenue retention has accompanied the introduction of the cost recovery policy, in addition to assurances that overall levels of public funding for health will remain unchanged. In other countries (e.g. Ethiopia, Namibia, Malawi, and Eritrea) revenues collected by government health facilities still revert to the Ministry of Finance. This practice means that cost recovery in health is neither an instrument of transferring access rights to the underserved nor an earmarked revenue-raising device for health. Revenue retention within the health sector, to better achieve health objectives, is, therefore, an important *quid pro quo* in the negotiation of subsidy-reducing pressures between Ministries of Health and Ministries of Finance. A variety of mechanisms exist for sharing fee revenue between the facility making the collection, the district,

potential users. This last condition suggests that the equity rationale for implementing fees for publicly provided health services may be strongest for relatively isolated communities, or where private alternatives for equivalent services are very expensive in terms of both monetary price (travel and fee) and the amount of time needed to use these providers.

There is little evidence of experiences where mechanisms function successfully, consistently, and cost-effectively to identify the poor for exemption from fee payment so that their access to necessary care is not inhibited. This does not mean that exemptions do not work and should be abandoned. More research is needed to identify the effect of exemption measures on the utilization of services by the poor in the hopes of illustrating the institutional features that facilitate good performance.

2.8. Conclusions

Cost recovery policies have wide-ranging impacts on people's health-seeking behaviour; a focus on the revenue-raising objective alone is dangerously narrow. Nevertheless, there is now widespread acceptance (in Africa and elsewhere) that cost recovery has some role to play in the financing and allocation of health services. This represents a major change from the early 1980s. From recent experience it can be seen that the trade-off between raising money and achieving more equitable access may be sharp unless several accompanying measures are in place. Also, it has been seen that small amounts of money at local level can make an important contribution to service availability. The major lessons from experience draw attention to the difficult process of converting revenue gains into service quality and/or accessibility improvement. It is now clear that a composite package of accompanying organizational and managerial changes is needed to support successful cost recovery policy if its most obvious predicted effect—reducing demand by those least able to pay—is to be avoided.

This review has illustrated several conditions that are associated with the capacity of fee systems to make a positive contribution to the goals of health sector reform. The most important conditions relate to cost recovery policy, managerial capacity, and institutional development. In terms of policy, sustained progress towards reform goals of equity and efficiency requires that some or all fee revenues be retained at the collecting facility and translated into quality improvement, and that periodic adjustment of fee levels be an integral part of fee systems. The managerial and institutional capacity must exist to use the retained revenues promptly to improve the quality of care in a manner that is perceptible to the local population, and in such a manner that the net private costs of gaining access to effective care are reduced. Local institutions (banks, for example) for the investment of collected revenues also need to be in place to prevent losses that are due to inflation.

Without other accompanying reforms, charging users of government health facilities is unlikely to yield substantial progress towards equity and efficiency. Associated policy measures include changes in resource allocation in favour of first-contact facilities, bypass charges for persons using referral facilities for first-contact care, and a waiver of fee payment in hospitals for persons who have been referred from first-contact facilities. Such a package of reforms may be facilitated by an organizational structure wherein overall management, including resource allocation authority, is vested in a single institution responsible for the health of the population in a defined geographic area. Such a structure should facilitate co-ordination of services across providers better than do administrative structures organized on the basis of specific facilities.

The fact is that managerial capacity in ministries of health is typically weak—particularly in sub-Saharan Africa. There is thus limited prospect in the short term for nationally administered schemes of cost recovery to be important sources both of additional finance and of improvements in the quality of care and access to it. However, in the context of longer-term organizational and financing change and institutional development, cost recovery may well have a role to play in ensuring that those who can afford to pay for care do, that low efficacy services are provided at full cost where they are financed through the public sector, and that the price signals facing consumers reinforce a rational allocation of health resources.

References

Abel-Smith, B. and Creese, A. L. (eds.) (1989). *Recurrent Costs in the Health Sector: Problems and Policy Options in Three Countries.* (WHO, Geneva).

Akin, J., Birdsall, N., and de Ferranti, D. (1987). *Financing Health Services in Developing Countries: An Agenda for Reform.* (World Bank, Washington, DC).

Arrow, K. (1963). 'Uncertainty and the Welfare Economics of Medical Care'. *American Economic Review,* 53: 941–73.

Barer, M. L., Evans, R. G., and Stoddart, G. L. (1979). 'Controlling Health Care Costs by Direct Charges to Patients: Snare or Delusion?' *Occasional Paper* no. 10 (Ontario Economic Council, Ontario).

Barnum, H. and Kutzin, J. (1993). *Public Hospitals in Developing Countries: Resource Use, Cost, Financing* (Johns Hopkins University Press, Baltimore and London).

Bennett, S. (1989). 'The Impact of the Increase in User Fees: A Preliminary Investigation'. *Lesotho Epidemiological Bulletin,* 4.

—— and Banda, E. Ngalande (1994). 'Public and Private Roles in Health: A Review and Analysis of Experience in Sub-Saharan Africa'. *Current Concerns,* SHS Paper 6, WHO/SHS/CC/94.1 (Division of Strengthening Health Systems, WHO, Geneva).

Bitran, R. A. *et al.* (1986). 'Zaire Health Zones Financing Study' (John Snow Inc., Arlington, Va.).

Brunet-Jailly, J. (1991). 'Health Financing in the Poor Countries: Cost-Recovery or Cost Reduction?' World Bank Policy, Research, and External Affairs Working Paper 692, (World Bank, Washington, DC).

Bumgarner, J. R. (ed.) (1992). *China: Long-Term Issues and Options in the Health Transition* (World Bank, Washington, DC).

Creese, A. L. (1991). 'User Charges for Health Care: A Review of Recent Experience'. *Health Policy and Planning*, 6(4): 309–19. Also available as SHS Paper 1 (Division of Strengthening Health Services, WHO, Geneva).

de Ferranti, D. (1985). 'Paying for Health Services in Developing Countries: An Overview'. World Bank Staff Working Paper 721 (World Bank, Washington, DC).

Evans, R. G. (1993). 'User Fees for Health Care: Why a Bad Idea Keeps Coming Back'. Working Paper No. 26, Programme in Population Health (Canadian Institute for Advanced Research, Ottawa).

Fiedler J. L. (1993). 'Increasing Reliance on User Fees as a Response to Public Health Financing Crises: A Case Study of El Salvador'. *Social Science and Medicine*, 36(6): 735–47.

Gertler, P. and Van der Gaag, J. (1990). *The Willingness to Pay for Medical Care* (Johns Hopkins University Press, Baltimore and London).

Gilson, L. (1988). *Government Health Care Charges: Is Equity Being Abandoned?* EPC Publication 15 (London School of Hygiene and Tropical Medicine, London).

Griffin, C. C. (1989). *Strengthening Health Services in Developing Countries through the Private Sector*. International Finance Corporation Discussion Paper 4. (World Bank, Washington, DC).

——(1992). *Health Care in Asia: A Comparative Study of Cost and Financing* (World Bank, Washington, DC).

Jimenez, E. (1987). *Pricing Policy in the Social Sectors*. (Johns Hopkins University Press, Baltimore and London).

Korte, R., Richter, H., Merkle, F., and Görgen, H. (1992). 'Financing Health Services in Sub-Saharan Africa: Options for Decision-Makers during Adjustment'. *Social Science and Medicine*, 34(1): 1–9.

Kutzin, J. and Waters, H. (1994). 'Health Sector Financing and Sustainability in Sub-Saharan Africa: A Strategic Framework for Setting Priorities'. Document prepared for the US Agency for International Development Health and Human Resources Analysis for Africa (HHRAA) Project (USAID, Washington).

Litvack, J. I. and Bodart, C. (1993). 'User Fees and Improved Quality of Health Care Equals Improved Access: Results of a Field Experiment in Cameroon'. *Social Science and Medicine*, 37(3): 369–83.

McPake, B. (1993). 'User Charges for Health Services in Developing Countries: A Review of the Economic Literature'. *Social Science and Medicine*, 36(11): 1397–1405.

——Hanson, K., and Mills, A. (1992). 'Experience to Date of Implementing the Bamako Initiative: A Review and Five Country Case Studies'. Health Policy Unit, Department of Public Health and Policy (London School of Hygiene and Tropical Medicine, London).

————(1993). 'Community Financing of Health Care in Africa: An Evaluation of the Bamako Initiative'. *Social Science and Medicine*, 36(11): 1383–95.

Mwabu G. M., Ainsworth, M., and Nyamete, A. (1993). 'Quality of Medical Care and Choice of Medical Treatment in Kenya: An Empirical Analysis'. Technical

Working Paper 9. Human Resources and Poverty Division, Africa Technical Department (World Bank, Washington, DC).

Nolan, B. and Turbat, V. (forthcoming). 'Cost-Recovery in Public Health Services in Sub-Saharan Africa'. Economic Development Institute (World Bank, Washington, DC).

Shepard, D. S., Vian, T., and Kleinau, E. F. (1990). 'Health Insurance in Zaire'. Policy, Research, and External Affairs Working Paper 489. (World Bank, Washington, DC).

——Carrin, G., and Nyandagazi, P. (1993). 'Household Participation in Financing of Health Care at Government Health Centres in Rwanda' in A. Mills and K. Lee (eds.), *Health Economics Research in Developing Countries* (Oxford University Press).

UNICEF (1991*a*). Bamako Initiative Management Unit, Sitrep 002/91, New York.

——(1991*b*). 'Strengthening Health Services: Community Cost-Sharing and Participation'. Paper prepared for Informal Session on the Bamako Initiative, UNICEF Executive Board Meeting, 24 April 1991 (UNICEF, New York, mimeo).

Vogel, R. (1990). 'Trends in Health Expenditure and Revenue Sources in Sub-Saharan Africa'. Background paper prepared for the Africa Health Policy Study (World Bank, Washington, DC).

Waddington, C. J. and Enyimayew, K. A. (1990). 'A Price to Pay, Part 2: The Impact of User Charges in the Volta Region of Ghana'. *International Journal of Health Planning and Management* 5(4): 287–312.

Weaver, M., Handou, K., and Zeynabou, M. (1990). 'Patient Surveys at Niamey National Hospital: Results and Implications for Reform of Hospital Fees'. Prepared under USAID Project 683–0254 (Abt Associates, Bethseda, Md).

WHO/National Health Systems and Policies (1994). Report of an Intercountry Meeting on Public/Private Collaboration for Health. WHO/SHS/NHP/94.2, Windhoek, Namibia, 4–8 October 1993.

WHO/UNICEF (1989). 'The World Economic Crisis and its Impact on Health and Health Services: Evidence and Requirements for Action'. Paper prepared for Joint Committee on Health Policy, January (WHO, Geneva).

World Bank (1980). *Health Sector Policy Papers*, 2nd edn., (World Bank, Washington, DC).

——(1993). *World Development Report 1993: Investing in Health.* (Oxford University Press, for World Bank, Washington, DC).

Yoder, R. A. (1989). 'Are People Willing and Able to Pay for Health Services?' *Social Science and Medicine*, 29(1): 35–42.

Yu Dezhi (1992). 'Changes in Health Care Financing and Health Status: The Case of China in the 1980s'. *Innocenti Occasional Papers EPS 34* (UNICEF, Florence).

3

Lessons from Cost Recovery in Education

JANDHYALA B. G. TILAK

In policy terms, neo-liberals and structuralists differ primarily in the extent to which they advocate state involvement in market processes (see Colclough 1991*a*: 1). This chapter attempts to assess the arguments of these two schools as they have been applied to education. Specifically, it examines the several approaches to cost recovery in education, particularly focusing upon their effects on equity and efficiency.

3.1. Cost Recovery in Education

Discussion of cost recovery is of relatively recent origin. It was long held that the benefits of education are large and widespread, and that the investments made in education are eventually recovered by society through increased labour productivity and higher tax receipts by the government, suggesting no need for specific measures to *directly* recover the investments made in education. As Mishan (1969) observed of higher education, '[it] is an investment that will pay for itself; [it] will increase the earnings of the beneficiary students and the government will recover its costs through consequent higher tax receipts'. However, over the last two decades, economic adversity and a growing disillusionment with the role of the state have together prompted a search for new ways of financing education, particularly in countries of the South.

Without implicating any with the opinions expressed here, I gratefully acknowledge the helpful comments and suggestions on earlier versions of the paper made by Malcolm Adiseshiah, V. N. Kothari, N. V. Varghese, Christopher Colclough, and by other participants at the IDS Workshop, particularly Mark Bray, David Theobald, Keith Lewin, Charles Griffin, and Martin Greeley.

3.1.1. The case for cost recovery

While revenue considerations form the most important rationale for imposing user fees, some advocates also argue that they improve quality, quantity, and equity in education (World Bank 1986, 1988; Psacharopoulos and Woodhall 1985; Thobani 1984*a*; and McMahon 1988). The main arguments in favour of cost recovery in education can be briefly summarized as follows.

1. In the light of recession and the need to constrain public spending, public budgets will not be able to meet the social demand for education without significant levels of cost recovery. In its absence, education is likely to be characterized by underinvestment (Psacharopoulos 1986: 563). Cost recovery measures will thus allow an increase in access to education (Mingat and Tan 1986*b*; Jimenez 1989)

2. It is held that public subsidization of higher education is often regressive. Owing to the fact that tertiary students are often from richer households, such subsidies increase inequalities, via the positive impact they have on students' future earnings. Cost recovery measures can reduce this regressive tendency in the public financing of education, and can improve equity in the distribution of public resources (Psacharopoulos 1977; Blaug 1982, 1992; Mingat and Tan 1986*a*; Jimenez 1994).

3. As the price elasticity of demand for education is estimated to be less than unity (Handa 1972; Chutikul 1986), it is argued that cost recovery measures will not lead to a significant fall in enrolments, and accordingly are capable of generating substantial resources for education (Jimenez 1986, 1987, 1989).

4. However, to the extent that demand for higher education is price-elastic, cost recovery measures could contribute to a fall in graduate unemployment, by reducing demand (Muta 1990: 35). Differential fees can be used as a tool for planning higher education by influencing demand for various courses/ subject specialisms (Panchamukhi 1983).

5. Some advocates argue that cost recovery measures can contribute to an improvement in the quality of education, by providing better and more serious students in the system, who will be diligent about their studies and vigilant about costs. Resulting pressures on teachers and educational administrators can help to improve the internal efficiency of education. It is further argued that goods or services provided free are not valued by consumers, and that fees make people value education, and ensure regular attendance by students.[1] By making education expensive from the students' point of view, the 'baby sitting' role of education will be reduced, discouraging students from wasting time (McMahon 1988), and 'excessive consumption' of higher education may be reduced (Stiglitz 1986: 316).

[1] Note that these arguments are not new: the Woods Despatch in 19th-c. British India made the same arguments.

6. Another argument used in favour of cost recovery policies points to the evidence for high private rates of return to education (Psacharopoulos 1993), which suggests that students would be willing to pay. More generally several modelling approaches have suggested that households are willing to pay modest fees—even for primary and secondary schooling—and that this willingness is not adequately tapped (Gertler and van der Gaag 1988; Gertler and Glewwe 1990). Hence cost recovery is not only desirable, but it is also feasible.

3.1.2. The case against cost recovery

Important arguments against cost recovery include the following.

1. The benefits of education are not restricted to the students; the neighbourhood or externality effects of education are so large (see Blaug 1970: 108) that measures to achieve high levels of cost recovery are inappropriate. State funding of education is necessary to capture these externalities. In its absence, social investment in education would remain sub-optimal.

2. Education is not only a quasi-public good[2] (Blaug 1970: 107; Levin 1987; Tomlinson 1986), but also a merit good, consumption of which is socially beneficial, but provision of which in a free market would be at sub-optimal levels (Musgrave 1959; Arcelus and Levine 1986). This is because consumers may not be aware of the full benefits received from such goods, and hence their provision may need to be financed by the state. Cost recovery approaches here would be counter-productive.

3. Some have argued that, since any method of cost recovery restricts demand for education, and since education is a merit good, it should not be rationed on the basis of ability to pay by the consumers (Weisbrod 1988). Exclusion of the poor from the consumption of education will reduce both equity and efficiency in society.

4. The price elasticity of demand for education differs according to income. If fees were imposed contemporaneously with an increase in the supply of places, total enrolments might even rise (e.g. Tan *et al.* 1984). But this result could still be consistent with enrolments among the poor being reduced. Thus, the introduction of cost recovery measures may result in a significant, and undesirable, change in the social composition of the student population (see Colclough 1996).

5. The argument that cost recovery in higher education will reduce (both present and future) income inequalities is based on the evidence that a substantial number of such students is drawn from higher income groups. But one reason why poor students do not gain access in large numbers to higher

---

[2] In a strict sense, education is not a public good, but its associated externalities bring some 'public good' characteristics. See Blaug (1970: 107).

education is precisely because it is already costly: there are high non-tuition costs to students, including opportunity costs, even if tuition costs are nil. The introduction of cost recovery measures would, therefore, aggravate the high-income bias in the distribution of enrolments.

6. With respect to the improvement in the quality of education, some have argued that, since the ability to pay and the ability to learn are not necessarily positively correlated, the introduction of charges need not lead to higher cognitive achievements, even if the diligence of students were, in general, to increase (see Colclough 1991*b*: 202).

3.1.3. An assessment of claims and counter-claims

The debate between the two sides has intensified in recent years (Hinchliffe 1993). How far are the claims and counter-claims valid? While evidence exists on each side, some points stand out clearly, which may help in making an objective assessment.

The case for cost recovery in education is centrally based on the premiss that governments, particularly those in developing countries, do not have adequate resources at their disposal, and that the scope for restructuring public budgets, so as to increase substantially the allocation to education, is limited. This premiss has rarely been critically examined, although the possibility of restructuring public budgets by withdrawing public resources from less productive sectors, and their reallocation towards human development sectors, has been stressed by some (e.g. UNDP 1991, 1992). Others (e.g. Looney 1990; Hess and Mullan 1988) have focused on military expenditure, pointing to the trade-off between public spending on the military and on education.

Early evidence from several countries (Table 3.1) suggested that the distribution of education subsidies was on the whole equitable, with the distribution of primary education subsidies being highly progressive, and the distribution of secondary subsidies being somewhat progressive. However, the distribution of higher education subsidies was largely skewed in favour of the richer groups. It can be seen that in almost all countries the richest 20 per cent of the population captured far more than 20 per cent of the available education subsidies. An exception is given by India, where positive discriminatory policies and a relative democratization of higher education have brought greater access to middle-income groups. Elsewhere, the table suggests a bias in access to higher education among the rich. On the other hand, after a careful review of several studies, and after standardizing their results, Leslie and Brinkman (1988: 118) found that 'higher education in most cases does contribute to progressivity and moreover when the analytical methods employed are most advanced, progressivity is found without exception'.

The claim that cost recovery measures will improve internal efficiency in

TABLE 3.1   Distribution of education subsidies by income group (%)

Country	Year	Education level	Shares of the population		
			Bottom 40%	Middle 40%	Top 20%
India	1978	Elementary	61	31	8
		Secondary	51	34	15
		Higher	33	49	18
		All levels	45	40	15
Uruguay	1982	Basic	77	22	7
		Secondary	46	43	12
		Higher	14	52	34
		All levels	52	34	14
Argentina	1980	Basic	64	27	9
		Secondary	47	39	14
		Higher	17	45	38
		All levels·	48	35	17
Costa Rica	1982	Basic	62	31	7
		Secondary	45	43	11
		Higher	17	41	42
		All levels	42	38	20
Malaysia (1)	1974	Primary	50	40	9
		Secondary	38	43	18
		Higher	10	38	51
		All levels	41	41	18
Malaysia (2)		Higher	30	35	35
Chile	1982	Basic	65	30	5
		Secondary	49	42	10
		Higher	12	34	54
		All levels	48	34	18
Colombia	1974	Primary	59	36	6
		Secondary	39	46	16
		Higher	6	35	60
		All levels	40	39	21
Dominican Republic	1980	Basic	31	48	21
		Secondary	22	46	32
		Higher	2	22	76
		All levels	24	43	33
Indonesia[a]	1978	Primary	51	27	22
		Jr secondary	45	21	33
		Sr secondary	22	23	55
		Higher	7	10	83
		All levels	46	25	28

[a] Indonesia: under 'Middle 40%' it is middle 30%: and under 'Top 20%' it is top 30%.
Source: Tilak (1989a: 55).

education is also unlikely. Students and households already incur significant costs of education (non-fee direct, and opportunity costs) in developing countries. Several estimates (Tilak 1991, 1993*a*; World Bank 1993) revealed that student household expenditure on education already equalled or exceeded that spent by governments.[3] Further, in the case of poorer students, fees may compel them to take up part-time work (Eisemon 1992: 14), resulting in less time being left for their studies. As a result, the overall internal efficiency of education may actually decline.

The relationship between cost recovery measures and the supply of education is least well supported by empirical evidence. Political economy factors may prevent the supply of education facilities being increased with cost recovery, and, even if that happened, 'higher supply strongly biased toward more privileged groups may be worse than lower supply' (Stern 1989: 145).

The use of rate of return estimates to support arguments for cost recovery is also questionable. First, there is a fairly consistent trend, noticeable from a range of countries, for private returns to fall—as illustrated for higher education in Table 3.2. Such returns would fall more sharply with the introduction of cost recovery measures,[4] bringing unpredictable implications for demand. Second, the estimated social rates of return to education are not *true* social returns: except for tax revenues, none of the benefits received by society at large are taken into account in their estimation; i.e., the externalities associated with education are not included.[5] Hence the difference between estimated public and private rates cannot be used as a valid justification for cost recovery policies (see also Leslie 1990).

Arguments for cost recovery measures underplay the externality and quasi-public good benefits of education,[6] and emphasize the role of the price mechanism, the private sector in general, and the putative need for a reduced role of the state. But the externalities or spill-over benefits of education are likely to be large (Summers 1987). The presence of an educated labour force increases the productivity of the less educated as well (Johnson 1984; Lucas 1988), which is an important externality. Besides, a large body of evidence exists on the effects of education on income distribution, infant mortality, life

---

[3] e.g., Tilak (1991) found that household expenditures on education in India were sizeable and comparable to public expenditures on education; household costs, including opportunity costs, exceeded the government (institutional) costs by two to four times. In the case of higher education, household expenditure per student in Kerala was Rs5566, compared with public institutional expenditure of Rs5718 in 1985–6 (Tilak 1993*a*: 60). In Jamaica household expenditures per student (about US$205) were much higher than public unit expenditures (about US$100) in 1990. In Jamaican community colleges, household expenditures are about 3.5 times higher than public expenditure (World Bank 1993: 38). More evidence is discussed later in this chapter.

[4] See Creedy (1995) for a theoretical analysis of the varying effects of surcharges on rates of return to education.

[5] This was Schultz's (1971: 172) argument for the need to 'repair' the estimates of social rates of return. It remains valid today.

[6] Further, Bates (1993: 10) argues that cost recovery measures remove the 'social' nature from the economics of social goods.

TABLE 3.2 Declining private returns to
higher education in selected countries (%)

	Year	Rate of return
Japan	1967	10.5
	1980	8.3
Mexico	1963	29.0
	1984	21.7
Pakistan	1975	27.0
	1979	6.3
Greece	1962	14.0
	1977	5.5
Philippines	1985	14.0
	1988	11.6
Taiwan	1970	18.4
	1972	15.8
Uruguay	1979	20.0
	1989	12.8
Venezuela	1957	27.0
	1989	11.0

Source: Psacharopoulos (1993: 55–6).

expectancy, health conditions, fertility rates, and population control.[7] In addition, in the case of higher education, 'dynamic externalities', associated with increasing the stock of knowledge in society (Stewart and Ghani 1992), may be very important.[8]

Further, that education is a merit good is also well recognized. Some people may be ignorant of the benefits of education, but even where not they may be influenced negatively by its long gestation period, and may not be ready to take the risk of investing in education, whose benefits are not certain to them. The experience of developing countries with respect to the universalization of first level of education confirms this. Some poor households are reluctant to invest even in primary education, as they fail to foresee its benefits. It is widely held that full cost recovery in the case of merit goods is not justified, as it would result in sub-optimal levels of social investment.

To conclude, it seems that the general case against cost recovery is very strong. However, there may be a case for its limited use where it is partial,

[7] Weale (1993: 736) argues that these externalities are particularly important in developing countries. See Bowen (1988) and Leslie (1990) for recent elaborate descriptions of externalities in education.

[8] See Schultz (1990) and Birdsall (1988) on the externalities of higher education. Very few believe that externalities in higher education are negligible (see Arrow 1993).

confined to higher levels of education, and supplemented by measures to protect access by the poor. In the following section we concentrate on a few methods of cost recovery, and critically examine evidence from a selection of countries on their relative effects.

3.2. Methods of Cost Recovery:
Fees, Loans, and Earmarked Taxes

3.2.1. Student fees

One of the most important methods of cost recovery in education is the introduction of student fees. During the 1980s, fees were introduced in several countries, even in primary education—some on the basis of the recommendations of international institutions like the World Bank (e.g. Malawi from 1984 to 1994),[9] and some based upon entirely domestic considerations (e.g. China).[10] Criticism of the social and economic consequences of such policies led some to retract their earlier positions, arguing that user charges should be applied only at higher education levels (Jimenez 1989: 112). However, fees and charges at primary and secondary levels remain in place in many countries of the South.

Low price elasticities of demand for education (Jimenez 1987: 80–1; 1989: 116) are quoted in support of fees, but very few detailed estimates are available.[11] Jimenez (1989) referred to estimates in Peru, Mali, and Malawi. In all three cases, and in others (e.g. Chutikul 1986 for Thailand), demand was found to be relatively inelastic to price (fee, or distance to school in Mali). However, several studies found serious adverse demand effects of fees in lower levels of schooling: falls in gross enrolment ratios, and even in overall enrolments, were reported in response to increased fees in Nigeria (Hinchliffe 1989), Mali (Stewart 1994), and Jamaica (Cornia *et al.* 1987), and reduced growth in enrolments was detected in Ghana (Lavy 1992)[12] and Malawi (Bray

---

[9] See Thobani (1983, 1984*a*, *b*) and Klees (1984); see also Tilak (1989).

[10] In China the laws were changed in favour of introduction of fees. After the change, as much as 7.9% of the total expenditure on basic education was generated through student fees by1988. See Ahmed *et al.* (1991).

[11] Birdsall (1982) has reviewed several studies on determinants of enrolment or educational attainment, but many of these studies have not included a price variable. Jimenez (1989) also reported only three estimates. Further, the elasticities were measured in response to small changes in fees. But substantial levels of increases in fees might well produce high elasticity coefficients. For instance, Jimenez (1987: 82) calculated that significant increases in fees in Malawi would lead to a decline in enrolments by 22–57% in primary schools and by 52–91% in secondary schools. Their subsequent removal in 1994 led to increased enrolments of one-third (Colclough 1996).

[12] Logistic regressions of school enrolment in rural Ghana (Lavy 1992: 18) produced clearly negative and statistically significant coefficients for fees in primary and middle schools, after controlling for student, household, community, and school factors, though the absolute levels of fees were believed to be 'negligible' from the perspective of Western standards (US$0.40 in primary and US$1.00 in middle level schools).

TABLE 3.3   Distribution of enrolments in education in India, by household
expenditure quintiles, 1986–7

Quintile group (%)	Government			Private		
	Primary	Secondary	Post-secondary	Primary	Secondary	Post-secondary
Rural						
0–20	22.6	15.2	11.2	21.0	13.7	9.2
20–40	23.6	18.1	12.7	19.7	16.5	12.3
40–60	22.2	20.9	18.6	21.1	20.7	15.8
60–80	19.1	24.2	23.6	20.3	24.8	26.3
80–100	12.5	21.7	34.0	17.9	24.3	35.4
Urban						
0–20	31.8	19.9	9.4	18.4	13.2	8.1
20–40	32.9	26.6	14.1	22.5	19.3	10.4
40–60	19.3	24.5	19.4	22.0	23.0	17.3
60–80	11.9	19.3	25.4	21.7	25.4	27.5
80–100	4.1	9.6	31.8	15.4	19.1	36.7

Source: NSSO (1991: S-34 and S-89).

1987). By the same token, the positive effects of a reduction or abolition of fees on enrolments have also been documented for Botswana and Malawi (Colclough 1996: 17–18).

Income elasticities of demand are additionally important. Generally, the demand for education is found to be highly income-elastic, even in the absence of direct cost recovery measures. The elasticity is evident even from frequency tables such as that for India given in Table 3.3.[13] The table suggests that demand for secondary and higher education is a clear increasing function of household income—particularly so since household size declines with income. Although precise estimates of income elasticities are not available, Appleton *et al.* (1990) showed that income is an important determinant of enrolling in, and completing, the primary, lower secondary, and upper secondary schooling in Côte d'Ivoire. A high income elasticity obviously raises further questions about the wisdom of increasing the fees faced by the poor.

It is interesting to note that, while the earlier international declarations and conventions sought to assure free and compulsory education for all, the term 'free' began to be used more sparingly in the 1980s.[14] Organizations like the

13 For comparable data for Brazil, see Birdsall (1982: 6).

14 e.g., compare the *World Declaration on Education for All* (WCEFA 1990), and the *Delhi Declaration* (EFA 1993), with the United Nations *Declaration of Human Rights* (UN 1948), and the *Convention on the Rights of the Child* (UN 1989b), among many other UN and UNESCO resolutions.

World Bank favoured, in the earlier years, the introduction of fees in primary education,[15] simultaneously opposed and supported the same later,[16] and subsequently distanced itself from the practice.[17] However, the introduction of fees in higher education became an important condition for securing loans to the sector from the World Bank (Hinchliffe 1993: 185).[18] These changes in policy stance were, in turn, reflected in fairly frequent policy reversals over fees by national governments.[19] They also resulted in a mushrooming of private schools charging high fees—mostly in (but not necessarily confined to) urban areas—and in the introduction of various kinds of fees in public schools.[20]

While most observers and agencies now agree on the need to provide free primary education, there remains more debate about the post-primary levels. But the intra-sectoral dependencies are rarely acknowledged: if fees are high in secondary education, enrolments in primary education may fall, since the latter may be demanded in order to secure entry into secondary education rather than to lead directly to the labour market. High fees in higher education may reduce demand for secondary education in a similar fashion. A majority of countries now charge fees for higher education—some very small nominal amounts, and some reasonably large. For example Spain, Belgium, and Switzerland charged up to US$5,000 per student in 1987 (see Eicher and Chevaillier 1993: 465).[21] Fees also vary by discipline, by region, and by socioeconomic categories of the student population.

International evidence on fees given in Tables 3.4 and 3.5 shows that, among public higher education systems where data are available, only South Korea and Chile recover more than a quarter of their total public expenditure on higher education through fees. In many of the countries shown, including several OECD member states, the proportion of fees in total expenditure is negligible. Rates of cost recovery are low too even among private institutions

---

[15] Initially using Mali as an example, the World Bank (Birsdall 1983*a*, *b*) stressed that there existed considerable scope to increase cost recovery in primary education in several countries. This was further developed in the case of Malawi (see Thobani 1983). See also Bray (1987: 122), Bray and Lillis (1988), and Jones (1992: 248).

[16] e.g., the World Bank (1986: 23) observed that, 'in general, increased private financing at the primary level is not recommended since it might interfere with universal coverage—a socially desirable goal'; but also argued that it 'could increase efficiency within schools' (p. 23) and 'improve the future distribution of income' (p. 24). Around this time, the Bank gave its support to fees in primary education in Malawi, Mali, Lesotho, and other countries.

[17] e.g., most recently the Bank has not only advocated fee-free primary schooling, but targeted subsidies to households unable to support the other direct or indirect costs of sending their children to school (World Bank 1994*b*: 105).

[18] Fewer and fewer Bank loans by the end of the 1980s were free of the obligations imposed by loan conditionalities to promote privatization and expansion of user charges (Jones 1992: 249).

[19] See Bray (1987) for a description of such shifts in Nigeria, Ghana, and Kenya.

[20] The World Bank (1986) showed that, in 21 out of 36 countries on which information was available, there were user charges in primary education.

[21] Some countries first abolished and then reintroduced fees in higher education; e.g., tuition fees were phased out in Australia in 1974, but were reintroduced in 1989.

TABLE 3.4   Share of fees in costs of higher education in selected countries (%)

Developing countries[a]	Share	Developed countries	Share
Sri Lanka	[b]	Norway (public institutions) (1987)	0.0
Tanzania	[b]	Australia (1987)	2.1
Bolivia	1.0	France (1975)	2.9
Pakistan	2.1	(1984)	4.7
Philippines		Germany (1986)	0.0
Public (1985)	10.9	Canada (mid-1980s)	12.0
Private (1977)	85.0	Netherlands (1985)	12.0
Nepal (1986–7)	4.4	Spain (mid-1980s)	20.0
PNG (1988–9)	4.4–9.0	Japan	
Brazil	5.0	Private 4-yr institutions (1971)	75.8
Malaysia	5.8	(1985)	65.8
Thailand	6.9	Public institutions (1970)	2.0
Costa Rica	8.0	(1987)	8.8
Guatemala	10.0	All institutions (1971)	31.7
Nigeria	12.4	(1985)	35.8
Indonesia	13.0		
Turkey	15.0		
India (1984–5)	15.0	UK	
South Korea (1985)		Universities (1970–1)	12.6
Public	49.6	(1988–9)	6.4
Private	82.3	Polytechnics (1982–3)	15.0
Chile (1990)	34.2	(1987–8)	14.0
Public	38.5		
Private	95.0		
Philippines			
Private (1987)	2.3–2.5	USA	
Public (1985)	10.9	Private institutions (1969–70)	38.6
All (1985–7)	2.5–5.0	(1984–5)	38.7
Pakistan (1987–8)		Public institutions (1969–70)	15.1
Colleges	7.4	(1984–5)	14.5
Universities (general)	1.9	All institutions (1969–70)	20.5
Universities (technical)	1.3	(1986)	22.4
Colombia			
Public universities (1987)	9.6	Soviet Union (early 1980s)	0.0
Private universities (1989)	81.0	Hong Kong (1988–9)	6.3–12.2
Venezuela (1986)		Singapore (1992)	< 20.0
Public	3.8		
Private	83.0		

[a] Around 1980 unless specified.
[b] Nil or negligible.

Sources: Hong Kong: Bray (1993: 37); Korea: Eicher and Chevaillier (1993: 462); Singapore: Selvaratnam (1994: 81); UK: Williams (1992: 6–7); Chile: Brunner (1994: 230); others: Tilak (1993*b*: 20).

TABLE 3.5   The contribution of students/families
(fees) to the recurrent budgets of selected African
universities

University (country)	Year	Share (%)
Botswana	1991	12.6
Ghana	1990	1.2
Lesotho	1991	14.0
Malawi	1991	4.0
Swaziland	1991	0.0
Zimbabwe	1991	6.0
Kenyatta (Kenya)	1991	0.0[a]
Ibadan (Nigeria)	1990	5.3[b]
Nsukka (Nigeria)	1991	2.0[c]
Obafemi Awol (Nigeria)	1991	0.0
Makerere (Uganda)	1991	2.0[c]
Copperbelt (Zambia)	1991	8.0
Witwatersrand (South Africa)	1991	27.9

[a] Fees were to be introduced in 1991–2.
[b] Fees are for post-graduate students only.
[c] Fee is raised, but 'paid' by the state.
Source: Blair (1992: 20).

in some countries—although more than 80 per cent of costs are recovered in private universities in Venezuela, Colombia, Chile, and South Korea.[22]

Second, quite apart from the incidence of tuition fees, the private costs of education—particularly at tertiary levels—are often high.[23] For example, in India, while tuition fees are a small proportion of the total costs of higher education, the addition of other fees—in particular those paid to undertake examinations—causes fee income to represent a sizeable proportion of total recurrent costs. Furthermore, non-tuition costs, such as those for textbooks, transport, and other out-of-pocket expenses, are usually significant, as are opportunity costs. The available evidence suggests that students and/or families incur considerable costs on both counts, particularly in developing countries.[24] For example, in India, of the total social costs of higher education (comprising students' plus institutional costs, net of transfers), students' direct costs account for about 30 per cent, and opportunity costs a further 40 per cent. Thus, private costs form about 80 per cent of the total social costs of

---

[22] Lee (1987) estimated that tuition fees in private higher education in South Korea formed about 75% of the costs. In the education system as a whole, students and parents met about 25% of the total costs of public schools, and 79% of those in private schools in 1988. See also Dong-Kun and Jooing-Ryul (1990: 54).

[23] See Johnstone (1992*a*: 31–9) for some evidence on a few developed countries.

[24] See n. 3 for India, Tilak (1994) for Cambodia, and Kotey (1992) for Ghana.

TABLE 3.6   Private and social costs of higher education in
India and the USA (%)

	Private costs			Institu-tional costs	Total social costs
	Direct costs	Forgone earnings	Total		
India (1978)					
Higher education					
General	31.0	55.4	87.5	12.5	100
Professional	54.5	28.8	83.3	6.7	100
USA (1988)					
Higher education[a]	3.9	39.1	43.0	57.0	100

[a] College and universities/institutions of higher education (public and private).
Source: India: Tilak (1987); USA: Cohn and Geske (1990).

TABLE 3.7   Share of household expenditure
in total national expenditure on education in
selected countries

Country	Year	Share (%)
Netherlands	1986	3.5
France	1985	5.1
UK	1986	10.1
Australia	1986	16.4
USA	1986	24.1
Zimbabwe	1985	26.5
Thailand	1986	26.5
Colombia	1983	28.6
India	1985–6	50.3

Source: United Nations (1989*a*: tables 2.1 and 2.5).

higher education in India, compared with about 43 per cent in USA (Table 3.6).

Some cross-country data are presented in Table 3.7 which show household educational expenditure, as a proportion of total (public plus private) expenditure on education. It can be seen that in India households incur as much expenditure on education as the government.[25] More generally, in the poorer countries (e.g. Thailand, Zimbabwe, Colombia, and India), households shoulder a greater part of the expenditure on education than in the more

[25] These data were confirmed in a more recent study (Tilak 1991).

developed countries shown (Netherlands, France, UK, Australia, USA). Accordingly, while there may be scope for increased fees in higher education in the South, such changes may be counter-productive unless the magnitude of direct costs already met by households is recognized.

An important question, in this context, concerns whether or not fees, where they are introduced/increased, should be uniform for all. In countries like India, where the proportion of students from lower and middle-income groups combined is roughly half of the total (Tilak 1993*a*), a discriminatory fee structure may be preferred.[26] Such a mechanism minimizes the perverse effects of public subsidization of higher education and can be based upon the costs of education, the ability to pay, and future lifetime earnings associated with a given type of education. Discriminatory pricing may also be more efficient than uniform fees since it is capable of providing additional resources in comparison with unitary pricing approaches.

3.2.2. Student loans

Loans are an important measure to accompany increases in fees, so that poor students are not forced out of higher education. Loans provide an important equity measure as well as a strategy to improve efficiency (Blaug 1970; Woodhall 1983; Psacharopoulos and Woodhall 1985; Mingat *et al.* 1986*c*). But their use has increased well beyond the fifty or so countries having loans schemes in the 1980s (Albrecht and Ziderman 1991: 3), partly as a consequence of widespread constraints on public spending.[27]

Loans shift the fee burden from the present generation (government or parents) to future direct beneficiaries. There are two main types. Mortgage-type loans involve repayment of *fixed* equal amounts in regular instalments, irrespective of the earnings levels of graduates; on the other hand, income-contingent loans require payment of a given *proportion* of graduates' income as loan repayment, based on the principle of the ability to repay.

In an important study, Woodhall (1983) argued that, among other benefits, loans increase access to higher education, reduce the extent of redistribution of resources from the poor to the rich, increase the diligence and efficiency of students, and provide flexibility in financing full-time or part-time studies in government or private institutions. She later argued (Woodhall 1989) that income-contingent loans do not necessarily discourage low-income students or women from pursuing higher education. They are often said to provide a fair and cheap means of expanding the tertiary sector (Barr 1988; 1991).

There are, however, several problems associated with student loans. First, the uncertainty associated with the returns to investment in higher education

---

[26] See McMahon (1988), Johnstone (1992*b*), and Tilak and Varghese (1985) for further discussion of discriminatory pricing models.

[27] See Woodhall (1990, 1991*a, b,* 1992) for details on several countries.

acts as a deterrent to borrowing, particularly among the poor. Also, the introduction of loans increases both actual and perceived costs, in comparison with grants (Colclough with Lewin 1993: 172), which further reduces the demand for higher education, particularly among poor families (e.g. as in Jamaica: World Bank 1993), thereby exacerbating inequalities in access to education. These incentive effects are hardly desirable, as warned long ago by the Robbins Committee (1963: para. 647).

Second, the credit market in many developing countries is not developed enough to easily sustain an educational loans scheme (Arrow 1993: 9). Even where this is not so, private lending institutions may seek security, or collateral, which poorer students, for whom the programme is mainly meant, may not be able to provide (Nerlove 1975; Stiglitz 1986: 309). Thus, loan schemes may not easily or sharply change the socioeconomic background of tertiary students.

The third, and most important, problem faced with respect to student loans in most developed and developing countries relates to their non-repayment. In India, of the total investment of Rs.869 million made on student loan programmes during 1963/4–1987/8, only 5.9 per cent was recovered. In recent years recovery rates have improved somewhat, but to at most around 15 per cent (Tilak 1992). High default rates and losses to governments are well documented (Woodhall 1990, 1991a, b, 1992). In recent years, for example, every student in Kenya has received a loan, 94 per cent of which has not been subsequently recovered. The costs of administration of loans—for personnel and office expenses and attempts at recovery—are also high. While there is some evidence that the costs of administration of income-contingent loans may be small (as in Australia and Sweden), the administrative costs of mortgage-type loans can represent up to one-fifth of the value of loans made (Table 3.8). If such costs are added to the loss to the government because of defaulters, the total loss amounts to 103 per cent in Kenya and 108 per cent in Venezuela (i.e., it would actually have been cheaper for those countries to provide tertiary education free). Even Colombia, where its second-generation scheme was believed to be yielding adequate returns, the rate of recovery was scarcely more than 50 per cent. Although reforms have improved rates of cost recovery in Colombia, Brazil, and Jamaica, default rates remain high.[28] Further, Albrecht and Ziderman (1993: 83) estimated that, in some countries where rates of cost recovery are among the highest in the world, only between 2 per cent (Colombia) and 14 per cent (Quebec, Canada) of instructional costs are recovered from loan recipients.

[28] Based on simulations of behavioural responses, Mingat and Tan (1986c: 282) argue that the potential rate of cost recovery, under what appear to be bearable terms of repayment, is substantial in Asia and Latin America, but not in Africa. In fact, it may never be feasible to recover all of the investments made in loans. For example, the World Bank (1993: 183) estimated that, given the need for subsidization of interest rates and longer periods of repayment, the recovery of loans in Latin America and Caribbean countries could at best be in the range of 40–75%.

TABLE 3.8   Student loan programmes and government losses in selected countries

Country	Year	% of students with loans	Government loss (%) on account of:			Rate of recovery[d] (%)
			Default	Adminis-tration	Default and adminis-tration	
Mortgage loans[a]						
Colombia I	1978	—	76	11	87	13
Colombia II	1985	6	38	9	47	53
Sweden I	1988	—	62	8	70	30
Indonesia	1985	3	61	10	71	29
USA	1986	28	41	12	53	47
Hong Kong	1985	26	43	4	47	53
UK	1989	7	30	11	41	59
Norway	1986	80	33	15	48	52
Denmark	1986	—	56	6	62	38
Finland	1986	—	46	6	52	48
Brazil I	1983		94	4	98	8
Brazil II	1989	25	65	6	71	21
Jamaica I	1987	20[b]	84	8	92	8
Jamaica II	1988	—	62	8	70	30
Barbados	1988	—	18	15	33	67
Kenya	1989	100	94	9	103	−3
Canada[c]	1989	59	31	6	37	63
Chile	1989	—	69	13	82	18
Japan	1989	19	51	9	60	40
Venezuela	1991	1	98	10	108	−8
Honduras	1991	1	53	20	73	27
Income-contingent loans[a]						
Australia	1990	81	52	5	57	43
Sweden II	1990	—	30	3	33	67

[a] I and II refer to situations where the loan programmes underwent reform.
[b] 1985
[c] Quebec
[d] Rate of cost recovery refers to average loan recovery ratios as a percentage of loan amount, default, and administration costs.
Source: Albrecht and Ziderman (1991: 5, 15; 1993: 80) and World Bank (1994*a*: 47).

Worries about student indebtedness led to a reduction in interest rates in Sweden, where all students receive loans. Other countries often provide interest-free loans. But very low rates of interest make student loans 'inefficient': where inflation is significant, repayment terms in excess of ten years (which are common) result in efforts to recover loans being highly cost-ineffective.[29] These problems have led to growing pressures to move away from loans, and to reconsider grants, in Sweden and elsewhere (Morris 1992; Shackleton 1993).

Finally, over the short and medium terms, expenditure savings to the public sector arising from student loans are particularly elusive. Colclough (1993: 209–10) has estimated that, if loans were typically taken out to cover four years of study with a 20-year pay-back period, the government would not recover even 50 per cent of the initial generation of student loans until 14 years after the start of the scheme. This is exclusive of rebates for unemployment (etc.) and defaults. Barr (1993: 725) estimated that the loans programme in the UK will produce 'no cumulative net savings for at least 25 years'. After a thorough review of 24 loan programmes in 20 countries, Albrecht and Ziderman (1991: iii) concluded that, 'in general, developing country loan programmes to date have not reduced significantly the government's fiscal burden for higher education' and that the scope for increased effectiveness of the programme is also restricted. Hence student loans cannot be a short-term or a medium-term solution to the problems of resource scarcity in higher education, and given, *inter alia*, the levels of default, loans can never become self-financing.

Thus, there are at least two basic inherent weaknesses underlying the philosophy of loans. First, the idea of a loan scheme presupposes a fairly strong relationship between education, employment, and earnings. When higher education does not guarantee employment, students may be dissuaded from borrowing to finance their studies, particularly those from relatively poorer sections of the community. Second, financial returns to the government are undermined by high costs and low repayment rates. On the whole, it seems that, while investment in higher education may yield high returns, investment in loans for higher education may not.

3.2.3. Earmarked taxes

As an alternative to the public financing of higher education from general tax revenues, various forms of earmarked taxes can be used. At least three kinds of such taxes can be identified.

The payroll tax

While in the cases of fees and loans the costs of higher education are planned to be recovered from the students or their parents, other measures aim at recovering costs from the users of the graduates. Payroll taxation, for example,

---

[29] This leads some (e.g. Johnstone 1986) to argue in favour of using grants or direct subsidies rather than interest-subsidized loans.

can be designed as an education-specific tax levied on those who employ educated workers. The basic argument is that those who employ a highly educated labour force, and profit therefrom, should be required to pay for part of the costs of production of this 'human capital'. Such taxes would be some proportion of the wage bill paid to graduates, or other categories of educated labour, with tax rebates being payable if firms contributed directly to the education of these employees. The amount of tax levied would be based on the cost of education and (in the case of a graduate payroll tax) the number of graduates employed (Colclough 1990). Resources accruing to the fiscus would provide a contribution to higher education costs on an annual basis.

Payroll taxation has not been widely used, and where it has this has usually been for the purpose of financing training, rather than higher education (see Ziderman 1989; Middleton *et al.* 1994: 121–6). Albrecht and Ziderman (1991) cite two cases which are close to being an education-specific payroll tax. In Ghana, employers of graduates who have taken student loans contribute 12 per cent of wages paid to a national security fund, which, in turn, is redirected to the education budget. And in China, employers repay the loans taken out by their employees when they were students. Further, Eicher and Chevaillier (1993: 467) point out that in France payroll tax arrangements allow firms to pay a proportion of their due tax in the form of an unrestricted grant to institutions of their choice. Although the tax is compulsory, choice exists as regards the method of payment, and its ultimate beneficiary.

One effect of payroll taxation on graduates is that it might work as a disincentive to employ them. Depending upon the elasticity of substitution between different levels of worker, employers would have an additional incentive to employ less expensive skills (or skills which were embodied in people who had acquired them by a different route). In countries with unemployment of graduates, this may not be desirable. However, in the relatively large number of developing countries having a shortage of graduates, the incentives to economize on their use provided by payroll taxation may well be beneficial.[30]

Graduate tax

An alternative approach—similar, in principle to income-contingent loans—is a graduate tax, first proposed by Glennerster *et al.* (1968), whereby graduates would pay a proportion of their incomes for a part or whole of their working lives, as partial repayment for the costs of their education. Such a tax has useful features: unlike loans, there would be no capital indebtedness, and therefore minimal disincentive effects for individuals; equally, the tax could be progressive, with the tax rates rising for the higher paid.[31]

[30] This argument is developed by Colclough (1990).
[31] One example of such a tax is the proposed, but as yet not implemented, graduate income tax in Argentina; see Gertel (1991: 76–7).

Colclough (1990) and Albrecht and Ziderman (1991) show that the possibility of revenue generation is higher in cases of payroll and graduate taxes respectively than in the case of loans, in addition to their being more equitable. Ziderman (1989) argues that in the case of training such a tax may be relatively more efficient than most alternatives. The experience with graduate/payroll taxes is as yet limited. Their appeal is strong, although budget administrators do not in general favour earmarked taxes owing to the lack of flexibility they impose upon public spending patterns.[32]

On the other hand, the difference between graduate taxation and a well-designed income tax seems to be not great, except for the fact of earmarking of the graduate tax. For example, Arrow (1993: 9–10) suggests a higher income tax rate for higher educated workers, on the grounds of its being 'the most practical way of securing repayment'. Friedman (1962: 105) argued similarly that the graduate should be required to pay a specified proportion of his earnings, in excess of a specified sum, which could be combined with income tax. Furthermore, some graduate taxes and fees are rather similar in both their nature and effects. For example, the deferred fee charges introduced in 1986 in Australia amounted to a graduate tax; while the graduate tax introduced in 1989 provided a choice to pay an 'up-front' fee on entering higher education instead of paying tax.

Educational cess taxes

Educational cess taxes have been used by several countries. A cess is an earmarked levy, payable by all households in a given locality, the revenues from which would be used for a specific purpose, such as education. An educational cess tax is not restricted to the households with past or present students enrolled in schools. Usually a cess is levied as a small fraction of some other tax. For example, a cess for public financing of libraries may be attached to a professional tax or to an urban property tax. In rural areas a cess may be levied as a proportion of land revenue. China introduced an education levy[33] in 1986, which financed 16–17 per cent of total expenditure on basic education in China in 1988 (Ahmed *et al.* 1991). India has levied education cess taxes in several states. These were imposed, collected, and used by local governments, largely as a surcharge on land revenue, for the development of school education. However, the revenue generated was not satisfactory and the taxes were subsequently abolished.

An advantage sometimes claimed by proponents of education cess taxes is that, since the revenues are generated and used at local levels, the potential for their efficient utilization is high. This characteristic helps to ensure community

---

[32] See McCleary (1991) for a recent survey.

[33] This was a surcharge on the amount of product tax, value added tax, and business tax, paid by work units and individuals.

participation in education, thereby improving the internal efficiency of the system by making teachers more accountable to the community. Nevertheless, education cess taxes imposed on all households would be regressive—even if the effect were small in practice.

In general, these and other earmarked taxes link decisions about raising resources and decisions regarding their allocation in ways that risk rigidity in the allocation of resources, and a less flexible prioritization of public choices. On the other hand, as traditional funding sources have become threatened, revenue assigned from specific sources in these ways can help education spending to increase. An alternative would be to impose them selectively, for example on the households whose children go to schools; however, the distinction between fees and earmarked taxes would then disappear.

Generally, earmarked taxes for education and cesses have a limited tax base, and with some, such as graduate tax, revenues build up only slowly. Hence revenue from these sources would remain supplementary to, rather than substitutes for, general tax revenue, as a means of financing of education. Furthermore, such taxes often incur significant costs of administration and collection which, given limited revenues, may substantially undermine their efficiency (McCleary 1991).

3.3. Conclusion

Cost recovery measures risk increasing inequalities in society. Such risks can be reduced by properly designing loans and scholarships, albeit at the cost of reducing revenues raised. There can, of course, be a case for scholarships/grants, even where education is provided free, in order to help poor (or otherwise disadvantaged) students to meet the direct and opportunity costs of education. The case for targeted scholarships becomes stronger with the introduction of cost recovery measures. However, fees are levied (or made known) at the time of entry into higher education, whereas scholarships are awarded only after admission has been gained. Thus, unless scholarship programmes are imaginatively designed, they will be unable to correct the access of poor students to higher education—or, indeed, to other levels. Furthermore, the targeting of scholarships has been administratively difficult and inefficient in many developing countries. Hence universal subsidization is often preferred to targeting subsidies.

An attempt is made to provide a summary 'balance sheet' of cost recovery measures, based upon the arguments examined in this chapter, in Table 3.9. It shows that some measures (e.g. full-cost fees) have high potential for resource generation, but their adverse effects on equity are significant. Some (e.g. loans and graduate taxes) are easily feasible in terms of implementation, but their potential for resource generation is not high. Full-cost fees and loans may improve internal efficiency, but their impact on equity is mixed, as is their

TABLE 3.9   Efficiency of alternative measures of cost recovery

	Potential resource generation	Internal efficiency	Equity	Feasibility	Current use
Fees					
Token fees	··	··	+	++	++
Substantial levels of					
Uniform fees	+	··	–	++	++
Discriminatory fees	+	+	++	+	+
Full-cost fees	++	++	– –	– –	+
Student loans	+	+	+	+	++
Payroll tax	++	··	+	++	– –
Graduate tax	++	··	+	++	··
Educational cess	+	··	··	+	+

Notes:
+ Reasonably high   ++ Very high
– Reasonably low   – – Very low
·· Not significant or doubtful

feasibility. Among the various measures discussed here, discriminatory fees are to be preferred to uniform levels of fees, from the perspectives of both equity and resource generation. But administrative problems are more severe with respect to discriminatory, as opposed to uniform, fees. Both are also likely to meet with student and parent resistance, although less so in the case of discriminatory fees. Student loan programmes are attractive since cost recovery is postponed until the graduates are able to pay, although the experience of several countries with loan programmes is not encouraging as regards repayment. But graduate/payroll taxes appear superior to both loans and fees, with respect to efficiency in administration, scope for introducing progressiveness, and generating revenues. Nevertheless, revenues may remain limited compared with the total needs of higher education, unless tax rates are high. Such taxes can be earmarked, to prevent the revenues disappearing into the general revenue pool. Accordingly, a strategy of funding general education out of general tax revenues based upon a progressive scale, and of financing higher education out of a mix of general and specific tax instruments, is likely to remain the best option in many developing countries for some time to come.

References

Ahmed, M., with Cheng, K. M., Jalaluddin, A. K., and Ramachandran, K. (1991) *Basic Education and National Development: Lessons from China and India.* New York: UNICEF.

Albrecht, D., and Ziderman, A. (1991) 'Deferred Cost Recovery for Higher Education: Student Loan Programs in Developing Countries', Discussion Paper no. 137, Washington, DC: World Bank.

———— (1993) 'Student Loans: An Effective Instrument for Cost Recovery in Higher Education?' *World Bank Research Observer*, 8 (1): 71–90.

Appleton, S., Collier, P., and Horsnell, P. (1990) 'Gender, Education, and Employment in Cote d'Ivoire', SDA Working Paper no. 8, Washington, DC: World Bank.

Arcelus, F. J., and Levine, A. L. (1986) 'Merit Goods and Public Choice: The Case of Higher Education', *Public Finance*, 41 (3): 303–15.

Arrow, K. J. (1993) 'Excellence and Equity in Higher Education', *Education Economics*, 1 (1): 5–12.

Barr, N. (1988) *Student Loans: The Next Steps.* Aberdeen: Aberdeen University Press.

—— (1991) 'Income-Contingent Student Loans: An Idea Whose Time has Come', in Shaw (1991: 155–70).

—— (1993) 'Alternative Funding Sources for Higher Education', *Economic Journal*, 103: 718–28.

Bates, R. (1993) 'Education Reform: Its Role in the Economic Destruction of Society', *Australian Administrator*, 14 (2–3): 1–12.

Birdsall, N. (1982) 'Child Schooling and the Measurement of Living Standards', LSMS Working Paper no. 14. Washington, DC: World Bank.

—— (1983a) 'Strategies for Analyzing Effects of User Charges in the Social Sectors', CPD Discussion Paper no. 1983–9, Washington, DC: World Bank.

—— (1983b) 'Demand for Primary Schooling in Rural Mali: Should User Fees be Increased?' Washington, DC: World Bank (mimeo).

—— (1988) 'Public Spending on Higher Education in Developing Countries: Too Much or Too Little?' Washington, DC: World Bank, 23 August (mimeo).

Blair, R. (1992) 'Financial Diversification and Income Generation at African Universities', AFTED Technical Note no. 2. Washington, DC: World Bank.

Blaug, M. (1970) *An Introduction to Economics of Education.* London: Allen Lane.

—— (1982) 'The Distributional Effects of Higher Education Subsidies', *Economics of Education Review*, 2 (3): 209–31.

—— (1992) 'The Overexpansion of Higher Education in the Third World', in *Equity and Efficiency in Economic Development: Essays in Honour of Benjamin Higgins* (ed. D. J. Savoie and I. Brecher). London: Intermediate Technology Publications, pp. 232–44.

Bowen, H. R. (1988) *Investment in Learning.* San Francisco: Carnegie Council.

Bray, M. (1987) 'Is Free Education in the Third World Either Desirable or Possible?' *Journal of Education Policy*, 2 (2): 119–29.

—— (1993) 'Financing Higher Education: A Comparison of Government Strategies in Hong Kong and Macau', in *Economics and Financing of Education: Hong Kong and Comparative Perspectives* (ed. M. Bray). Education Paper no. 20. Hong Kong: University of Hong Kong, pp. 32–50.

—— and Lillis, K. (eds.) (1988) *Community Financing of Education: Issues and Policy Implications in Less Developed Countries*. Oxford: Pergamon.

Brunner, J. A. (1994) 'Chile: Government and Higher Education in Government', in *Government and Higher Education Relationships across Three Continents* (ed. G. Neave and F. A. V. Vught). Oxford: Pergamon, pp. 225–40.

Chutikul, S. (1986) 'The Effect of Tuition Fee Increases on the Demand for Higher Education: A Case of a Higher Education Institution in Thailand'. Institute of Development Studies, Sussex (mimeo).

Cohn, E. and Geske, T. G. (1990) *Economics of Education*, 3rd edn. Oxford: Pergamon.

Colclough, C. (1990) 'Raising Additional Resources for Education in Developing Countries: Are Graduate Payroll Taxes Preferable to Student Loans?' *International Journal of Educational Development*, 10 (2–3): 169–80.

—— (1991a) 'Structuralism versus Neo-liberalism: An Introduction', in Colclough and Manor (1991: 1–25).

—— (1991b) 'Who Should Learn to Pay? An Assessment of Neo-Liberal Approaches to Education Policy', in Colclough and Manor (1991: 197–213).

—— (1996) 'Education and the Market: Which Parts of the Neo Liberal Solution are Correct?' *World Development*, 24 (4): 589–610.

—— with Lewin, K. (1993) *Educating All the Children: Strategies for Primary Schooling in the South*. Oxford: Clarendon Press.

—— and Manor, J. (eds.) (1991) *States or Markets? Neo-Liberalism and the Development Policy Debate*. Oxford: Clarendon Press.

Cornia, G. A., Jolly, R., and Stewart, F. (1987) *Adjustment with a Human Face*. Oxford: Clarendon Press.

Creedy, J. (1995) *The Economics of Higher Education: An Analysis of Taxes versus Fees*. Aldershot, Hants: Edward Elgar.

Dong-Kun, J. and Kim Jooing-Ryul (1990) 'Education in Korea: Equity vs. Efficiency', *Korean Journal of Policy Studies*, 5: 53–68.

EFA (1993) 'Education for All: Summit of Nine High Population Countries', *Delhi Declaration*. New Delhi: EFA.

Eicher, J.-C., and Chevaillier, T. (1993) 'Rethinking the Finance of Post-Compulsory Education' *International Journal of Educational Research*, 19 (5): 448–70.

Eisemon, T. O. (1992) 'Private Initiatives and Traditions of the State Control in Higher Education in Sub-Saharan Africa', *PHREE Background Paper*. Washington, DC: World Bank.

Friedman, M. (1962) *Capitalism and Freedom*. Chicago: University of Chicago Press.

Gertel, H. P. (1991) 'Issues and Perspectives for Higher Education in Argentina in the 1990s,' *Higher Education*, 21 (1): 63–81.

Gertler, P., and Glewwe, P. (1990) 'The Willingness to Pay for Education in Developing Countries: Evidence from Rural Peru', *Journal of Public Economics*, 42 (3): 251–75.

—— and van der Gaag, J. (1988) 'Measuring the Willingness to Pay for Social Services in Developing Countries', LSMS Working Paper no. 45. Washington, DC: World Bank.

Glennerster, H., Merrett, S., and Wilson, G. (1968) 'A Graduate Tax', *Higher Education Review*, 1 (1): 26–38.

Handa, M. L. (1972) *Toward a Rational Educational Policy*. Toronto: Ontario Institute for Studies in Education.

Hess, P., and Mullan, B. (1988) 'The Military Burden and Public Education Expenditures in Contemporary Developing Nations: Is There a Trade-off?' *Journal of Developing Areas*, 22 (4): 497–514.

Hinchliffe, K. (1989) 'Economic Austerity, Structural Adjustment and Education: The Case of Nigeria', *IDS Bulletin*, 20 (1): 5–10.

—— (1993) 'Neo-Liberal Prescriptions for Education Finance: Unfortunately Necessary or Inherently Desirable?' *International Journal of Educational Development*, 13 (2): 183–7.

Jimenez, E. (1986) 'Public Subsidization of Education and Health in Developing Countries: A Review of Equity and Efficiency', *World Bank Research Observer*, 1 (1): 111–29.

Jimenez, E. (1987) *Pricing Policy in Social Sectors: Cost Recovery for Education and Health in Developing Countries*. Baltimore: Johns Hopkins University Press for the World Bank.

—— (1989) 'Social Sector Pricing Policy Revisited: A Survey of Some Recent Controversies', *Proceedings of the World Bank Annual Conference on Development Economics*, pp. 109–38.

—— (1994) 'Financing Public Education: Practices and Trends', in *The International Encyclopedia of Education* (ed. T. Husen and T. N. Postlethwaite). Oxford: Pergamon, pp. 2310–16.

Johnson, G. E. (1984) 'Subsidies for Higher Education', *Journal of Labor Economics*, 2 (3): 303–18.

Johnstone, D. (1986) *Sharing the Costs of Higher Education: Student Financial Assistance in the United Kingdom, the Federal Republic of Germany, France, Sweden and the United States*. New York: College Entrance Examination Board.

—— (1992a) 'International Comparisons of Student Financial Support', in Woodhall (1992: 24–44).

—— (1992b), 'Tuition Fees', in *The Encyclopedia of Higher Education* (ed. B. Clark and G. Neave). Oxford: Pergamon, pp. 1501–09.

Jones, P. W. (1992) *World Bank Financing of Education: Lending, Learning and Development*. London and New York: Routledge.

Klees, S. (1984) 'The Need for a Political Economy of Education: A Response to Thobani', *Comparative Education Review*, 28 (3): 424–40.

Kotey, N. (1992) 'Students Loans in Ghana', *Higher Education*, 23 (4): 451–9.

Lavy, V. (1992) 'Investment in Human Capital: Schooling Supply Constraints in Rural Ghana', LSMS Working Paper no. 93. Washington, DC: World Bank.

Lee, K. (1987) 'Past, Present and Future Trends in the Public and Private Sectors of Korean Higher Education', in *Public and Private Sectors in Asian Higher Education*. Hiroshima: Research Institute for Higher Education, Hiroshima University, pp. 49–70.

Leslie, L. L. (1990) 'Rates of Return as Informer of Public Policy with Special Reference to the World Bank and Third World Countries', *Higher Education*, 20 (3): 271–86.

—— and Brinkman, P. (1988) *The Economic Value of Higher Education*. New York: Macmillan.

Levin, H. J. (1987) 'Education as a Public and a Private Good', *Journal of Policy and Management*, 6 (4): 628–41.

Looney, R. E. (1990) 'Defense Expenditures and Human Capital Development in the Middle East and South Asia', *International Journal of Social Economics*, 17 (10): 4–16.

Lucas, R. E. (1988) 'On the Mechanics of Economic Development', *Journal of Monetary Economics*, 22 (1): 3–42.

McCleary, W. (1991) 'The Earmarking of Government Revenue: A Review of Some World Bank Experience', *World Bank Research Observer*, 6 (1): 81–104.

McMahon, W. (1988) 'Potential Resource Recovery in Higher Education in the Developing Countries and the Parents' Expected Contribution', *Economics of Education Review*, 7 (1): 135–52.

Middleton, J., Ziderman, A., and Adams, A. V. (1994) *Skills for Productivity*. New York: Oxford University Press for World Bank.

Mingat, A., and Tan, J.-P. (1986a) 'Who Profits from Public Funding of Education? A Comparison of World Regions', *Comparative Education Review*, 30 (2): 260–70.

—— (1986b) 'Expanding Education through User Charges: What Can be Achieved in Malawi and other LDCs?' *Economics of Education Review*, 5 (8): 273–86.

—— (1986c) 'Financing Public Higher Education in Developing Countries: The Potential Role of Loan Schemes', *Higher Education*, 15 (3–4): 283–97.

Mishan, E. J. (1969) 'Some Heretical Thoughts on University Reform', *Encounter*, March.

Morris, M. (1992) 'Student Aid in Sweden', in Woodhall (1992: 85–119).

Musgrave, R. A. (1959) *The Theory of Public Finance*. New York: McGraw-Hill.

Muta, H. (ed.) (1990) *Educated Unemployment in Asia*. Tokyo: Asian Productivity Organisation.

Nerlove, M. (1975) 'Some Problems in the Use of Income-Contingent Loans for the Finance of Higher Education', *Journal of Political Economy*, 83: 157–83.

National Sample Survey Organisation (NSSO) (1991) 'Participation in Education', *Sarvekhsana* (New Delhi) 14 (46).

Panchamukhi, P. R. (1983) 'Education and Employment: Problems and Prospects in the International Order', in *Education and the New International Order* ed. J. V. Raghavan. New Delhi: Concept for National Institute of Educational Planning and Administration, pp. 50–64.

Psacharopoulos, G. (1977) 'The Perverse Effects of Public Subsidization of Education, or How Equitable is Free Education?' *Comparative Education Review*, 21 (1): 69–90.

—— (1986) 'The Planning of Education: Where Do We Stand?' *Comparative Education Review* 30 (4): 560–73.

—— (1993) 'Returns to Investment in Education: A Global Update', PPR Working Paper (WPS 1067). Washington, DC: World Bank.

—— and Woodhall, M. (1985) *Education for Development*. New York: Oxford University Press for the World Bank.

Robbins Committee (1963) *Report of the Committee on Higher Education*. London: HMSO.

Schultz, T. W. (1971) *Investment in Human Capital: The Role of Education and Research*. New York: Free Press.

—— (1990) *Restoring Economic Equilibrium: Human Capital in the Modernizing Economy*. Oxford: Basil Blackwell.

Selvaratnam, V. (1994) 'Innovations in Higher Education: Singapore at the Competitive Edge'. Technical Paper no. 222. Washington, DC: World Bank.

Shackleton, J. R. (1993) 'Student Assistance in Sweden: Lessons for the UK', *Higher Education Review*, 26 (1): 54–63.

Shaw, G. K. (ed.) (1991) *Economics, Culture and Education: Essays in Honour of Mark Blaug*. Aldershot, Hants: Edward Elgar.

Stern, N. (1989) 'Comment on Social Sector Pricing Policy Revisited', *Proceedings of the World Bank Annual Conference on Development Economics*. 139–42.

Stewart, F. (1994) 'Education and Adjustment: The Experience of the 1980s and Lessons for the 1990s', in *Market Forces and World Development* (ed. P. Prendergast and F. Stewart). New York: St Martin's Press, pp. 128–59.

—— and Ghani, E. (1992) 'How Significant are Externalities for Development?', *World Development*, 19 (6): 569–94.

Stiglitz, J. (1986) *Economics of the Public Sector*. New York: W. W. Norton.

Summers, A. (1987) 'Comment', *Journal of Policy Analysis and Management*, 6: 641–3.

Tan, J.-P., Lee, H. K., and Mingat, A. (1984) 'User Charges for Education: The Ability and Willingness to Pay in Malawi', Staff Working Paper no. 661. Washington, DC: World Bank.

Thobani, M. (1983) 'Charging User Fees for Social Services: The Case of Education in Malawi', Staff Working Paper no. 572. Washington, DC: World Bank.

—— (1984a) 'Charging User Fees for Social Services: Education in Malawi', *Comparative Education Review*, 18 (2): 107–21.

—— (1984b) 'A Reply to Klees', *Comparative Education Review*, 18 (3): 441–3.

Tilak, J. B. G. (1987) *Economics of Inequality in Education*. New Delhi: Sage, for the Institute of Economic Growth.

—— (1989a) 'Education and its Relation to Economic Growth, Poverty and Income Distribution: Past Evidence and Further Analysis', Discussion Paper no. 46. Washington, DC, World Bank.

—— (1989b) 'Financing and Cost Recovery in Social Sectors in Malawi', Washington, DC: World Bank (mimeo).

—— (1991) 'Family and Government Investments in Education', *International Journal of Educational Development*, 11 (2): 91–106.

—— (1992) 'Student Loans in Financing Higher Education in India', *Higher Education*, 23 (4): 389–404.

—— (1993a) 'Financing Higher Education in India: Principles, Practice and Policy Issues', *Higher Education*, 26 (1): 43–67.

—— (1993b) 'International Trends in Costs and Financing of Higher Education: Some Tentative Comparisons Between Developed and Developing Countries', *Higher Education Review*, 25 (3): 7–35.

—— (1994) *Financing Education in Cambodia*. Manila: Asian Development Bank, and Brisbane: Queensland University of Technology.

—— and Varghese, N. V. (1985) 'Discriminatory Pricing in Education', Occasional Paper no. 8. New Delhi: National Institute of Educational Planning and Administration (mimeo).

Tomilinson, J. R. G. (1986) 'Public Education, Public Good', *Oxford Review of Education*, 12: 211–22.

UNDP (1991, 1992) *Human Development Report.* New York: Oxford University Press.

United Nations (UN) (1948) *Declaration of Human Rights.* New York: UN.

—— (1989a) *National Accounts Statistics,* New York: UN.

—— (1989b) *Conventions on the Rights of the Child.* New York: UN.

World Conference on Education for All (WCEFA) (1990) *World Declaration on Education for All.* New York: WCEFA.

Weale, M. (1993) 'A Critical Evaluation of Rate of Return Analysis', *Economic Journal*, 103 (418): 729–37.

Weisbrod, B. A. (1988) *The Non-Profit Economy.* Cambridge, Mass.: Harvard University Press.

Williams, G. (1992) *Changing Patterns of Finance in Higher Education.* Buckingham: Open University Press, for the Society for Research into Higher Education.

Woodhall, M. (1983) 'Student Loans as a Means of Financing Higher Education: Lessons from International Experience', Staff Working Paper no. 599. Washington, DC: World Bank.

—— (1989) 'Loans for Learning: The Loans versus Grants Debate in International Perspective', *Higher Education Quarterly*, 43 (1): 76–87.

—— (1990) *Student Loans in Higher Education: 1, Western Europe and the USA.* Paris: Unesco–International Institute for Educational Planning (IIEP).

—— (1991a) *Student Loans in Higher Education: 2, Asia.* Paris: Unesco–IIEP.

—— (1991b) *Student Loans in Higher Education: 3, English-Speaking Africa.* Paris: Unesco–IIEP.

—— (ed.), (1992) *Student Loans in Developing Countries,* Special Issue of *Higher Education*, 23 (4).

World Bank (1986) *Financing Education in Developing Countries: An Exploration of Policy Options.* Washington, DC: World Bank.

—— (1988) *Education in Sub-Saharan Africa: Policies for Adjustment, Revitalization and Expansion.* Washington, DC: World Bank.

—— (1993) *Caribbean Region: Access, Quality, and Efficiency in Education.* World Bank Country Study. Washington, DC: World Bank.

—— (1994a) *Higher Education: The Lessons of Experience.* Washington, DC: World Bank.

—— (1994b) 'Priorities and Strategies for Education'. Education and Social Policy Department, World Bank, Washington, DC (draft).

Ziderman, A. (1989) 'Payroll Taxes for Financing Training in Developing Countries', Working Paper (WPS 141). Washington, DC: World Bank.

PART III

Public versus Private Alternatives

4

Private Health Care and Public Policy Objectives

SARA BENNETT

4.1. Introduction

Historically, the debate about the appropriate roles for public and private sectors in health care has been polarized, with participants forcefully expounding the virtues of the private sector and the great shortcomings of the public sector, or vice versa.[1] However, during recent years the tone of this debate has changed; it has been recognized that neither a purely private nor a purely public health care system may be appropriate. In a predominantly private system, there will be a continuing role for government in regulation and incentive setting. In a predominantly public system, elements of the market may be incorporated or private organizations co-opted to enhance efficiency. The focus of this paper is the 'pure private system' with both private finance and private provision, and in particular the relationship between such pure private systems and government.

Since the mid-1980s several countries which previously had extremely limited or totally forbidden private for-profit practice (such as Malawi, Tanzania, and Mozambique) have taken measures to encourage private providers. These measures rarely take the form of privatization observed in other sectors, that is the sale of assets; instead, regulatory liberalization and

---

[1] The debate within the health sector is clearly linked to the broader debate about the appropriate role of government in the economy. Pro-marketeers form part of a line of liberal thought which can be traced back to Adam Smith. Anti-marketeers are often linked to socialist and collectivist ideologies. Debate within the health sector became most intense during the 1960s, with critics of socialized medicine arguing that health care was much like any other good and therefore could be provided through the market (see e.g. Lees 1960; Friedman 1962). Anti-marketeers instead argued that health care was so different from other consumer goods that market provision was inappropriate (see e.g. Titmuss 1963; Arrow 1963). This debate took place largely in industrialized countries. International health policy statements of the time, and until quite recently, tend to envisage policy implementation in an entirely public health care system (see e.g. WHO 1978).

fiscal incentives are used to encourage private sector growth. Moreover, many lower and middle-income countries already have substantial private sectors. Particularly in India, South-East Asia, and to a lesser degree sub-Saharan Africa, the private sector has become extremely important. In India for example it is estimated that more than three-quarters of illness episodes are treated in the private sector (Bhat 1993). On the continent of Asia (excluding India and China), approximately 60 per cent of total health expenditure is private; in sub-Saharan Africa the corresponding figure is 44 per cent; and in Latin America and the Caribbean, it is 40 per cent (World Bank 1993). In many countries rapid private sector growth has occurred not as a result of explicit policies to promote the private sector, but primarily because of a perceived low quality of care in the public sector. Those advocating expansion of the private sector have, at the very least, drawn attention to a substantial health care resource which was previously relatively neglected by government. Acknowledgement of the potential contribution of this resource raises new questions of regulation, co-ordination, and incentive setting.

Section 4.2 reviews the theoretical arguments put forward in favour of private sector development, and in Section 4.3 recent evidence on the degree to which the arguments are well founded is examined. The evidence suggests that the extent to which the private sector contributes to the identified goals of increased efficiency, equity, resource availability, and consumer choice depends to a considerable degree on the setting in which it operates. Section 4.4 discusses the various factors influencing the way in which the private sector behaves and how government may attempt to alter them so as to ensure that the private sector contributes to government health goals. Finally in Section 4.5 the problems associated with state governance of the private sector and government capacity to perform its new roles effectively are considered.

The primary focus of the paper is clinical (both preventive and curative) care. While all evidence suggests that non-clinical services such as water supply and sanitation, education, and shelter play a more important role in improving a population's health status, the different properties of these goods means that a distinct set of arguments is required. A wide variety of providers deliver clinical care, including for example small private clinics, large mission hospitals, sophisticated investigation centres, and corner shop drug stores. It is often useful to distinguish between organizations and individuals motivated by profit and those professing other sorts of motivations such as altruism or proselytism. The latter category is referred to as non-profit.

4.2. The Theoretical Arguments

Four main neo-liberal arguments have been put forward to support the expansion of private health care systems. This section examines the principal arguments and counter-arguments. Evidence is considered in Section 4.3.

4.2.1. Efficiency and quality

Neo-liberal arguments hold that the private sector is more technically efficient than the public sector (World Bank 1987: 39). Economic theory explains this with reference to the profit incentive. The profit incentive induces firms to minimize costs for a given level of output. In a competitive market, firms that do not behave in this efficient way will make negative profits and be driven from the market place. The question of quality is inextricably linked to that of efficiency. Given a fixed level of costs, competitive for-profit firms should maximize quality for a given level of output.

A number of counter-arguments have been posed. First, in many developing countries competitive conditions (with a large number of buyers and sellers) may not prevail. Second, many hospitals are non-profit and thus may not behave as economic theory predicts. Third, and most critically, informational problems may jeopardize an efficient outcome, even in a market that would outwardly appear to be competitive. Consumers find it difficult to judge the quality of health care both in advance and ex post, this is particularly true with respect to clinical aspects.[2] Therefore providers may:

1. compromise clinical aspects of quality of care in order to reduce costs;
2. provide unnecessary but profit-augmenting services and investigations;
3. charge prices that are higher than would be charged in a competitive market.

The naked self-interest implied by the actions described above may be tempered by professional ethics, but the final balance between these two counter-posing forces, ethics and profit, is unclear.

It could be argued that, even if the relatively affluent who opt out of public care pay more than the competitive price for private care, some social gain remains because the public sector is thereby relieved of some of its burden. But this ignores the possibility that inefficient provision of care at the individual level may have implications for the service as a whole, including that which is publicly provided. First, extreme examples of low-quality care in the private sector may ultimately place a greater burden on the public sector as poorly treated private patients turn to the public sector. Second, as consumers find it difficult to judge quality of care, providers may try to distinguish themselves by signalling quality through, for example, the acquisition of high-technology equipment (Robinson 1988). Once several firms do this, signalling levels must be raised further in order to attract consumers, equilibrium is not achieved,

---

[2] In some industrialized countries this problem may be alleviated by large institutional purchasers of health care (such as insurance organizations) acting on behalf of consumers and selecting good providers. In developing countries insurance is more limited and the market model is simpler, generally with a direct exchange of services for a fee.

and an amount in excess of that which is socially optimal is spent on health care.

Closely allied to the efficiency and quality argument is that of increased responsiveness to consumer preferences. Private providers will ensure that services more closely match consumer demands, in terms of politeness of staff and appropriate opening hours, than the notoriously inflexible and discourteous public sector service. Although patient perceptions of quality should clearly influence provider behaviour, there is a danger that patients lacking information may demand inappropriate services such as unnecessary drug prescriptions.

More recently, the emphasis of the neo-liberal argument has shifted to suggest that there will be gains in allocative efficiency from private sector growth. If the private sector is able to provide 'non-essential' services, then the resources freed in the public sector can be targeted on priority health interventions. The World Bank (1993) suggests that priority health interventions include all quasi-public goods, goods with strong externalities, and interventions that are socially, highly cost-effective. For low-income countries the basic package would cover maternal health, family planning, tuberculosis and sexually transmitted disease (STD) control, and the treatment of childhood diseases. A common criticism made of developing countries' health care expenditure patterns is that too much is spent at the hospital, rather than at the primary level. Promotion of the private sector may thus also redress this imbalance. However, evidence to support the claim of over-expenditure on hospitals is mixed.[3]

4.2.2. Equity

Growth of the private sector and the transfer of the demand of the affluent from public to private sectors (particularly for more sophisticated clinical services), it is argued, will free up government resources to meet the needs of the poor (World Bank 1993: 11). There are a number of points on which this thesis might falter. First, it is conceivable that the affluent have previously influenced the distribution of health care resources and thus enjoy privileged access to the public sector, under which circumstance it may be the poor who have to resort to private care. Second, even if the affluent do switch and resources are freed, it is questionable whether the government will succeed in redirecting resources to the underprivileged. Public choice arguments emphasizing government's vulnerability to capture by powerful interests still hold; professional groupings may continue to demand government funding of high-technology services (Birdsall and James 1992). Finally, if the affluent do desert the public sector, then in the medium term standards of care may

---

[3] See Ch. 10 below for a fuller discussion of the evidence.

decline as the articulate middle class no longer voices its concerns (Chandra and Kakabadse 1985). Poorer groups with less voice will also choose to exit to the private sector.

4.2.3. Increased resources for health

An increased private sector implies more private resources flowing into health care and implicitly less pressure upon government resources (World Bank 1987: 39). For many governments of developing countries, this is perhaps the most attractive of all four arguments. Counter-arguments have stressed that a successful private sector depends critically on willingness and ability to pay, at least among some parts of the population. An increase in the size of the private sector may increase competition for inputs which in turn drives up factor prices. Thus, although there is an increase in the financial resources available, this does not lead to a proportional increase in inputs or outputs. Rather, new resources pay higher rents to factors. This is particularly a concern where relatively inelastic factors (such as doctors) are in short supply.

Even in a situation where there is an adequate supply of factor inputs, prices (both in terms of price per individual service and price per case) may be driven upwards by private sector expansion. The problem of imperfect information (as discussed in Section 4.2.1), combined with the common form of payment in the private sector, i.e. fee-for-service, creates incentives for providers to over-service clients and may enable them to charge more than the efficient rate. Thus, under certain conditions, private sector growth will succeed in increasing the resources available for health care but will also generate cost-containment problems.

It is also feasible that increased private resources allow central government to reduce the level of public resources for health, so that there is no net gain in resource availability, but rather a shift in the composition of funding. This is not intended by donor agencies and international financial institutions, but it would appear difficult to guarantee that it does not occur.

4.2.4. Consumer choice

Consumer choice may be seen as a 'good' in its own right, enhancing liberty and allowing individuals to select products or services that match their own preference patterns. In some industrialized countries consumer choice has been viewed in this manner (Minford 1991; Saltman and von Otter 1989), but this is rare in developing countries, where consumer choice is often seen more as a luxury good. Indeed, it is the relatively affluent who are likely to benefit most from increased choice; those without the ability to pay for private care will still be denied choice.

Second, consumer choice is the principle mechanism driving competitive markets towards an efficient outcome. However, if there are serious informational gaps on the part of consumers, then increased consumer choice may negatively affect consumer welfare. Without government intervention in the market, consumers are likely to make inappropriate choices about the quantity and quality of health care services they consume.

4.2.5. Other concerns

The above four points present the principal arguments in favour of an increased private sector role in health. In addition to the counter-arguments already mentioned, there are three further traditional arguments limiting the private sector role.

The first of these concerns the under-provision of services with externalities or with a quasi-public good nature. There are many services in the health sector with high degrees of externalities, including immunization, all forms of communicable disease control, and family planning. The aggregate need for these services tends to be highest in the poorest countries, where communicable diseases are the most important cause of morbidity and mortality. Economic theory would suggest that the private sector is likely to under-provide services such as immunization where the benefits do not accrue to the individual consumer alone. A related point is that private practice, by its very nature, could be thought to be in conflict with the objectives of public health in the sense that private practitioners may be reluctant to provide required preventive services such as immunization or health education, since these services may reduce future demand (see e.g. Roemer 1984).

It is unclear how serious a problem these two factors comprise. There is increasing evidence that private practitioners do provide certain public health services such as immunization and family planning, where the public recognizes the benefit of such services and is willing to pay for them (Lewis and Kenney 1988; Thomason 1994). Birdsall and James (1992) argue that changing epidemiological patterns, particularly in lower middle-income countries, mean that services with quasi-public good characteristics are of declining importance. Furthermore, most neo-liberal arguments recognize at least a vestigial role for the state in ensuring the effective provision of a core of services to promote public health. This may be achieved by direct state provision or possibly through subsidies, incentive payments, and public information encouraging the private provision of such services.

It has been shown above that the major arguments in favour of encouraging private provision of health services in less developed countries centre around expected improvements in technical and allocative efficiency. The arguments against such policies, on the other hand, focus upon various aspects of market failure as the main rationale for continued public provision.

In addition, a range of political economy considerations suggest that new sources of funding will not necessarily be spent in ways that are socially desirable. There is, however, a final concern as to whether developing country governments have the capacity—quite apart from the willingness—to influence private sector behaviour so that it contributes to public health goals. How effectively can governments co-ordinate health policies between public and private sectors? To what extent can the public sector ensure that private providers locate in under-served areas, or that they follow the same im-munization guidelines as government, or that they pass valid health statistics to the ministry of health? These are central issues which are returned to in-depth in Section 4.5.

4.3. The Evidence

It should be clear from the preceding discussion that the claims made for the private sector have different types of status; some depend upon concurrent changes in government policy, others upon certain external conditions. Table 4.1 describes the status of the various claims about the private sector and thus the type of evidence required to support or refute the claims. For example, equity is unlikely to be enhanced by private sector expansion unless there is also a shift in the pattern of government finance so as to benefit the poor. Evidence supporting the claim is thus required to show that, when private

TABLE 4.1 Status of claims concerning the private sector

Claim	Claim dependent upon:		Evidence required
	Government policy	External factors	
Efficiency			
Technical efficiency	None	Competition and absence of severe market failure	Relative efficiency of public and private sectors Evidence of market failure
Allocative efficiency	Reallocation of government resources to cost-effective interventions	Broader political economy/civil society	Cost-effective shift in government resource use
Equity	Reallocation of government resources to the poor	Broader political economy/civil society	Extent to which governments have been willing and able to shift resources to the poor
Increased resources	Maintenance of government funding	Limited price inflation Ability to pay among users	Patterns of government funding after private sector expansion Factor price change Ability to pay Patterns of service use
Consumer choice	None	Choice depends on ability to pay	Ability to pay for private care Patterns of service use

sector expansion has freed government resources, it has been feasible to shift such resources to health care for the poor. Increasingly, promoting the role of the private sector is not seen on its own as a way to ameliorate problems in the health sector. Rather, it is viewed as one of a package of complementary policies which together are sometimes referred to as health sector reform. Until now few countries have embarked on a programme of health sector reform, and of those that have it is still too early to evaluate the success of the reform package and the role of the private sector in particular.

The following discussion is based upon the structure of Table 4.1.

4.3.1. On efficiency and quality

Public/private comparisons

Numerous studies have attempted to compare efficiency and quality in public and private sectors. But health care is an extremely diverse commodity, and conclusive evidence requires that quality of care, case-mix, and severity of illness are all controlled for. Inevitably, developing country studies with this level of sophistication are few and it is difficult to draw conclusions. Furthermore it is not always clear how complete the costings are.

On balance, Table 4.2 suggests that private providers are more efficient, but all of the studies cited refer to private not-for-profit providers, suggesting that differences in efficiency are not due to the profit motive. They do not, therefore, provide an adequate test of the neo-liberal case. Perhaps factors such as freedom from bureaucratic constraints or commitment of staff, which could be improved in the public sector, are more important. A study in Thailand found cost per bed per day in for-profit hospitals to be twice as high as non-profit facilities although quality of care in both was acceptable (Phijaisanit *et al.* 1985).

Several authors attribute lower unit costs in private hospitals to lower wages or lower levels of staffing (e.g. Berman and Dave 1990; DeJong 1991). It is unclear how these affect standards of care. Recent evidence suggests that there is a considerable degree of market segmentation between public and private sectors (and within the private sector) which makes it essential to consider case-mix and severity. A recent study in Bangkok showed that cases seeking private sector care tended to be less serious, with poorly defined complaints which had far shorter lengths of hospital stay (Bennett and Tangcharoensathien 1993). This division is partly due to higher private sector fees. In addition, the private sector may offer higher confidentiality and thus attract people with sexually transmitted diseases or the victims of household violence. If the private sector is treating completely different types of case from the public sector, and thus offering a different set of services, then straightforward comparisons are invalid.

TABLE 4.2   Studies comparing public and private efficiency and quality in developing countries

Author	Country	Comparison	Results	Quality controls
Mills (1990)	Malawi	Govt and NFP hospitals	No difference in efficiency	None
Berman and Dave (1990)	India	Govt and NFP hospitals	NFP hospitals had considerably lower unit costs	None
Alailima and Mohideen (1984)	Sri Lanka	Govt and NFP hospitals	NFP hospitals cheaper	None
Gilson (1992)	Tanzania	Govt and NFP dispensaries	NFP facilities had significantly lower costs than government	Quality not controlled but addressed separately Structural aspects of quality better at missions for curative, at govt for MCH
Bennett (1989)	Lesotho	PHC services in govt and NFP health centres	No significant difference	None
Mitchell *et al.* (1988)	Papua New Guinea	Govt and NFP health centres	Recurrent costs of NFP (excluding depreciation) 18% cheaper	Quality issues addressed separately Quality of care at missions higher

Notes:
NFP: not-for-profit.
MCH: mother and child health.
PHC: primary health care.

Moreover, comparisons of efficiency should not take place without reference to the environment in which providers are operating. Comparisons of for-profit and non-profit hospitals in the USA found the for-profit to be less efficient, but attributed this principally to the fact that services (at the time) were reimbursed on a cost-plus basis, so that profit-maximizing agents were delivering as many services as possible at the highest possible price (Gaumer 1986). Ongoing work in South Africa suggests that management strategies at private hospitals vary considerably according to the incentives and disincentives faced.[4]

Evidence of market failure

Because of the difficulty of making comprehensive comparisons of public and private providers, several studies have addressed the efficiency question by identifying and examining instances where private providers may abuse their

---

[4] Personal communication, A. Mills and J. Broomberg.

informational advantage over patients in a way that is likely to damage efficiency and/or lower the quality of care.

In terms of compromising clinical standards in order to lower costs, there is a lot of anecdotal evidence but few hard facts. Much of this anecdotal evidence comes from India, where there are great concerns about unethical practices and low standards of care in the private sector. Interviews with key informants in Bombay revealed poor waste disposal practices, unacceptable levels of hygiene (sterilizing operating theatres on a weekly basis), and the use of inappropriate residential buildings for clinic and nursing home premises, as the main concerns (Yesudian 1994). Such extreme examples of poor quality care may ultimately place greater pressure on public health care services. In Zimbabwe, South Africa, India, and Thailand there is evidence that private sector providers heavily depend upon relatively untrained staff with limited supervision from physicians (Bennett *et al.* 1994).

By contrast, a number of studies have argued that over-servicing is a serious problem in the private sector. In Brazil the high rate of Caesarian sections among private maternity patients was partly attributed to the financial incentives for providers to operate rather than allow normal deliveries (Barros *et al.* 1986). In a study of private physicians in a slum area of Bombay it was found that drug prescriptions did not match WHO recommended practices; a larger number of more costly items was prescribed (Uplekar 1989*a*, *b*). Yesudian (1994) describes 'cut practice' in Bombay where unnecessary referrals and investigations are recommended with the prescribing practitioner getting a cut of the provider's fee. In Thailand this practice is referred to as 'liang jai' meaning literally 'to feed an illness'.

In terms of price, a comparison of fees charged to insured inpatients in Bangkok showed private sector fees to be approximately three times higher, for comparable diagnoses, despite much shorter lengths of stay in the private sector and the fact that public hospitals were fully recovering recurrent costs (Bennett *et al.* forthcoming). However, without greater knowledge of the costs of private hospitals, in particular capital costs, it is difficult to determine the extent to which these fees differed from competitive, marginal cost, pricing.

Finally there is some evidence of distortions at the market level. In particular some middle income countries with substantial private sectors are beginning to become concerned about rates of technology accumulation and escalating health care costs. In both Korea and Thailand the availability of certain high technology equipment is the same or greater than that in most European countries, despite the fact that GNP per capita is much lower (Yang 1993; Nittayaramphong and Tangcharoensathien 1994). Such high levels of high-technology equipment may lead to the provision of unnecessary, and potentially dangerous, medical investigations and interventions. Moreover, it is likely to increase the costs of health care. In Thailand, just over 6 per cent of GNP was being spent on health care in 1992; it is estimated that this figure will top 8 per cent by 2000. There are no clear-cut rules as to what an 'appropriate level' of health sector expenditure is, but very high rates of expenditure are problematic as they are likely to place pressure upon the payer of health care services. In the USA, once health expenditure grew to more than 10 per cent of GDP there was considerable concern, and consequently political pressure, from small businesses who found their profit margins squeezed by high health care premiums (Economist 1991). In many developing countries the concern is compounded by the inefficient and inequitable nature of health care expenditure; health care inflation is driven by the high-technology hospital care that is provided for the affluent minority.

Such evidence does not suggest that the private sector is more or less efficient than the public; there is substantial evidence documenting inefficiency in the public sector (see Chapter 10 below). However, the examples discussed here do indicate that the profit motive may be accompanied by adverse effects of which governments should be aware.

4.3.2. On equity

Despite claims by some neo-liberals that promoting the private sector may be an effective way to allow a government to shift resources to the poor in order to promote equity, this rarely seems to have been an explicit policy pursued by government. Instead, strong private sectors have developed for ideological reasons (as in Chile), for pragmatic reasons (as in Zimbabwe), or without a conscious government policy (as in Thailand). None the less, the experience of each of these countries sheds light on the probable effects of privatization upon equity.

In Chile in the late 1970s an ideologically driven privatization programme was adopted in the health sector, along with other social sectors. The main thrust of the programme was to expand private insurance and promote private provision for the middle classes (Viveros-Long 1986). At the same time, the government re-targeted limited public sector resources on high-priority primary and preventive services such as maternal and child health, and devolved funding for primary care. This strategy has reaped considerable improvements in health process and health status indicators in Chile; for example, Chile has the highest immunization coverage rate in Latin America and the Caribbean although it does not have the highest per capita income.

However, problems associated with the privatization policy have emerged. First, the healthier and wealthier members of the population tend to elect to have private health insurance. The removal of this group from the main social insurance scheme means that risks can be less widely shared and there is greater inequity than there would otherwise have been (World Bank 1993). Second, funding for public curative health services is extremely limited, and those groups without any insurance have access only to very poor standards of care. Government health staff are extremely demoralized and there has

TABLE 4.3   Hospitalization by household income groups in a
northern Thai town

Income quintile	N	Admission rate (%)	% admission in each sector	
			Public	Private
1 (lowest)	62	9.9	59.3	37.0
2	58	8.2	44.1	50.8
3	67	8.9	26.7	68.0
4	70	9.2	16.9	80.3
5 (highest)	84	9.7	18.6	75.6

Source: Pannurunothai (1993).

been a series of protests and strikes by public sector doctors, lowering standards of care still further (Chaudhary 1992). The under-funding of public curative care is not a direct result of privatization, but the philosophy behind the privatization programme has promoted the notion that hospital-level curative care is not a right, but rather a consumer good which must be purchased.

In Thailand there has not been an explicit privatization policy within the health sector, but during the 1980s there was a concerted effort to increase the accessibility of health services to the rural poor. While government focused on this objective, growing wealth in urban areas, combined with unchanging levels of public health services, led to rapid private sector expansion. The number of private hospital beds grew from 2,050 in 1970 to 12,777 in 1989. Over half of the private beds are in Bangkok (Nittayaramphong and Tangcharoensathien 1993). Evidence suggests that, although access to care has improved for everyone over the past decade, there are now considerable differences in patterns of utilization between the rich and the poor (Table 4.3). Admission rates are roughly the same for different income groups, but among low-income groups the majority of hospitalizations take place in government hospitals whereas higher-income groups use principally private hospitals. Detailed comparative analyses of the quality of care in public and private hospitals are not available. It is clear that in some respects, such as in terms of promptness and politeness, private sector care is of a higher standard. But it is not proven that the clinical quality of care differs substantially between sectors, hence equity may not have been adversely affected.

In Zimbabwe, at Independence the government faced a difficult decision as to whether the existing substantial private for-profit sector should be allowed to continue to operate freely. It was decided that a liberal policy would allow government to focus its attentions on the poor. Recent data show that 37 per cent of health care expenditure is private; however, this covers only 10 per cent of the population (MOH, Zimbabwe 1993). The growth of the private sector has effectively 'crowded out' the public sector; it is estimated that 40 per cent of doctors work full-time in the private for-profit sector (Chandiwana and Chiutsu 1993), leading to shortages of physicians in the government sector; 75 per cent of these private doctors are located in the two major cities of Harare and Bulawayo. Despite these skewed statistics, Zimbabwe has one of the best records of improvements in health indicators since Independence in the whole of sub-Saharan Africa. Like Chile, its immunization coverage is virtually the best on the continent, although per capita income is not the highest.

The lessons from Chile, Thailand, and Zimbabwe suggest that privatization may form a useful part of a strategy to re-target government resources and bring about health status improvements, even for the poor. However, this achievement comes at a price: that of increasing inequity in the accessibility of care and in the quality of care (at least with respect to some aspects) accessed by different income groups. Privatization has a 'tiering' effect. Often there are just two tiers: those who can afford private sector care and those who cannot. In Chile, where there is greater income inequity than the other countries, a rather more sophisticated tiering has developed distinguishing three levels: those with private insurance, those with national health insurance, and those without insurance. Tiering appears inevitable; in order for people to be willing to pay for private sector care, quality, at least in some respects, must be higher.

The privatization strategy targets more government resources at the poor while allowing growing differences in the type of health care which different income groups access. The acceptability of this strategy will vary between countries. It will vary with society's concept of social justice and how utilitarian this is in approach. It will vary with income distribution; for example, the strategy may be more acceptable if the majority of the population continue to use government services (as in the UK), rather than just a weak and marginalized minority. It may also vary with the income level of a country. In poor countries a privatization strategy accompanied by a reallocation of government funding may be critical in enabling government to provide a basic package of services to all. In wealthier countries which have already secured provision of basic services, greater emphasis may be placed upon equity of care given to different income groups.

4.3.3. On additional resources

There are no longitudinal studies examining changes in total funding levels in response to increased private sector funding; however, there are some cross-country studies examining the relationship between total health sector expenditure and the composition of expenditure between public and private sectors. Early econometric analyses covering mainly industrialized countries suggested that those countries which had a higher share of government finance for health also had higher health sector spending as a percentage of GNP (Leu 1986). However, a more recent and better specified model by Gerdtham *et al.* presents the opposite conclusions, suggesting that those countries with higher shares of private spending also have higher total spending (McGuire *et al.* 1993).

Such statistical approaches fail to address the question of government commitment to health sector funding; if governments promote the private sector but also maintain or increase public sector funding, then it would appear most likely that total resources would increase.

Ability to pay is a real constraint to increasing resources in some countries. In Chile in the early 1990s, more than a decade after the reforms began, only 11.5 per cent of the population had bought private health insurance (WHO 1993a). Privatization was markedly slower than anticipated because policy implementation coincided with economic recession, limiting people's ability to pay. Furthermore, with similar policies being pursued in other sectors, there were many new demands on household budgets. By the mid-1980s overall health spending had altered very little, and if anything had fallen, as contraction of the government budget had not been matched by private sector growth (Viveros-Long 1986). Discussing the experience of Singapore, Ruderman (1988) notes that 'privatization of health care has limits that are imposed by the realities of the marketplace'. The size of the private sector is likely to be limited by the number of relatively wealthy persons who can afford to use it.

Competition over scarce resources, particularly doctors, is a problem for many countries with a growing private sector. Owing to wage rigidity in the public sector, it is rare that government can compete in wages (although perquisites such as government housing and future training opportunities may be extremely attractive) and braindrain from public to private sectors occurs. The problem takes two different forms. In some countries doctors are allowed to maintain both public and private sector jobs and there is a danger that public sector duties are neglected in favour of profit-making private activities. In Thailand a recent survey showed that Ministry of Public Health doctors could nearly triple their salaries through private sector work (Chunharas *et al.* 1990). On average, Ministry of Public Health doctors worked an extra 26 hours per week in the private sector, totalling a staggering 84 hour week.

Alternatively, where public doctors are forbidden from holding private sector jobs as well, doctors may quit the public sector to work privately full-time. As Table 4.4 indicates, in many countries a substantial proportion of doctors work in the private sector. In countries such as India, where there is an excess supply of doctors, this is less of a concern. In Malawi it is thought that the majority of private practitioners are elderly doctors who have retired

TABLE 4.4   Private for-profit physicians in selected countries

Country	No. of private doctors	No. of private 'GPs'	Private as % of country's doctors
Papua New Guinea	61	61	25
South Africa	11,650	8,000	59
Pakistan	n/a	38,000	n/a
Zimbabwe	505	n/a	40
Malawi	35	35	16
Bombay (India)	20,000	14,000	n/a

Source: Bennett and Zwi (1993).

from public service.[5] In Zimbabwe, however, there are acute shortages of doctors in the public sector which have led the MOH to recruit physicians from overseas (MOH Zimbabwe 1993).[6]

Banning the private sector entirely also creates problems. In Tanzania, following a 1977 ban on private for-profit activities, an estimated 200 doctors left the country (WHO 1991). It may therefore be better to retain skilled personnel within the country even if they work in the private sector.[7]

4.3.4. On choice

The fact that an increased private sector enhances consumer choice is less debatable than some of the other assertions made, although as noted previously ability to pay may seriously constrain the choice of many people. Few studies have investigated the value placed by consumers on freedom to choose their health care provider. Some studies in the industrialized world (e.g. Lupton *et al.* 1991; Hibbard and Weeks 1987, 1989) indicate that, because of the agency relationship between patient and doctor, people are reluctant to regard a consultation with their doctor as a consumer transaction and thus are unlikely to exercise consumer choice. For example, in one survey of more than 300 households selecting new general practitioners in the UK, 66 per cent exercised little active choice of doctor, simply going to the closest one or the only one which they knew (Salisbury 1989). However, there is virtually no evidence on the extent to which patients in developing countries approach health care providers with a consumerist ethos. Given the asymmetries of

[5] Personal communication, E. Ngalande-Banda.

[6] The shortage of physicians in Zimbabwe is due not only to internal braindrain between public and private sectors, but also to migration within the region.

[7] Competition for other inputs such as drugs and maintenance services has not been studied, but the relatively elastic supply of such services probably means that it is not so problematic.

information mentioned earlier, the interpretation of the welfare effects of this increased choice remain ambiguous.

4.3.5. Summary

From the limited evidence available we conclude that:

1. The evidence on standards of efficiency and quality in the private sector relative to the public sector is inconclusive but suggests that private *non-profit* providers may be more efficient and offer a higher quality of care.
2. Damaging failures in the market for health care services may occur as the result of problems of imperfect information.
3. Promoting the private sector may increase accessibility to services and/or quality of care for the poor in absolute terms, but differences in access and quality of care provided to rich and poor are likely to increase.
4. Government commitment to maintaining existing public funding levels is critical if total health sector resources are to increase.
5. Private providers are likely to bid up certain factor prices, thereby decreasing public sector purchasing power and possibly adversely affecting standards of care in the public sector. A concomitant shift in inputs from public to private sector will occur.
6. Consumer choice normally increases with privatization, but with ambiguous implications for consumer welfare.

4.4. Government Influences on Factors Affecting Private Sector Behaviour

In Section 4.3 it became clear that there are important contextual factors affecting private sector behaviour, three of the most important of which are market structure, the regulatory framework, and the socioeconomic environment. Government is unlikely to be able to determine all of the relevant factors affecting private sector behaviour, but it does have considerable influence over some of them. Moreover, in formulating pro-private policies, government needs to be aware of existing conditions which will affect the way in which private sector providers operate, and to adapt policies accordingly.

4.4.1. Market structure

The nature of the market, and in particular the type of competition in a market, is likely to affect the profitability, efficiency, and quality of care delivered by private providers. Traditional industrial economics suggests that the structure of the market, that is the number of firms and their respective market shares, will influence the way in which the market operates. Those markets that approach the perfectly competitive model, having a large number of buyers and sellers, are likely to work better than those where power is concentrated in the hands of a few sellers. In health care, measures of market concentration are problematic, because health care providers offer a huge range of services, from basic oral rehydration therapy to complex neuro-surgery. Different services will have different geographical market areas and different market structures. Despite a lack of empirical data on market structures in health care, it seems likely that those services with substantial sunk costs and economies of scale (such as neuro-surgery) will be much more concentrated than markets for simpler forms of health care.

The successful functioning of the market will also be affected by the severity of the informational imbalance between patient and physician. For certain primary care services that consumers use frequently, they may be able to judge the quality of care received, and friends and relatives may also be able to offer advice. Pauly and Satterthwaite (1981) describe these types of health service as reputation goods. The problem of asymmetric information is probably greatest for rarely used sophisticated, curative services, where the consumer is almost entirely dependent upon the physician for advice.

The 1993 *World Development Report* proposes that essential clinical care and public health measures be financed by government, whereas 'non-essential' services should be left to the private sector. By contrast, it is the basic services, such as maternity care and treatment of sexually transmitted diseases, that the private sector is most active in providing. In many developing countries the difficulty of raising capital, combined with limited ability to pay among the population, constrains private sector activity at the hospital and referral levels (Viveros-Long 1986; Ngalande-Banda and Simukonda 1994; Thomason 1994). Moreover, from the analysis above it would appear that the market for basic health services is likely to function better than that for more sophisticated care.

The quality (and possibly price) of care provided in the private sector is also likely to be influenced by the quality and price of that in the public sector.[8] Several countries, including Malaysia, have indicated that maintaining adequate standards of government care is part of a strategy to discipline private providers and to prevent excessive 'tiering'. It would seem therefore that there are advantages in terms of both equity and efficiency to a government maintaining provision of the whole range of health care services, rather than segmenting the market by type of service.

The structure of factor markets will also affect the success with which pro-private policies are pursued. In many developing countries government has a

---

[8] See Hammer (1993) for a full discussion of the interactions between public and private sector prices and the policy implications for government.

virtual monopoly on the production of professional health personnel, and also fully funds their training. Thus, if braindrain occurs, the private sector receives subsidized inputs. There may be good reasons why responsibility for training should ultimately rest with government (see Section 4.4.2), but the private sector could help to pay for basic training. Such an arrangement might help to increase the supply of physicians in countries where there are shortages.

4.4.2. The framework of regulations and incentives

There will always be some aspects of health care that consumers are unable to judge for themselves and which thus may not be properly provided under a free market. Hence a regulatory framework is required to ensure that care of an appropriate quality, quantity, and price is offered. The term 'regulation' is a fairly narrow and negative one identifying the set of rules by which private providers must abide. In reality, government has a much broader set of tools, including for example incentive-setting, policy statements about private sector responsibilities, etc., which together define the framework within which the private sector operates. Recently there appears to have been a shift from a regulatory approach to influencing the private sector to a more incentive-based one (WHO 1993*b*).

The ministry of health (MOH) may exercise regulatory authority itself or it may delegate it to other actors such as professional councils. There is a wide range of regulation that may be brought to bear in the health sector, including:

- registration of facilities with the ministry of health to control the number and distribution of private providers;
- establishment of minimal structural requirements to ensure an adequate quality of care;
- control of the acquisition of equipment and expansion of existing facilities;
- price regulation;
- control over procedural aspects of quality of care through investigation of complaints, review of medical records, etc.

Most developing countries exercise some form of regulation. In particular, it is very common for private health care facilities to have to register with the MOH and individual providers with the medical or relevant professional council. For example, in Thailand there are structural requirements specifying the minimum floor space per bed and maximum ratio of beds per toilet. Jordan and Iran have an agreed fee schedule for private practitioners which is negotiated annually between the MOH and private doctors. Whether price regulations are actually complied with in these countries is not clear. Regulatory systems depend critically upon consumers being aware of their rights and being sufficiently confident to complain if they receive low-quality care. This condition is least likely to be met when there are big social, economic, or ethnic differences between patient and health care provider. Hence it would seem that regulation is likely to work better for the rich than for the poor.

Governments may also influence provider behaviour by restructuring incentives. The form of payment mechanism used is perhaps the most obvious incentive; fee-for-service payment mechanisms are likely to encourage providers to give as many services as possible, whereas capitation-based payment will help contain costs. The Thai social security scheme was designed with cost containment in mind and pays providers on a capitation basis. Uninsured patients, however, are likely to pay for care out-of-pocket on a fee-for-service basis. It is difficult for government to alter this, and thus structuring incentives through payment mechanisms becomes a viable option only when a significant proportion of the population is covered by insurance.

Several developing country governments have provided incentive payments or subsidies (financial and in-kind) to private providers to encourage them to offer preventive services and services with positive externalities. For example, Iran, Nigeria, and Zimbabwe have all provided free vaccines to private providers (WHO 1991). Economic theory would suggest that goods with externalities should be subsidized in order to ensure an optimal level of consumption. But if the service is already being provided by government at a subsidized price, then the argument for a general subsidy to private practitioners who provide such a service is less clear. Even without subsidy, some sections of the population would have sought the service in the private sector. By offering a general subsidy to private practitioners, government subsidizes those who were willing to pay the full private sector price as well as those who were not; public funds may be better spent on improving government services or increasing consumer knowledge about the service. A number of factors, including the extent of externalities associated with a good and its price elasticity of demand, will determine whether or not it is worthwhile for government to subsidize the good's provision by the private sector.

Non-financial incentives also affect the way private providers behave. Some innovative schemes are emerging; in Mexico an accreditation scheme is being developed (Garner and Lorenz 1992). This is a voluntary scheme for public and private hospitals which has been organized by a non-government organization. Hospital managers can request accreditation under the scheme. If they are approved by the accreditation agency, then they may gain extra custom because of the advantageous reputation that the scheme confers. In Zimbabwe private sector doctors are able to take up training opportunities organized by the government (WHO 1991). It is felt that this encourages them to behave as responsible members of the health care sector.

A further underlying consideration affecting provider behaviour is that of professional ethics. There has been limited work on how professional ethics are formed, but it would seem that training, existence of a monopoly position, and penalties for abuse of power are likely to influence the strength of professional ethics. Increasingly in developing countries, physician education is being privatized. Three new private medical schools have been established in Malaysia in the past couple of years.[9] In Mexico it has been suggested that, even with MOH control over medical curricula, the course content at private medical schools has encouraged a less altruistic approach to medicine (WHO 1991).

4.4.3. Socioeconomic conditions

A number of different aspects of the socioeconomic conditions within a country will affect the success with which privatization policies are pursued and how well the private sector operates. Important aspects of socioeconomic conditions are income levels, income distribution, education, freedom of the media, and the institutions of civil society.

These factors are likely to interact in quite a complex manner. For example, the key to any success in the promotion of the private sector is the existence of an ability and a willingness to pay for private health care among at least some part of the population. In wealthier countries this ability to pay may exist concurrently with a fairly equitable pattern of income distribution. In poorer countries, however, ability to pay will only exist if income distribution is heavily skewed. In such societies where income inequalities are most marked, it is most likely that some of the adverse effects of privatization, particularly the tiering of health care services, are likely to be observed.

In terms of how well the private sector functions, education, the media, and the richness of civil society are likely to be important factors. Previous parts of this section have already shown how important an informed and relatively well educated population is, both to the efficient functioning of markets and to an effective regulatory system. Furthermore, in a country with an educated populace and rich civil society, consumer groups supporting consumers are more likely to evolve. In India, consumer groups have played a key role in ensuring that medical malpractice cases receive a fair hearing (*Times of India* 1992). Finally, a free and fair press may help to focus public attention on poor performance in both public and private health care sectors and thus create pressure for greater public accountability.[10]

[9] Personal communication, Syed Aljunid.
[10] This is similar to the role that Drèze and Sen (1991) attribute to the media in the prevention of famines.

4.4.4. Summary

From the discussion above, a set of conditions emerges which would appear to enhance the chances of private sector expansion leading to greater efficiency, without having negative effects upon equity. These conditions include the existence of a sub-section of the population who are able and willing to pay for private care, the absence of great inequities, appropriate incentive and regulatory structures for health care providers, strong professional ethics, informed consumers and active consumer organizations, and relatively high standards of care in the government sector.

From this list, it would appear that in the poorest countries of the world the conditions for a successful privatization programme are most limited. In particular, ability to pay is low, consumers are in a weak position, doctors are in short supply and the standard of care in government services is low. In newly industrializing economies many of the conditions are better (supply of doctors, standards of government care, and ability to pay tend to be higher), but low professional standards and inequitable income distributions may be problematic. The conditions for successful private sector involvement would appear to be strongest in developed market economies. Thus, those countries that are most short of resources, and in which external advocacy in support of promoting the private sector has been strongest, are also those that are least likely to be able to manage such a private sector.

Problems with the internal coherence of the neo-liberal arguments also emerge. Neo-liberal arguments suggest that privatization policies may promote both equity and efficiency. Concerns about the equity and cost effectiveness of services suggest that government should focus its efforts on a basic package of primary care leaving the private sector to provide more sophisticated services. But realistically, providers of more sophisticated care are unlikely to be able either to establish themselves or to operate profitably without government subsidy. Moreover, in terms of efficiency, markets for rarely used sophisticated services are likely to operate less well than those for primary care. There is a conflict between the objectives of achieving cost-effective and equitable government expenditure and the arguably more important objective of achieving efficient and equitable provision in the sector as a whole.

4.5. Government Capacity to Regulate and Set Incentives

In terms of the delivery of social services, government has at least three roles it may play; it may provide the service itself, it may let the market provide the service, or it may regulate private provision (Stiglitz 1989). Choice of which strategy to adopt is not straightforward. Market failure in the health sector indicates that private supply is likely to prove sub-optimal, but the problems commonly observed in government health care systems indicate that they are also unlikely to achieve optimality. Regulatory approaches are also problematic; there is always a cost to regulatory activity and regulation may fail to achieve the desired outcome. Government must question whether the cost of intervening in the market-place outweighs the benefits of intervention. Unfortunately, there is very little empirical evidence to guide governments in making such decisions. Research on regulatory arrangements in the health sector of industrialized countries is extremely limited, and there is even less evidence on the success (or otherwise) of regulation in developing countries.

The precise form of regulatory action varies between countries, but a number of core regulatory strategies can be identified. These strategies, and the requirements they place on government capacity, are reviewed below.

4.5.1. Regulatory strategy and government capacity

At least two objectives of health sector regulation can be identified: consumer protection and cost containment. The former objective stems from problems of asymmetric information in the health sector and is probably relevant to countries at all stages of development. Cost containment, on the other hand, is primarily an issue in middle and high-income countries where there is greater ability to pay for health care. Regulation related to either objective may concern itself with the price, quantity, or quality of care. If quality is the focus of regulatory activity, then regulation may address structural measures of quality, procedural measures, or outcome measures. Consumer protection may take the form of legal protection for consumers, machinery for redress, or the availability of independent information to guide consumers. A further aspect of regulation which differs across countries is the organization responsible for enforcing regulation; this responsibility may lie with government, a professional body, or a quango; it may be centralized or decentralized.

Despite the range of regulatory choices, there are strong similarities across countries in the form of regulation adopted. However, the extent of regulatory intervention varies, corresponding both to the socioeconomic status of a country and (to a lesser extent) to the size and nature of the private sector.

Virtually all countries attempt to prevent the delivery of care of an unacceptably low standard, particularly where it may actually cause harm to the patient. Two main strategies are evident: first, the establishment of structural requirements which must be met in order to operate a health facility, and second, a complaints system which responds to accusations of malpractice. Both these measures have limited informational requirements and thus are relatively easy for government or professional organizations to implement; however, their goals are also modest. Structural aspects of care, such as the space per bed, adequacy of hygienic arrangements, etc., are the aspects of care which consumers find easiest to judge; and, because consumers are able to judge these aspects, most private providers will ensure that they are of an adequate quality. Structural quality regulation is probably of most value in situations where private providers compete for low-income customers on the basis of price, instances of which have been described in countries such as India and Pakistan (Garner and Thaver 1993).

The next level of regulatory intervention in the market focuses on over-provision of services, but again considers only structural aspects of quality. Such regulation aims both to control costs and to protect consumers from receiving unnecessary services. Private providers are required to seek government permission before investing in major pieces of equipment or infrastructure. Legislation similar to this exists in the USA, France, and Belgium (Havighurst 1986; Lacronique 1982; Van den Heuvel and Sacrez 1982). However, it is difficult to implement such regulation in an entirely objective manner. Although in principle it is possible to compute the optimal number of facilities or items of equipment for a given population, the analysis is complex, requiring factors such as differing epidemiological patterns, population densities, factor prices, etc., to be taken into account. As governments rarely have the capacity to complete the analysis properly, scope remains for a degree of subjectivity in the final decision which is open to manipulation by political and business interests (Havighurst 1986).

The most sophisticated level of regulation consists of a medical review or audit, which focuses on health care procedures and attempts to ensure that all procedures given are both necessary and appropriate. These approaches have substantial informational requirements. For medical review private providers must routinely supply information on diagnoses, procedures undertaken, length of stay, patient characteristics, etc. Either this information is computerized with outliers then selected for closer examination, or cases are randomly selected and assessed (Wahn 1992; Peachey *et al.* 1992). During internal medical audit, hospital staff will review cases treated by a particular hospital department and discuss the strengths and weaknesses of the procedures adopted. This process may be reinforced by an external audit which periodically tests the completeness and accuracy of internal audit (Lembcke 1956). Approaches such as these are most viable in countries with extensive health insurance coverage where participation as a provider in the scheme can be made conditional upon co-operation in the provision of information or the implementation of medical audit procedures. Countries without such schemes would probably find it very difficult to get reliable information from private providers.

Price regulation may also be used as a means both to protect consumers and to control costs. There are however a number of problems inherent in its implementation. With the heterogeneous standards of care provided in developing countries, different fixed price schedules probably need to be established for different providers. Without an established social health insurance system, it is difficult for government to enforce such regulation. Furthermore, there is a danger that provider groups are strong enough to negotiate fixed prices, which protects their profits rather than consumer welfare. Finally, as experience in Zimbabwe shows, price regulation alone is unlikely to prevent cost inflation unless the quantity of services can also be controlled (Chandiwana and Chiutsu 1993).

More positive approaches to influencing private sector behaviour, such as setting financial incentives or accreditation schemes, may help develop greater trust between government and providers, and will also encourage providers to give information to government. However, government faces similar problems to those outlined above in the verification of such information.

4.5.2. Regulatory experiences

There is very limited evidence about the success with which health sector regulation has been enforced in developing countries, but the few examples available are illuminating.

In India, where there is a very large private sector, considerable regulatory problems have emerged. Medical councils are the main authority for maintaining adequate standards of health care. However, many people in India came to feel that the councils were not giving a fair hearing to malpractice cases. Cases were being delayed, evidence was being lost, and the final penalty imposed upon health care providers often seemed risible in comparison with the seriousness of the malpractice committed (*Times of India* 1992). Considerable media coverage was given to allegations of unfair treatment made by people taking malpractice cases to the Medical Council. Several consumer groups were formed to advocate stronger regulation of private providers and offer support to complainants in malpractice cases. Finally, a legal ruling was made that cases against private practitioners could also be brought under the Consumer Protection Act, the same act which covers the purchase of most consumer items. This has outraged private practitioners in India, resulting in strike action and demonstrations (*Times of India* 1993). The situation has not yet been resolved.

Similar problems have occurred in Zimbabwe, where the Medical Council was accused of 'hushing up' malpractice cases to protect the future custom of the provider and the reputation of the profession (MOH, Zimbabwe 1993). Elsewhere in sub-Saharan Africa regulatory authority has barely been developed. For example, in Ghana, although various medical councils responsible for regulation have been established for many years, only recently have they started to receive funding.[11]

In Thailand private providers may be regulated either through professional

---

[11] Personal communication, George Dakpallah.

legislation falling under the Medical Council or through the 1963 Medical Institutions Act enforced by the Ministry of Public Health. However, complaints in the press about recent unethical behaviour (such as refusing treatment to emergency patients who are unable to pay in advance) have been targeted at hospital managers and administrators. No action can be taken against such behaviour; the Medical Institutions Act does not cover procedural aspects of the quality of care regulation and the Medical Council has authority only over doctors (Cheang 1992).

There is also increasing evidence from the industrialized world of problems associated with health sector regulation. Foremost among these complaints is a tendency not to consider the lay perspective and to be more concerned with maintaining the reputation of the profession than confronting and resolving problems (Moran and Wood 1993). Studies of industrial regulation in developing country economies have highlighted problems including the limited regulatory capacity of government, the resource costs of information collection, and problems of regulatory capture, particularly where the individuals or organizations being regulated are politically powerful (Adams *et al.* 1992).

In many developing countries, ministries of health have notoriously weak information systems which rarely cover the private sector and have substantial problems in processing and analysing even the available public sector information. Reports may be out-of-date and information may be fragmented between different vertical programmes. In such a context, expanding information systems to cover the private sector would be a formidable task. The greatest hope for success in this area lies in the development of social health insurance schemes. Under such schemes it is possible to withhold payment if data are not provided or appear unreliable.

The experience of regulatory failure in India suggests that regulatory authorities may be concerned more with protecting those whom they are supposed to be regulating than with protecting consumers. This problem is well recognized in the literature. Regulation can be viewed as a good, like any other consumer good, which different groups within society want to purchase (Tomlinson 1993). In the health care context it would appear that the medical and other health professions probably have the greatest interest in health sector regulation. Moreover, the health professions tend to be highly organized and thus in a much better position to influence the form the regulation takes. Similar arguments are echoed in public choice theory, which suggests that bureaucrats, in this case members of regulatory authorities, tend to promote their own interests rather than the wider good of society as a whole.

4.5.3. Implications for government policy

Many of the current directions of reform in the health sector (such as user fees, internal markets, etc.) raise critical questions about the capacity of government to fulfil its new responsibilities. This is particularly true of the promotion of the private sector and regulation. Greater capacity is required in the areas of management, economics, strategic planning, and law. Vague exhortations to regulate need to be backed up by detailed guidance on what should be regulated and how. Existing regulatory instruments need to be more effectively operated. Government may need to monitor the activities of regulatory agents to ensure that they perform their job in a satisfactory manner, or indeed may need to establish its own mechanisms to regulate procedural aspects of care and investigate complaints. Evidence suggests that the larger the number of regulatory agencies, the less susceptible they are to regulatory capture (Propper 1993). There may also be more innovative approaches to regulation, such as greater decentralization of regulatory authority, in order to generate greater local accountability.

By its very nature, regulation is political; the regulatory agencies and regulatory processes that develop depend principally on the relative power of different actors. More problematic is the fact that individual and political interests may interfere in the operation of the regulatory system. Regulatory systems in health care are particularly susceptible to this because of the scope for subjective interpretation of regulations. This problem is exacerbated by the often close links (and sometimes direct involvement) of public sector policy-makers with the private sector. Fair regulation requires transparent and independent decision-making.

4.6. Conclusions

Despite (or perhaps because of) the fact that public health care providers are a relatively recent phenomenon compared with providers in the private sector, research during the past few decades has ignored the private sector, focusing instead upon government activities. National government and donor interest in the private sector is relatively recent. Moreover, until a few years ago the debate about the relative roles of public and private sectors was largely ideologically driven, and thus little empirical evidence was sought. Hence data on the private sector in health care and its relationship with government are astoundingly scarce. There are limited data on comparative cost structures and case-mix in public and private sectors, and upon the impact of private sector growth upon equity and upon resource availability. There is virtually no evidence on the success (or otherwise) of government regulatory and incentive-setting strategies in developing countries. Far more evidence is required before satisfactory answers can be found to many of the questions raised in this chapter.

The most common reason for promoting the private sector is to attract more funding to the health care sector. If there is ability and willingness to pay, at least among a portion of the population, then this strategy is likely to be successful—but at a price. First, it seems inevitable that there will be an increase in inequity, even if access of the poorest to health care services is improved in absolute terms. Second, claims of greater efficiency in the private sector are either unproven or of dubious reliability. Efficiency benefits are likely to materialize only if government is an effective regulator.

Perhaps the most important lesson emerging is that the wisdom of promoting the private sector can be assessed only on a case-by-case basis. Different countries, and even different regions within countries, will have different socioeconomic characteristics, different sets of professional ethics, different market structures, and different health status objectives which will affect both the way in which the private sector operates and the degree to which it meets government goals and objectives. Second, in developing policy about the role of the private sector, different types of health sector services need to be disaggregated; a service such as immunization has completely different characteristics to one such as cardiac surgery. Neo-liberal arguments currently advocate public sector financing, and possibly provision, for a package of basic preventive and curative services, while more complex services are left to the private sector. Such a strategy ensures that public finances are focused on the most cost-effective interventions, but fails to ensure that the sector as a whole will operate in the most efficient manner.

There are many obstacles to effective regulation by government within the health care sector, and there are likely to be considerable costs associated with the establishment and exercise of regulatory power, in particular with respect to information collection. The expansion of government's role as purchaser of health care through health insurance schemes may potentially assist it in its regulatory role by lowering the cost of information collection. However, many dimensions of imperfect information remain and mean that a certain trust must exist between government and the private sector. Such trust may be facilitated through greater consultation between the two sectors.

The tasks placed upon government, if it is to be a truly effective regulator and enabler, are substantial. New skills need to be developed within the public sector, and fair and independent regulatory systems developed. Promotion of the private sector, like other alternative modes of social sector funding advocated, still leaves substantial and difficult responsibilities with government. It must not be seen as a way to reduce the burden that government bears.

References

Adams, C., Cavendish. W., and Mistry, P. S. (1992) *Adjusting Privatization: Case studies from Developing Countries*, James Currey, London.

Alailima, P. and Mohideen, F. (1984) 'Health sector expenditure flows in Sri Lanka', *World Health Statistics Quarterly*, 37(4): 403–20.

Arrow, K. (1963) 'Uncertainty and the welfare economics of medical care', *American Economic Review*, 53(5): 941–73.

Barros, F. C., Vaughan, J. P., and Victora, C. (1986) 'Why so many Caesarean sections? The need for further policy change in Brazil', *Health Policy and Planning*, 1(1): 19–29.

Bennett, S. (1989) 'The immunization and diarrhoea control programmes, a unit cost study', *Lesotho Epidemiological Bulletin*, 4(1): 15–20.

—— and Tangcharoensathien, V. (1993) 'Health insurance and private providers: a study of the Civil Servants' Medical Benefit Scheme in Bangkok, Thailand', *International Journal of Health Planning and Management*, 8: 137–52.

—— and Zwi, A. (1993) 'The private sector and public health', in Health Economics and Financing Programme (eds.), *Report of the Workshop on the Public/Private Mix for Health Care in Developing Countries*. London School of Hygiene and Tropical Medicine, London.

—— Dakpallah, G., Garner, P., *et al.* (1994) 'Carrot and stick: state mechanisms to influence private provider behaviour', *Health Policy and Planning*, 9(1): 1–13.

—— Tangcharoensathien, V., Mills, A., and Nittayaramphong, S. (forthcoming) 'Using insurance fund records to investigate the private health care market', *Social Science and Medicine*.

Berman, P. and Dave, P. (1990) 'Experiences in paying for health care in India's voluntary sector' in P. Dave (ed.), *A Report on the National Workshop on Health Financing in the Voluntary Sector*, Voluntary Health Association of India and the Ford Foundation, New Delhi.

Bhat, R. (1993) 'The private health care sector in India: some policy concerns', Research paper no. 54, Takemi Program in International Health, Harvard, Boston.

Birdsall, N. and James, E. (1992) *Health, Government and the Poor: The Case for the Private Sector*. World Bank, Washington, DC.

Chandiwana, S. and Chiutsu, A. (1993) 'The public/private mix for health care in Zimbabwe', in Health Economics and Financing Programme (eds.), *Report of the Workshop on the Public/Private Mix for Health Care in Developing Countries*, London School of Hygiene and Tropical Medicine, London.

Chandra, J. and Kakabadse, A. (1985) *Privatization and the NHS: The Scope for Collaboration*, Gower, Aldershot, Hants.

Chaudhary, V. (1992) 'Chile's economic boom fails to improve health care', *British Medical Journal*, 305: 1113.

Cheang, Wee Soo (1992) 'No cash, No cure', *The Nation* (Bangkok), 25 June.

Chunharas, S., Wongkanaratanakul, P., Supachutikul, A., *et al.* (1990) *An Appropriate Remuneration for Doctors in Thailand: A Research Report* (in Thai), Medical Council, Bangkok.

DeJong, J. (1991) 'Non-governmental organizations and health delivery in Sub-Saharan Africa', Population, Health, and Nutrition Working Paper, World Bank, Washington, DC.

Drèze, J. and Sen, A. (1991) 'Public action for social security: foundations and strategy' in E. Ahmad, *et al.* (ed.), *Social Security in Developing Countries*, Clarendon Press, Oxford.

Economist (1991) 'Health care: a spreading sickness', *The Economist*, 6 July 1991

Friedman, M. (1962) *Capitalism and Freedom*, University of Chicago Press.

Garner, P. and Lorenz, N. (eds.) (1992) 'Managing and financing urban health systems', World Development Report Urban Health Consultations Working Group no. 2, Department of Public Health and Policy with the Swiss Tropical Institute, Basel.

—— and Thaver, I. (1993) 'Urban slums and primary health care: The private doctor's role', *British Medical Journal* 306: 667–8.

Gaumer, G. (1986) 'Medicare patient outcomes and hospital organization mission', in Institute of Medicine, *For-Profit Enterprise in Health Care* National Academy Press, Washington, DC.

Gilson, L. (1992) 'Value for money? The efficiency of primary health facilities in Tanzania', Ph.D. thesis, University of London.

Hammer, J. S. (1993) 'Prices and protocols in public health care', Population, health and nutrition department working paper, World Bank, Washington, DC.

Havighurst, C. C. (1986) 'The changing locus of decision making in the health care sector', *Journal of Health Politics, Policy and Law*, 11: 697–735.

Hibbard, J. H. and Weeks, E. C. (1987) 'Consumerism in health care: prevalence and predictors', *Medical Care*, 25(11): 1019–32.

—— —— (1989) 'Does the dissemination of comparative data on physician fees affect consumer use of services?' *Medical Care*, 27(12): 1167–74.

Lacronique, J.-F. (1982) 'The French health care system', in G. McLachlan and G. Maynard (eds.), *The Public/Private Mix for Health*, Nuffield Provincial Hospitals Trust, London.

Lees, J. (1960) 'The economics of health services', *Lloyds Bank Review*, 56(26).

Lembcke, P. A. (1956) 'Medical auditing by scientific methods, illustrated by major female pelvic surgery', *Journal of the American Medical Association*, 162: 646–55; reprinted in J. Frenk *et al.* (eds.), *Health Services Research: An Anthology*, Pan-American Health Organization, Washington, DC.

Leu, R. (1986) 'The public–private mix and international health care costs', in A. Culyer and B. Jonsson (eds.), *The Public–Private Mix of Health Services*, Blackwell, Oxford.

Lewis, M. A. and Kenney, G. (1988) *The Private Sector and Family Planning in Developing Countries: Its Role, Achievements and Potential*, Urban Institute, Washington, DC.

Lupton, D., Donaldson, C., and Lloyd, P. (1991) 'Caveat Emptor or blissful ignorance? Patients and the consumerist ethos', *Social Science and Medicine*, 33(5): 559–68.

McGuire, A., Parkin, D., Hughes, D., and Gerard, K. (1993) 'Econometric analyses of national health expenditures: can positive economics help to answer normative questions?' *Health Economics*, 2: 113–26.

Mills, A. (1990) 'Economics of hospitals in developing countries', *Health Policy and Planning*, 5(3): 203–18.

Minford, P. (1991) 'The role of social services a view from the New Right', in M. Loney *et al.* (eds.), *The State or the Market: Politics and Welfare in Contemporary Britain*, Sage, London.

Ministry of Health (MOH), Zimbabwe (1993) 'Intercountry meeting on public/private collaboration for health: country report on Zimbabwe', unpublished paper presented at WHO regional meeting, Windhoek, Namibia.

Mitchell, M., Donaldson, D., and Thomason, J. (1988) *Papua New Guinea Rural Health Services Cost Study*, Management Sciences for Health, Boston.

Moran, M. and Wood, B. (1993) *States, Regulation and the Medical Profession*, Open University Press, Buckingham.

Ngalande-Banda, E. E. and Simukonda, H. P. M. (1994) 'The public/private mix in the health care system in Malawi', *Health Policy and Planning*, 9(1): 63–71.

Nittayaramphong, S. and Tangcharoensathien, V. (1993) 'Thailand: private health care out of control?' *Health Policy and Planning*, 9(1): 31–40.

Pannurunothai, S. (1993) 'Equity in health: the need for and the use of public and private health services in an urban area in Thailand', Ph.D. thesis, University of London.

Pauly, M. V. and Satterthwaite, M. A. (1981) 'The pricing of primary care physicians' services: a test of the role of consumer information', *Bell Journal of Economics*.

Peachey, D. K., Henderson, G., Weinkauf, D., and Tsianidis, J. (1992) 'Can medical review committees control overservicing?' *Canadian Medical Association Journal*, 146: 693–4.

Phijaisanit, W., Phijaisanit, P., Boonyaratapan, *et al.* (1985) 'Investor owned and not-for-profit hospitals; a comparison study in Bangkok 1981', *Journal of the Medical Association of Thailand*, 68(6): 292–7.

Propper, C. (1993) 'Quasi-markets and regulation', in J. le Grand and W. Bartlett (eds.), *Quasi-Markets and Social Policy*, Macmillan, London.

Robinson, J. (1988) 'Hospital quality competition and the economics of imperfect information', *Milbank Quarterly*, 66(3): 465–81.

Roemer, M. I. (1984) 'Private medical practice: obstacle to health for all', *World Health Forum*, 5: 195–210.

Ruderman, P. A. (1988) 'Health planning in Singapore: limits to privatization', *Journal of Public Health and Policy*.

Salisbury, C. J. (1989) 'How do people choose their doctor', *British Medical Journal*, 299: 608–10.

Saltman, R. B. and von Otter, C. (1989) 'Public competition versus mixed markets: an analytic comparison', *Health Policy*, 11: 43–55.

Stiglitz, J. (1989) *The Economic Role of the State*, Basil Blackwell, Oxford.

Thomason, J. (1994) 'A cautious approach to privatization in Papua New Guinea', *Health Policy and Planning*, 9(1): 41–9.

Times of India (1992) 'Ethics in medical profession: need for prescription of conduct', *The Times of India*, 26 October 1992, Bombay.

—— (1993) 'For Delhiites, it could have been worse . . .', *Times of India*, 18 September 1993, New Delhi.

Titmuss, R. (1963) *Essays on the Welfare Side*, 2nd edn., Allen & Unwin, London.

Tomlinson, J. (1993) 'Is successful regulation possible? Some theoretical issues', in R. Sugden (ed.), *Industrial Economic Regulation: A Framework and Exploration*, Routledge, London.

Uplekar, M. (1989*a*) 'Implications of prescribing patterns of private doctors in the treatment of tuberculosis in Bombay, India', Research paper no. 41, Takemi Programme in International Health, Harvard School of International Public Health, Boston.

—— (1989*b*) 'Private doctors and public health: the case of leprosy in Bombay, India', Research paper no. 41, Takemi Programme in International Health, Harvard School of International Public Health, Boston.

Van den Heuvel, R. and Sacrez, A. (1982) 'Cost containment in health insurance: the case of Belgium', in G. McLachlan and A. Maynard (eds.) *The Public/Private Mix for Health*, Nuffield Provincial Hospitals Trust, London.

Viveros-Long, A. (1986) 'Changes in health financing: the Chilean experience', *Social Science and Medicine*, 22(3): 379–85.

Wahn, M. (1992) 'Controlling overservicing by physicians: review of office practices in Manitoba', *Canadian Medical Association Journal*, 146: 723–8.

World Bank (1987) *Health Financing: An Agenda for Reform*, World Bank, Washington, DC.

—— (1993) *Investing in Health: World Development Report 1993*, World Bank, Washington, DC.

WHO (1978) *Alma-Ata 1978: Primary Health Care*, WHO, Geneva.

—— (1991) *Interregional Meeting on the Public/Private Mix in National Health Systems and the Role of Ministries of Health*, WHO, Geneva.

—— (1993a) *Evaluation of Recent Changes in the Financing of Health Services*, WHO, Geneva.

—— (1993b) *Public/Private Collaboration for Health*. Report of an intercountry meeting, Windhoek, Namibia, WHO National Health Systems and Policies, Geneva.

Yang Bong-Min (1993) 'Medical Technology and inequity in health care: the case of Korea', *Health Policy and Planning*, 8(4): 385–93.

Yesudian, C. A. K. (1994) 'Behaviour of the private sector in the health market of Bombay', *Health Policy and Planning*, 9(1): 72–80.

5

The Cost Effectiveness of Public and Private Schools: Knowledge Gaps, New Research Methodologies, and an Application in India

SAJITHA BASHIR

5.1. Introduction

Private provision and funding at all levels of education is widespread in developing countries, but research on the comparative performance and costs of the private and public sectors is surprisingly sparse. A recent study which reviewed the size of the private sector in 35 countries found that most developing countries in the sample have large private sectors at the secondary level accounting for at least 20 per cent of total enrolment (James 1987). Moreover, in almost all these countries, the private sector either receives no public funds or is only partially subsidized and hence operates under conditions that differ considerably from those facing public schools. In several countries, there also exists a category of private schools which are almost entirely unregulated. By contrast, in industrialized countries the private sector is both heavily subsidized and tightly regulated, approximating the public sector in its input and output characteristics. Developing countries, therefore, appear to present a wide variety of private systems of provision and financing, yet their characteristics have only recently begun to be studied systematically.

This paper reviews existing knowledge about the performance of public versus private schools, the appropriateness of the research methodologies used, and the policy implications of results regarding cost effectiveness. Important methodological and conceptual problems are discussed, focusing upon a series of major studies undertaken in the USA which have been subjected to great criticism and reanalysis. The results of similar studies conducted in developing countries are also presented. This is followed by a brief exposition of new research methodologies which enable a more appropriate conceptualization of school effects and statistically more valid methods of estimating sector effects. An application of these methods, in a study of government-aided and unaided schools at the primary level in the state of Tamil Nadu in India, is presented, together with a discussion of its implications for policy. Our work shows that private schools are not unambiguously more cost-effective than public schools, even when attention is focused on only one outcome of schooling, namely cognitive achievement.

5.2. Issues of Methodology

The economic debate over public versus private provision of education dates back at least as far as the classical economists, and the main arguments that are being currently advanced for private schooling, as for private financing in general, remain the arguments advanced by Adam Smith: greater efficiency and responsiveness to consumer needs. The necessity to compete for students would cause private schools to provide the type of service required by families and to adopt more effective and economical teaching practices, staffing patterns, and educational materials (World Bank 1992). It is also argued that promotion of private schools will encourage public schools to become more efficient as the latter compete for students with private schools.

Classical economists who opposed Adam Smith's reasoning did so on the grounds that the majority of consumers, the labouring classes, lacked the information about education to make rational choices in their own interest regarding the content of education (cf. J. S. Mill: 'the uncultivated cannot be competent judges of cultivation'). Privately provided education that was driven purely by consumer demand would not have the characteristics (as reflected in the curriculum, the teaching of moral values, etc.) that were considered desirable for society. It was therefore incumbent on the more cultivated people, who also controlled state policy, to assist consumers by providing the appropriate kind of education free of cost at least up to the elementary level. The debate centred on the 'right' content of education and on whether public authorities or private providers should be entrusted with the task of ensuring this content. The adoption of more or less universal public, or publicly financed, school education in most industrialized countries by the end of the nineteenth century made this debate somewhat redundant. When the debate resurfaced in the early 1980s in the context of growing fiscal constraints worldwide, research concerns focused upon testing empirically whether private schools are more efficient than public schools in producing certain defined and measurable cognitive skills, rather than on the relative merits of the content of education provided by public and private schools.

Thus, much of the recent debate has centred on the methodology of making valid comparisons of public and private sector performance using quantitative indicators of educational inputs and outcomes. Three main methodological issues have dominated the research on the public/private differential. The first of these revolves around the appropriate definition and measurement of school outputs. Schools produce multiple outcomes in both the cognitive and non-cognitive domains. Further, the real concern in making school comparisons is not about pupil performance on a test *per se* but about future performance in the labour market. Practical considerations and difficulties involved in measuring affective outcomes, however, require comparisons between public and private sectors to be made on the basis of the academic achievement of pupils in one or two subjects while they are still in school. It is also extremely difficult to relate current school characteristics to performance in the labour market a decade or two later (Harbison and Hanushek 1992). The basic assumption is that the academic outcomes currently produced by schools are correlated with labour market outcomes in the future. At the primary school level, the focus on acquisition of cognitive skills is more easily justifiable, since it is correlated not only with future performance in the labour market but also with the ability of pupils to continue in school. At higher levels, however, it appears more difficult to justify the evaluation of sectors on the basis of one or two measures of cognitive achievement alone, when the important outcome may be other skills and aptitudes demanded in the labour market.

Cognitive outcomes are usually measured by achievement on a standardized test in a particular content area. In principle, scientifically constructed, carefully administered and well interpreted tests can provide accurate measures of pupil performance in the particular content area. In practice, the reliability and validity of the measuring instruments are often the most crucial elements in determining the soundness of inferences about relative performance. Moreover, a scientifically drawn sample with reasonably large sample sizes of schools and pupils is necessary in order to draw generalizations. Both these factors have serious cost implications which inhibit studies on the cost effectiveness of education or limit the validity of their conclusions.

The second set of methodological issues arises from the fact that comparisons of public and private schools in non-experimental settings (that is, when students cannot be randomly assigned to schools within sectors) necessitate effective statistical controls over the intake characteristics of pupils and other factors that may affect pupil outcomes but cannot be attributed to the policies of the schools themselves. Randomized experiments would assist in making stronger causal inferences, but even in such cases, it may not be possible to control for all factors experimentally. Since randomized experiments can play only a limited role in educational settings, the main conceptual and methodological question is how to characterize the private sector effect when data are collected from schools as they exist, and to elaborate on the inferences that can be made about observed relationships. Although there is a broad con-sensus that pupil background factors, including variables relating to the home environment, individual motivation, and community characteristics, should be 'controlled', there is little agreement on the precise delineation of these variables and how they should be measured. The result is that individual researchers have resorted to constructing and measuring variables for specific contexts which reduce the comparability of studies done in different social and cultural settings.

Some analysts have also discussed the conceptual impossibility of separ-ating out the intake characteristics of pupils from the effects of school inputs and hence of making any kind of comparisons of schools from observed data. Murnane (1981) argues that 'selection mechanisms, the factors that influence which children attend which schools, and educational programmes are not analytically distinct', because selecting the right mix of students is an import-ant way to improve the effectiveness of a programme, to attract more mo-tivated and skilled teachers, and to raise teacher morale. The only meaningful comparison would be to 'analyse the effectiveness of the two types of schools in carrying out the same tasks with the same tools and with the same children', and no data collected from existing situations can answer this question.

Without an explicit model of how learning outcomes are produced, a great deal of caution must be exercised in making causal inferences from observed behavioural relationships in non-experimental settings. Murnane's criticism was directed against those researchers who, basing themselves on an observed statistically significant private school effect, concluded that private schools could effectively serve a clientele different from the one they currently serve. Such a conclusion would be valid only under the assumption that 'the regres-sion relationship accurately describes the mechanics of a rigid educational process' (Lockheed and Longford 1989), an assumption that is clearly un-tenable.

A third set of methodological questions relates to the appropriate statistical method for estimating sector effects which is also linked to the more funda-mental issue of how school effects are conceptualized. Initial studies on school effects used single-level regression models, where pupil and school variables are regressed on a measure of achievement and the coefficients of these variables are estimated using ordinary least squares (OLS). One line of criticism stressed the pitfalls of using this technique specifically in the context of public/private comparisons because of bias resulting from self-selection (Barnow *et al.* 1980; Goldberger and Cain 1982; Willms 1984). The estimates of the private school effect will be biased if there are other excluded variables that are related to both achievement and attendance in private schools. Examples of omitted variables which might account for both higher achieve-ment and attendance in a private school are innate ability and motivation. More motivated students with greater parental support may either themselves choose or be selected into private schools, so that some of the private school effect should in fact be attributed to students rather than to the school.

A more fundamental criticism appertains to the very conceptualization of school effects underlying the use of OLS and its basic assumption that pupil factors and educational inputs exert the same effect on pupil outcomes irrespective of the particular school that the pupil attends. Another basic assumption is that all explanatory variables have been measured. The vast literature on school effects, on the other hand, shows that individual schools do have a powerful effect on students' performance and that individual schools not only affect mean outcomes, but also differentially affect students of different social and academic backgrounds. However, almost all commonly measured school and teacher characteristics are poor proxies for the inputs that enter students' classroom experiences (Hanushek 1986).

The first observation indicates that the individual effect of each school on average performance or on the distribution of scores within each school must be explicitly modelled. The use of OLS techniques imposes the restriction of homogeneity of regression. If the true relationships between the explanatory and dependent variables differ across schools, estimating a common relationship across all schools can distort the effect of individual variables.

The second observation implies that, since many school-level variables cannot be measured, the correlation of residuals within each school must also be explicitly taken into account. If all class-level or school-level variables that affect outcomes were observed, pupils would differ only by the individual error component. If these variables are not all measured, as is usually the case, they are absorbed into the error term. Correlation between two observations within a school arises because one component of the error term is common to all pupils in a school, since the same value on each of these omitted variables is ascribed to all of them. In such situations, the use of OLS techniques, which ignore the clustering of pupils within schools and the correlation of the residual terms, leads to incorrect estimates for the standard errors of school-level coefficients and wrong inferences about the statistical significance of the latter. The estimated standard errors will be too small and the risk of Type I errors inflated.

The unmeasured component of the 'school effect' need not arise only from factors that can be ascribed to school practices. Intra-school correlation in residuals can also arise because of the way in which students have been assigned to schools. In rural areas in developing countries, for instance, the catchment area of a village school will typically comprise people who are relatively homogeneous in characteristics such as social and ethnic background, educational level, occupation, attitude and commitment to education, and other home environment factors. The variation in these characteristics will tend to be more pronounced between villages than within villages. Thus, pupils in a typical village school are likely to be more homogeneous than pupils in different schools. These omitted common background characteristics again give rise to intra-school correlation in the within-school residuals.

Finally, the proportion of the total variation in test scores which is due to variation between schools and that which is due to variation between pupils within schools are unknown when OLS techniques are used. The variation in scores between schools is the only component that can be explained by school-level factors. Where the proportion of between-school variance is small, the model will typically explain a relatively small part of the *total* variation, although it may explain a large proportion of the variation that can be explained by all school-level factors. Since OLS analysis does not provide estimates of the variance components, judgements about the adequacy of the models must necessarily be more limited. All these methodological problems are well illustrated in the review of research that follows.

5.3. Review of Public/Private Differences in Achievement

5.3.1. Evidence from developed countries

The systematic study of school effects and of the relative performance of public and private schools is a recent development even in industrialized countries. Papers submitted to the International Congress for School Effectiveness and the annual meetings of the American Educational Research Association reveal that, by and large, the research on school effects has been confined to Anglo-Saxon countries (Scheerens 1992). Investigation of public–private school differences has been undertaken in only a few cases even in these countries, while similar research in developing countries has been even more rare.

Research on the nature of differences between public and private schools began with the study by Coleman *et al.* (1982) of American high schools. Under the High School and Beyond (HSB) project, a very large sample of 58,728 American high school students in 893 public schools, 84 Catholic schools, and 38 non-Catholic private schools was surveyed in 1981. The authors' conclusions regarding the greater effectiveness of private schools for students from low socioeconomic backgrounds were based on the difference in the predicted performance of the average public school student and the expected achievement if he or she were to attend a private school. Predicted scores were derived from regression equations computed separately for public and private school students, using 17 family background variables to control for pre-existing differences between students entering the two sectors. The private school effect was attributed to certain definable 'school policies', such as academic tracking, the school's emphasis on homework, the disciplinary climate, and attendance policies, the conclusion being that public schools which emulated these policies could achieve the superior results of private schools.

Coleman's study highlighted the three main methodological issues referred to above. The dependent variables used to measure the outcomes of high school appeared to be outcomes of elementary education, while the background variables used in Coleman's analysis to control for differences between public and private school students prior to their entering high school excluded certain important variables such as a measure of prior attainment (Goldberger and Cain 1982).

The HSB dataset was subsequently re-analysed by a number of researchers; the results indicated the necessity for exercising caution in interpreting estimated parameters of empirically constructed models of achievement. A re-estimation of Coleman's model by Noell (1981) with the inclusion of four additional student variables (gender, region, handicap status, and college expectations in eighth grade) lowered the private school effect. Another line of criticism challenged the conceptualization of the variables used to describe 'school policy' (Goldberger and Cain 1982). Most of these variables were derived from students' perceptions about the behaviour of their teachers and fellow students, which might easily be attributed to the social composition of the school. Although such variables are clearly attributes of the school, and are of considerable interest to parents when selecting schools, it is highly debatable whether they can be considered elements of 'school policy'. Murnane (1984) further argued that 'school policy' can only be taken to mean a set of actions which can be spelt out and which school administrators can be asked to carry out; if this set of actions produces higher outcomes, the policy can be considered effective. The variables used to describe school policy in Coleman's study could not be defined in this manner. Furthermore, the treatment of the student's track status—whether the student was in an academic, general, or vocational track—was especially controversial. In the Coleman study, the student's track status was treated as a school policy variable, although it could clearly reflect initial abilities and aptitude, in which case it should be treated as a control variable. Comparison of performance of students in the academic track alone, who were likely to be more alike in their initial abilities and interests, showed that the private school effect was statistically insignificant (Willms 1982).

The neglect of contextual effects of social class was another limitation of the study (Murnane 1983). The question posed by Coleman was: What would the achievement of an average public school student be if he or she attended a Catholic or a non-Catholic private school? Taking into account the differences in the regulations faced by the two sectors and in the characteristics of the clients they serve, the more appropriate question would be: What would the achievement of an average public school student be if he or she attended a private school and took along his/her public school classmates? Murnane reconducted Coleman's analysis introducing average socioeconomic status of the class as another explanatory variable. The Catholic–public school gap shrank by 60 per cent, although the difference remained statistically significant. In the case of other private schools, the predicted test score was actually lower than the predicted public school score.

Goldberger and Cain (1982) argued that failure to control for selectivity bias undermined many of the substantive conclusions put forward by Coleman *et al.* In particular, selection effects might explain the better performance of minority students in Catholic schools: the few minority students who do enter these schools tend to be the most motivated and academically oriented, who would have performed well in any school. Correction for self-selection, by explicitly modelling sector choice using Heckman's two-stage method, was used by Noell (1982) to re-analyse Coleman's model. The analysis yielded substantially lower effects for private schools compared with the original study.

An important reanalysis of the HSB data was done by Willms (1984), who examined differences between individual schools in both sectors. Separate within-school regressions were fitted for all 958 schools in the analysis, using four control variables to account for initial differences between students in their background. Thus, each school was characterized by a different intercept as well as a different slope. A school effectiveness score was calculated for the average student, using the estimated parameters for the within-school regression. The effectiveness scores were then averaged for the different sectors. Since many schools served students only from high socioeconomic status (SES), Willms estimated separate sets of effectiveness scores for both public and private sectors at five different SES levels. The results revealed a wide range in school effectiveness within each sector at each of the SES levels; at the fiftieth percentile in SES, for example, the range within either sector was 'over 40 times the small differences between them'.

5.3.2. Evidence from developing countries

Initial research in developing countries, using variants of the original Coleman model, with corrections for self-selection, also seemed to indicate the superiority of private schools. However, unlike the American HSB dataset, these data were not re-analysed and hence the conclusions could not be verified under alternative model specifications. Psacharapoulos (1987) examined differences between public and private secondary schools in Tanzania and Colombia, using a single pupil-level regression, controlling for student's sex, father's education and verbal and mathematics aptitude. The model was similar to that used in the original Coleman study. A positive private school effect was detected for academic subjects and a negative effect for vocational and technical subjects. The Tanzanian data were analysed separately for academic, commercial, technical, and agricultural schools, because of curriculum specialization in all Tanzanian secondary schools. Separate regressions were fitted for each of these different types of schools; again a similar result was noted, with a positive private sector effect for academic subjects and a negative effect for vocational subjects. However, the number of schools within each stream was very small, ranging from 7 to 18, which meant that much of the variation in pupil scores was likely to be within schools. Appropriate adjustment for this would most probably have reduced the private school effect. Further, no school composition variables were included that might have partly explained the sector differences.

Subsequent studies have concentrated on the need to correct for self-selection bias; Jimenez *et al.* (1988*a*) found a positive private school effect, after correcting for family background, in a study of eighth-grade students in Thailand. This study employed a variety of controls for characteristics of students entering the eighth grade, including achievement at the beginning of eighth grade, father's occupation and mother's education, gender, language used at home, age, hours of extra tutoring, and an index of parental encouragement. Separate regressions were fitted for public and private sectors; estimated private school effects, computed as the difference in predicted scores at two different reference points, were strongly positive. However, inclusion of the average pre-test score reduced the private–public differential by two-thirds. In the next stage of the analysis, variables describing school characteristics were added. Although relatively few variables were statistically significant,[1] and only one of the statistically significant school characteristics could be described as a 'policy' variable, inclusion of these variables virtually eliminated the private sector advantage.

Jimenez and Cox (1989), in their study of secondary schools in Colombia and Tanzania, found that there was a strong private school advantage after controlling for student background and two important school characteristics (teacher salaries and the teacher–student ratio). No peer group effects were included in the final model.

Jimenez *et al.* (1991*b*) discovered a private school advantage in the Dominican Republic, even for non-elite private schools, using a sample of 2,472 students in 76 urban schools. An important feature of this study was that it distinguished between two types of private schools ('high status' and 'low status') and fitted choice equations for each sector. Very few school or classroom variables could be identified to explain the private school effect. In

---

[1] In public schools, these were district per capita income, enriched mathematics class, and maintaining order in the classroom; in private schools they were school enrolment size, male teacher, and maintaining order.

the non-elite schools, no teacher or teaching variable was statistically significant, while only one was significant in public schools and two in the elite schools. However, inclusion of peer group effects (the average pre-test score and average years of parental education) significantly diminished the private school advantage. In the final model, the selection terms for type of school became insignificant, indicating that peer group variables may have captured their effect.

Differences in achievement between public and private schools in five districts of Madhya Pradesh in India were analysed by Govinda and Verghese (1991) using a simple regression model estimated by ordinary least squares. Tests were constructed to measure the mastery of competencies in mathematics and language expected at the end of the primary cycle. Based on a sample of 2,159 pupils in 59 schools, this study found that, after controlling for student background characteristics, performance of pupils in private unaided schools was considerably higher, in both mathematics and language, than that of pupils in either private aided or government schools. The private school effect was denoted as the coefficient for the sector variable (coded as a dummy variable). Regression analysis was conducted separately for each locality, as the localities surveyed varied from extremely backward regions (including a predominantly tribal locality) to major cities. Statistical controls for pupil characteristics included a measure of mother's education, gender (in mathematics), repetition, and attendance in pre-school. Of the numerous school and teacher variables examined, only the level of general education of the teacher emerged as a factor influencing pupil achievement in all localities, while teacher training status was significant only in urban areas. Possession of all prescribed textbooks was the third identified determinant of pupil achievement. A private school effect was noted even after adjusting for differences in these school inputs.

All the studies mentioned above, with the exception of Govinda and Verghese (1991), were conducted at the secondary level. To the extent that there is greater self-selection of students at this level because of the large number of drop-outs, the importance of statistical controls for intake characteristics is all the greater than at the primary level, where it can be more safely assumed that pupils are at approximately the same level at the age of entry (Mingat and Tan 1988). However, this latter assumption may not be valid if there is 'coaching' of pre-primary students to gain entry into selective private schools, a phenomenon that is quite widespread in developing countries.

The common methodological strand in all the above studies is the use of single-level regression models of achievement, with correction for self-selection in some cases. The studies reviewed above thus seemed to indicate better results for private schools. We now turn to the study of school effectiveness using multi-level modelling techniques which address some of the conceptual shortcomings of the OLS models.

5.3.3. New approaches to studying school effects: use of multi-level models in the research on the public/private differential

One way of dealing with the correlation of residuals within schools and the consequent underestimate of standard errors is to aggregate all observations to the school level. A major shortcoming of such aggregation is that the within-school variation is completely ignored (Aitkin and Longford 1986) and the effect of pupil-level variables on individual outcomes cannot be ascertained. Nor can the variation in these within-school relationships be examined. Other problems of interpretation also arise, since the same variable may denote two different constructs when aggregated and when measured at the individual level (Burstein 1980). The average socioeconomic status of a school is an indicator of school resources; conceptually it can have a different impact from that of the individual pupil's socioeconomic status, which is a proxy for the resources available at home. Models using school means alone cannot take account of situations where a pupil's outcome is influenced both by his or her socioeconomic status and by the average socioeconomic status. Hence, aggregation can take care of one statistical problem, but only by reducing the possibility of discovering relationships of substantive interest.

An alternative procedure is to estimate separate regressions for different schools. The handicap of this method of analysis is that it makes use of the within-school variation only. Relationships among schools in the within-school parameters cannot be explored since the between-school variation is ignored. A specific topic of interest would be whether the estimated regression coefficients for pupil background variables within each school vary systematically with school-level characteristics. Another problem in using separate regressions is that, typically, the sample size within schools will be small, leading to considerable sampling variability in the regression coefficients.

The application of multi-level estimation techniques has enabled researchers to address both the heterogeneity of within-school regressions and the correlation of the residuals within one school. These models are called multi-level because they postulate random errors at more than one level (pupil, class, and/or school). Their advantage over conventional single-level models is that they can explicitly model differences between schools as well as the intra-school correlation and provide estimates of variance components at each level.

The heterogeneity of parameters across schools is explicitly modelled by assuming a different regression for each school. In a simple two-level model, for example, the pupil–level model consists of the regression of the pupil's test score on pupil characteristics. The parameters of this regression are assumed to vary across schools. It is thus possible to model the fact that gender or socioeconomic status (pupil characteristics) may produce different effects on achievement depending on the school that the pupil attended. Some of this variability in the within-school parameters can be assumed to have a systematic component which is due to school-level factors; part of the variability in parameters is assumed to be stochastic (a random effect which is unique to each school) because it is usually not possible to identify all school-level factors. The school-level model postulates that the parameters of the within-school regressions are outcomes of observed and unobserved school characteristics. The random effects associated with the between-school relationship imply that the intra-school correlation in test scores is also explicitly taken into account. The model is called a 'two-level model' because it comprises residual error terms at two levels, the pupil level and the school level.

Finally, variance-explained statistics can be computed for each level, enabling a better interpretation of the explanatory power of school-level factors. Models can be extended to include more than two levels (for instance, school, class, and pupil, or district, school, class, and pupil), but in practice problems of data collection, small sample sizes at the higher levels, and difficulties of statistical estimation of parameters usually limit the number of levels that can be included.

The use of multi-level models enhances the richness of analysis and interpretation by enabling more flexible modelling of all the variation in the data. It also has implications for the definition of school and sector 'effectiveness'. If both the intercept and the slope parameters of the within-school regression in a two-level model are assumed to vary across schools and involve a random component, the 'effectiveness' of a school has to be measured on more than one dimension. Hierarchical models thus enable school effectiveness to be described in more ways than one. This is a better representation of the real world, where clearly different schools have different types of effects, one of them being to modify the influence of pupil background characteristics on achievement. For example, if the background variable measures socio-economic status, some schools may have smaller slopes than average, indicating that they equalize the performance of pupils from different strata. An effective school may be defined as one that has a high mean outcome (intercept) and a small value for the coefficient of the background variable.

Further, the effect of a school on the intercept and slope of the within-school regression can be conceptually decomposed into that which is attributable to school practice and policy variables and that which is due to variables such as school composition, location, and the characteristics of the community. The first group of variables is of interest to policy-makers because they can be modified by the actions of educational authorities. The second group of variables cannot be changed by such actions. Nevertheless, the effects of these compositional variables are of interest to families because they can choose schools with better compositional characteristics that raise achievement. Both sets of indicators are valid for different groups of people, but comparisons between schools or between groups of schools will be affected by the precise indicator that is used. Thus, the application of multi-level modelling techniques can have substantive effects on the estimation and interpretation of school and sector effects. Below we review studies that have used hierarchical linear modelling (HLM) techniques to analyse sector differences.

A re-analysis of the HSB data using a multi-level model was undertaken by Lee and Bryk (1989). The student-level predictors were minority status, socio-economic status, and academic background (the latter being a composite of variables indicating educational experiences and aspirations prior to entering high school). In the between-school model, the school-level predictors for each of the parameters in the pupil-level model were sector, the social and academic composition of schools (defined as the school means for SES and academic background and the proportion of minority students), the perceived quality of instruction, the disciplinary climate of the school, the academic emphasis in the school, and the curricular structure. Though a positive unconditional sector effect (that is, the effect of sector when no other school-level explanatory variables were included in the between-school model) was noted for private schools, this was reduced when the social and academic composition of schools (peer group effects) were included. Sector effects also were partly explained by various school practices, such as the average number of mathematics courses taken, the average amount of homework, staff prob-lems, and disciplinary climate. The authors note, however, that many of these variables cannot be unambiguously described as 'school policy' variables and may also reflect characteristics of the student body.

Multi-level models have also been used in more recent studies of public–private differences in developing countries. Riddell and Nyagura (1991) studied 33 schools and 5,293 pupils, using longitudinal data on English and mathematics achievement. They found that school type explained almost the entire residual school variance, after controlling for initial achievement. Six different school types were considered—schools that formerly catered exclusively to the European population, schools that formerly catered ex-clusively to the African population in rural and urban areas respectively, high fee-paying private schools, mission schools, and new district council schools. Individual coefficients for the school type variables were not significant, but their simultaneous contrast showed that the effect of school type was significantly different from zero. Since individual coefficients could not be used to gauge sector effects, schools were ranked on the basis of residual variances, after adjusting for significant pupil-level and school-level variables. It was found that district council schools were more effective in promoting learning gains, given their lower levels of initial achievement, while high fee-charging schools and the former exclusive government schools catering to Europeans (which were more like selective private schools) performed poorly, given their initial intake.

A study by Lockheed and Bruns (1990) found, for a sample of 66 Brazilian schools, that students in private schools outperformed those in public schools in mathematics, after holding constant family background factors, but this did not hold true in Portuguese. Lockheed and Zhao (1993), in a study of science and mathematics achievement in 214 schools in the Philippines, produced similar results: students in private schools outperformed those in national public schools in mathematics, but there was no private school effect in science (after controlling for background factors). However, with the inclusion of peer group effects, the sector effects disappeared almost entirely. A large part of the between-school variance in achievement remained unexplained, even after the inclusion of material and non-material inputs, indicating the existence of unmeasured school effects.

A few tentative conclusions emerge from this discussion of the literature on public–private differences. First, studies using multi-level models have not shown an unambiguously positive effect for the private sector in developing countries, although initial studies using single-level models seemed to show that private schools were more effective. Second, irrespective of whether OLS or multi-level modelling techniques were used, the inclusion of peer group characteristics and certain non-manipulable school variables appear to reduce, or virtually eliminate, the private school advantage. Third, and again irrespective of the statistical technique employed, very few variables that can be conceptually identified as 'school policy' variables have been shown to explain the variation in school outcomes. This means that, although we know that some schools, and types of school, are more effective than others, we still know very little about what contributes towards greater effectiveness. The construction of achievement models continues to rest largely on empirical foundations and hence leaves ample room for model misspecification and consequent bias in the estimation of parameters and sector effects. Moreover, despite the superiority of multi-level models over conventional OLS models, their use does not overcome the overarching problems regarding the validity of outcome and intake measures, the correct specification of models, and the interpretation of results.

5.3.4. Unit costs in public and private schools

Apart from methodological controversies surrounding the study of school effects, a major shortcoming of many studies has been the lack of comprehensive information on costs. Few studies on the comparative effectiveness of public and private schools have evaluated the unit costs of schooling in the two sectors. Jimenez *et al.* (1991*a*), in their review of the relative efficiency of private and public schools in developing countries, based their conclusions on the findings of four studies, all of which were sponsored by the World Bank. These studies share the same methodology in comparing effectiveness but exhibit considerable variation in their treatment of costs. Cost estimates in the study of Colombian and Tanzanian secondary schools (Jimenez and Cox

1989) were imprecise because many private schools did not provide the required information. In the study of secondary schools in the Philippines (Jimenez *et al.* 1988*b*), owing to the unavailability of school-level data, unit costs in the public and private sectors were derived using data for all schools in the country. Only two studies, conducted in the Dominican Republic and Thailand (Jimenez *et al.* 1989; Jimenez *et al.* 1988*a*), collected data on costs from each school in the sample.

The most important limitation of the data in all the above-mentioned studies was that they pertained to institutional costs alone. No estimate was made of direct private expenditures on books, supplies, uniforms, and travel, or of the indirect costs associated with schooling (the opportunity costs of students' time). At the secondary level, on which the above studies were focused, private costs are likely to be substantial and, in particular, opportunity costs are likely to be the biggest component of non-fee costs (Jimenez 1987). In their review, Jimenez *et al.* (1991*a*) surmised that inclusion of private costs would not significantly change their broad conclusions regarding the greater cost effectiveness of private schools. Without adequate data on the size and structure of private costs, however, the evidence is far from conclusive on this point. Direct private costs tend to be relatively high in private schools, while indirect costs too will not be negligible if the private schools cater to poor students who face opportunity costs. Conclusions regarding the relative cost effectiveness of private schools can be radically altered from the standpoint of families or of society, if higher total private costs in these schools outweigh the effect of lower institutional costs.

5.4. Unaided, Aided, and Government Schools in Tamil Nadu

5.4.1. School characteristics

The main objective of our study was to investigate whether the performance of private schools, as measured by the academic achievement of their pupils at the primary level, was superior to that of public schools and whether they operated at lower unit costs.[2] The state of Tamil Nadu in India offers an interesting setting for studying the comparative performance of public, private aided, and unaided schools. Public schools are entirely financed by the state government, while aided schools operate under private managements which finance the initial and on-going capital costs but receive government funds to cover salaries of all sanctioned teachers and recurrent expenditure on non-teacher inputs. Unaided schools are completely self-financing; an important distinguishing feature of these schools is that they offer instruction in

---

[2] A full description of the research, including details of instruments, test administration, and data collection and verification, can be found in Bashir (1994).

English, while publicly funded schools teach in Tamil. While public schools dominate primary level enrolments with 68 per cent of the total, private aided schools also have a significant presence with a share of 28 per cent. Unaided schools account for only 4 per cent of enrolment at this stage, but this sector has grown rapidly since the early 1980s (and continues to do so) following relaxation of government regulations and implicit official encouragement. Furthermore, the proportion of pupils in primary classes in unaided schools may be larger than indicated by official data as many unaided secondary schools have 'unrecognized primary sections' which are not formally registered with the Department of Education.

Distinctions between the three types of school are very pronounced and can be classified into three broad categories: those relating to management practices that are amenable to policy manipulation, those arising from aspects of policy that are inflexible given the commitment to universal primary education, and those arising from the differing constituents of demand for education.

Public schools are managed in a centralized fashion with a uniform curriculum, timetable, school hours, and textbooks. The hiring of teachers and their allocation to individual schools is also done in a centralized manner following rigid specifications regarding educational qualifications and training. A uniform set of educational aids is supplied to all schools. Headteachers are not involved in adapting the syllabus, the hiring of teachers, or the purchase of learning materials, nor do they have access to any funds. Aided schools are similar to public schools in that they must follow the same curriculum, syllabus, textbooks, and eligibility criteria for teacher recruitment. However, the decision to hire teachers rests with managements. The latter can also finance additional teacher posts and other recurrent expenditure from their own funds. Teachers in public and aided schools form part of the civil service and salary scales are linked to the civil service pay structure. Unaided schools, on the other hand, are free to choose among any of the recognized syllabi, hire and fire teachers, set salary scales, determine fees, select textbooks, and decide on the composition of expenditures and the mix of inputs. Government regulation is confined to ensuring that prescribed standards for physical infrastructure and initial endowments are adhered to through annual inspections (though often these regulations are not enforced).

A second set of distinctions arises from the differing policy objectives for the three types of school. These affect both the socioeconomic composition in the three sectors and certain school characteristics. Public schools are the main means by which the commitment to universal primary education has been implemented. Tamil Nadu has attained near universal gross enrolment rates at the primary level, and much of the expansion has occurred in the public sector with the provision of primary schooling facilities within 1 kilometre of every village and a substantial programme of incentives (including free midday meals, textbooks, and uniforms) to encourage attendance. In a state characterized by very high levels of poverty and deprivation (MIDS 1988), this has meant that the majority of the child population in public schools is drawn from extremely underprivileged, undernourished, and impoverished sections of the population. A large number of children are also first-generation learners. Further, public schools cannot refuse entry to any child irrespective of his or her prior educational attainment. These characteristics of public schools cannot be altered without compromising the commitment to universal access.

Although there is considerable overlap in the clientele served by public and aided schools (since all publicly funded schools are open to all children), the latter tend to be located in larger villages and semi-urban areas (for historical reasons) and hence serve a somewhat more prosperous population. After the recent phase of expansion, unaided matriculation schools are also increasingly serving the lower middle classes and the better off farmers in rural areas; nevertheless, in general, children of agricultural labour households, the Scheduled Castes, and urban manual workers in the unorganized sectors are not represented in these schools since they cannot bear the direct and indirect costs of schooling.

Certain school characteristics, notably school size and the number of teachers, are also affected by the differing policy goals. Given the size of the state and the numerous small habitations, the criteria for school location in the public sector have resulted in multi-grade schools and a large number of very small schools. The lack of a 'critical mass' of teachers is known to affect school effectiveness adversely (Raudenbush *et al.* 1991). Most public schools offer only classes 1 to 5, while aided and unaided schools serving larger populations offer classes from 1 to 12.

The third set of distinctions results from the nature of demand for the education provided in the different sectors. The majority of children in public schools, and to a lesser extent in aided schools, will drop out after five years of schooling to take up work in the household or in traditional occupations. This factor must clearly influence the motivation of the child as well as the degree of parental support he or she receives, while it also indirectly influences teachers who tend to concentrate their efforts on those students with greater aptitude and who are likely to continue to higher levels, neglecting the vast majority. In unaided schools, on the other hand, although there are different components of demand (for English language skills, for the particular curriculum offered, and for better quality education), all children intend to continue their education for 12 years.

Comparisons of public and private schools must take into account the differing characteristics of the pupils entering these schools as well as the differing regulatory framework facing them. The public sector cannot choose the social composition or location of schools or differentiate between pupils with varying levels of motivation, all of which are factors affecting achievement. These factors must be controlled in a statistical analysis in order to understand whether different management practices contribute to differential performance. The complexity of the interaction of these factors and the difficulties in measuring many of these variables can hardly be overstated.

The difference in the medium of instruction in publicly funded schools and unaided schools also introduces formidable conceptual problems in setting up an appropriate analytical framework and in the interpretation of results. In the former it is Tamil, the mother tongue of the majority of the population; in the latter it is English, which is neither the native tongue nor a language with which most parents (even those who send their children to unaided schools) are familiar, and to which children receive little exposure outside the school environment. When standardized achievement tests are used as the measure of school outcomes, the language of test administration can crucially affect inferences about the comparative performance of the sectors. This issue is dealt with in greater detail in the next section.

5.4.2. Research design and instruments

Multi-stage stratified random sampling was used to select a sample of 113 rural and urban schools, of which 65 were public, 28 aided, and 20 unaided schools. The total sample comprised 72 rural schools and 41 urban schools. At the first stage, four districts, one from each of the geographical regions of Tamil Nadu, were randomly selected along with the capital city, Madras. Within districts, one-fifth of the community development blocks (rural) and one or two urban areas were selected. For the selected blocks and towns, the sampling frame consisted of all recognized public and private aided schools with a primary section (Classes 1–5). Schools were stratified on the basis of management and a proportionate sample was selected from each of the strata. An additional random sample of 20 unaided schools was proportionately drawn from each of the districts and the capital city.[3]

Within each selected school, one fourth-grade class was selected (using simple random sampling if there was more than one section). A maximum of 25 students per class and five teachers handling primary classes were also selected. Random sampling was used when the number of students/teachers exceeded the desired number. A total of 2,735 pupils were administered the

---

[3] There are three categories of unaided schools in Tamil Nadu, differentiated by the syllabus they offer. These are matriculation schools, schools affiliated to the central boards of education, and Anglo-Indian schools. Of these, the matriculation schools constitute the largest category and serve a broader cross-section of the population in both rural and urban areas, while central schools and Anglo-Indian schools cater to highly selective populations (families employed in central government service or from Anglo-Indian background) and are located in only a few urban areas. The sample of unaided schools was therefore drawn from the population of matriculation schools, and hence all the results pertaining to unaided schools refer to this target population alone.

tests in intact groups within each school. Instruments for collecting information on pupil background, teachers, and schools were developed and all data were collected through individual interviews or directly from school records.

Standardized achievement tests for mathematics, reading comprehension and Word Knowledge developed by the National Council of Educational Research and Training (NCERT) in New Delhi were used to measure the academic performance of pupils. The tests were constructed for use in the countrywide survey of primary school attainment in 1991 conducted by the NCERT. They were based on the competencies in language and mathematics expected to have been attained by the end of Class 4, which are largely common to all states and to all syllabi. The mathematics test consisted of 40 items, while the other two tests comprised 44 and 40 items respectively. Both the mathematics and reading comprehension test questions were in multiple choice format. The format of the reading comprehension test was a set of six short passages, each followed by a set of questions; pupils could refer back to the passage as often as they wished while answering the questions.

Measures of school effectiveness depend importantly upon the intake variables that are used as controlling factors. It is common, in the literature on school effects, to control for student background characteristics, although there is no universally accepted method of how best to measure them. Ideally, a measure of prior achievement in mathematics or reading comprehension would have been most appropriate. In cross-sectional studies, however, such measures of prior attainment are usually not available, and it is necessary to use variables that may serve as proxies. At primary level, in particular, it is usually not possible to obtain a measure of prior attainment, and most studies have assumed that pupils entering primary school are similar in their initial attainments (Mingat and Tan 1988).

One response in the literature has been to use the results of verbal or mathematics aptitude tests as a proxy for prior abilities (e.g. Psacharopoulos 1987). In the present study, an indicator of verbal ability was included as a proxy for differences in prior attainment, and was measured by a score on a Word Knowledge test. In earlier surveys conducted by the International Association for the Evaluation of Educational Achievement (IAEEA), the score on the Word Knowledge test had been found to be highly correlated with verbal ability (Thorndike 1973). The score on this test had also been used as a proxy for students' ability in comparing the performance of schools in the IEEA survey of science achievement (Choppin 1974). In Tamil Nadu, private schools tend to select for Class 1 on the basis of performance in oral tests. An indicator of verbal ability should thus be helpful in controlling for such pre-existing differences.

Since the language of instruction differs between the unaided schools and the public and aided schools, the language of test administration can critically affect the validity of the test scores. In the case of mathematics, in which pupils are expected to demonstrate their ability to solve problems presented in the language in which they were taught, the most appropriate course was to administer the test in the language of instruction: Tamil in public and aided schools and English in unaided schools.

In the case of reading comprehension skills, however, the choice was between administering a test in Tamil in public and aided schools and in English in unaided schools, or administering a common test in Tamil to all pupils, provided the selected pupils in unaided schools had been instructed in Tamil as a second language for at least four years. The disadvantage of the first method is that English is a second language to which few children get exposure outside the school; pupils in unaided schools could therefore be handicapped in a test of reading skills administered in English *vis-à-vis* pupils in other schools who would have received far greater exposure to Tamil outside the school environment. For these reasons, it was decided to administer a common test in Tamil to all pupils to test reading comprehension skills. The Word Knowledge test was therefore also administered in Tamil. Consequently, only those pupils in unaided schools who had studied Tamil for at least four years were selected. (Most pupils do take Tamil as a second language, while some take Hindi; hence, the selection process would not have affected the representativeness of the pupil sample.)

5.4.3. Important findings on sector effects

Overall performance in mathematics and reading comprehension was extremely low, with mean scores in the range of 30–35 per cent of the respective total test score. When judged by the mean scores, the performance of pupils in unaided schools was, on the whole, not appreciably higher than that of pupils in public schools. Apart from mean scores, subscores were arrived at by grouping individual items on the two tests by levels of difficulty.[4] Analysis of subscores in mathematics and reading comprehension revealed that more pupils in unaided schools had acquired some knowledge of *basic skills* in these content areas. By contrast, a large proportion of government school pupils, especially in urban areas, demonstrated no knowledge of even those competencies which should have been acquired in an earlier class. This suggests that unaided schools may be offering a different 'service mix' from that provided in public schools, with greater emphasis on all or almost all pupils acquiring basic skills (which, however, may be well below the requirements of the official curriculum on which the achievement tests were based). If this proposition is true, it has implications for assessing the effectiveness of schools using the total score of a pupil on a standardized achievement test.

---

[4] In mathematics, items were divided into three groups based on competencies which should have been mastered by Classes 3, 4, and 5 respectively (on the basis of the Minimum Levels of Learning developed by NCERT 1991). In reading comprehension, items were divided into three main reading skills: 'noting details', 'understanding', and 'inference'.

Basic descriptive data confirmed the differences between the three sectors highlighted above. Unaided schools are relatively more advantaged in terms of the background of the pupils and the kind of educational support they receive outside school (educated parents, families employed in the organized sector, prior attendance in pre-school, regular attendance in school, extra tuition, access to other reading materials, etc.), the number and quality of their teachers (almost all were graduates), the level of material inputs, and the quality of their physical facilities. Pupils in government schools are not only poor and disadvantaged, but they also absent themselves from school to participate in paid and unpaid household work. Aided schools occupy an intermediate position in terms of their social composition. On the other hand, the hours of official teaching time and the number of textbooks possessed by pupils (two major inputs) are very similar across the three sectors.

The regression analyses used a two-level model to analyse the determinants of mathematics and reading comprehension achievement. At the pupil level, pupil scores in mathematics and reading comprehension, respectively, were separately regressed on four pupil variables having earlier run a more general model with many other variables. Word Knowledge score, gender, whether a repeater, and high educational aspirations emerged as the best predictors.[5] Two parameters of the within-school regressions were treated as random: the intercept, which represents the school mean achievement, and the slope of the Word Knowledge score. At the school level, these random parameters were modelled as functions of school characteristics and composition. Potential school-level explanatory variables were divided into conceptually distinct categories, such as sector, the physical facilities of schools, school size and macro characteristics, the characteristics of teachers, the activities of head-teachers, and the composition of the school. Within each category, a subset of variables was selected primarily on empirical grounds. The model yields estimates of the fixed parameters for both the within-school and between-school regressions as well as estimates of the random effects (the pupil-level and school-level residual variance components).

The regressions were run separately for rural and urban areas. A preliminary analysis using ordinary least squares revealed a structural difference in the parameters of the two regressions in rural and urban areas respectively. Variance components analysis in the two-level models also revealed there was greater between-school variation in scores in rural areas compared with urban areas. Based on these findings, it was decided to conduct the analysis

---

[5] The rationale for the exogeneity of the Word Knowledge score has been treated earlier. In common with other studies, repetition is used as an additional proxy for prior abilities: while it is likely to be true that less able children repeat grades more frequently, this does not imply endogeneity with regard to a model explaining achievement levels. Those who repeat have had more years in school than those who do not, which in a complete model might lead us to expect a positive rather than a negative relationship between repetition and achievement. Equally, the aspirations variable is judged to be more strongly related to parental background and educational achievement than to in-school achievement effects alone.

separately for rural and urban areas. The details of model building and variable selection are given in Bashir (1994). The list of explanatory variables and the 'final' models are given in this chapter's appendix tables and the main findings are discussed below.

Since both the intercept and the Word Knowledge slope were treated as random parameters, the effect of school variables can be analysed in terms of both the mean school outcome and the distribution of outcomes within schools (the slope of the Word Knowledge score). The data generated by the survey did not permit any substantive conclusions to be drawn regarding the effects of school variables on the slope of the Word Knowledge score. More substantive results were obtained for the factors influencing school mean achievement.

Explanatory variables included in the model for mean achievement were those indicating whether the school was multi-grade, whether the school had only two teachers,[6] the number of teachers, the average teaching experience, the proportion of teachers with high scores on a simple test in mathematics,[7] one indicator of physical facilities (unpartitioned classrooms), and variables describing headteacher activities which proxy management practices. School composition variables included the male literacy rate (in rural areas only), the average socioeconomic status of pupils (in urban areas), and the average academic composition of pupils in the class. Most common indicators of teaching resources (such as pupil–teacher ratio and per-pupil expenditures) were not included in the final models, since they exhibited very low correlation with the achievement scores.

Since the statistical tests used in hierarchical linear models are more stringent than in the case of OLS, it is usually difficult to identify statistically significant school-level predictors, especially when there is a high degree of intra-school correlation. In the sample of schools and pupils tested in Tamil Nadu, the between-school variation ranged between 34 and 59 per cent for the two achievement tests in rural and urban areas, which indicates large intra-school correlation. As the appendix tables show, however, several important school variables have been found to be significant predictors of achievement. The most consistent of these are the variables denoting headteacher activities, such as motivation and commitment of the headteacher, the frequency of school meetings, and the amount of time that the headteacher spends outside school hours on school-related activities. These variables should be viewed as rather crude proxies for complex management processes which enable headteachers and teachers to adapt the educational programme to the specific school context and the learning abilities of pupils and to establish sound relationships among themselves as well as between the school and the community.

---

[6] These two variables were included only in the rural models, since they are not relevant in urban areas.

[7] This was included in the model for mathematics achievement only.

Equally importantly, the effects for the sector variables were consistent in rural and urban areas and for achievement in both content areas. Unaided schools and aided schools were coded as dummy variables with the public sector constituting the reference category. Although 'unconditional' sector effects (that is, when no other school variables were included in the model) were positive and significant, the coefficient for unaided schools was negative and large when these variables were included in the regression, while the effect for aided schools was consistently positive (except for Tamil in rural schools, where there was a very small negative effect). Moreover, the negative effect for unaided schools was larger in reading comprehension achievement than in mathematics achievement.

The sector coefficient is usually interpreted as the effect of management practices, a positive effect indicating the superiority of private management practices (Mingat and Tan 1988). This seems a plausible explanation of the positive effect noted for aided schools, which are similar to public schools in almost every aspect except the greater degree of control by private managements. However, if the same interpretation were to hold for unaided schools, the negative value would indicate that, after making allowance for measurable school inputs, headteacher and student characteristics, other practices in unaided schools were less effective. In this case, the greater managerial flexibility and the degree of close supervision of classroom teaching do not induce better performance: they may result in practices that are not conducive to the educational process, such as teachers feeling harassed and having less secure tenure, which leads to high teacher turnover and low morale.

However, unaided schools also differ from other types of school in the medium of instruction. Thus, a plausible explanation for the negative sector coefficient in the case of mathematics achievement could be that the language of instruction hampers the acquisition of skills in mathematics because English proves a stumbling block for both pupils and teachers alike. Despite the fact that most teachers handling primary classes in matriculation schools have graduate or postgraduate education, they lack proficiency in English language, especially in spoken English. Classroom interaction is severely impeded when neither teachers nor students have mastery over the language, resulting in a tendency towards the rote learning of facts.

In the case of reading comprehension, the even stronger negative unaided sector effect probably reflects the fact that little emphasis is placed on the acquisition of reading skills in Tamil in the curriculum of unaided schools. The issue is how this result should be interpreted in the context of comparing the relative effectiveness of the three sectors in producing reading comprehension skills. This is an important question in many developing countries, where public schools typically offer instruction in the native language while private schools use a medium of instruction that is not the mother tongue (usually English or French). In the case of Tamil Nadu, it could be argued that the instructional objectives differ across the sectors since children in unaided schools do not need to acquire the same level of proficiency in reading and comprehending Tamil as do children in other schools. However, the reading comprehension test was developed to test *basic* cognitive skills such as noting details, understanding the main idea, and drawing inferences from a short passage. To the extent that the objectives of instruction in reading and comprehending connected prose in Tamil at the primary level are similar and that the skills described above are expected of all pupils who have received formal instruction in the language for four years, whether the language has been used as a medium of instruction or taught as a subject only, a common test in Tamil provides a sound basis for making valid comparisons of sectors. Nevertheless, the difficulties in interpretating test scores require caution in drawing generalizations about the relative effectiveness of sectors, particularly in the development of language skills. I return to this question in the discussion of policy implications.

5.4.4. Effectiveness indicators for mean outcomes

The school-level models provide the basis for developing measures of school and sector effectiveness. Taking the statistical models discussed above as 'true models' of mean achievement, each individual school's mean achievement depends on the school variables in the model, their respective estimated coefficients, and the unique (random) school effect. We may then conceive of two effectiveness indicators: one that uses the predicted mean obtained by including all school-level variables, and one that uses the predicted mean obtained by excluding the effects of school composition (which cannot be manipulated by policy) and including only the effects of manipulable 'policy' variables. We could interpret these two scores as being of interest to different groups of people. The first score is of interest to parents, who would attribute the effects of all factors to the schools themselves and might therefore rank schools on the totality of these factors. From a policy point of view, however, it does not make sense to attribute to schools the effects that are really due to their composition and community characteristics. It seems inappropriate to 'reward' or 'penalize' schools on compositional factors which affect school (and hence sector) mean outcomes, but which, strictly speaking, are not manipulable by policy. We could therefore derive the mean score that is the sum of the effects of school variables alone. School effectiveness scores can then be averaged for the different sectors to yield two sets of sector effectiveness scores, including and excluding the effect of school composition variables respectively.[8]

---

[8] Strictly speaking, the effectiveness indicator should comprise not only the effect on the school mean (intercept) but also the effect on the Word Knowledge slope, which was also specified as a random parameter. However, as no school-level variables could be found to explain the variation in slopes, the latter effect was ignored.

Sajitha Bashir

TABLE 5.1 Effectiveness indicators

	Mathematics		Reading comprehension	
	Indicator 1	Indicator 2	Indicator 1	Indicator 2
Rural				
Unaided	19.03	16.41	17.35	14.34
Aided	14.78	15.58	13.01	14.50
Public	12.96	13.23	14.06	14.31
Urban				
Unaided	13.13	12.29	12.93	9.79
Aided	13.44	13.16	15.33	15.91
Public	10.22	10.86	10.92	13.27
Effectiveness ratios (as ratios of public sector means)				
Rural				
Unaided	1.47	1.24	1.23	1.00
Aided	1.14	1.18	0.93	1.10
Public	1.00	1.00	1.00	1.00
Urban				
Unaided	1.28	1.13	1.18	0.74
Aided	1.32	1.21	1.40	1.20
Public	1.00	1.00	1.00	1.00

The two average scores are referred to below as Effectiveness Indicator 1 (including the effects of school composition) and Indicator 2 (excluding these effects), respectively. The school composition variables were those measuring the average academic composition of the class, the average socioeconomic status of pupils, and the male literacy rate of the village. Table 5.1 presents the sector effectiveness scores derived by using these indicators. (The figures have been obtained by computing the predicted means using the models in the appendix tables.)

The second half of the table displays each predicted mean as a ratio of the respective public sector mean. For mathematics achievement in rural areas, for example, the ratio for Indicator 1 (which includes the effect of all variables) is 1.47 for unaided schools, revealing that mean performance is 47 per cent higher relative to public schools. When the effect of school composition is excluded, the ratio drops to 1.24. In the case of reading comprehension, the 23 per cent achievement advantage of unaided schools reduces to nil when school composition variables are excluded. For mathematics achievement in urban areas, the relative effectiveness of unaided schools drops from 1.28 to 1.13. In reading comprehension achievement, rural unaided schools display no advantage over rural public schools when compositional variables are excluded, and in urban areas they are actually less effective than public schools.

In the case of rural aided schools, their relative standing in both mathematics and reading comprehension achievement *vis-à-vis* public schools increases when school composition variables are excluded. This means that school composition variables in rural aided schools actually pull down their predicted performance. However, in urban areas the relative effectiveness of aided schools declines when school composition variables are excluded, although they continue to be more effective than public schools.

Excluding the effect of school composition variables thus reduces the effectiveness of the unaided schools relative to public schools. Of special interest is the change in the relative ranking of sectors in reading comprehension achievement: in rural areas unaided schools, which are superior to aided schools when the effect of compositional variables is included, become less effective than the latter when this effect is removed; in urban areas they are more effective than public schools in the first case, but become less effective than the latter in the second case.

The general conclusion from this analysis of effectiveness indicators for school means is that, *when school compositional variables are excluded*, rural and urban aided schools are relatively more effective than their public school counterparts in both curricular areas. Their relative advantage is greater in urban areas and in mathematics. Aided schools are relatively more effective than unaided schools as well, except for mathematics achievement in rural areas. On the other hand, it is only in mathematics achievement that unaided schools are more effective than public schools; in this subject, their relative effectiveness is greater than that of aided schools in rural areas only. In reading comprehension achievement, their performance is either on a par with (in rural areas) or less than (in urban areas) that of public schools.

5.4.5. Comparisons of costs

Conclusions regarding the relative 'costliness' of education in unaided, aided, and public schools depend in large measure on the type of costs being considered. They also depend on whether relative costs are evaluated from the standpoints of the government, private households, or society. Many previous studies have used institutional costs as the basis for comparisons, motivated mainly by practical rather than theoretical considerations. The extensive data collected from school accounts and pupil and headteacher interviews for this study indicate that other elements of costs (expenditures on textbooks and supplies, which may be borne by either families or the government, and private opportunity costs) are not only sizeable but also vary in magnitude and incidence across sectors.

Table 5.2 presents the ratios of different categories of average annual unit costs (per pupil cost) in each sector relative to those in public schools for rural and urban areas respectively. Five different average cost measures are

TABLE 5.2   Ratios of sectoral average unit costs[a] (relative to public sector unit cost)

	(1) Institu-tional	(2) Private direct	(3) Total direct	(4) Total private	(5) Grand total (3) + (4)
Rural					
Unaided	0.81	19.32	1.44	1.51	0.91
Aided	0.94	1.06	0.96	1.01	0.99
Public	1.00	1.00	1.00	1.00	1.00
Public (in rupees)[b]	798	69	971	1,275	2,177
Urban					
Unaided	0.94	29.33	1.48	1.76	0.92
Aided	0.76	1.47	0.83	1.00	0.91
Public	1.00	1.00	1.00	1.00	1.00
Public (in rupees)[b]	820	55	989	1,201	2,135

[a] Definitions of costs are as follows: *Institutional costs* include funds spent on purchase of labour and material inputs for the school by the school management and/or the government; they exclude the cost of inputs supplied to individual pupils such as textbooks and notebooks. *Private direct costs* include all direct costs that are borne by households, including the cost of tuition fees, textbooks, educational materials and uniforms. In all publicly funded schools, households do not bear any expense for any of these items apart from nominal charges for annual examination papers, etc. *Total direct costs* incorporate institutional costs and the cost of textbooks, educational materials, and uniforms, irrespective of who finances these costs. *Total private costs* comprise the private direct costs and the average opportunity cost of children's labour; this was estimated using reported incidence of work for payment, unpaid household work, and imputed or actual weekly earnings. Total direct and indirect costs represent the sum of direct costs and opportunity costs.
[b] The public sector average unit cost for each category is given in rupees for reference.

displayed as defined in the table. It can be seen that unit costs in rural aided schools are only slightly lower than those in public schools, irrespective of the cost measure used. This similarity reflects the parallelism of policy regimes (with respect to staff salaries and material inputs) and of social composition in the two sectors. In urban areas, aided schools enjoy a more substantial cost advantage over public schools when institutional costs (column (1)) and total direct costs (column (3)) are compared, mainly because of their higher pupil–teacher ratio.

Institutional unit costs in unaided schools are lower than in public schools in both rural and urban areas and in rural aided schools, despite the fact that the pupil–teacher ratio in the unaided sector is about half that in the publicly funded sectors. The main reason for this cost differential is the low level of teachers' salaries in the unaided sector, which range between one-fifth and one-half of salaries in the publicly funded sectors. This latter phenomenon is in turn a manifestation of the rigidities in the labour market for teachers. In the publicly funded sectors, teachers' salaries are linked to the civil service pay structure; hence they are comparatively high and, more importantly, are not related to supply and demand for teachers. It can be shown that current budgetary constraints on public secondary education and past policies of encouraging subsidized higher education have created the present situation of excess supply of teachers with graduate-level training and education. (For a more complete discussion, see Bashir 1994.) This excess supply is therefore available to work in the unaided sector for at least a few years at extremely low salaries. Hence, the lower institutional unit costs in the unaided sector can be attributed to a number of government policies governing other levels of education; the implication is that, if these policies are changed in such a manner as to reduce the excess supply of graduate teachers, the unit cost in the unaided sector is likely to rise on account of a rise in teachers' salaries.

Private direct costs are substantially higher in the unaided sector because the cost of textbooks, uniforms, and supplies are entirely borne by households; in public and aided schools, these costs are defrayed by the government. If charges for additional tuition, transportation costs, and unreported extra levies, which are common in unaided schools, but for which data could not be collected during this survey, were also included, private direct costs (and hence total direct costs) in this sector would be even higher.

The total direct unit cost (which comprises all costs apart from private opportunity costs) is higher in unaided schools because the costs of textbooks, uniforms, and other materials utilized in this sector more than compensate for lower institutional costs.

When opportunity costs are imputed and total private costs are used, the cost differential between the unaided sector and the other two sectors is considerably reduced. This is not only because the estimated opportunity cost for pupils from low-income households is relatively high, but also because there is a far greater proportion of such pupils in government and aided schools. Hence the average opportunity cost is higher in the latter and comparable to private direct costs in the unaided sector. In terms of absolute magnitude, the estimated forgone earnings of children who reported work for payment represented about one-third of the annual earnings of adult male agricultural labourers. In fact, opportunity costs may be higher for certain groups of children depending on whether child labour is a substitute for adult labour (as in the case of girls who look after siblings, thereby releasing the mother for paid work) or whether keeping the child in school implies forsaking seasonal migration. In such cases, the relevant opportunity cost would be not the child's own earnings, but the forgone earnings of the mother or of the household, respectively.

In summary, therefore (Table 5.2), for unaided schools the cost advantage relative to public schools is greatest in rural areas when institutional costs are compared. The cost disadvantage is greatest for unaided schools when private direct costs (column (2)) are compared. (They are between 19 and 29 times higher than in public schools.) When total direct costs are compared, the unit cost in the unaided sector is between 44 and 48 per cent higher than in public schools. If private costs (including opportunity costs) are used (column (4)), the unit cost in unaided schools is about 50 per cent higher than in public schools. Finally, the unit cost measure, which incorporates all direct and indirect costs (column (5)), is very similar across all three sectors, with unaided schools and urban aided schools enjoying a small advantage over public schools. However, as noted earlier, inclusion of transportation costs, extra unrecorded 'donations', and private tuition, which are almost mandatory in some unaided schools, would have raised the total unit cost in the unaided schools.

5.4.6. Comparing costs and effectiveness: implications for policy

Table 5.3 presents the results on costs and effectiveness for the three sectors in rural and urban areas. The entries in the table show the incremental costs and the incremental achievement in terms of raw scores for each sector relative to the public sector (following Psacharapoulos and Woodhall 1985). The incremental costs (in percentage terms) are derived from the cost ratios in Table 5.2 and the incremental advantage in mean achievement score is based on the predicted mean scores, after excluding the effect of social composition variables.

A number of comparisons can be made depending on the costs that are used, but here we focus on total direct costs, which are the most comprehensive and reliable, in order to highlight the main issues. For an extra cost of 44 per cent (in rural areas), the increase in the adjusted mean achievement score

TABLE 5.3   Incremental costs and incremental achievement scores

	Incremental costs (as % of public sector costs)			Incremental advantage in mean achievement score	
	Total direct	Total private	Total direct + indirect	Mathem- atics	Reading comprehension
Rural					
Unaided	−19	+44	+51	−9	+3.2	0
Aided	−6	−4	+1	−1	+2.4	+0.2
Public	—	—	—	—	—	—
Urban					
Unaided	−6	+48	+76	−8	+0.1	−3.7
Aided	−14	−17	—	−9	0	+2.4
Public	—	—	—	—	—	—

for unaided schools is 3.2 points in mathematics achievement; in reading comprehension achievement there is no net gain. In urban areas, the extra cost of 48 per cent is associated with a negligible increase in mathematics achievement score and a decline of 3.7 points in reading comprehension. Aided schools display an increase of 2.4 points in mathematics (rural) and 2.4 points in reading comprehension (urban) and negligible increases in achievement in reading comprehension (rural) and mathematics (urban). Moreover, these increases are associated with a unit cost that is 4 per cent lower in rural areas and 17 per cent lower in urban areas.

Thus, the general conclusion is that aided schools are unambiguously more cost-effective than public schools because costs are lower while predicted achievement is either higher than or the same as in public schools. For unaided schools, modest gains in achievement are linked with substantial cost increases of about 45 per cent.

This discussion should serve to highlight the pitfalls of drawing very generalized inferences from a single summary indicator. Had institutional costs alone been used as the basis of comparisons in this study, private unaided schools might have been considered more cost-effective. Further, the conclusions would have depended on the particular achievement score that was considered as the outcome measure. In mathematics, unaided schools are more effective than public schools in rural areas and at least as effective as them in urban areas. However, in Tamil reading skills, the predicted mean for unaided schools is lower than that in public schools. Because of the greater consistency of results for aided schools, and because the curriculum, language of instruction, and other conditions are virtually identical to those in public schools, the conclusions regarding the greater cost effectiveness of aided schools rest on stronger empirical foundations.

In comparing schools and sectors on the basis of the effectiveness indicator, an implicit assumption is that the school-level model for each random coefficient has been correctly specified. If there were prior knowledge about the determinants of school mean achievement (or of the coefficients of pupil background variables), the problem of misspecification would not arise. In practice, the models are derived through a mixture of *a priori* reasoning and empirical testing. There often remains uncertainty about what the 'true' model is. Misspecification of the school-level model will lead to bias in the estimates of the coefficients for the school-level variables if these omitted variables are correlated with one of the explanatory variables, and hence to a bias in the estimates of the effectiveness measures.

For instance, we can consider the case where one school policy variable, effective leadership by the headteacher, and one school composition variable, the average socioeconomic status of pupils, have been included in the model for school means. Suppose, however, that the 'true' model also includes the effect of teacher proficiency in subject matter. If more able teachers are recruited into schools with a better social composition, the omitted variable will be positively correlated with the school composition variable. If the coefficients of both variables in the 'true' model are positive, exclusion of the teacher proficiency variable will increase the estimated effect of social composition and lower the value of the effectiveness indicator (the predicted mean adjusted for social composition). Part of the effect on mean achievement is being wrongly attributed to social composition, when in fact it is due to the presence of more able teachers. Similarly, a bias can occur if some social composition variables have been omitted, which will tend to overstate the 'school effect'.

The possibility of model misspecification arises because there is no strong theory to guide the selection of explanatory variables. Such problems arise in OLS regression analysis as well and are highlighted here to show that models estimated by multi-level modelling techniques suffer from the same limitations. The main point is that conclusions regarding the relative effectiveness of schools and sectors must necessarily remain tentative in the absence of an underlying theory of school effectiveness.

Nevertheless, if these caveats are borne in mind, the findings of this study do suggest some issues for policy. A superficial inference would be that aided schools should be encouraged while unaided schools should be curtailed. This does not seem to be a viable policy option because of the nature of aided schools in Tamil Nadu which were established several decades ago by highly motivated individuals or institutions, at a time when public education was scarce, with the aim of providing education to specific linguistic, religious, or social groups and often without direct pecuniary objectives in mind. Unless similar conditions obtain today, it is not possible to know whether managements of new aided schools would have the same characteristics as those of existing ones. A plausible conjecture is that they would not, because the motivation of new entrepreneurs is unlikely to be the same as that of the founders of existing aided schools.

Similarly, a policy that curtailed the unaided sector on the grounds of its low cost effectiveness on measures of cognitive achievement would ignore the multiple outcomes of these schools. As noted earlier, insurance against repetition and drop-out is an important source of demand for these schools. Another major component of the demand for unaided schools is English-medium instruction, which is not offered in publicly funded schools at the primary level. As long as labour market outcomes are more favourable for those who know some English, there will be a strong private demand for this kind of education.

Policies for encouraging the unaided sector must also take into account the effects of other policies that are being considered simultaneously for higher and secondary education. It has been pointed out that lower institutional costs in unaided schools are largely on account of low teachers' salaries, and that policies that might affect the pool of unemployed graduates would also alter relative costs. Since proposals for increased privatization are usually accompanied by policies to reduce public budgets, and hence subsidies for higher and secondary education, the entire policy package needs to be considered, in order to understand the dynamic effects on subsectors.

At the same time, the results of this analysis indicate that in Tamil Nadu the continued encouragement of the unaided sector as in the past is not advisable. Pupil performance appears to be severely impeded by the difficulties of learning in a second and largely unfamiliar language. Unaided schools attempt to overcome these difficulties by lengthening the instructional time (through extra tuition) and imposing a heavy burden of homework on pupils, but these strategies have a deleterious effect on the normal growth of children. Measures are therefore required to improve the performance of unaided schools.

The low levels of performance of pupils in all three sectors also raise more fundamental concerns regarding the appropriateness of the curriculum and the differences in the 'service mix' offered by the three sectors. Standardized achievements tests are based on the official curriculum, which reflects what should have been taught in schools rather than what is actually taught. In the absence of periodic evaluations of achievement at the primary level, the divergence between the official and actual curriculum tends to be large. The low levels of performance indicate that the official curriculum is probably pitched at too high a level; at any rate, it is hardly related to what is transacted in the classroom. The analysis of subscores on the two tests, however, reveal that there are some important differences in the degree of mastery at different skill levels. In unaided schools, most pupils demonstrate mastery of the basic skills expected by the end of Class 3; in public schools, few can demonstrate the required degree of mastery of even these basic skills, which means that many pupils will drop out or repeat another year.

One possible interpretation is that unaided schools offer an educational service which, though not adhering to the official curriculum for each class, ensures that all or most children acquire the skills necessary to continue in school. In other words, what is taught in unaided schools mirrors more closely private demand, which in turn is regulated by the labour market and the kind of criteria it uses for selecting employees (for example, credentials for completing school/college rather than mastery over the official curriculum). In public schools, on the other hand, where there is no such targeting, the best pupils will succeed, but the majority will not acquire even rudimentary skills of literacy and numeracy.

If the aim of policy is to ensure that all pupils acquire a certain minimum set of skills, and assuming that unaided schools provide this mix of services, the choice may be one of expanding access to unaided schools for low-income pupils (through stipends) or of ensuring that public schools also provide a similar mix of services. The implementation of the first option encounters many practical hurdles because of the presence of opportunity costs which are difficult to identify and offset for individual pupils. In particular, there is the danger that if a uniform stipend is offered children who are relatively better off and who face lower opportunity costs will benefit, while those who are poorer will still be deterred because the stipend is not enough to cover the opportunity costs. In such cases, the policy of expanding access to unaided schools can lead to a greater segregation of pupils along socioeconomic lines in two different types of school; this would have cumulative negative effects on public schools, which would become increasingly confined to the most deprived strata.

For all practical purposes, the public sector will continue to dominate primary education, and improving its effectiveness remains the best means of offering education in basic skills to all children. The second policy option is therefore a more desirable and feasible one. The specific measures required to alter the service mix in the public sector would have to be identified; it would definitely involve reformulating instructional objectives and ensuring that teaching adheres closely to these objectives, with supporting changes in teacher training, academic supervision, and evaluation of learning outcomes. The costs of these specific strategies would need to be evaluated, but this analysis shows that, as long as unit costs do not increase by more than about 45 per cent above current levels (this being the difference in direct costs between the unaided and public sectors), improving the quality of public education would still be a more cost-effective strategy.

TABLE 5A.1   Explanatory variables included in the HLM analysis

Variable	Symbol of variable	Unit of measure-ment	Whether included in HLM analysis Rural		Urban	
			Math	RC[a]	Math	RC[a]
Within unit (pupil-level)						
1. Unaided school	WORD KNOWLEDGE	Score	*	*	*	*
2. Repeater	REPEATER	1,0	*	*	*	*
3. Girl	GIRL	1,0	*	*	*	*
4. Wants to study up to class 12 or beyond	HIEDASP	1,0	*	*	*	*
Between unit (school-level)						
1. Unaided school	UNAIDED	1,0	*	*	*	*
2. Aided school	AIDED	1,0	*	*	*	*
Teacher resources						
3. School is multigrade	MULTIGRADE	1,0	*	*	—	—
4. School has only two teachers	TWOTCH	1,0	*	*	—	—
5. Number of teachers	TEACHERS	Number	*	*	*	*
6. Average teaching experience	AVGEXP	*	*	*	*	*
7. Proportion of teachers who scored at least 4 (out of 5) on maths subject matter questions	FRHISCOR	0.00–1.00	*	—	*	—
Headteacher characteristics						
8. Headteacher's self-motivation	HMSELF	1,0	*	*	—	—
9. Headteacher meets with teachers regularly	MEETCH	1,0	—	—	*	*
10. Total hours spent by headteacher on academic tasks (excluding teaching duties)	TOTHRS	Hours	*	*	*	*
Physical facilities						
11. At least one class without partition	NOPART	1,0	*	*	—	—
School Composition						
12. Average SES	AVGSES	0.00–1,001	*	*	*	*
13. Average word knowledge score	AVGWK	Score	*	*	*	*
14. Male literacy rate	MLITRCY	(%)	*	*	—	—

[a] Reading comprehension
* Indicates that the variable was included in the model.

	Mathematics achievement score		Reading comprehension achievement score	
	Coefficient	s.e.	Coefficient	s.e.
Fixed effects				
Pupil-level variables				
REPEATER	−0.61 (−2.54)	0.240	−0.45 (−1.62)	0.276
HIEDASP	0.59 (2.48)	0.237	0.25 (0.94)	0.272
GIRL	0.26 (1.20)	0.221	0.48 (1.91)	0.253
School-level effects for mean				
INTERCEPT	12.23 (12.17)	1.004	13.75 (20.44)	0.673
UNAIDED	−1.74 (−0.63)	2.740	−3.29 (−1.27)	2.595
AIDED	1.94 (1.61)	1.204	−0.45 (−0.39)	1.130
TWOTCH	2.38 (1.71)	1.394	3.17 (2.41)	1.316
TEACHERS	0.07 (0.86)	0.086	0.14 (1.68)	0.082
FRHISCOR	1.67 (1.19)	1.400	—	—
HMSELF	1.20 (1.02)	1.185	1.32 (1.17)	1.121
TOTHRS	0.36 (3.11)	0.115	0.15 (1.37)	0.110
MLITRCY	0.11 (2.60)	0.041	0.70 (1.70)	0.04
AVGWK	0.53 (4.46)	0.119	0.84 (7.63)	0.110
School-level effects for word knowledge				
INTERCEPT	0.22 (6.35)	0.034	0.29 (7.82)	0.037
UNAIDED	0.02 (0.13)	0.138	0.24 (0.61)	0.150
AIDED	−0.02 (−0.38)	0.066	−0.08 (−1.18)	0.07
Random effects				
Pupil-level	17.86		23.72	
School mean	15.55		14.13	
WK slope	0.04		0.04	

TABLE 5A.3 Urban schools 'final' model coefficients, standard errors (*t*-statistics)

	Mathematics achievement score		Reading comprehension achievement score	
	Coefficient	s.e.	Coefficient	s.e.
Fixed effects				
Pupil-level variables				
REPEATER	−0.64	0.295	−0.62	0.403
	(−2.16)		(−1.55)	
HIEDASP	0.56	0.295	1.26	0.401
	(1.92)		(3.14)	
GIRL	0.51	0.261	1.02	0.355
	(1.96)		(2.89)	
School-level effects for mean				
INTERCEPT	12.05	1.082	13.40	1.308
	(11.13)		(10.24)	
UNAIDED	−3.49	1.851	−4.65	2.528
	(−1.89)		(−1.84)	
AIDED	1.61	1.007	1.77	1.336
	(1.60)		(1.33)	
TEACHERS	0.03	0.014	−0.01	0.020
	(2.33)		(−0.64)	
AVGEXP	−0.19	0.067	−0.11	0.092
	(−2.82)		(−1.20)	
FRHISCOR	1.46	1.057	—	—
	(1.39)			
MEETCH	0.42	0.083	1.85	1.128
	(0.51)		(1.64)	
TOTHRS	0.18	0.065	−0.05	0.089
	(2.84)		(−0.60)	
AVGSES	−0.71	0.751	0.92	1.025
	(−0.95)		(0.89)	
AVGWK	0.47	0.112	0.65	0.152
	(4.20)		(4.26)	
School-level effects for word knowledge				
INTERCEPT	0.16	0.048	0.29	0.065
	(3.36)		(4.45)	
UNAIDED	0.12	0.068	0.11	0.091
	(1.83)		(1.22)	
AIDED	−0.02	0.074	0.02	0.100
	(−0.25)		(0.24)	
Random effects				
Pupil-level	13.04		24.29	
School mean	4.23		7.78	
WK slope	0.02		0.03	

References

Aitkin, M. and Longford, N. (1986). 'Statistical Modelling Issues in School Effectiveness Studies'. *Journal of the Royal Statistical Society*, 149(1): 1–43.

Barnow, B. S., Cain, G., and Goldberger, A. (1980). 'Issues in the Analysis of Selectivity Bias'. In E. W. Stromsdorfer and G. Farkas (eds.), *Evaluation Studies Review Annual*, v. Beverly Hills: Sage.

Bashir, S. (1994). 'Public versus Private in Primary Education: Comparisons of School Effectiveness and Costs in Tamil Nadu'. Unpublished Ph.D. dissertation, London School of Economics.

Behrman, J. R. (1993). 'Measuring the Cost-Effectiveness of Schooling Policies: Revisiting Issues of Methodology'. Paper presented at International Symposium on the Economics of Education, 19–21 May 1993. Manchester: British Council.

Blomqvist, A. and Jimenez, E. (1989). 'The Public Role in Private Post-Secondary Education: A Review of Issues and Options'. PPR Working Paper no. 240. Washington, DC: World Bank.

Bock, R. D. (ed.) (1988). *Multilevel Analysis of Educational Data*. San Diego: Academic Press.

Bolger, N. and Kellaghan, T. (1990). 'Method of Measurement and Gender Differences in Scholastic Achievement'. *Journal of Educational Measurement*, 27 (2): 165–74.

Bosker, R. and Scheerens, J. (1990). 'Issues in the Interpretation of the Results of School Effectiveness Research'. *International Journal of Educational Research*, 13: 745.

Bryk, A. S. and Raudenbush, S. W. (1988). 'Toward a More Appropriate Conceptualization of Research on School Effects: A Three-Level Hierarchical Linear Model'. *American Journal of Education*, 7 (1): 65–108.

———— (1989). 'Methodology for Cross-Level Organizational Research'. In S. B. Acharach (ed.), *Research in the Sociology of Organisations*, vii: 233–73. Greenwich, Conn.: Jai Press.

———— (1992). *Hierarchical Linear Models*. Newbury Park, Calif.: Sage.

Burstein, L. (1980). 'The Analysis of Multi-level Data in Educational Research and Evaluation'. *Review of Research in Education*, 8.

Carr-Hill, R. (1987). 'Ideology and Inference: A Comment on the Evidence on Private versus Public Schools'. *International Journal of Educational Development*, 7 (2): 133–5.

Choppin, B. (1974), 'The Introduction of New Science Curricula in England and Wales', *Comparative Education Review*, 8(2): 196–206.

Chubb, J. E. and Moe, T. M. (1990). *Politics, Markets and America's Schools*. Washington, DC: Brookings Institution.

Colclough, C. and Manor, J. (eds.) (1991). *States or Markets? Neo-liberalism and the Development Policy Debate*. Oxford: Clarendon Press.

Coleman, J. S., Hoffer, T., and Kilgore, S. (1982). 'Cognitive Outcomes in Public and Private Schools'. *Sociology of Education*, 55 (2/3): 65–76.

Cuttance, P. (1985). 'Frameworks for Research on Effectiveness in Schooling'. In D. Reynolds (ed.), *Studying School Effectiveness*. London: Falmer Press.

Desai, U. (1991). 'Determinants of Educational Performance in India: Role of Home and Family'. *International Review of Education*, 37 (2): 245–65.

Fuller, B. (1985). 'Raising School Quality in Developing Countries: What Investments Boost Learning'. Education and Training Department, Discussion Paper EDT7. Washington, DC: World Bank.

—— (1986). 'Is Primary School Quality Eroding in the Third World?'. *Comparative Education Review*, 30 (4): 491–507.

Goldberger, A. S. and Cain, G. (1982). 'The Causal Analysis of Cognitive Outcomes in the Coleman, Hoffer and Kilgore Report'. *Sociology of Education*, 55 (2/3): 103–22.

Goldstein, H. (1984). 'The Methodology of School Comparisons'. *Oxford Review of Education*, 10 (1): 69–79.

—— (1987). *Multilevel Models in Educational and Social Research*. New York: Oxford University Press.

—— (1991). 'Multilevel Modelling of Survey Data'. *The Statistician*, 40: 235–44.

Govinda, R. and Verghese, N. (1991). *The Quality of Basic Education Services in India: A Case Study of Primary Schooling in Madhya Pradesh*. Paris: International Institute of Educational Planning, and New Delhi: National Institute of Educational Planning and Administration.

Gray, J. (1988). 'Multilevel Models: Issues and Problems Emerging from their Recent Application by British Students of School Effectiveness'. In R. D. Bock (ed.), *Multilevel Analysis of Educational Data*. San Diego: Academic Press.

Hanushek, E. A. (1979). 'Conceptual and Empirical Issues in the Estimation of Educational Production Functions'. *Journal of Human Resources*, 14 (3): 351–88.

—— (1986). 'The Economics of Schooling: Production and Efficiency in Public Schools'. *Journal of Economic Literature*, 24: 1141–77.

Harbison, R. W. and Hanushek, E. A. (1992). *Educational Performance of the Poor: Lessons from Rural Northeast Brazil*. New York: Oxford University Press.

Heyneman, S. P. (1986). 'The Search for School Effects in Developing Countries: 1966–1986'. World Bank EDI Seminar Paper no. 33. Washington, DC: World Bank.

—— and Loxley, W. (1983). 'The Effect of Primary School Quality on Academic Achievement Across 29 High and Low Income Countries'. *American Journal of Sociology*, 88 (6): 1162–94.

Hough, J. R. (1991). 'Input–Output Analysis in the UK: A Review Essay'. *Economics of Education Review*, 10 (1): 73–81.

James, E. (1987). 'The Public/Private Division of Responsibility for Education: An International Comparison'. *Economics of Education Review*, 6 (1): 1–14.

—— (1991). 'Private Finance and Management of Education in Developing Countries: Major Policy and Research Issues' (mimeo). Paris: International Institute of Educational Planning.

—— (1992). 'Public Policies Towards Private Education: An International Comparison' (mimeo). Washington, DC: World Bank.

Jimenez, E. (1987). *Pricing Policy in the Social Sectors*. Baltimore: Johns Hopkins University Press.

—— and Cox, D. (1989). 'The Relative Effectiveness of Private and Public Schools: Evidence from Two Developing Countries'. Living Standards Measurement Study, Working Paper no. 60. Washington, DC: World Bank.

—— Lockheed, M. E., and Wattanawaha, N. (1988a). 'The Relative Efficiency of

Private and Public Schools: The Case of Thailand'. *World Bank Economic Review*, 2 (2): 139–64.

Jimenez, E., Paqueo, V., and de Vera, M. L. (1988*b*). 'Does Local Financing Make Primary Schools More Efficient? The Philippine Case'. World Bank Policy, Planning, and Research Working Paper 69, Washington, DC.

—— Lockheed, M. E., and Paqueo, V. (1991*a*). 'The Relative Efficiency of Private and Public Schools in Developing Countries'. *World Bank Research Observer*, 6 (2): 205–18.

—————— Luna, E. and Paqueo, V. (1991*b*). 'School Effects and Costs for Private and Public Schools in the Dominican Republic'. *International Journal of Educational Research*, 15: 393–410.

Lee, V. and Bryk, A. S. (1989). 'A Multilevel Model of the Social Distribution of High School Achievement'. *Sociology of Education*, 62 (3): 172–92.

Levin, H. (1991). 'Economics of Educational Choice'. *Economics of Education Review*, 10 (2): 137–58.

Lockheed, M. E. and Bruns, B. (1990). 'School Effects on Achievement in Secondary Mathematics and Portuguese in Brazil'. Population and Human Resources Department, PRE Working Paper no. 25. Washington, DC: World Bank.

—— and Hanushek, E. (1988). 'Improving Educational Efficiency in Developing Countries: What Do We Know?' *Compare*, 18 (1): 21–38.

—— and Longford, N. T. (1989). 'A Multilevel Model of School Effectiveness in a Developing Country'. Discussion Paper no. 69. Washington, DC: World Bank.

—— and Zhao, Q. (1993). 'The Empty Opportunity: Local Control of Secondary Schools and Student Achievement in the Philippines'. *International Journal of Educational Development*, 13 (1): 45–62.

—— Fuller, B., and Nyirango, R. (1988). 'Family Background and Student Achievement'. Population and Human Resources Department, PPR Working Paper no. 27. Washington, DC: World Bank.

—— Verspoor, A. *et al.* (1991). *Improving Primary Education in Developing Countries*. New York: Oxford University Press.

Madaus, G. F., Kellaghan, T., Rakow, E. A., and King, D. J. (1979). 'The Sensitivity of Measures of School Effectiveness'. *Harvard Educational Review*, 49 (2): 207–30.

Madras Institute of Development Studies (MIDS) (1988). *Tamil Nadu Economy: Performance and Issues*. New Delhi: Oxford and IBH.

Mingat, A. and Tan, J. P. (1988). *Analytical Tools for Sector Work in Education*. Baltimore: Johns Hopkins University Press.

Murnane, R. J. (1981). 'Evidence, Analysis and Unanswered Questions'. *Harvard Educational Review*, 51: 483–9.

—— (1983). 'How Client Characteristics Affect Organisation Performance: Lessons from Education'. *Journal of Policy Analysis and Management*, 2 (3): 403–17.

—— (1984). 'A Review Essay: Comparisons of Public and Private Schools: Lessons from the Uproar'. *Journal of Human Resources*, 19 (2): 263–77.

—— (1986). 'Comparisons of Private and Public Schools: The Critical Role of Regulations'. In D. C. Levy (ed.), *Private Education: Studies in Choice and Public Policy*. New York: Oxford University Press.

Noell, J. (1981). 'The Impact of Private Schools when Self-Selection is Controlled: A Critique of Coleman's "Public and Private Schools" '. Washington, DC: US Department of Education.

—— (1982). 'Public and Catholic Schools: A Reanalysis of Public and Private Schools'. *Sociology of Education*, 55: 123–32.

National Council of Educational Research and Training (NCERT) (1991). *Minimum Levels of Learning at the Primary Stage*. New Delhi: NCERT.

—— (1992). 'Attainments of Primary School Children in Various States of India, 1991', draft manuscript. New Delhi: NCERT.

Psacharapoulos, G. (1987). 'Public versus Private Schools in Developing Countries: Evidence from Colombia and Tanzania'. *International Journal of Educational Development*, 7 (1): 59–67.

—— and Woodhall, M. (1985). *Education for Development: An Analysis of Investment Choices.* New York: Oxford University Press.

Raudenbush, S. W. (1988). 'Educational Applications of Hierarchical Linear Models: A Review'. *Journal of Educational Statistics*, 13 (2): 85–116.

—— and Bryk, A. S. (1986). 'A Hierarchical Model for Studying School Effects'. *Sociology of Education*, 59 (1): 1–17.

—— Eamsukkawat, S., Di-Ibor, I., Kamali, M., and Taoklam, W. (1991). 'On-the-Job Improvements in Teacher Competence: Policy Options and Their Effects on Teaching and Learning in Thailand'. Working Paper Series no. 889. Washington, DC: World Bank.

Reynolds, D. and Reid. K. (1985). 'The Second Stage: Towards a Reconceptualization of Theory and Methods, in School Effectiveness Research'. In D. Reynolds (ed.) *Studying School Effectiveness*. London: Falmer Press.

Riddell, A. R. (1988). 'School Effectiveness in Secondary Education in Zimbabwe: A Multilevel Analysis'. Unpublished doctoral dissertation, Institute of Education, University of London.

—— (1989*a*). 'Focus on Challenges to Prevailing Theories: An Alternative Approach to the Study of School Effectiveness in Third World Countries'. *Comparative Education Review*, 33 (4): 481–97.

—— (1989*b*). 'Response to Heyneman'. *Comparative Education Review*, 33 (4).

—— and Nyagura, L. M. (1991). 'What Causes Differences in Achievement in Zimbabwe's Secondary Schools?' Working Papers Series no. 705. Washington, DC: World Bank.

Saraswathi, L. S. (1989). 'Medium of Instruction in Tamil Nadu'. In P. R. Panchmukhi (ed.) *Studies in Educational Reform in India*, iv. Pune: Himalaya Publishing House.

Scheerens, J. (1992). 'Educational Productivity Issues in Western Europe'. In D. W. Chapman and H. J. Walberg (eds.), *Advances in Educational Productivity*, ii. Greenwich, Conn.: Jai Press.

Schiefelbein, E. and Simmons, J. (1981). 'The Determinants of School Achievement: A Review of the Research for Developing Countries', IDRC-TS24E. Ottawa: International Development Research Centre.

Sussangkarn, C. (1993). Public/Private Provision of Education and Thai Economic Development: Issues and Future Strategy'. Paper presented at International Symposium on the Economics of Education, 19–21 May 1993. Manchester: British Council.

Thorndike, R. L. (1973). *Reading Comprehension Achievement in Fifteen Countries: An Empirical Study.* New York: John Wiley.

Veles, E., Schieferbein, E., and Valenzuela, J. (1993). 'Factors Affecting Achievement in Primary Education: A Review of the Literature for Latin America and the Caribbean'. HRO Working Paper no. 2. Washington, DC: World Bank.

Willms, D. J. (1982). 'Achievement Outcomes in Public and Private Schools: A Closer Look at the High School and Beyond Data'. California Institute for Research on Educational Finance and Governance, Stanford University.

—— (1984). 'School Effectiveness within the Public and Private Sectors'. *Evaluation Review*, 8 (1): 113–35.

—— (1985). 'Catholic-School Effects on Academic Achievement: New Evidence from the High School and Follow-up Study'. *Sociology of Education*, 58: 98–114.

Windham, D. M. and Chapman, D. W. (1990). *The Evaluation of Educational Efficiency: Constraints, Issues and Policies*, xiii, *Advances in Educational Productivity*. Greenwich, Conn.: JAI Press.

World Bank (1992). 'Public Schools and Private: Which are More Efficient?' *World Bank Policy Research Bulletin*, 3 (1).

6

Who Really Pays for Education? The Roles of Government and Families in Indonesia

ELIZABETH M. KING

6.1. Introduction

There are a number of commonly assumed, or stylized, facts about the finance of public and private schools which are seldom questioned. One is that, since primary (or basic) education is usually compulsory and governments take it upon themselves to be the major provider of schools and teachers at this level, public basic education is free. Another is that private education is funded primarily by private individuals or organizations, and generally caters to those who can afford to pay high fees.

In this study I examine these stylized facts about public and private education in the context of Indonesia and find that they over-simplify reality. As in many other countries, public education is not free, even to the poor, and private schools receive substantial support from the state. I examine the structure of education costs in public and private schools and the sharing of these costs by government and households; I also address the hypothesis that public expenditures are generally pro-poor.

The next section of this paper describes the expansion of education in Indonesia and the diversity in the progress attained by 1989. This is followed by a discussion of the role of the state in the provision of schools at different levels of education, and by an examination of the education costs that are borne directly by families. There then follows a discussion of the level of subsidies provided by the government and their distribution among the rich and the poor. Public and private schools are then compared with respect to the support they receive from the government, private households, and other funding sources.

I use expenditure data from central government sources, as well as survey data from several others: the Socioeconomic Survey of 1989 (Government of

Indonesia 1989; henceforth SUSENAS 1989), which included a special module on educational attainment and detailed education expenditures by households;[1] the 1990 Potensi Desa Survey (Government of Indonesia 1990; henceforth PODES 1990), a community-level survey which includes data on the number of schools; and the 1991/2 Indicators of Quality Survey, conducted by the Ministry of Education and Culture (Government of Indonesia 1991/2; henceforth MOEC), which collected data on inputs, and the sources and uses of funds by schools.[2]

6.2. Why Who Pays Matters

The way in which schools are financed has implications for the equity, the efficiency, and the effectiveness of schools. The role of the state is considered critical in broadening access to basic educational services because capital markets generally do not exist to allow poor students to borrow against their future earnings, and because individuals themselves do not consider the net benefits to education beyond their perceived net private gain and, therefore, underinvest. These are the common justifications for the existence of public schools and for why public schools should charge minimal fees.

The idea public schools benefit the poor more than private schools do is based, however, on the assumption that the poor enrol in public schools in larger numbers than do the rich. Yet there are several reasons why the poor may not be able to afford, or may even be excluded from, public education, and why private schools may be more accessible at times. First, even if public schools were to charge minimal fees, since there are a multitude of other costs besides school fees that are associated with school attendance, and which have to be balanced against perceived benefits to schooling, public education may be too costly to draw the poorest students. Especially at the secondary and tertiary levels, the enrolment rates of the poor can fall far below those of the nonpoor. At these levels, the incidence of public expenditures can appear pro-rich. Second, public schools in most developing countries do charge fees, officially or otherwise. 'Non-official' fees might include a one-time registration fee or mandatory contributions in cash or in kind from families. According to various studies cited in a review by Tsang (1994), private spending

---

[1] Enrolment rates are computed using the sample expansion (weighting) factors for individuals included in SUSENAS 1989. The resulting enrolment statistics are thus representative of the population of Indonesia. The three different types of enrolment measures are defined in Table 6.1. Often the focus is on the gross enrolment rates rather than the other two enrolment rates because the gross rates include all those enrolled in school for the year. By definition, the gross rates for an education level can exceed 100% because children younger or older than the standard ages may be enrolled at that level.

[2] The Survei Sosial Ekonomi Nasional, or SUSENAS, which is undertaken by the Central Bureau of Statistics, covered about 148,000 individuals in about 32,700 households throughout the country in 1989.

accounted for about 30 per cent of the total cost of public primary schools in Thailand and Colombia; about three-quarters of public expenditures for primary education in two provinces in China; 30 per cent in Pakistan; and 110, 51, and 32 per cent for Brazil, Colombia, and Chile.

Many countries rely on private schools to reach populations not adequately served by the public school system, such as remote rural areas, girls, and ethnic or religious minorities. These schools are not necessarily for-profit schools, but are simply non-governmental schools. Examples abound in sub-Saharan African countries where there is a long tradition of schools founded by religious organizations. In Bangladesh and Pakistan, schools run by local non-governmental organizations serve rural areas where there are no public schools, especially for girls.

But even for-profit schools can play a role in broadening access to education. Particularly at the post-primary levels, the supply of public school places in many countries is limited relative to the total demand for education, and students must compete, usually through entrance tests, to enter. The result is that public school places are rationed to the best students who mostly belong to the richer groups, while low-cost, lower-quality private secondary and tertiary institutions meet the excess demand from less able students. The fact that there are usually two types of for-profit private schools—one heavily funded and controlled and the other, unsubsidized and unregulated—is often forgotten (James 1991). Numerous private schools do not fit the stereotype of high-fee, high-quality private schools. In many instances, these are low-cost schools of dubious quality that do not meet the requirements for registration. For many poor students, however, these private institutions may be the only means to pursue a secondary or a tertiary degree.

How schools are financed is related not only to equity but also to schools' effectiveness and efficiency. Some studies have found that private schools may have a productive edge over public schools. For several developing countries, Jimenez *et al.* (1991) have estimated that the unit costs for private schools are about 15 per cent smaller than for public schools. One way to interpret this cost difference is that, for the same unit cost, private schools provide more learning than public schools do. Although the evidence is mixed, some researchers have argued that this relative efficiency comes from private schools having both the incentive and the autonomy to operate efficiently and effectively.

Another reason why private schools might be more effective and efficient is that, by relying on private sources of finance, they are subjected to closer scrutiny by parents and students. Some argue that those who manage the school are not as important to securing improvements in efficiency as those who finance it (Jimenez *et al.* 1988; James *et al.* 1993). The importance of local control in school management is also the cornerstone of the education decentralization reform that is sweeping many countries. As a way to improve school productivity, central governments are giving local school districts and public schools themselves more decision-making authority, including the right (and the responsibility) to supplement public subsidies with local resources. The critics of this reform argue, however, that greater reliance on local financing will result primarily in wider disparities among schools, with poor schools not being able to raise enough resources to take advantage of the greater autonomy given them (Lockheed and Zhao 1993).

I now turn to the case of Indonesia, where the division between public and private schools is not clear-cut, and where the question regarding the right mix of public and private provision and public and private funding is relevant.

6.3. Progress and Diversity in Education in Indonesia

Indonesia has achieved dramatic progress in both education and literacy levels since the 1960s. Between 1960 and 1989, the net enrolment rate rose from 68 per cent in 1960 to 91 per cent in 1989 at primary level, and from about 6 to 68.4 per cent at secondary level. The primary net enrolment rate ranks Indonesia, a low-income country with a GNP per capita of $670 in 1992, alongside upper-middle-income countries which had an average net enrolment rate at primary level of 91 per cent in 1989.

To achieve this progress, there were large investments in school construction, and fees for primary schooling were abolished (in 1977) in a drive to achieve universal primary education. Since the early 1980s, the government has spent more than 3 per cent of gross domestic product annually on education, and about one-half of this education budget has been devoted to the primary level. Moreover, in its more recent (1994) campaign to extend

TABLE 6.1   School enrolment rates in Indonesia, 1989

	Age group/school level			
	7–12 Primary	13–15 Junior secondary	16–18 Senior secondary	19–25 Tertiary
Age-specific rate[a]	90.5	68.4	48.1	11.8
Gross enrolment rate (GER)[b]	105.3	59.1	40.0	5.4
Net enrolment rate[c]	89.4	40.2	27.3	4.8

[a] Age-specific enrolment rate is the ratio of total enrolees in an age group to the population in that age group.

[b] Gross enrolment rate is the ratio of all enrolees in a school level to the population in the official age group for that level.

[c] Net enrolment rate is the ratio of enrolees in a school level who belong only to the official age group for that level to the population in the same age group.

Source: computed by author using SUSENAS 1989.

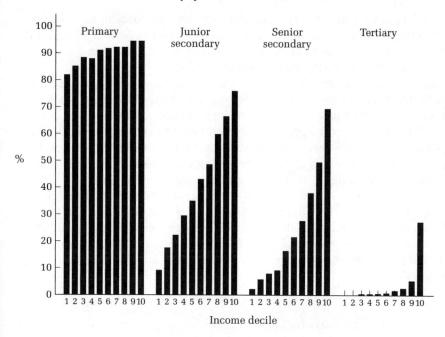

FIG. 6.1   Net enrolment rates, 1989
Source: computed from SUSENAS 1989

universal education up to junior secondary level (grades 7–9; ages 13–15), the government has indicated a commitment to continue to allocate substantial resources to education.

It is difficult, however, to expect that public resources will be sufficient to achieve the government's goal of a universal nine-year basic education within 10 to 15 years, while simultaneously improving the quality of that education. Despite the tremendous progress in primary education, there remain important concerns regarding the access of the poor to education of acceptable quality. There is evidence that some of the success in expansion of enrolments was achieved at the expense of the quality of instruction. Key inputs, such as textbook development, maintenance of classrooms and facilities, and teacher training, are said to have been underfunded by the government, and thus have had to be financed by local communities.

Moreover, as shown in Table 6.1, students begin to drop out in large numbers beyond the age group 7–12 years, and only slightly over two-thirds of those aged 13 to 15 years are likely to remain in school. Of children in this age group, 40.2 per cent were enrolled in junior or lower secondary schools, with the rest mostly still in primary schools. More children in the age group 16–18 leave schools, leading to a further drop in the enrolment rate to 48.1 per cent in 1989. Although this is the official age group for senior or upper secondary education, only 27.3 per cent were actually enrolled at this level, with a further 20 per cent still enrolled in lower secondary. About 12 per cent of those in the age group 19–25 attended school in 1989, less than 5 per cent of whom were enrolled in tertiary-level institutions.

Which groups drop out of school early and which stay in school are illustrated by comparing the enrolment rates among income deciles (Fig. 6.1). Income per capita and school enrolment are very clearly positively associated, with the gap between the poor and the rich being much wider at the higher education levels. Whereas at the primary level the net enrolment rate of the richest (top) decile is only about 15 per cent greater than the enrolment rate of the poorest (bottom) decile, it is almost nine times larger at the lower secondary level and 37 times larger at the upper secondary level. Even more stark is the contrast at the tertiary level: only 1 per cent of youths aged 19–25 in the bottom 60 per cent of the population were enrolled, compared with 27 per cent of those in the top decile. This statistic alone suggests that public subsidies for tertiary education must disproportionately benefit the richer groups.

6.4. The Government and the Supply of Schools

The level and distribution of school enrolments depend crucially on the availability of schools—how many there are relative to demand, and where they are situated. The central government, the main provider and financier of education in Indonesia, thus strongly influences access to schools. In the late 1970s, the government launched an aggressive school-building programme, especially in more remote areas. This programme continued through the 1980s, resulting in the building of enough schools to equalize the potential access to primary schools of children, irrespective of income, throughout the country. The beneficiaries of this programme are clear from Fig. 6.2. The average distance to the nearest primary school is about equal across income deciles. To achieve this in rural areas, which are less densely populated than urban areas, 1.6 more public schools per 1,000 school-age children were constructed in rural than in urban areas.[3]

At the secondary level, even including private schools, the average distance to the nearest school for the poorer income deciles is several times that for the richer income deciles. Moreover, urban residents are better served than rural residents, judging from the school–population ratio: there are seven more junior secondary schools and eight more senior secondary schools per 100,000 youths in urban areas than in rural areas. In addition, while private schools outnumber public schools—there are almost twice as many private junior secondary schools as there are public schools—they too are found with

[3] Data on population are given separately for the age group 7 to 15 in the PODES 1990.

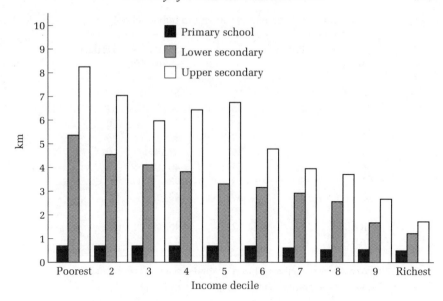

F IG. 6.2   Average distance to school, by education level and income decile
Source: computed from SUSENAS 1989

much greater density in urban than in rural areas: there are 36 more such private schools per 100,000 youths in urban areas than in rural areas.

As regards the characteristics of those who enrol, a very high proportion (87 per cent) of primary students are in public schools. Comparing income groups, there appears to be a slight preference among those in the richest 20 per cent as well as in the poorest decile for private schools (Table 6.2). However, while the richest group will be attending the high-cost, high-quality schools of their choice, the poorest group is likely to be attending the only primary schools available to them, whatever the quality.

At the junior secondary level, there was a roughly equal split in enrolments between public and private schools, with the public share dominating, but with no clear relationship between income levels and the propensity to enrol in public education. At the senior secondary level, however, a pattern of the richer students preferring private schools strongly emerges: whereas 61 per cent of those in the poorest decile are enrolled in public schools, this is true of only 45 per cent of those in the richest decile. By contrast, at the tertiary level the relationship with income is reversed: a higher proportion in better-off families attend public institutions, thus providing further evidence that subsidies at the tertiary level are not egalitarian. As in many countries, the public universities in Indonesia tend to be of higher quality than private institutions because they have a limited enrolment capacity and thus ration their places through entrance tests. Students from richer families who have

TABLE 6.2   Share of enrolment in public schools (%)

Income decile	Primary	Junior secondary	Senior secondary	Tertiary
Poorest	86	57	61	—
2	89	55	60	—
3	90	55	47	0
4	90	57	42	0
5	90	56	37	0
6	89	57	40	22
7	89	58	43	17
8	87	57	43	45
9	85	59	44	43
Richest	71	52	45	35
TOTAL	87	57	43	36

Note: Income deciles are based on total expenditure per capita.

Source: computed by author using SUSENAS 1989.

also attended higher-quality primary and secondary schools are usually better prepared for these tests.

6.5. Private Costs of Schooling

The construction of school buildings and classrooms is not the only education expenditure of the government. Salaries and allowances for teachers account for a large proportion of the total government allocation for education, and have come to be increasingly regarded as squeezing out allocations for quality-enhancing educational inputs.

When fees were suspended in primary schools in 1977, the revenues from fees that financed non-salary school expenditures were replaced with a subsidy from central government under the recurrent budget and the annual development budget. The subsidies received by individual schools have been generally regarded as inadequate to support education of acceptable quality, however. Calculating from the central government accounts, in 1988 the expenditures for instructional inputs in primary schools totalled just Rp20,500 (or less than US$12 per year) for an average class of 30 students—that is, about US$0.40 per student. Allocations for school maintenance were only Rp25,000 per school per year.[4] Moreover, it has been difficult to ascertain

[4] The MOEC provides a relatively small fraction of the resources used to purchase critical pedagogical inputs, such as textbooks, teacher upgrading, and supervision. Inpres SD, a special development fund for primary education provided for by presidential decree, finances the construction and major renovation of school facilities, but provides only limited funds for recurrent

how much of the subsidy actually reached the schools, and even more difficult to verify that these funds were indeed spent on pedagogical inputs.

An important source of supplementary finance for schools has been the contribution of parents' associations, the BP3 (Badan Pembantu Penyelenggaraan Pendidikan). This contribution, which is generally considered mandatory, helps finance vital school activities and, at the same time, ensures parents' involvement in school programmes. The amount and use of the contribution, which is retained by the school and is wholly extra-budgetary, is determined jointly by parents and school principals. A uniform per-student contribution is established for each school, and there is no restriction on what this amount should be in public primary schools. While some schools in the poorest rural communities receive almost no BP3 contributions, collections in wealthier communities are as much as twenty times the size of the subsidy from the central government. Section 6.7 below, on sources of school funds, will present more specific estimates of the level of these contributions in primary schools.

In public secondary schools, too, BP3 contributions can be quite significant, often exceeding revenues from regular student fees.[5] According to an earlier study in the provinces of South Kalimantan, Aceh, and Central Java, BP3 contributions supported from 46 to 78 per cent of the non-salary operational expenditures of schools. These parental contributions are thus critical to the operations of schools. While secondary schools do charge regular tuition fees, the fee revenues are collected by the central government. They later come back to individual schools as a subsidy for their non-salary operational costs, but schools are reported to receive only about one-half of their total fee revenues, on average (World Bank 1989). The leakage is due partly to the fact that administrative costs at the district and provincial levels are also funded by the fee revenues.

Private schools account for a substantial share of secondary enrolments, but much less is known about their costs and financing. Although there are no BP3 fees, private schools impose entrance fees and monthly tuition fees. It is generally assumed that they cover all their operating expenditures by tuition charges. This is far from the truth for many schools. They receive some resources from the central government in the form of textbooks, and a certain number of public schoolteachers are officially seconded to private schools.

expenditures. For fiscal years 1989 and 1990, however, a large share of this allocation was earmarked to supplement the funds that primary education could spend for quality-enhancing school inputs. This amounted to an additional Rp310,000 per year for each primary school, an 80% supplement to the annual school subsidy.

[5] At the secondary level, the MOEC is responsible for the salaries of all full-time teachers. In addition, secondary schools receive a subsidy to meet their non-salary operational costs, and this is financed entirely from official student fees. Hence, while the subsidy for instructional costs at the primary level is a direct grant, the subsidy for secondary education is really a mechanism for redistributing resources from wealthier communities to less affluent areas. As with primary schools, the school allocations are based on an agreed-upon formula.

TABLE 6.3 Average per-child family expenditures for education ('000 rupiahs)[a]

Education level	Urban		Rural		Total	
	Public	Private	Public	Private	Public	Private
Primary	7.3	13.7	3.6	3.9	4.5	8.0
Junior secondary	17.2	20.9	11.2	11.7	13.7	15.7
Senior secondary	26.2	33.4	19.2	23.1	23.0	29.1
Tertiary	54.2	90.0	53.3	66.2	54.0	85.4

[a] These monthly expenses include all fees, outlays for uniforms, books and other learning materials, pocket money, and transportation costs.

Source: computed by author using SUSENAS 1989.

Many public schools share their buildings and facilities with private schools, which operate in the afternoons or evenings, while the public school operates in the morning. Moreover, a large but unknown proportion of public school-teachers 'moonlight' in private schools (Somerset 1992).

Household survey data corroborate school data on the importance of parental contributions in school budgets. They show that families incur non-trivial costs, especially at post-primary levels, whether they send their children to public or private schools. The average monthly cost of attending school varies widely not only among the different levels of education, but also between urban and rural students and between public and private students at the same school level. For example, primary school pupils in urban public schools spend, on average, twice the amount spent by public school pupils in rural areas; and primary school pupils in urban private schools spend 3.5 times more than those in rural private schools (Table 6.3). At all levels of education, urban students clearly spend more than rural students and private students spend more than public students; but the public–private difference in rural areas is very much smaller than that in urban areas. As a result, urban public school pupils actually spend more than rural private school pupils. Urban pupils, even in public schools, tend to spend more on books, other school materials, and uniforms than do rural pupils.

Wealthier students spend much more on education per year than do poorer students. The ratio of these outlays per student between the top and the bottom income deciles is 6 at the primary level, 3.7 at the lower secondary level, 4.5 at the upper secondary level, and 3.6 at the tertiary level.[6] Even when only fees (e.g. admissions, examinations fees) are considered (and more 'voluntary' expenses such as sports equipment are excluded), these ratios remain large: at the primary level the ratio is 9.6. Moreover, these differences

[6] The ratio is between the top decile and the third lowest decile for tertiary education. There are no data corresponding to the bottom two deciles in the population.

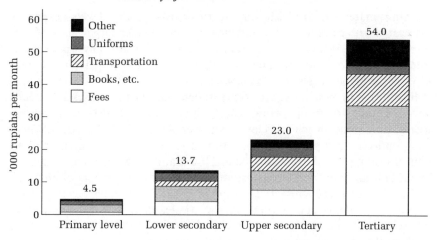

FIG. 6.3 Family education expenditures for public education, by type
Source: computed from SUSENAS 1989

are not simply due to the student's choice of attending a public or a private school; even among those enrolled in public institutions, there remain significant, albeit smaller, disparities than among those enrolled in private institutions. These disparities may be interpreted as differences in the quality of schooling. The household survey I use did not collect school quality data, so this interpretation cannot be ascertained.

One of the policies being considered by the government in promoting enrolment at the junior secondary level is to abolish tuition fees in public schools, as had been done at the primary level. To what extent will such a policy reduce household education expenditures? In public primary schools, about 50 per cent of spending is devoted to just a few items—uniforms (31 per cent), and textbooks and other learning materials (18 per cent) (Fig. 6.3); all fees together account for just 18 per cent. In private schools, fees account for 29 per cent of expenditures, and uniforms and books for 41 per cent. At the post-primary levels, the share of fees increase steeply while that of uniforms and learning materials diminish. At the junior secondary level, fees account for one-third of spending by public school students, and textbooks for 12 per cent. If the government were to abolish tuition fees in junior secondary schools, it would not be reducing out-of-pocket expenditures by one-third, however, since on average less than two-thirds of fees pertain to tuition or BP3 contributions. There would still be fees for admission, examinations, and participation in school activities. Expenditures by private school students mostly go to fees (45 per cent); textbooks account for the same share as for primary students.

At the tertiary level, 47 per cent of out-of-pocket spending in public institutions is allocated to fees while only 8 per cent goes to books and other learning materials. In addition, at the post-primary levels, expenses associated with travel to and from school become a much larger share of out-of-pocket costs. Whereas transportation costs account for only 1 per cent of total expenses for primary education, they represent 8–16 per cent of total expenses at higher levels.

In addition to monetary costs to the student and the family, school attendance also involves an opportunity cost which is associated with alternative uses of time spent for school-related activities. According to SUSENAS 1989 data, on average, a primary school student spends about one-quarter of an hour travelling to and from school daily; lower and upper secondary students, about half an hour; and tertiary students, about three-quarters of an hour. Although urban secondary students might spend 5–8 minutes less than rural secondary students commuting, on the whole, there is surprisingly little difference between urban and rural students with respect to travel time. Rather, the greatest variation in travel time can be seen among income deciles. The overall pattern reveals that wealthier students have longer travel time than do poorer students. For example, at the upper secondary level, the daily travel time of students who belong to the topmost income decile is more than ten minutes longer than that of students in the poorest decile. This means that the threshold travel time at which wealthier students would choose to stop schooling is greater than that for poorer students, for whom either the transportation cost of the extra travel time or the opportunity cost associated with it represents a more significant increment to the total cost of attending school.

6.6. Public Subsidies for Education

It has been demonstrated above that the government supplies the large majority of school places to primary pupils and has all but removed the fees that primary pupils must pay. At the post-primary levels, the roles of the family and the private sector are much greater. This section examines the level of public subsidy at all education levels. Using the government recurrent budget allocations for education and data on the fee structure across income groups, the amount of government subsidy per capita for public education can be estimated for each education level. The estimates assume that government funds go only to public school students (since there is no clear existing formula for determining subsidies to private schools).

In 1989, the total recurrent expenditures by the government amounted to Rp1,799 billion (or approximately $900 million) for primary education, Rp573 billion for junior secondary education, Rp398 billion for senior secondary education, and Rp309 billion for tertiary education—a total of Rp3,079 billion for all education levels (World Bank 1992). Cost recovery was fairly modest at 16.3 per cent, but this was due primarily to a cost recovery

TABLE 6.4   Relative subsidy per capita in public schools by
income deciles

Income decile (poorest = 1.0)	Primary	Junior secondary	Senior secondary	Tertiary
Poorest	1.00	1.00	1.00	—
2	1.01	1.01	1.05	—
3	1.05	1.03	1.14	1.00
4	1.02	1.02	1.00	0.99
5	1.06	1.03	1.09	0.99
6	1.05	1.01	1.01	0.97
7	1.06	1.04	1.16	0.91
8	1.02	0.99	1.10	0.93
9	1.01	0.99	1.11	0.92
Richest	0.98	0.94	1.03	0.79

Note: Income deciles are based on total expenditure per capita.

Source: computed by author using SUSENAS 1989.

ratio of 8 per cent at the primary level. At the higher levels, fees accounted for more: 22.7 per cent at the junior secondary level, 31.9 per cent at the senior secondary level, and 33.5 per cent at the tertiary level.

How are public subsidies distributed across income groups? To compute the level of subsidy per capita for each income level, the fees collected in public schools and recovered by the central government must be considered.[7] Since data do not permit the government recurrent budget to be allocated by income decile, the enrolment share in public schools and the level of fees in those schools will determine the distribution of subsidies per capita. In Table 6.4, the per capita subsidy for each income decile is compared with the estimated subsidy for the poorest decile. The pattern that emerges is a fairly equal distribution at the primary and senior secondary levels, a slightly pro-poor bias at the junior secondary level, and a more significant pro-poor bias at the tertiary level where the richest groups receive per capita subsidies of approximately 79 per cent of those received by the third poorest decile.

---

[7] This calculation involved using data on fees paid by families from SUSENAS 1989. Although the survey questionnaire provides for a detailed breakdown of fees, I retained some aggregation because of the frequency of missing data. I used three broad categories of fees: (1) fees for entry and registration; (2) tuition fees, BP3 contributions, and others; and (3) examination fees. I assumed that category (2) is recovered by the central government, while the rest are retained by the school or local government. As BP3 contributions are also retained by primary schools, I inferred the BP3 portion of category (2) from the primary school survey data from MOEC. To differentiate the level of BP3 contributions by income decile, I assigned schools to income deciles using the average household expenditure per capita of the sub-district in which they are located. The data for primary schools are then applied to junior secondary schools as well; this assumption is likely to underestimate the BP3 share at the junior secondary level.

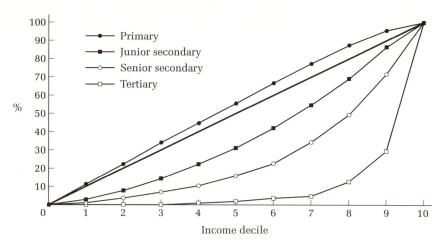

Fɪɢ.6.4   Subsidies for public education (Cumulative shares by income decile)
Source: computed from SUSENAS 1989

It is also of interest to examine the distribution of subsidies, by income group, in aggregate rather than in per capita terms. Here, a strong pro-poor bias emerges at primary level because primary school-age children represent twice as large a fraction of the population in the poorest deciles as among the richest, and because gross enrolment rates and the public share of enrolment differ little across the income distribution.

However, at post-primary levels, any pro-poor bias in terms of per capita expenditures disappears when the total subsidy amounts are considered. The pro-rich bias of total public spending for secondary and tertiary education is due to much higher enrolment rates at these levels for better-off youths, together with high but relatively constant public sector shares of enrolment across income deciles, and an age distribution of youths in better-off families that is skewed towards older age groups. The result of these factors is that the poorest decile receives a total subsidy of Rp17.8 billion at the junior second-ary level, Rp4.6 billion at the senior secondary level, and Rp0.6 billion at the tertiary level (for the third poorest decile). In contrast, the total amount of the subsidy for the richest decile is 4.2 times larger for junior secondary educa-tion, 21.2 times larger for senior secondary education, and 289 times greater at the tertiary level.

The Lorenz curves showing the distribution of the total education subsidy by income decile further illustrates these points (Fig. 6.4). The distribution of the subsidies for primary education lies above the 45° diagonal line, indic-ating that the poorer groups receive larger shares of the total than the rich. By contrast, the fact that the subsidy for post-primary levels is skewed sharply towards the better-off population is indicated by the relevant curves being well below the diagonal line.

A policy of abolishing fees at the junior secondary level to promote universal nine-year basic education would be likely, initially, to worsen the position of the curve for that level. The slightly pro-poor bias of the per capita subsidy for junior secondary education would disappear as all tuition fees in public schools are abolished. Since enrolment rates for the poor are not likely to increase immediately, the total subsidy will also more greatly favour the rich.

6.7. Sources of Funds of Primary Schools

A final perspective offered here on the financing of education in Indonesia is that from the school. How are public and private schools funded? Thus far, receiving a public subsidy has been identified with attendance at a public school. Yet, the government provides subsidies also to private schools, usually in the form of assigning civil service teachers to them, allowing them to convene in public school buildings, and offering them funds of up to Rp70,000 for repairs and major rehabilitation of school properties. Indeed, when funding is considered along with management, one obtains a more accurate picture of the proportion of students who receive public subsidy.

The 1991/92 MOEC school survey provides a rare opportunity to obtain systematic and more detailed data on how schools finance their operations and how they spend their revenues and subsidies. Unfortunately, the MOEC data are available for only 15 of the 27 provinces in the country and they pertain only to primary schools.[8] None the less, by revealing a wide diversity in the means whereby public and private primary schools are financed, the data suggest a need to rethink the conventional definition of public and private schools.

The data indicate that primary schools operate on an average budget of Rp104,643 per pupil (or about $50 per pupil), ranging between Rp76,488 (about $40) in South Sumatra and Rp159,556 ($80) in North Sulawesi. Across regions, the average expenditure per pupil is highest in the Jakarta area, but schools outside Java operate on fairly similar revenues and subsidies per pupil (Table 6.5). On average, public schools, which account for 95 per cent of all schools included in the survey, spend about 6 per cent less per pupil than do private schools. A larger difference is observed between rural and urban schools, with rural schools operating with 89 per cent the per-pupil budget of urban schools.

Central government allocations account for an average of 91 per cent of

---

[8] The 15 included provinces are: Aceh, Bengkulu, West Sumatra, and South Sumatra in the island of Sumatra; Central Java, Jakarta, West Java, and Yogyakarta in the island of Java; Bali; South Kalimantan and East Kalimantan; Maluku; East Nusa Tenggara; and North Sulawesi and South Sulawesi.

TABLE 6.5   Average school budget per pupil (rupiahs)

Region	Type of school[a]				Total[a]
	Public	Private	Rural	Urban	
Jakarta	116,252	111,729	92,951	118,826	115,529
	(2,318)	(441)			(2,759)
Other Java	97,609	92,870	96,342	104,581	97,519
	(44,163)	(849)			(45,012)
Outside Java	114,181	117,775	111,788	126,777	114,483
	(27,042)	(2,482)			(29,529)
Indonesia	104,290	111,462	102,227	115,311	104,643
	(73,528)	(3,772)			(77,300)

[a] Numbers in parentheses are the number of schools in each category. About 500 schools do not have a rural/urban designation and are omitted from the corresponding columns.

Source: computed by author using the Ministry of Education and Culture 1991/2 Indicators of Quality Survey (GOI 1991/2).

school budgets. This share is highest outside Java, at 96 per cent, and lowest in Jakarta schools, at 61 per cent. Partly explaining this variance is the relatively greater number of private schools in Jakarta; whereas 16 per cent of all primary schools are private schools in Jakarta, less than 2 per cent are private in the other provinces of Java and about 8 per cent outside Java.

On average, public schools obtained 92 per cent of their funding from government allocations, but private schools are also heavily subsidized, deriving 70 per cent of their budgets from government subsidies. There is, however, considerable variance across regions (Table 6.6). Public schools in Jakarta depend on the government for only 70 per cent of their funding, while public schools in other Java provinces and provinces outside Java derive 91 and 96 per cent of their funding, respectively, from the central government. The regional diversity among private schools is even greater. The shares of the government subsidies in private school budgets are 8, 51, and 87 per cent in Jakarta, other Java, and outside Java provinces, respectively. These numbers suggest that, outside the Jakarta area, the government relies on private schools to provide education to more remote rural areas, but that it heavily supports the existence of this small number of schools.

The sources of school funding indicate that, at least at the primary level, in provinces outside Java there is little difference in the source of funding of private and public schools. With respect to the income distribution of public subsidies for education, this result implies that the Lorenz curve for primary education in Fig. 6.4 would show an even more pro-poor curve for primary education, since private schools attended by the poor, especially in rural

TABLE 6.6   Share of government
subsidies in school budgets (%)

Region	Type of school				Total
	Public	Private	Rural	Urban	
Jakarta	71.0	8.1	63.4	11.8	61.0
Other Java	90.7	51.3	91.4	69.8	90.0
Outside Java	96.5	87.4	96.5	91.5	95.8
Indonesia	92.2	70.0	93.2	86.6	91.2

Source: computed by author using the Ministry of Education and Culture 1991/2 Indicators of Quality Survey (GOI 1991/2).

areas, are almost as heavily subsidized as the public schools. However, this effect would not be dramatic, since the enrolment share in private schools is quite small at the primary level.

6.8. Conclusion

Among the reasons for studying the respective roles of the state and families in the financing of education are to review the stylized facts about the differences between public and private schools and to assess the equity rationale for a stronger public presence in education. At least with respect to financing, public schools are often not as clearly differentiated from private schools as is usually assumed. In Indonesia, many rural private schools are as dependent on subsidies from the central government, as are urban public schools. Studies that have found this dichotomy of schools to be helpful in explaining differences in technical efficiency thus need to assess whether it is the nature of school management rather than the sources of school finance that leads to any apparent private school advantage.

For Indonesia, one lesson is that government resources alone may prove insufficient to achieve present expansion goals for basic education, especially in view of the need also to upgrade the quality of such education. We have seen that communities and families even now supplement school funds and, with the greater emphasis on investments in human capital in Indonesia, they may well be willing to contribute further in the future. On a per capita basis, the poor benefit from subsidies as much as do the rich. However, total subsidies at the post-primary levels are overwhelmingly pro-rich because those who complete the primary level and pursue further education belong to the richer segments of the population. Thus, there is a need to target subsidies for post-primary education in order to reverse their current strong pro-rich bias. The government was able to achieve this with relative success at the primary level. It should ease the burden of junior secondary education for the poorest, going beyond the mere provision of schools and the abolition of tuition fees for all.

References

Government of Indonesia (GOI) (1989). *Survei Sosial Ekonomi Nasional* (SUSENAS). Jakarta: GOI Central Bureau of Statistics.

—— (1990). *Sensus Penduduk: Potensi Desa* (PODES). Jakarta: GOI Central Bureau of Statistics.

—— (1991/2). *Kuestioner Data Indikator Mutu* (MOEC). Jakarta: GOI Ministry of Education and Culture.

James, E. (1987). 'The Public/Private Division of Responsibility for Education: An International Comparison', *Economics of Education Review*, 6(1): 1–14.

—— (1991). 'Public Policies Toward Private Education', *International Journal of Educational Research*, 15: 359–76.

—— King, E. M., and Suryadi, A. (1993). 'Finance, Management, and Costs of Public and Private Schools in Indonesia'. Paper presented at the International Symposium on the Economics of Education, Manchester, 19–21 May; forthcoming in *Economics of Education Review*.

Jimenez, E., Paqueo, V., and de Vera, L. (1988). 'Does Local Financing Make Primary Schools More Efficient? The Philippine Case', PPR Working Paper no. 69, World Bank.

—— Lockheed, M., and Paqueo, V. (1991). 'The Relative Efficiency of Private and Public Schools in Developing Countries', *World Bank Research Observer*, 6(2): 139–164.

Lockheed, M. and Jimenez, E. (1994). 'Private and Public Secondary Education in Developing Countries', HRO Working Papers, HROWP 43, World Bank.

—— and Zhao, Q. (1993). 'The Empty Opportunity: Local Control of Secondary Schools and Student Achievement in the Philippines', *International Journal of Educational Development*, 13(1): 45–62.

Somerset, A. (1992). 'Secondary Teachers in Indonesia: Supply, Demand and Initial Preparation'. Mimeo.

Tsang, M. C. (1994). 'Private and Public Costs of Schooling in Developing Countries,' *International Encyclopedia of Education*, 2nd edn., viii: 4702–8. Oxford, UK: Pergamon Press.

World Bank (1989). *Indonesia: Basic Education Study*. Washington, DC: World Bank.

—— (1992). *Indonesia: Public Expenditures, Prices and the Poor*. Washington, DC: World Bank.

PART IV

Spreading the Burden

7

Community Financing of Education: Rationales, Mechanisms, and Policy Implications in Less Developed Countries

MARK BRAY

The evidence on the social and economic impact of community financing approaches in education is fairly limited. I reviewed the evidence in the mid-1980s (Bray 1986; Bray with Lillis 1988), and this paper re-examines the topic in the light of literature that has appeared since those two books were written. In general the subject remains disquietingly neglected, and the present paper restates many of the earlier conclusions. However, some additional material has emerged, which contributes both to a better description of different systems and to a clearer understanding of issues.

The paper begins with a conceptual framework comprising definitions and models of financing. It then focuses in turn on the mechanics of community financing in different parts of the world, and on issues of quality and equity. Section 7.6 comments on questions of government guidance and control. Finally, the paper draws out some of the main policy implications as they appear in the mid-1990s.

7.1. The Conceptual Framework

7.1.1. Definitions

The title of this paper contains two words which require definition: 'community' and 'financing'. A considerable literature exists on the nature of communities (see e.g. Ryba and Kallen 1975; Dore 1981; Kotzé 1987; Anderson

1991). Hillery's classic paper notes as many as 94 alternative definitions, and points out (1955: 113) that the list is still not exhaustive.

Without going too deeply into this debate, for present purposes a community may be defined as a group of people who share social, economic, and cultural interests and/or attributes. This overall definition embraces several major types of community.

1. Probably the most common conception is of the *geographic community*, which may refer to the individuals living in a village, district, or suburb. These are relatively small geographic areas, and are the levels with which this paper is most concerned.
2. Alternatively, a community can be formed from *ethnic, racial, and religious groups*. Thus, it can refer for example to Tamil, Gikuyu, or native American peoples; to Chinese, Europeans, or Latin Americans; and to Christians, Mormons, Jews, or Muslims. These groups may also be subdivided so that, for instance, within Christian communities there may exist separate communities of Roman Catholics, Baptists, Methodists, and Anglicans.
3. Some communities are subdivided by *sex and age*. In all parts of the world, males and females, and children, youths, the middle-aged, and the elderly meet in separate communities for particular purposes. Women's groups may be a strong force for development; and in parts of Africa formally constituted age grades play a major part in community projects.
4. Communities may also be based on *common occupations or experience*. Tailors, truck drivers, and academics, for instance, may form themselves into communities. The Rotary and Lions Clubs are communities of businessmen which often assist local schools. Common ties arising from past connections are exemplified by communities of ex-servicemen and, in the context of education, Old Students' Associations.
5. Communities can also arise from *shared family concerns*. Among the most important for school support are Parents' Associations, based on adults' shared concerns for the welfare of their children.
6. Finally, communities may arise from general *shared philanthropy*. Many schools are run by bodies which were created to fund and run schools but which have no other community functions.

Turning from the concept of community to that of financing, although in most contexts financing implies provision of direct monetary contributions, much community support for education is in non-monetary form. Land, labour, and materials have costs associated with their provision, and would have to be purchased if they were not provided directly. Thus, the paper is concerned with both monetary and non-monetary support for schools.

Finally, the paper is concerned mainly with community-supported formal primary and secondary schools. In many countries, considerable community contributions are made to pre-primary and post-secondary institutions, to non-formal education, and to alternative formal systems such as Koranic schools and Roman Catholic seminaries. Discussion of community support in these areas is beyond the scope of the present paper.

7.1.2. Community financing *v.* government and private financing

The proportions of community and government financing in individual schools may vary widely. To conceptualize this, one may build up a model as in Fig. 7.1. Fig. 7.1(*a*) shows the range of options in two dimensions. On the left are schools that are entirely self-financed and receive no government support, and on the right are schools that are entirely financed by government with no community support. In between is a series of combinations. Of course, not all countries have schools occupying all points in the spectrum; and the centre of gravity may vary widely in different national systems.

Since Fig. 7.1(*a*) takes no account of private, profit-making schools, part (*b*) of the figure adds an extra wing to the model. Because in some countries even profit-making schools receive government grants, the private school wing also contains a range of situations. In contrast to the non-profit-making system, it is difficult to envisage a situation in which the government pays more than 50 per cent grants. Accordingly, the line separating government from non-government finance is not a true diagonal.

Figure 7.1(*c*) takes this model one stage further to allow for intermediate situations. Four situations are illustrated by different arrangements to secure new school buildings. A profit-making businessman who wished to erect a new school building might take a bank loan and subsequently repay it from pupils' fees. This extreme could not be described as community financing, and is outside the boundaries of this paper. The second option in the diagram is an intermediate one in which a school is non-profit-making but is run from a trust. The Kamuzu Academy in Malawi, for example, is said to have been funded entirely from trust funds set up by President Banda. Such an arrangement does not fall within the category of community support as defined in this paper. The same might apply to mission schools in Africa or elsewhere which obtain funds for buildings or running costs from their mother churches or from parishes overseas, though this example is perhaps less clear-cut. A third example, with a stronger element of community support, is where new buildings are erected by the pupils' parents, either directly or by employing a contractor to do so on their behalf. Finally, the most community-oriented type is a school in which the buildings are erected by the whole community, both parents and non-parents.

Just as a particular school could be located anywhere along the spectrum

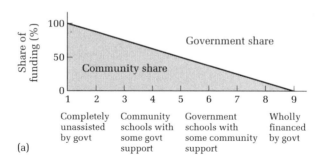

(a)

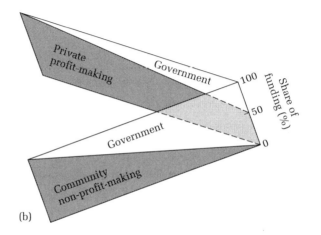

(b)

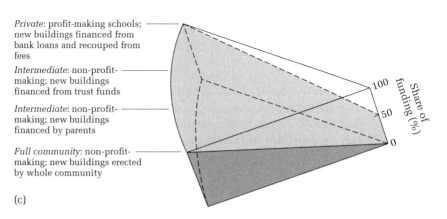

(c)

FIG. 7.1   Community and government financing
(*a*) Model 1   (*b*) Model 2   (*c*) Model 3

in part (*a*), the same holds true of the three-dimensional model in part (*c*). Individual countries usually have clusters of school types which can be placed in different parts of the model. This paper is concerned mostly with the full-community end of the spectrum, but must also recognize intermediate types.

Linking to an allied body of literature, many authors have analysed the range of characteristics and types of private education (e.g. James 1988, 1991; Walford 1989; Cummings and Riddell 1994; Bashir, Ch. 5 above). Community financing may be seen as a subset of private schooling in so far as private education is taken to encompass all non-government provision. However, community schools must be distinguished from other types of private institution. Schools operated by entrepreneurs as profit-making businesses are clearly distinct from community-financed schools. Also distinct are not-for-profit institutions financed entirely from fees. The most important characteristic of community financing is that at least some resources are gained as contributions from the broader community, as opposed to just pupils and their families.

7.2. Rationales and Extent of Community Financing

From the viewpoint of the communities themselves, the chief reason for undertaking community financing projects is to secure a service that is not provided by the government or any other organization or individual (Assié-Lumumba 1993: 7–15). In some cases government schools may be available, but are not of the type or quality desired by particular religious or racial groups. In other cases government provision is judged quantitatively inadequate, and community financing seeks to reduce the shortfall. In the latter case, community financing may supplement provision in existing schools, or it may lead to the creation of completely new institutions.

From the viewpoint of governments, community financing may be considered desirable because it reduces pressure on the government purse. It is also sometimes argued that community financing can improve the impact of education. It is suggested that people who directly pay at least small amounts for education and other services come to value those services more highly than when they are handed out anonymously and apparently without cost. Self-help projects can also promote desirable forms of social cohesion, though of course none of these are automatic outcomes of community financing schemes.

The extent of community financing varies widely both within and between countries, and at different times. It is usually hard to form precise estimates of the extent, not only because of the paucity of data but also because of the difficulty of assigning monetary values to non-financial contributions.

Nevertheless, examples from widely scattered contexts indicate that contributions can be considerable.

Kenya, for example, has become particularly well-known for its self-help projects. The movement there is known as *harambee*, commonly translated as 'let's pull together' (Abreu 1982; Hill 1991; Bradshaw 1993). At least in rural areas, communities are usually expected to take responsibility for the construction and maintenance of primary schools. Recent policy changes have blurred the distinction between types of secondary school, but in 1987, *harambee* secondary schools comprised nearly three-quarters of the total (Mwiria 1990: 355). Some of the *harambee* schools were aided by the government (almost 44 per cent of all secondary schools), but others (almost 29 per cent) were unaided. Ten years earlier, unaided *harambee* schools had comprised 10.5 per cent of the total, with aided *harambee* schools comprising just 0.5 per cent. In addition, by the mid-1980s 15 *harambee* institutes of technology had been constructed and managed by communities. Furthermore, some have argued that it is now time for Kenyans to use *harambee* as an alternative way to finance universities (Olembo 1992: 105).

In neighbouring Uganda, where government provision of education all but collapsed during the 1970s and 1980s, parents and broader communities have been estimated to contribute approximately 80 per cent of the costs of running primary schools, and 60 per cent of the costs of operating secondary schools (Opolot 1994: 26). Less dramatic but nevertheless highly significant figures from Chad indicate that in 1991/2 at the primary level community schools formed 22.4 per cent of the total, and catered for 9.3 per cent of pupils (Esquieu and Péano 1994: 24); and in Malawi community primary schools, unassisted by the government, comprised 20.5 per cent of all primary schools in 1992/3 and enrolled 9.5 per cent of all primary pupils (Malawi 1993: 8, 30). Scattered reports also indicate high levels of community financing in other African countries (see e.g. Moorad 1989; Chung 1990; Kemmerer 1992; Olembo and Harrold 1992; Wetta and Ilboudo 1993).

Turning to Asia, J. Robinson (1991: 167) reports that in China's Yunnan Province there were, in the late 1980s, over 46,000 community-employed primary schoolteachers, while in 36 mountainous areas of Fujian Province there were 32,100 such teachers. In Vietnam, one survey of five provinces estimated that communities contributed 26 per cent of the total costs of primary education (Rorris and Evans 1994: 50); in Cambodia, family expenditures on primary education in 1992/3 were typically between four and nine times the level of government expenditures, and the gap was even wider at the secondary level (Cambodia 1994: Annex 1/5; Tilak 1994: 108, 140, 173); and in 1991 Bhutan had 84 lower primary community schools compared with 138 government full primary schools and just 14 government junior high schools (Irvine 1992: 3). These are scattered examples, and patterns are far from uniform throughout geographic regions. However, they do indicate that community financing is significant in at least some countries.

7.3. Mechanisms of Community Financing

The mechanisms for generating resources are diverse, and depend, among other factors, on cultural contexts and the inventiveness and enthusiasm of the organizers. Although it is impossible here to present a full portrait, some common strategies may be highlighted.

In many institutions, even in community-run schools, fees are the largest source of income and are especially important for recurrent costs. Sometimes the fees are quite high, and raise major questions of equity. Issues linked to fees or 'user charges' for education are controversial and have attracted extensive discussion in the literature (e.g. Thobani 1984; Lewin with Berstecher 1989; Colclough 1991; Hinchliffe 1993). Much of this debate is as relevant to community-financed schools as to others. Cornia (1987: 170) represents community financing as an *alternative* to user charges, yet in many schools user charges and community financing go together.

Communities may also raise resources by imposing taxes. Igwe (1988) indicates that in his village in Eastern Nigeria community members are taxed by the Council of Elders. Men are generally taxed at higher rates than women, and age groups are a valuable vehicle for collection of the taxes. Sons and daughters who are no longer resident in the village may also be taxed, with the sanction of ostracism in the event of non-payment. Hill (1991) makes similar comments about Kamba communities in Kenya. He reports that, when money was urgently needed, the enforcers would go round the homes of defaulters at night:

They first asked politely for the payment and, if this was paid to them, collected in addition a payment of one shilling for their services. If it was not paid, they seized some item of the defaulter's property and took it away. . . . Most of these items were later reclaimed by the owners and the dues paid, plus the *askaris'* 'expenses', but some were sold in the village later as the owners refused to pay up. (Hill 1991: 188)

Some communities, alternatively, decide to tax beer, vehicles, or market stalls and traders. These measures are usually based on the assumption that people who consume luxury items or operate businesses have more money than the average person, and can afford to give extra support to their schools.

For capital works, launching ceremonies are among the most prominent ways to generate funds. According to one account,

people compete to see who will donate the highest amount. There is a similar competition among the age groups. Everybody in the community endeavours to donate some amount, no matter how big or small, and each donation is announced over the public address system. By the general spirit of the people, it is better to be dead than to be alive and not able to contribute to the development of one's village or clan. (Igwe 1988: 112)

Although for obvious reasons the organizers of launching ceremonies pay close attention to the potential for attracting large individual gifts, in many contexts the bulk of project income comes from small donations. One study from India reports that:

under the Gudiyatttam Town Teachers Association Centre conference, Rs. 72,000/- were collected for 20 schools. The analysis of the donors revealed that only 5.3% of the donors contributed more than Rs. 25/- each. 41.1% of the contributions came from people who contributed Rs. 0.50 to Rs. 0.99 each. (Nayar and Virmani 1978: 56)

Other ways to raise resources include levies on alumni, collections from church congregations, and mobilization of Parent–Teachers' Associations (PTAs). As mentioned above, contributions are not necessarily in cash. Community members may help construct or repair buildings, may donate animals, and may provide transport for teachers, students, and school supplies. In some communities, women cook meals on a voluntary basis; and many communities provide lodging for pupils whose homes are distant from the schools. Occasionally, community members also help with teaching at little or no charge. Instances of this can be cited from countries as diverse as Cameroon, China, and Dominica (Bray with Lillis 1988: 45).

Reference to Parent–Teachers' Associations draws attention to the extent to which the community may be narrowly or widely defined and perceived. For obvious reasons, it is easier to persuade parents to take an interest in school affairs than adults who are not parents. Schools in Papua New Guinea have bodies called Parents' and Citizens' Associations rather than Parent–Teachers' Associations; but even there the main interest comes from parents rather than from other members of the community (Preston 1991). A similar observation has been made with reference to Botswana by Tsayang and Yoder (1991: 15). Elsewhere, however, community involvement tends to be much broader. This is particularly evident in parts of Nigeria and Kenya.

Communities are also sometimes able to obtain resources from governments on a 'matching grants' basis. In Lesotho, for example, the government has met 75 per cent of building costs but has expected communities to meet the remaining 25 per cent. In one state of India, proportions have been one-third community to two-thirds government, but grants have also varied according to the wealth of each area. Comparable policies in China are known as 'fishing': the government fund is the 'bait' able to attract the 'fish' of much larger contributions from the communities. This terminology has a rather negative flavour which could imply an element of exploitation by the government. However, Cheng explains that the policy may be viewed positively as well as negatively. The three possible responses that he identifies are as follows:

First, some prosperous localities are glad to take the opportunity to gain ownership of their schools. In this case, the 'bait' acts as an incentive to local initiative. Second, in localities where the governments are used to issuing top-down directives the local contribution is mandatory. This has created much resentment among the people. . . . Third, some poorer areas are genuinely unable to match the 'bait'. (Cheng 1990: 63)

In the last case, the policy is particularly problematic because it exacerbates inequalities.

Finally, it is common for governments to provide annual recurrent grants for materials and other needs, to pay teachers' salaries, and to give non-financial assistance, while expecting communities to meet capital costs. Payment of teachers' salaries is especially important, since they are usually by far the largest single item of expenditure. Many governments also provide advice on building designs, procurement of supplies, fund-raising, accounting, and other matters.

7.4. Issues of Quality

When discussing quality, it is necessary to evaluate the inputs and processes of school systems as well as their outputs. Where community resources supplement government ones in existing institutions, it may be assumed that the community initiatives improve quality. Different concerns arise when schools operate entirely outside the government system. Although such schools may be qualitatively excellent, they are more likely to be problematic. Questions then arise about whether such institutions should be allowed to operate at all.

The most detailed data on qualitative issues in relation to community financing again comes from Kenya. Wellings (1983: 19–20) pointed out that most pupils in *harambee* secondary schools were there by default, having failed to gain places in government institutions. *Harambee* schools also tend to have inferior facilities. The Ministry of Education in Kenya used to grade the infrastructure of secondary schools from A to D. Of the 416 institutions inspected in 1978, 27 per cent of maintained schools were graded A, but only one *harambee* school was accorded this rank. At the other extreme, only 7 per cent of maintained schools were graded D, compared with 84 per cent of unaided schools (UNICEF 1984).

Harambee schools also tend to be deficient in the quality of their teachers. In 1982, 87.3 per cent of unaided *harambee* secondary schoolteachers were untrained, compared with just 15.4 per cent of those in government schools. Furthermore, although it was actually against the law, some *harambee* schools even employed staff with only the Kenya Certificate of Education. With such deficiencies in input and process, it is not surprising that *harambee* schools have performed poorly. In 1984, only 17 *harambee* institutions were among the top 300 schools as measured by results of the Kenya Certificate of Education, and 246 of the 337 institutions at the bottom of the ranking were *harambee* schools (Lillis and Ayot 1988: 125–7).

Comparable situations are found in other countries. A study in Chad indicates that, at the primary level,

Community schools are developing considerably but in a somewhat unsystematic manner in villages, where they make up for the absence of public schools. Once the embryo of a school has been financed, often under precarious conditions and with a pupil intake that exceeds the capabilities of a teacher with little experience, the village community waits for the State to take over . . . to enlarge the school and provide trained teachers. Placed in varying degrees under the responsibility of inspectors, who are sometimes faced with a *fait accompli*, these schools cover only the early years of primary education. The State is not able, at the present time, to follow up all these local initiatives, many of which stagnate in unsatisfactory conditions. (Esquieu *et al.* 1993: 4)

The study adds that community schools lack qualified teachers, textbooks and other teaching materials. In 1992 only 38 per cent of community schoolteachers held the Brevet d'Etudes du Premier Cycle (gained after four years of secondary education) or a higher qualification, compared with 67 per cent of teachers in the public sector and 77 per cent in the urban private sector.

Similarly, government officials in Bhutan found in the early 1990s that many community schools 'continue to be located in empty village houses . . . temples or simple huts which are found to be most unsuitable for proper learning purposes' (Bhutan 1992: 24). These comments were echoed in a report produced in the same year:

Community schools are currently operating as second-class schools. . . . They are officially denied some of the support services of larger schools, are staffed by the least experienced teachers, and are poorly supported in terms of adequate facilities, staffing and supplies. (Gyamtsho *et al.* 1992: 16)

The situation has since improved (Bray 1995); but the 1992 report added that schools were constructed in remote areas by people 'whose leaders have little or no prior experience of modern education, and who . . . do not know what a school should look like, what goes on in schools and why their children need a basic education' (Gyamtsho *et al.* 1992: 16).

Similar observations have been made in Botswana. In that country the community junior secondary schools receive a great deal of government assistance, but are nevertheless perceived as inferior in quality. As a result, they find it difficult to attract the best pupils and teachers (Moorad 1989; Tsayang and Yoder 1991; Ruda 1993). In Malawi, the contrast is even more stark since the unassisted community schools receive no help from the government and are severely starved of resources (B. Robinson *et al.* 1994: 47–63).

A further qualitative issue is also linked to the location and size of schools. In general, research evidence suggests that, the closer the schools are to community members' residences, the stronger will be community ties, especially in rural areas (see e.g. Mbithi and Rasmusson 1977: 152–3). However, this sometimes leads to inappropriate siting of schools and to unnecessary fragmentation in which two or more schools are constructed to serve communities which could easily be served by one school. This point highlights the need for certain government controls, which will be given further comment below.

7.5. Issues of Equity

Community financing can raise major problems of equity. The most obvious difficulty, already noted in the Chinese example, is that some communities are in a better position to help themselves than are others. Community financing can perpetuate inequalities because the rich are able to make stronger investments in their future and therefore to maintain their lead.

The dimensions of inequality may be both geographic and social. Beginning with the former, regional inequalities have been demonstrated in many countries. For example, it is no coincidence that in the mid-1980s Tanzania's prosperous Kilimanjaro region had 20.1 per cent of the country's secondary schools even though it had only 5.3 per cent of the population, and that 68.0 per cent of those secondary schools were in the unaided self-help category (Galabawa 1985: 17). Comparable developments have been noted in the Anambra State of Nigeria, where:

the parts of the State where education was first established showed the initial interest in the scheme [for secondary education expansion through self-help], while other areas followed; a natural consequence since secondary education can only be useful to children who have completed their primary education. The disadvantage, however, is that in the less developed part of the state, where many children . . . do not reach Primary 6, the lack of secondary schools continues, without the impetus of a local school to encourage parents to educate their children. (Okoye 1986: 272)

Similar points have been made in Kenya, where disadvantaged districts have remained disadvantaged because they had low incomes in the first place and therefore found it difficult to embark on self-help. Mwiria (1990: 358) observes that, partly because of *harambee*, a child born in Central Province has a much better chance of going to secondary school than a child born in North Eastern Province. In Zimbabwe, the government has attempted to overcome severe discrepancies by establishing a Disadvantaged Schools Programme for communities that are extremely poor. However, even the Minister of Education has noted that this fund is small and therefore limited in effectiveness (Chung 1990: 194).

Regional disparities may overlap with rural–urban disparities. The tendency here is for inequalities to be compounded rather than reduced by government policies (see e.g. Tsang and Wheeler 1993: 115). Because it is usually more difficult to foster community initiatives in urban than in rural areas, governments commonly provide extensive resources for the urban schools while expecting the rural ones to help themselves.

Further issues are raised by the inequalities that exist within rural or urban areas. Tensions may be particularly acute when these are linked to fees, and although at first sight involvement of the broad community (as opposed to just parents or others who are direct beneficiaries) would seem to be a mechanism for reducing social inequalities, matters do not always work out that way. This point was made clearly in one Kenyan case study in the mid-1970s, which highlighted issues that are still relevant two decades later. The study concerned two schools in Western Kenya which the communities constructed in the face of major difficulties. Ultimately, both schools were opened. However,

in both instances the villagers who had helped to put them up have been dismayed by the high school fees charged when the schools started to operate. The fees have been so high that only the very prosperous can now send their children to them. The majority of the people, who are living more or less below the poverty line, have therefore to suffer the agony of watching children from all over the district . . . receive the 'precious' education in 'their' schools for which they had sold their only chickens and crops in order to raise funds at the time of building. Education, for them, has become the domain of the rich, and since some of them are already aware that education is the key to a better life in the future, they feel cheated and robbed. This is borne out by the fact that in 1974 the fees at each of these schools were K.Shs.900 per annum, without uniform, bedding, utensils and most of the textbooks, in an area where the average per capita income for a year is less than K.Shs.400. (Bray *et al.* 1976: 232)

A similar point has been made in the context of Zimbabwe, where communities commonly make decisions by simple majority voting (Chung 1989). Sometimes the 51 per cent are the wealthy, and the relatively poor 49 per cent have little choice. A related observation has been made even more starkly with reference to Uganda, where executives of Parent–Teachers' Associations may not be properly representative and may not conduct meetings in a free and fair way. Members of PTA executives are often from among the socially and economically advantaged groups, and it is not uncommon for powers to be abused. When it comes to finance, in the worst cases the executives may:

set and pass estimates and then call a general meeting to discuss the estimates. In an attempt to ensure that the estimates are approved, short notices for the general meeting are given to parents denying them the opportunity to reflect upon the agenda, and the actual meeting is usually stage managed by the organisers. Speakers are determined in advance, supporters scattered all over the audience to allay any suspicion and occasionally when some critic is chosen, (s)he is interrupted, booed or the views simply ignored by the chairman. To give the meeting credibility, a motion is put to vote and at times the chairman uses the discretion to force the meeting to endorse minority views. Complaints to challenge the irregularities and undemocratic processes are not tolerated through points of order and/or points of information technicalities. Parents who get tough with figures are accused of not having the school at heart and can be frankly told to withdraw their pupils from the school. Delaying tactics are employed so that financial statements (almost all not audited) are brought in late when the audience is tired and hungry or when others have already left. (Opolot 1994: 112–13)

The writer of this account indicated that such irregularities had not gone unnoticed by parents. He observed that two categories of parents could be identified: those who advocate increases in PTA contributions and who always 'win', and the generally poorer parents, who are against the 'unfair' increases in PTA contributions. The majority of parents, he indicated, see PTA annual general meetings as forums for increasing parental contributions to the schools. 'Most parents go simply to hear what they have to pay, but quite a number simply don't turn up at all' (Opolot 1994: 113).

Geographic and social inequalities may be even stronger when they are linked to racial or religious groups. Schools catering for the children of expatriates exist throughout the world. Also widespread are schools that cater for ethnic and religious minorities. Examples include South Asian communities in East Africa, and Chinese communities in such countries as Fiji, Malaysia, and the Philippines. As regards religious minorities, Ismaili communities have, for example, financed education in such countries as Pakistan, India, Bangladesh, and Uganda. Seventh Day Adventists are active in countries as far apart as Solomon Islands, Malawi, and Montserrat; and various types of Christian schools are found almost everywhere.

7.6. Guidance and Control

Recognizing the valuable but potentially problematic nature of community financing, the questions arising include what governments can do to maximize benefits and minimize problems, and how authorities can find the optimum balance between encouraging initiatives and preventing problems of low quality and serious inequity. The locus of the optimum balance varies markedly according to the nature of the society. In parts of eastern Nigeria, the tradition of self-help is so strong that it seems to flourish under almost all circumstances. Mongolia, by contrast, has almost no comparable tradition, and projects there would require much more careful nurture.

Controls on schools may be both direct and indirect. Most governments require all schools to be registered, including ones that are independently managed and financed. Governments do this in order to facilitate enforcement of regulations on quality, and to help assess the geographical coverage of schooling. Some governments also enforce regulations on fees and levies, either prohibiting them altogether or setting ceilings. Authorities also commonly require schools to present audited accounts. This not only provides a check on activities but may also encourage community financing, since members know that there is less danger of their contributions being misappropriated.

Indirect ways to influence the education sector include grants and technical advice, workshops for teachers and managers, and curriculum control through examinations. Many governments also encourage both higher quantity and better quality by offering to take over schools that are in the right places and have satisfactory facilities. To some communities, of course, government take-over is a threat rather than a benefit; but many communities aspire to relieve themselves of a burden by asking the government to take over the institutions.

To tackle the problems of regional inequalities, special grants may be made available to disadvantaged communities. In many countries the government also aspires to ensure that needy schools get good teachers. The government of Bhutan (1992), for example, announced that only the best trained national teachers would be sent to community schools. This is easier to announce than to implement, but it does at least indicate some commitment. The authorities also required district education officers and inspectors to make regular visits, and to provide frequent in-service workshops for community schoolteachers.

In the Anambra State of Nigeria, the government has also been able to influence communities through its control of admissions. Concerning secondary schools, it has been observed that:

As the government could not compel communities to build schools, or to complete schools they had started, the only control available was not to allocate Class I students to the community school at the beginning of the year. . . . Warnings of this were given to both the community and the school at each stage, and well ahead of time, with conditions that were to be met if such a penalty was to be avoided. Community leaders were often grateful to receive this notice in writing, as the letter could then be read out at the monthly Town Union meeting, and the necessary contributions or assistance would be forthcoming. (Okoye 1986: 268)

However, while such strategies may be useful in particular communities at particular times, insistence on controls is sometimes difficult. In some contexts, corruption is a major problem which subverts good intentions. In other settings, carefully laid administrative endeavours are subverted by political forces. Assié-Lumumba (1993: 10) makes this point with reference to Madagascar. The point has also been made in Kenya, where Keller (1980) has highlighted the qualitative problems arising from proliferation of *harambee* schools, but has added that in some instances the politicians have been unable to control the situation. Keller quoted the Kenyan Minister for Labour as saying:

they are a political thing and even though I am not very happy with what they are doing, I myself am building these schools . . . this is political and cannot be helped. (Keller 1980: 52; emphasis in the original)

This type of situation is not confined to Africa. Concerning the South Pacific, Hindson (1985: 291–3) documents problems encountered by the government of Kiribati, which has been anxious both to promote balanced regional development and to limit investment in academic secondary education until it could be justified by expansion of the cash economy. Because the government refused to build new secondary schools in the main island, various communities decided to open their own. Between 1978 and 1984, schools were opened by the Mormons, the Catholics, adherents to the Church of God, and the Seventh Day Adventists. Although the schools undermined government policy, which aimed to contain the threat of educated unemployment, for political reasons the government felt unable to prohibit them—especially since they were entirely funded with non-government money. A similar situation has been described in India by Nayar and Virmani (1978: 46).

7.7. Conclusions: What We Ought to Know and What We Think We Know

The 1988 book on which much of this paper is based concluded with an observation about the paucity of research evidence from a sufficient range of countries:

[More] detailed analysis of specific contexts is urgently required. This book has drawn on literature which is wide but mostly superficial. Writing this book has therefore been like assembling a jigsaw with half the pieces missing. (Bray 1988: 218)

The book noted that governments often quote their own expenditure data as if that is all that is spent on education in their countries, and that many authorities are disquietingly ignorant of the nature and impact of self-help projects. One reason for the ignorance is that self-help does not cost governments anything. Most items that do appear in official budgets are scrutinized much more carefully. Yet it is precisely *because* self-help efforts do not cost governments money that they deserve more careful investigation.

Returning to the topic in the mid-1990s, a review of recent literature shows insufficient attempts to close the knowledge gaps. A few pieces have been added to the jigsaw, but many pieces are still missing. There is a need for more detailed study of the factors leading to success or failure of initiatives in communities of different types. Also needed is a deeper understanding of the range of models for community financing, of the mechanisms for such financing, and of the impact of community financing initiatives on quality and equity.

Despite these knowledge gaps, however, some things are clear. Above all, community financing is not a panacea. In most cases it should be treated as a stop-gap measure, ameliorating the impact of deficiencies in government provision. For example, the Minister for Education in Zimbabwe, speaking in 1989, identified the impact of community financing on equity, as *the* major problem facing the educational authorities in that country (Chung 1989). Her views would no doubt be echoed elsewhere. While at first sight community financing might seem to be a mechanism through which a broad social base can support the education of needy people and thus promote equity, closer examination reveals that it is more likely to do the opposite. Most community-financing initiatives seem to exacerbate rather than reduce regional and sub-regional inequalities. Also, while for example Kenya's *harambee* schools have given access to people who would otherwise have been denied it, evidence also exists that poor people have been taxed in order to pay for the education of the relatively rich.

A related aspect concerns attempts to universalize education. While at first sight community financing would seem to provide additional resources which extend access, the picture may not be so simple. The fact that many community schools have to charge fees may in itself exclude the poorest members of the community. Problems also arise from management disputes in community-resourced schools (see e.g. Mannathoko and Odharo 1992: 92; Opolot 1994: 113). Case studies in Papua New Guinea (Preston 1991: 283) provide examples of schools being closed because the communities refused to provide labour and other inputs to maintain buildings, and of children being sent home from school as a sanction against their parents' failure to make the contributions that had been demanded.

A further question, linked partly to the definitions of community raised at the beginning of this paper, concerns catchment areas and inclusiveness/ exclusiveness. While communities may be defined in religious, racial, occupational, and other terms, they are most commonly defined according to geographic criteria. One consequence of allowing communities free rein to establish their own schools may be the creation of a large number of small and inefficient institutions with overlapping catchment areas.

Community enthusiasm and morale also may be critically linked to enrolment patterns. This has been noted in Botswana by Moorad (1992: 30). He observed that initially only pupils who did well in their Primary School Leaving Examination were admitted to the community junior secondary schools (CJSSs), and that in many instances the villages closest to the schools did not have enough pupils with the required passes to fill the schools. As a result, the schools drew significant proportions of intakes from more distant areas. The result appears to have been very detrimental to general levels of community enthusiasm (see also Ruda 1993: 46).

Further questions concern resource generation and use. On the one hand, community projects can mobilize resources for educational use which could never be accessed through the government's taxation system (Mbithi and Rasmusson 1977: 16). Yet on the other hand, even labour has an opportunity cost. As noted by Colclough with Lewin (1993: 175), unless great care is taken over timing and other factors, there will almost certainly be a cost in forgone agricultural or other output.

Finally, tricky issues surround the question about precisely what powers should be devolved to community bodies and what responsibilities should be retained or assumed at the government level. Psacharopoulos *et al.* (1986: 34) present a rather broad recommendation for decentralization in order to 'give parents and students a greater role in choosing the quality and type of education they want and the means of delivery'. Colclough and Lewin, wisely, are more cautious. They suggest that:

the devolution of responsibility for some aspects of schooling provision is less damaging than others. In general, the provision of those aspects of the infrastructure, the quality of which are not likely to be causally associated with cognitive outcomes (some buildings, latrines, sports facilities) is less risky and inequitable than the devolution of responsibility for other items (teachers' salaries—and thus the proportion of teachers trained/untrained—school textbooks, and other learning materials) which are so associated. (Colclough with Lewin 1993: 175)

Even this, however, is a rather general statement which can only be of use when interpreted in the light of other social and economic factors specific to particular contexts. While some communities respond to, and can be trusted with, a considerable devolution of responsibility, initiatives in other communities require much more careful nurture and/or control.

References

Abreu, E. (1982): *The Role of Self-Help in the Development of Education in Kenya 1900–1973.* Nairobi: Kenya Literature Bureau.

Anderson, B. (1991): *Imagined Communities: Reflections on the Origin and Spread of Nationalism*, rev. edn. London: Verso.

Assié-Lumumba, N'Dri T. (1993): *Coûts, Financement de l'Education de Base et Participation des Familles et Communautés Rurales dans les Pays du Tiers Monde.* Paris: Institut International de Planification de l'Education.

Bhutan (Government of) (1992): *Eighth Quarterly Policy Guidelines and Instructions.* Thimphu: Department of Education.

Bradshaw, Y. W. (1993): 'State Limitations, Self-Help Secondary Schooling, and Development in Kenya', *Social Forces*, 72: 347–78.

Bray, M. (1986): *New Resources for Education: Community Management and Financing of Schools in Less Developed Countries.* London: Commonwealth Secretariat.

—— (1988): 'Policy Implications and Conclusions', in M. Bray with K. Lillis (eds.), *Community Financing of Education: Issues and Policy Implications in Less Developed Countries.* Oxford: Pergamon Press, pp. 203–18.

—— (1995): *The Costs and Financing of Primary Schooling in Bhutan.* Thimphu: UNICEF/Department of Education, Royal Government of Bhutan.

—— with Lillis, K. (eds.) (1988): *Community Financing of Education: Issues and Policy Implications in Less Developed Countries.* Oxford: Pergamon Press.

—— Dondo, J. M. C. and Moemeka, A. A. (1976): 'Two Case Studies from Nigeria and Kenya', in K. King (ed.), *Education and the Community in Africa.* Edinburgh: Centre of African Studies, University of Edinburgh, pp. 217–38.

Cambodia (Royal Government of) (1994): *Rebuilding Quality Education and Training in Cambodia.* Phnom Penh: Ministry of Education, Youth and Sports, with assistance from UNESCO under UNDP contract and with the collaboration of AIDAB and UNICEF.

Cheng Kai-ming (1990): 'Financing Education in Mainland China: What are the Real Problems?' *Issues and Studies* (Taipei), 26(3): 54–74.

Chung, F. (1989): 'Government and Community Financing of Education in Zimbabwe', paper presented at a conference sponsored by the UK Forum on Education and Development, Oxford University.

—— (1990): 'Government and Community Partnership in the Financing of Education in Zimbabwe', *International Journal of Educational Development*, 10(2/3): 191–4.

Colclough, C. (1991): 'Who Should Learn to Pay? An Assessment of Neo-liberal Approaches to Education Policy', in C. Colclough and J. Manor (eds.), *States or Markets? Neo-liberalism and the Development Policy Debate*. Oxford: Clarendon Press, pp. 197–213.

Colclough, C. with Lewin, K. M. (1993): *Educating all the Children: Strategies for Primary Schooling in the South*. Oxford: Clarendon Press.

Cornia, G. A. (1987): 'Social Policy-Making: Restructuring, Targeting, Efficiency', in G. A. Cornia, R. Jolly, and F. Stewart (eds.), *Adjustment with a Human Face: Protecting the Vulnerable and Promoting Growth*. Oxford: Clarendon Press.

Cummings, W. K. and Riddell, A. (1994): 'Alternative Policies for the Finance, Control and Delivery of Basic Education', *International Journal of Educational Research*, 21: 751–84.

Dore, R. (1981): 'Introduction', in R. Dore and Z. Mars (eds.), *Community Development*. London: Croom Helm.

Esquieu, P. and Péano, S. (1994): *L'Enseignement privé et spontané dans le système educatif Tchadien*, Rapport de Recherche no. 103. Paris: Institut International de Planification de l'Education.

—— Jallade, L., and Péano, S. (1993): 'The Place of Private and Community Education in Chad', *IIEP Newsletter*, 11(3): 3–5.

Galabawa, J. C. J. (1985): 'Community Financing of Schools in Tanzania', paper presented at the Commonwealth Secretariat workshop on Community Financing of Schools, Gaborone, Botswana.

Gyamtsho, T., Passang, S., Norbu, P., and Irvine, J. (1992): 'Report of Field Visits to Selected Schools in the Bumthang, Tongsa and Shemgang Dzongkhags'. Thimphu, Bhutan: Department of Education.

Hill, M. J. D. (1991): *The Harambee Movement in Kenya: Self-Help, Development and Education among the Kamba of Kitui District*. LSE Monographs on Social Anthropology, no. 64. London: Athlone Press.

Hillery, G. A. (1955): 'Definitions of Community: Areas of Agreement', *Rural Sociology*, 20(2): 111–23.

Hinchliffe, K. (1993): 'Neo-liberal Prescriptions for Education Finance: Unfortunately Necessary or Inherently Desirable?' *International Journal of Educational Development*, 13(2): 183–7.

Hindson, C. (1985): 'Kiribati: The Search for Educational Alternatives in a Pacific Micro-State', *International Journal of Educational Development*, 5(4): 289–94.

Igwe, S. O. (1988): 'Community Financing of Schools in Eastern Nigeria', in M. Bray with K. Lillis (eds.), *Community Financing of Education: Issues and Policy Implications in Less Developed Countries*. Oxford: Pergamon Press, pp. 107–16.

Irvine, J. (1992): 'Community Schools in Bhutan', paper presented to the Annual Conference of Dzongkhag Education Officers, Thimphu, Bhutan.

James, E. (1988): 'The Public/Private Division of Responsibility for Education: An

International Comparison', in T. James and H. M. Levin (eds.), *Comparing Public and Private Schools*, i. New York: Falmer Press.

—— (1991): 'Public Policies toward Private Education: An International Comparison', *International Journal of Educational Research*, 15(4): 359–76.

Keller, E. (1980): *Education, Manpower and Development: The Impact of Educational Policy in Kenya*. Nairobi: Kenya Literature Bureau.

Kemmerer, F. (1992): 'Community Support of Schools', in D. W. Chapman and H. J. Walberg (eds.), *Advances in Educational Productivity*, ii. Greenwich, Conn.: JAI Press, pp. 109–22.

Kotzé, D. A. (1987): 'Contradictions and Assumptions in Community Development', *Community Development Journal*, 22(1): 31–5.

Lewin, K. with Berstecher, D. (1989): 'The Costs of Recovery: Are User Fees the Answer?' *IDS Bulletin*, 20(1): 59–71.

Lillis, K. and Ayot, H. (1988): 'Community Financing of Education in Kenya', in M. Bray, with K. Lillis (eds.), *Community Financing of Education: Issues and Policy Implications in Less Developed Countries*. Oxford: Pergamon Press, pp. 117–29.

Malawi (Government of) (1993): *Basic Education Statistics 1993*. Lilongwe: Ministry of Education, Science and Technology.

Mannathoko, C. and Odharo, J. (1992): 'The Role of Boards of Governors in Botswana Community Junior Secondary Schools', in W. Kouwenhoven, S. G. Weeks, and C. Mannathoko (eds.), *Proceedings of the Comparative Education Awareness Seminar*. Gaborone: Botswana Educational Research Association.

Mbithi, P. M. and Rasmusson, R. (1977): *Self-Reliance in Kenya: The Case of Harambee*. Uppsala: Scandinavian Institute of African Studies.

Moorad, F. R. (1989): 'An Evaluation of Community Junior Secondary Schools in Botswana with Particular Emphasis on Community Participation and Decentralization', Ph.D. thesis, University of London Institute of Education.

—— (1992): 'Community Financing of Education in Botswana: A Literature Review', paper prepared for the Educational Research Network for East and Southern Africa (ERNESA) workshop on 'Financing Basic Education: Participation and Partnerships', University of Botswana, Gaborone.

Mwiria, K. (1990): 'Kenya's *Harambee* Secondary School Movement: The Contradictions of Public Policy', *Comparative Education Review*, 34(3): 350–68.

Nayar, D. P. and Virmani, K. G. (1978): *Management of Local Support to Education in India: A Case Study*. New Delhi: National Staff College for Educational Planners and Administrators.

Okoye, M. (1986): 'Community Secondary Schools: A Case-Study of a Nigerian Innovation in Self-Help', *International Journal of Educational Development*, 6(4): 263–74.

Olembo, J. (1992): 'Financing Education in Rural Africa: The Kenyan Case', in J. Olembo and R. Harrold (eds.), *Planning and Financing Rural Education in Africa*. Armidale, New South Wales: Commonwealth Council for Educational Administration.

—— and Harrold, R. (eds.) (1992): *Planning and Financing Rural Education in Africa*. Armidale, New South Wales: Commonwealth Council for Educational Administration.

Opolot, J. A. (1994): *Study on Costs and Cost-Effective Approaches to Primary Education in Uganda*. Kampala: UNICEF.

Preston, R. (1991): 'Organisational Perspectives on the Local Management of Schools: Papua New Guinean Perspectives', *International Journal of Educational Development*, 11(4): 275–88.

Psacharopoulos, G., Tan, J. P. and Jimenez, E. (1986): *Financing Education in Developing Countries: An Exploration of Policy Options*. Washington, DC: World Bank.

Robinson, B., Davison, J., and Williams, J. (1994): *Malawi Education Policy Sector Analysis*. Lilongwe: USAID.

Robinson, Jean (1991): '*Minban* Schools in Deng's Era', in I. Epstein (ed.), *Chinese Education: Problems, Policies and Prospects*. New York: Garland, pp. 163–71.

Rorris, A. and Evans, K. (1994): *Towards Universalised Primary Education in Vietnam: A Study of the Costs and Cost Effectiveness of the Primary Education System*. Hanoi: UNICEF.

Ruda, G. B. (1993): 'Implications of Community Financing of Community Secondary Schools in the North-Central and North-East Districts in Botswana', M.Ed. dissertation, University of Botswana.

Ryba, R. and Kallen, D. (eds.) (1975): *School and Community*. Sèvres: Comparative Education Society in Europe.

Thobani, M. (1984): 'Charging User Fees for Social Services: Education in Malawi', *Comparative Education Review*, 28(3): 402–23.

Tilak, J. B. G. (1994): *Financing Education in Cambodia*. Brisbane: Queensland Education Consortium/Manila: Asian Development Bank.

Tsang, M. C. and Wheeler, C. (1993): 'Local Initiatives and their Implications for a Multi-level Approach to School Improvement in Thailand', in H. M. Levin and M. Lockheed (eds.), *Effective Schools in Developing Countries*. London: Falmer Press.

Tsayang, G. and Yoder, J. (1991): 'Through their Eyes: Community Perceptions of the Community Junior Secondary School Policy in Botswana', *Boleswa Educational Research Journal*, 8: 1–17.

UNICEF (1984): *Situation Analysis of Women and Children in Kenya*. Nairobi: UNICEF Eastern Africa Regional Office.

Walford, G. (1989): *Private Schools in Ten Countries: Policy and Practice*. London: Routledge.

Wellings, P. A. (1983): 'Unaided Education in Kenya: Blessing or Blight?' *Research in Education*, 29: 11–28.

Wetta, C. and Ilboudo, E. K. (1993): *Cost-Effectiveness Study in Basic Education: Burkina Faso*. Ouagadougou: UNICEF.

8

Health Insurance: A Solution to the Financing Gap?

CHARLES NORMAND

8.1. Introduction

There are four main mechanisms for financing health care: government spending, social insurance, private insurance, and direct payments by patients. Social insurance provides access to a range of health services in exchange for an annual fee, normally calculated as a percentage of income. This system is often organized through employers, and the fee is not related to the risk of using health services. Private insurance is a normal commercial system in which the company insures individuals against the need to pay for health services. This normally takes into account the risks in setting the premium.

Most countries use a combination of these, but normally there is one mechanism that is dominant. For example, in northern and southern Europe government finance provides access to health services for the majority of the population; in Switzerland and the USA it is mainly private insurance, and in Germany and the Netherlands social insurance is dominant (Hurst 1991; US Congress Office of Technology Assessment 1995). Most African countries have a mixture of government finance and user fees, with only a small role at present for social insurance (Bendahou et al. 1994). Japan has a system based on social insurance (KEMPOREN 1992), and full coverage is now in place using social insurance in Korea, although significant user fees are still charged (Kwon 1991). Social insurance is being introduced in Thailand.

The choice of the main system of financing for health care depends on the history and development of services, the infrastructure of the health system, and political and cultural issues. Tax finance and social insurance both aim to give access to care on the basis of need, and the insurance contributions or tax are paid according to income. Under social insurance the patient has to be enrolled in the scheme, and normally has defined rights of access to care. Under both systems the provision of health services can be either public or private, or a mixture.

Whereas social insurance and tax finance have an element of solidarity (i.e. there is support from the rich and well to the poorer and sicker), private insurance in principle insures against the risk of any individual needing health care, but does not contain this element of mutual support. In fact, it is too difficult and too expensive to rate the risks for different individuals with such accuracy that it is purely a system of insuring for risks, but, in general, the premium paid reflects the likely need for services. So, for example, older people pay more for private health insurance than younger ones, and those with a record of illness pay more than those who are generally well. Under these circumstances, people on low incomes may be unable to afford insurance for comprehensive access to services.

User fees and charges, in common with private insurance, do not contain any systematic solidarity between richer and poorer, and the well and the sick. Patients or their families pay for whatever services are used. A major issue in user fees is the effects on equity of access (Thomason *et al.* 1994). However, it is quite common for user fees to be partly related to incomes, or for there to be exemptions for poorer people, so there can be some element of mutual support.

The pattern of health care finance in developed countries is premissed upon making access to a wide package of care free or nearly free at the point of use. Except in the USA and Switzerland, this is achieved via tax finance or social insurance. Middle-income countries tend to use a mixture of financing systems, with some people being guaranteed access. However, additional fees, and private or social insurance schemes, can increase the range of available services. Public sector provision in many poorer countries has faced reductions in resources resulting from falling national income, structural adjustment programmes, and changes in government priorities. In response, user fees are being increasingly resorted to, and often form a major part of funding of services.

This paper is concerned with the potential role of health insurance in contributing to the financing of access to care. There are many options for health sector finance, and these can be combined in ways that help to achieve health policy goals. The analysis starts from the premiss that the aims are to improve the health of the population and to provide services appropriate to needs. Choices for finance are analysed in the context of these objectives. The approach used is to consider general issues in health policy and health finance, to define and discuss options for financing services, and to examine in particular the potential role for health insurance. Both private and social health insurance will be discussed in the context of trying to achieve policy goals.

8.2. Health Policy, Health Financing, and Health Insurance

The debate in developing countries about social policy in general, and health policy in particular, takes place in the context of objectives and constraints that are a product of both internal and donor pressures (Foster *et al.* 1994). The demands of other policy objectives, especially that of achieving more rapid economic growth, may constrain the total level of finance for the health sector and the ways in which the resources can be mobilized. For example, the overall level of resources for social welfare programmes may be constrained by a perceived need to release resources for physical investment designed to produce more rapid economic growth. There is a coherent argument that, since health is positively affected by income, the priority must be to increase growth and thereby incomes. By this means, both health and other aspects of welfare can be increased. Since there is a fixed amount of resources available in the economy, lower levels of spending on health services can allow higher spending on investment in infrastructure and on productive capacity.

Nevertheless, the conviction that social sector spending crowds out productive investment that will generate growth is an argument about the level and not the mechanism of health services finance. If private spending on health services replaced public spending, this is likely to have very similar effects in terms of crowding out investment in more direct forms of productive capacity. On the other hand, some infrastructure spending produces facilities that have limited or no effect on the capacity of the economy to grow, and are therefore crowding out productive spending.

It is therefore important to be clear, in any discussion of financing health services, about whether the constraints are upon total spending or upon the choice of mechanisms for funding expenditure. If faster growth requires lower health sector spending, then the precise mechanism for mobilizing resources might be quite unimportant. However, there are also ways in which the mechanisms for raising funds can affect investment in productive capacity in the economy. The ways in which people spend extra income from lower taxes varies, with richer people more likely to save and invest, and poorer people more likely to use extra funds for current consumption. There may therefore be ways in which mechanisms of raising funds for health sector spending will affect economic growth. They may also, of course, have profound effects on the access to treatment and care for different sections in the population.

For the purposes of this paper, it will be assumed that in many countries the constraints on health expenditure come from the limits of existing mechanisms to raise adequate finance, and that additional finance is desirable. These constraints may be specific disincentive effects of particular sources of revenue, difficulty in collecting taxes, concerns about the quality of services financed by taxation, or the high administrative costs of user fees.

It is now well understood, if not always really accepted, that many of the most cost-effective health interventions are located in public health and primary care (World Bank 1993). This can easily be contrasted with the actual use of health sector resources, which are devoted mainly to curative care, and often to curative services that are relatively ineffective. It is therefore easy to argue against continuing the current patterns and mechanisms of health sector finance, since historically they have failed to focus resources where and for whom they would be most effective. The two main concerns are the inefficient use of resources and their inequitable distribution (World Bank 1993; Akin 1986). Removing state funding from inefficient and inequitable services can have little negative impact on society's health. However, such services are often valued by those who receive them, are popular, and are difficult to discontinue.

Recent debates about health financing in South Africa provide some insight into the issues of efficiency, access and equity (McIntyre *et al.* 1995; Committee of Inquiry into a National Health Insurance System 1995). It is very clear that the current use of government resources is inefficient and inequitable. Hospital facilities consume 76 per cent of the government budget for health services. Tertiary care facilities consume 44 per cent of the government budget, and 11 per cent is spent on non-hospital primary care (McIntyre *et al.* 1995). The aim of the reform is to provide more efficient services (in terms of both allocation and production) and greater equity (Committee of Inquiry into a National Health Insurance System 1995). However, there is great resistance to change, both from providers of hospital care and from the users of the services of secondary and tertiary care hospitals.

South Africa is an example of a country with very unequal distribution of incomes, and therefore great disparities in ability to pay for health care. Changes in the use of government funds for health services, along with the use of health insurance, can improve access to primary care and improve equity. However, the basic inequity in access to health services comes from the basic inequity in incomes. A sensible approach to government health policy is to manage inequity better, and to avoid further inequity being caused by government. Some of the discussion below of health insurance mechanisms is concerned with this type of objective, that is to say with trying to focus government funds on providing the most needed services, and avoiding further inequity. Accepting the inevitability of unequal access to care can allow policy to develop that minimizes the harmful effects. The aim should be to raise the standards of care for those with the worst access. To achieve this, it may or may not be necessary to make access worse for those with good access. It may be that good management of inequity may lead to more equitable outcomes than attempts to eliminate inequity altogether.

Much has been written about market failure in health care, and the particular characteristics of health care markets. It is argued that unregulated markets for health care fail owing to monopoly in the supply of services, uncertainty and risk concerning the need to use services, information asymmetries between health care professionals and patients, and time (Arrow 1963; Normand 1991). An element of monopoly in the supply of services comes from the need to licence professionals to ensure competence, and from some economies of scale in the provision of services. Information asymmetries mean that patients are less well informed about the disease and possible treatments than are the health care professionals. The uncertainty about the need for services means that in many years no service will be needed, but in some years there is a need for very expensive treatment. This requires either budgeting for the costs, or insurance. There is the related issue that need for treatment and care is often late in life when incomes are very low, and incomes (and therefore the ability to pay) are higher in middle age when needs for care are lower.

Much is made of the contrast between the relative certainty in the need for most other necessities, and the great uncertainty in the likely need for health care. It is certainly true that very acute illness, with very high costs of treatment, often occurs unexpectedly. However, much of the problem is not uncertainty, but the fact that the costs have to be paid at times when incomes are low. Cross-sectional data show that use of health services is concentrated in young and old, and around some key events. The variation in the intensity of need for services between individuals over a lifetime is smaller than the variation in intensity of need between individuals at a given point in time. The important issue for the design of health sector finance is the extent to which the problem is uncertainty (i.e. whether large expenditures for health services will ever be needed), and how much is simply the mismatch between the time when resources are available, and the time when they are needed. Government and health insurance financing of health services are concerned both with helping to insure against the risk of high costs in any given year, and with matching the timing of the need to pay for services and the availability of funds.

If the problem is mainly one of temporal mismatch, forced savings by individuals would be capable of meeting their health care costs. There are now several initiatives that focus on mobilizing resources to be available when needed, rather than on health insurance. The Singapore Medisave scheme is one version of this approach, under which families take part in compulsory savings for health care. This allows the risks to be shared within the family (i.e. the family fund is available to whoever in the family needs it), but there is no sharing of risk between families. No comprehensive evaluation of this has yet been carried out, but it is clear that much of the objective of achieving access to care has been achieved within this scheme without risk pooling and insurance.

There are potential difficulties with this approach, especially if family ties weaken and there comes to be a need to arrange access for those without family. There is also a problem for those without continuous employment, who may not be able to save enough to meet their subsequent needs. The higher the level of compulsory savings, the less the need for insurance, since large funds can pay for most needs, whereas small compulsory funds are likely to be depleted, and lead to a need for more insurance. Therefore the extent to which compulsory savings can be a substitute for health insurance depends on the required level of savings.

The most obvious advantages of compulsory savings systems, whether based on individuals, families, or local communities, are that the system is very transparent, and the ownership of health resources remains with those who save. Full access to care is not possible under compulsory savings, since there will always be people whose needs are greater than what can be afforded from their savings, so that there may be a requirement for complementary insurance. The real test will be how Medisave copes with the ageing population, and what measures are needed to cope with people (such as those who have no family or only intermittent employment) for whom the system fails to give adequate access to services.

Although there are no government plans for combined savings and insurance schemes in Singapore, some such mechanisms are emerging there, and it is likely that hybrid arrangements will be introduced, possibly by private insurers. There may come to be a particular need to have mechanisms to convert Medisave balances into insurance for single elderly people. Elements of compulsory savings are being discussed in other settings, such as in the medical aid schemes in South Africa and to complement social insurance in the Czech Republic.

It is suggested above that much of the challenge in health sector finance is the need to make resources available at the times when they are needed, and to some extent savings schemes can achieve this. They are likely to work best where incomes are relatively equal across the population, and where family or community ties are strong. Some health financing mechanisms aim to redistribute resources from richer to poorer. There is often confusion between two reasons for the absence of private medical insurance for poorer people— market failure and low incomes. The latter can be addressed only through some redistributive mechanism, whether or not this is part of a risk pooling (insurance) system. Much of the problem is not that the need is uncertain, but simply that, even given complete certainty, the cost of access to care is too expensive for many people to pay, even if payment can be spread over many years, and if risk and uncertainty are removed.

8.3. The Need for a Policy Environment

The debate about health sector reform, and in particular about alternative financing mechanisms for the health sector, is often conducted in the absence of a clear set of policy goals. The only way that alternative mechanisms can be properly compared and evaluated is to articulate the goals, and to analyse the alternative mechanisms in terms of their ability to meet the objectives.

Common versions of the goals of health policy are the two main dimensions of health—longer life and better quality of life—to be promoted by good public health services (such as environmental health), and widespread access to appropriate preventive health services and curative care. These goals would be most fully achieved by ensuring that access is on the basis of need, thereby securing the maximum potential impact of health services.

Resource constraints mean that it will never be possible to achieve the maximum possible health gain from services, but the objective of policy must be to make the greatest progress towards this objective. From the perspective of government, this allows a number of principles to be identified. First, any services that pay for themselves should be adopted, since these release resources. For example, services that prevent or reduce injuries from accidents can lower the need for treatment and care of accident victims, and thus be resource-releasing overall. Second, government resources should be spent to achieve the maximum health gain in terms of longer and better quality of life (however measured). Third, any other services that do some good, and that people are willing fully to pay for themselves, should be encouraged.

The logic of these three principles is that access to services will be based on a mixture of need and ability to pay. In most cases, maximizing the impact of health services conflicts with an objective of equal access for equal need. Some services are not sufficiently useful to justify public resources, but at the same time a number of people consider that the benefits justify the cost to themselves. Of course, even more would be achieved if these privately supplied additional resources were available for higher-priority uses, but that could not happen without the service purchased being supplied to the purchaser.

Despite the clear evidence to justify a greater priority for public health and primary care interventions in many countries, it is difficult in practice to redirect resources from secondary and tertiary care. Under these circumstances it can be important to analyse alternative financing systems in terms of their ability to shift resources, and especially government resources, towards their most effective use. It may be possible to change the basis of financing a service by, for example, shifting the burden to those who use it, even though it would not be feasible for the service to be discontinued. For example, it may be agreed that heart surgery is a low priority, and no further government funds should support it, but that those with insurance financing should still be allowed to buy it.

The political problems of removing government expenditure from low-priority health programmes should not be underestimated, because, normally, such programmes benefit relatively influential people. Perhaps more importantly, the general understanding among the population of the relative effectiveness of different health interventions is poor. Curative care is normally more visible and more plausible than public health and primary care interventions as sources of health gain, despite the evidence that the opposite is normally the case.

8.4. Financing as a Servant of Policy

There are some features of financing mechanisms that may be seen as desirable in themselves. Some would argue that they should be transparent, i.e. that they should allow choice or should encourage people to take responsibility for their health. However, it is important also to see financing mechanisms in terms of their role in helping to meet policy objectives. Debate about financing reform in many countries focuses on such features, but often fails to see the choice of financing mechanisms in terms of policy goals. There is no single financing mechanism that is clearly superior in terms of policy objectives, but it is possible to choose combinations of mechanisms that are likely to work better than others given the local circumstances and the declared goals of policy.

Managing inequity well means ensuring that differential access to services, and in particular the ability of those who can pay to get better services, does not adversely affect those on low incomes. There are many ways in which better services for some part of the population can lead to worse services for the rest. In particular, there is a risk of harm to care for poor people if there are government subsidies to all services, if there is a shortage of skilled human resources, if facilities are limited, or if there is a general rise in the cost of some inputs to health. Government subsidies come in many forms. For example, medical supplies (for whatever use) often enjoy preferential tax treatment, doctors are often trained at public expense, facilities are often built with subsidies, and funding for innovation and research can subsidize services. The importation of medical equipment in Thailand, using government subsidies, is an example of an incentive in the country's industrial policy being used to subsidize a particular type of health care.

Health services financed with private resources can divert skilled professionals away from providing other services which would generate a greater health gain. Staff can be diverted from primary care, and the cost of services can be bid up. It is therefore important to ensure that a policy of allowing managed inequity does not reduce the available resources for providing basic care. One simple test is whether or not there is spare capacity in the health sector (e.g. suitable facilities that are not in use, unemployed or underemployed professionals), since this can ensure that additional funding brings additional services. This kind of analysis has to look at components of the service and not simply the whole service.

The high cost of training health care professionals requires either that there is a subsidy to support training or that the incomes of professionals is high enough to pay for the training. If the state pays for the training, but the skills are then used for low-priority work, then the state is subsidizing this. It is very difficult in health to allow flexibility in the use of human resources, but to avoid subsidies to low-priority work. To an extent, this can be avoided by ensuring that the training subsidies are focused on skills needed for the provision of basic care.

The overall lesson is that it is generally desirable to allow additional resources to be spent on health, even if they will be used for relatively low priorities. However, the risk is that government resources are used to subsidize this relatively low-priority work, and can displace higher-priority work. The test that should be applied is whether the subsidy to any service could achieve more health gain if applied to another service.

8.5. Health Insurance—
Types, Options, and Constraints

Health insurance systems have one or more of the following objectives: spreading risk between individuals, mobilizing resources for health, and redistributing purchasing power. The market response to risk is insurance. Given an aversion to risk by the population (at least for certain types of risk), insurance benefits all those who participate. The most efficient insurance simply spreads risk. With perfect information about risks and costless markets, this can be achieved. On average participants in the system get out exactly what they put in (i.e. it is 'actuarially fair'). Compared with savings and self insurance, this approach is efficient, since it reduces the need to retain large balances in liquid forms. However, in reality there is imperfect ability to assess risk, and therefore there are some subsidies from lower to higher-risk individuals. Actuarially fair insurance allows individuals to buy the desired amount of goods for which the need is uncertain. It also serves as a mechanism to mobilize funds to pay for uncertain needs. It does not address the separate issue of limited access to care for poor people, since they cannot afford the premiums, and the system has no subsidies related to income. In practice, insurance markets do not work perfectly, since there are high costs of information for risk rating, so that few people are ever offered actuarially fair insurance. In extreme cases, no insurance market exists when risks rating is very costly (Akeloff 1970). Insurance can be expensive to administer (i.e. can have high transactions costs), owing not only to high costs of collecting and applying risk rating data, but also to the administration of claims.

Systems of insurance that require less information can be cheaper to operate. If access is to an agreed range of services, and all people pay the same premium (or at least pay a premium that is not rated for risk), then it is possible to have lower average premiums. Low-risk individuals lose relative to those with higher risks, but, if there is a sufficient saving in transaction costs, it can be in the interests of both high and low-risk people to limit or eliminate risk rating. Social health insurance operates on the basis that all those insured receive the same access to benefits, with no relationship between risk and the premium paid. In most social insurance schemes the premium is either fixed or paid as a proportion of salary. If the latter, there is a subsidy not only from low risk to high-risk members, but also from those on higher incomes to those on lower ones. The classic German style social insurance has contributions on the basis of ability to pay, and access to services on the basis of need.

Some systems of social insurance allow those on high incomes to opt out, and arrange their own insurance. This has the effect of weakening the degree of cross-subsidization in the system, since those who opt out have higher than average incomes, and a lower than average need for services. From the point of view of the insurance scheme, they are therefore ideal customers. In contrast to a tax financed system, where people opting out normally save the health services money, in the case of social insurance it is desirable from the point of view of the scheme to have no opt-out for those on high incomes.

Social insurance operates with no risk rating within the group covered by the scheme. However, it is possible to limit the degree of risk to the whole scheme by limiting the range of people who can become members. For example, a system for a professional group, such as lawyers, may be inherently less risky, since they have lower than average morbidity. A scheme for miners would have higher than average risk, and would therefore have higher than average premia. Countries that use social insurance as their main financing mechanism normally get round this by some system of levies on schemes for low risk people and subsidies for schemes for those with high risk. In principle, this means that the difference in the cost of insurance depends only on the efficiency of the insurance scheme, and not on the risks for those covered.

Social insurance has its origins in German industrial schemes in the nineteenth century (Kohler and Zacher 1982; International Labour Office 1984). Those covered were typically industrial workers, working for large companies. A levy on the payroll to provide social benefits was efficient and popular. It was cheap to collect, and there was little problem of compliance. A danger attending attempts to develop social insurance in developing countries is that the proportion of the population working in large, formal sector employment is typically small relative to the proportion working in agriculture and self employment. Alternative mechanisms for collection of funds may therefore be necessary, and it may not be possible to use payroll as the contributions base. The alternatives to payroll are likely to be a levy on the sale of agricultural products (especially seasonal ones), or on wealth (measured by land ownership), a fixed sum (regardless of income), or an amount related to taxable income.

Formal sector employment has several advantages for social insurance. In general, incomes are well defined and fairly stable. Large employers usually have information systems, payment systems, and systems for deducting taxes which can be adapted to assist with collection of contributions to social insurance. In contrast, it is always difficult to define the income of self-employed people, and their incomes frequently fluctuate. Incomes of people involved in farming vary with the climate, and income is normally received unevenly over the year. For all self-employed people there is some ambiguity between private income and income from the business. The effects are that it is difficult to assess the appropriate income-related contributions, and difficult and costly to collect contributions.

Measuring incomes in general is difficult and expensive. Evidence from Bulgaria (Bogetic and Hillman 1995: ch. 4) shows that the level of incomes of self-employed people is higher than is typically declared. However, income-related contributions depend on declared income. There are some advantages in trying to link contributions to a point in the cash-flow of small businesses. An example of this is the suggestion that contributions of cocoa farmers in Ghana could be collected as a levy on the sales of cocoa. In Hungary the health insurance fund found that many self-employed people declared an income which required payment only of the minimum contribution. The cost of collection of contributions is also important, and may mean that social insurance is too expensive to use in countries with poorly developed infrastructure or a large informal sector. In more developed country cases it is often possible to use an existing collection system, such as income tax or pension contributions, to collect health insurance payments.

8.6. Social versus Private—Solidarity Based or Risk Based

Health insurance can help in achieving health policy goals by increasing the overall resources for health, and by allowing existing resources to be used more effectively. Market failure limits the scope for private, actuarial insurance to achieve these goals, although there are some parts of the population in most countries that can and will seek private insurance. Private insurance schemes will inevitably aim to insure people with high incomes and relatively low needs. However, it is likely that some of the work that would be financed on private insurance would otherwise have been paid for by the state, so that private insurance can play a useful role in part-funding health care.

It is easier to envisage a significant role for social insurance in financing health care in developing countries, since the population who can make some additional contribution to resources through this mechanism is larger than for private insurance. Significant problems will remain, especially if the contributions base chosen is the payroll, since coverage and compliance will be limited. However, it is quite possible to use a range of ways for assessing contributions.

An additional advantage of social insurance, which is clearly important, but not easy to analyse, is the way in which some of the equity and cost-control features of state funding are combined with the traditions of insurance. Analytically, social insurance can look very similar to a system of tax finance. Participants have little or no choice on membership and the level of contributions, so that these are analytically similar to taxation. Benefits depend on need and not the level of contributions, which is common in tax-financed systems. However, the attitudes and rhetoric of social insurance can be more like private insurance (Normand 1992). The main ways in which this is seen are in the existence of specified rights, choices of where to be treated and by whom, and more participation in decision-making than is normal in tax-financed systems.

8.7. Coverage

The size and configuration of the formal sector can partly determine the scope for the development of health insurance. Estimates of the proportion of the population that could be covered by social insurance vary, but normally the starting point is the size of the formal sector and other organized groups. Even here it is not always clear which parts of the formal sector will be in a position to deliver social insurance.

If social insurance is to be considered within existing structures, it is likely that the easy-to-cover groups will comprise around 10–25 per cent of the population in developing countries (Bendahou *et al.* 1994). Many of these will already have some form of health insurance cover, for example senior government officials and members of armed forces. In South Africa a significant proportion of those in the formal sector are already covered by the medical aid schemes. One approach is therefore for social insurance to be developed around these existing schemes, providing a framework for their future development, and bringing in a wider range of members. As currently envisaged, social insurance has little to offer as a mechanism for subsistence or near subsistence farmers, self-employed people on low incomes, and the dependants of these people. However, this view is challenged by Arhin (1995), who reports a significant willingness to pay for health insurance, making it more likely that locally operated and controlled schemes could be made to work. Testing this would require carefully monitored experiments, since declared willingness to pay may, or may not, be real.

8.8. Access to Care for Insured

Health insurance is unlikely to offer a mechanism for universal coverage in developing countries, but both private and social insurance may play a useful role in supplementing other sources of revenue. I have suggested that the services financed by insurance will not be those that make the largest impact on the health of the population, but that they may, nevertheless, make a valuable contribution. The risk is that the relatively low-priority services are provided at the expense of those with higher priority, owing to the interaction of insurance financing and services financed within other schemes. This section considers the options for the provision of services, and how it may be possible to avoid insurance-funded developments damaging care for those most in need.

The choices for provision of services as between public and private sources should depend on their quality, their efficiency, and their relative costs. In addition, if services are to be provided on contract, there are needs for new legal frameworks, infrastructure, and skills to work within this model. The quality of services is important *per se*, but also in terms of persuading people to enrol in health insurance: if the volume and quality of services is the same whether or not insurance is bought, there is no incentive to join. However, even quite small improvements, such as good supplies of essential drugs, or quicker access to care, may be enough to encourage people to enrol. People enrolling in health insurance can release resources for those who do not, and so services can thereby be improved for both the insured and the uninsured.

Evidence on the efficiency of government, private for-profit, and non-profit providers is not clear. Government providers have often been so badly funded that it is difficult to judge how efficient they are. In some senses the comparisons are not important in a system of multiple sources of funding, since the best option is likely to be services provided on contract by public or private providers. Although the ownership of service providers is probably not very important, the form of the contract between funders and providers is, since it is that which determines the nature of care for the insured population. Costs, access to care, and quality of care are all likely to be affected by the form of contract for the supply of services. This will also be important in terms of the likely effects on services provided for those not covered by insurance. This is because the effective control of costs in the services provided under insurance may be important in containing overall health sector costs and therefore access.

It was suggested above that there are advantages in the provision of services on contract, whether by public or private providers. In some cases there is vertical integration of care, and a single organization will offer to collect contributions and provide care. The health maintenance organizations in the USA are examples of this. There are various different types of vertical integration: some are involved in all insurance and services work, and others operate joint finance and access (US Congress Office of Technology Assessment 1995). There can be efficiencies gained from integrating primary and secondary care. Since the same institution is paying, there is no advantage in shifting the costs from primary to secondary care providers or vice versa, thereby providing an incentive to provide care in the lowest cost setting. There is a danger in the integration of financing and services that the organization becomes dominated by provider interests.

Detailed analysis of the effects of different payment mechanisms shows that there is no one correct way to pay providers, but there some principles to follow (Normand and Weber 1994). The most important lesson is that any system of payment that has no overall budget limit will be associated with cost escalation. Although it may be possible to use financial incentives to achieve particular service delivery and behaviours, this should always be within the framework of overall financial limits. A second general principle is to keep the relationship as simple as possible. Payment systems based on very detailed classification of activities use significant resources in doing so, and there is no evidence that this avoids strategic behaviour by providers.

8.9. Services for Those without Insurance

Countries that use social insurance as the main mechanism for financing health care have to have mechanisms to provide cover for those who are young, retired, or unemployed. Normally this is a mixture of tax funding and payment from other social protection systems (pensions, unemployment insurance). Where insurance provides access for only part of the population, it is necessary to have some alternative that provides services for the remainder (probably the majority). There is a potential problem that the attraction of insurance may be better access to care, and good access for everyone therefore may undermine attempts to attract people to insurance.

The main options for those not covered are government funding, fees and charges, and various forms of community financing. Some form of community financing has elements of social insurance, and it may be possible to have common features between social insurance schemes for those in formal sector employment and some community financing. Since a major objective of insurance is often to find alternative financing for services currently provided by government, in principle there is then increased scope for government finance for services for those not insured. Politically it can be possible to remove state support for activities that benefit the relatively rich if alternative financing is put in place. It should therefore be possible for governments to redirect resources away from current uses. The scope for this may be limited, where government pays little of the cost of relatively low-priority services.

However, analysis of the patterns of government finance in many developing countries shows that more than half of the public funds are spent on services that are specified as low priority by government. Analysis of expenditure in South Africa shows how difficult it is in practice to move the resources, but it also indicates the potential gains from such policies (McIntyre *et al.* 1995). Recent (unpublished) work by the Health Economics

Unit in the Ministry of Health in Bangladesh indicates that there is scope for making more effective use of the government resources spent on health, and that better access to essential care would be possible with existing resources.

There have been many studies on the impacts of user fees (Gertler *et al.* 1987; Stanton and Clemens 1989; Waddington and Enyimayew 1989), and more recently of the mechanisms used in the Bamako Initiative where rural communities are required to pay part of the costs of care (McPake *et al.* 1993). For some parts of the population there is evidence that access can be improved using these mechanisms, although it is difficult to avoid some disincentives to use for those with very low incomes. Universal access for those without insurance will require at least some subsidy from government. Perhaps a more significant difficulty in giving access to care for those without insurance is to avoid the care being of very poor quality. Services specifically for the very poor are often poor services, staffed by relatively unsuccessful professionals, with low motivation and often supported by poor facilities, equipment, and access to drugs. A major advantage of providing access to care as insured people (but with the insurance paid by government) is that these problems can be avoided.

8.10. Conclusion

Social insurance provides near universal cover in some countries, but this is unlikely to be feasible in most developing countries. The reasons for this are that too many people work in the informal sector, income is too unequally distributed, and collection costs are too high. However, as a partial mechanism it can have a useful role. It is at its best in the relatively small formal sectors, and is most difficult and expensive to use in subsistence or near subsistence farming. However, modifications of the approach can be more widely applicable. There is a need for countries to analyse the potential role of social insurance within a framework of clear policy goals. The objective should be to manage inequity in such ways as to minimize the problems for those worst off, but not to try to give equal access to care for all.

The scope for private insurance is generally less than that for social insurance, so only very small parts of the population can be offered cover via this route. However, it is important to consider who are the people for whom cover would be provided, since they may be able to generate resources out of proportion to their numbers. If private insurance pays for those with high incomes, it may be possible to divert some of this resource to help meet other health policy goals.

Finally, the great diversity both between and within countries makes it difficult to identify a single financing mechanism that can satisfactorily provide access to care for all of the population in low and middle-income countries. It is therefore likely that a more complex pattern is needed, with elements of social insurance being present in many cases.

References

Akeloff, G. (1970) 'The market for "lemons" ', *Quarterly Journal of Economics*, 84: 488–500.

Akin, J. (1986) *Fees for Service and Concern for Equity for the Poor*, Technical Note Series. Washington, DC: World Bank.

Arhin, D. (1995) *Rural Health Insurance: A Viable Alternative to User Fees?* PHP Publication no. 19. London: London School of Hygiene and Tropical Medicine.

Arrow, K. J. (1963) 'Uncertainty and the welfare economics of medical care', *American Economic Review*, 53: 941–73.

Bendahou, T., Mach, E., Normand, C., and Cichon, M. (1994) *Health Care Under Social Security in Africa: Taking Stock of Experience and Potential*. Geneva: International Labour Office.

Bogetic, Z. and Hillman, A. (1995) *Financing Government in the Transition: Bulgaria*. Washington, DC: World Bank

Committee of Inquiry into a National Health Insurance System (1995) *Restructuring the National Health System for Universal Primary Health Care*. Pretoria: Department of Health.

Foster, S., Normand, C., and Sheaff, R. (1994) 'Health care reform: the issues and the role of donors', *The Lancet*, 344: 175–7.

Gertler, P., Locay, L., and Sanderson, W. (1987) 'Are user fees regressive? The welfare implications of health care financing proposals in Peru', *Journal of Econometrics*, 36: 67–88.

Hurst, J. (1991) 'Reforming health care in seven European nations', *Health Affairs*, 10(3): 7–21.

International Labour Office (ILO) (1984) *Introduction to Social Security*. Geneva: ILO.

KEMPOREN (National Federation of Health Insurance Societies) (1992) *Health Insurance and Health Insurance Societies in Japan*. Tokyo: KEMPOREN.

Kohler, P. and Zacher, H. (1982) *The Evolution of Social Insurance 1881–1981*. London: Francis Pinter.

Kwon, S. W. (1991) 'Distributional consequences of national health insurance in Korea', Korea Development Institute Working Paper no. 9110, Seoul.

McIntyre, D., Bloom, G., Doherty, J., and Brijlal, P. (1995) *Health Expenditure and Finance in South Africa*. Durban: Health Systems Trust and World Bank.

McPake, B., Hanson, K., and Mills, A. (1993) 'Community financing of health care in Africa: an evaluation of the Bamako Initiative', *Social Science and Medicine*, 36: 1383–95.

Normand, C. (1991) 'Economics, health and the economics of health', *British Medical Journal*, 303: 1572–7.

—— (1992). 'Funding health care in the United Kingdom', *British Medical Journal*, 304: 768–70.

—— and Weber, A. (1994) *Social Health Insurance: A Development Guidebook*, Geneva: World Health Organisation and International Labour Organisation.

Stanton, B. and Clemens, J. (1989) 'User fees for health care in developing countries: a case study of Bangladesh', *Social Science and Medicine*, 29: 1199–205.

Thomason, J., Mulou, N., and Bass, C. (1994) 'User charges for rural health services in Papua New Guinea', *Social Science and Medicine*, 39: 1105–15.

US Congress Office of Technology Assessment (1995) *Hospital Financing in Seven Countries*, OTA-BP-H-148. Washington, DC: US Government Printing Office.

Waddington, C. and Enyimayew, K. (1989) 'A price to pay: the impact of user charges in Ashanti-Akim district, Ghana', *International Journal of Health Planning and Management*, 4: 17–47.

World Bank (1993) *World Development Report*. Washington, DC: World Bank.

9

Financing Rural Health Services: Lessons from China

GERALD BLOOM

9.1. Introduction

There has been a considerable international effort to develop strategies for financing rural health services in poor and middle-income countries.[1] A number of options have been put forward which can be categorized by both source of revenue and institutional arrangements for fund management. The sources of revenue include national and local taxes, direct charges to patients, voluntary or compulsory prepayments earmarked for health, and transfers by international donors to health services. Possible financial managers include the government, formal sector bodies such as social security schemes, and community organizations.

Assessments of the above options have tended to ignore contextual issues such as strategies for reform of public finance, the public sector management system, the legal status of public and private institutions, the effectiveness of regulation, and the degree of social inequality (Bloom 1991; Kutzin 1995). As a result, writing on the issue of health finance in developing countries often has an abstract quality.

The aim of this paper is to demonstrate how the health sector is influenced by its environment, using China as an example. It begins by describing the organization of China's rural health services during the period of the command economy and outlining how they have been affected by the major economic

This paper has greatly benefited from the author's participation in the programme of research on rural health finance in which the School of Public Health of Shanghai Medical University and the Institute of Development Studies are collaborating. This work is funded by the International Health Policy Programme, the International Development Research Council of Canada, the British Council, and the Overseas Development Administration of the UK. I would like to acknowledge the useful notes on the original paper by Sara Bennett and the very helpful comments made by Christopher Colclough at several stages during the drafting process.

[1] The World Bank (1987, 1993) has published two major reports. There is now a large literature on the role of user charges (see Ch. 2 above), community financing (Abel Smith and Dua 1988), and insurance schemes (Ron et al. 1990 and Ch. 8 above).

and institutional reforms that have taken place. It then discusses the co-operative health care schemes, which the government had hoped would solve the problem of rural health finance, and seeks explanations for the failure of these schemes to spread. It concludes by highlighting the lessons to be learned about strategies for financing rural health services. $>$

9.2. China's Rural Health Services Before and After the 1980s

9.2.1. Rural health services in China's command economy

Prior to the economic reforms of the late 1970s, Chinese society was dominated by three institutions: the state bureaucracy, rural communes, and the Communist Party. The state bureaucracy, which included the large state-owned enterprises, was organized according to the principles of the command economy. The government was organized into national, provincial, and county levels. The national government set prices and levels of pay and controlled all investment decisions. Enterprises and lower levels of government were expected to fulfil plan targets and, in the case of the former, to transfer profits to the centre. The rural areas were organized into communes which managed collective production. They used a portion of their output to finance investment and local services, and distributed the remainder to their members in proportion to the number of workpoints they had accumulated. Members of a commune earned workpoints for time spent on collective activities. The number of points earned per hour or day varied with the task undertaken. The Communist Party played an important role in economic and social activities. Its cadres directly influenced decision-making in all institutions. The politicization of economic life reached its apogee during the late 1960s and early 1970s, when the Cultural Revolution put 'politics in command'.

By the end of the 1970s, the so-called 'three-tier health services' were well established throughout most of rural China. Approximately 85 per cent of villages had a health station staffed by one or more 'barefoot doctors'[2] who provided a combination of curative and preventive services; the township health centres provided referral services and supervised the village health workers; and the county health bureaux, the lowest level of the government system, planned and supervised the county's health services. A number of public health campaigns were organized under the technical leadership of the Ministry of Public Health (MoPH) and the political leadership of the Communist Party, which played an important role in mobilizing the population (Sidel and Sidel 1973).

---

[2] 'Barefoot doctors' were peasants who were given a short training course and then returned to their villages. They led local preventive programmes and public health campaigns and provided basic curative care. They worked part-time in health work and the rest of the time in agricultural production and were paid a share of collective production like all other commune members.

The three-tier health network provided a combination of preventive services and curative care for almost all of the rural population. This contributed, along with a number of other factors, to a dramatic improvement in health, in which life expectancy at birth rose from 35 years during the 1940s to 69 in 1990 (Ahmad and Hussain 1991; World Bank 1993; and Xu 1985).

Both the government and the communes supported the rural health services financially. The former paid the salaries of government employees and covered some of the operating costs of county-level facilities and preventive programmes. The latter paid non-government health workers, notably the barefoot doctors, a share of agricultural output much like any other member of the collective. Preventive services and consultations with barefoot doctors were supplied free or at very low cost, but patients purchased their own drugs and paid relatively low service charges for curative care at township and county-level facilities (Yu 1992). A portion of the charges was reimbursed by local co-operative medical schemes that were funded by the communes.

Health services for formal sector workers were funded quite differently. State-owned enterprises and the government paid for the medical care of their employees and, in some cases, their dependants, through the public sector medical scheme or labour insurance. These schemes, referred to collectively in this paper as 'work-related insurance', paid almost the entire cost of both outpatient and inpatient care. This care cost over four times as much per person as the rural health services, and covered 118 million people (excluding dependants) in 1981 (Prescott and Jamison 1984).

9.2.2. The impact of the transition to a socialist market economy

Since the late 1970s, China has been evolving from a command economy to what its political leaders refer to as a 'socialist market economy'. This has involved, among other things: a shift from collective to household agricultural production; the phasing out of price controls; the reform of state-owned enterprises to allow them to retain profits and give them independence from bureaucratic and political interference; the phasing out of job security and introduction of profit-related bonuses; the development of private and collectively owned enterprises; and the devolution of tax authority and public sector financial management.

The transition has taken place against a background of rapid economic growth, in which the gross national product increased by 9 per cent a year, in real terms, between 1978 and 1992 (SSB 1993). This growth has been uneven, and both inter- and intra-regional inequalities have increased (Howes and Hussain 1994). This paper focuses particularly on the poorest areas, where 10–15 per cent of the population lives. The following paragraphs outline the effect of these economic and institutional changes on the rural health services.

Increases in the cost of health care

The cost of rural health care has increased rapidly owing to rises in health worker pay, a growth in drug spending, and, in the richer areas, an increasing use of expensive technologies. The real pay of health care, sports, and social welfare workers increased by 84 per cent between 1981 and 1993 (Bloom *et al.* 1995).[3] In the richer areas average health sector earnings have grown more slowly than in sectors with fully deregulated prices. However, in poor areas health worker salaries have grown much more rapidly than average peasant income. This reflects the growing inequalities between industrialized and underdeveloped areas.

Drug expenditure has increased rapidly (Yu 1992). This is due partly to price rises, which were slightly greater than the rise in the consumer price index (SSB 1993), and also due to an increase in the amount of drugs prescribed and a greater use of expensive products.[4] The 15–20 per cent mark-up on drug prices has encouraged health facilities and individual practitioners to prescribe a large number of products (Zhan 1997). In addition, the increase has been encouraged by the termination of the State Pharmaceutical Company's monopoly of drug production. Many expensive drugs, often produced by joint ventures with foreign companies, are now on the market. This has made it possible to treat certain conditions more effectively, but there are many examples of expensive and dangerous drugs being used when cheaper, safer products would have been just as good.

Another factor behind the cost increases is the growing use of expensive technologies. Provincial price bureaux have kept fees for routine medical services low in order to minimize financial barriers to care. However, charges tend to be high for investigations or treatments not widely available prior to the 1980s (World Bank 1990). This has encouraged facilities to acquire new equipment. For example, Shanghai's hospitals have more than 30 CAT scanners (equipment for carrying out specialized X-ray examinations). Many smaller hospitals are also upgrading the sophistication of their equipment, for example purchasing powerful X-ray machines, ultrasound equipment, and automated laboratory equipment.

Increased reliance on user charges

Government funding of health services has lagged behind the salary increases. Hospitals and health centres derive an increasing share of their budgets from

---

[3] The basic salaries of government employees are set on a national scale and individual facilities top them up with a bonus, the size of which depends on their financial situation.

[4] Gu *et al.* (1995*b*) report that drug spending by county hospitals in three poor counties in 1992 was four or more times the levels in 1981. After the increase in the pharmaceutical price index was taken into account, this was equivalent to almost a doubling of the value of drugs used in two of the hospitals and a much greater increase in the third. Health centres also reported substantial increases, but not as large as the hospitals.

fees for services and the sale of drugs. For example, a study of three poor counties by Gu *et al.* (1995*b*) found that between 1981 and 1992 the contribution of user charges to facility budgets rose from 63 to 78 per cent for county hospitals and from 61 to 74 per cent for township health centres.

The charges to patients have risen substantially. For example, in two poor counties the real charge for an average outpatient visit (including drugs) rose by 20 per cent at health centres and 80 per cent at hospitals between 1981 and 1992. The real charge for an average admission to a county hospital rose by 450 per cent.[5]

Most villages no longer pay their local health workers a salary, and the majority of co-operative medical schemes have collapsed. One reason for this is that township governments and village committees no longer retain a share of agricultural production and have been unable to raise enough taxes to compensate (Shue 1984; Kelliher 1992). In addition, there has been a political reaction against institutions established during the Cultural Revolution.

In many parts of the country, the only government support for village health services are the small payments made to health workers for preventive work. In 1987, 94 per cent of the income of health stations in moderately poor counties came from patients (Tang *et al.* 1994). Most village health workers depend on consultation fees and profits from drug sales to finance their health work.[6]

Increased autonomy of health service providers

Administrative and political authorities have less influence over health service providers than previously. First, the government has radically devolved financial management. Each tier funds its own facilities, so that provinces fund referral hospitals, counties fund general hospitals, and townships fund health centres. The only money provided by national or provincial health departments for rural health services are construction grants and subsidies for preventive programmes. Higher levels no longer determine expenditure plans or set compulsory performance targets, and the vertical lines of authority are much weaker.

Second, government has reduced the power of members of administrative and political structures to interfere in the management of enterprises (Hussain 1990). Enterprises retain their profits and use them to finance investments and pay bonuses or fringe benefits to their employees. Managers of health facilities have powers similar to managers in other sectors.

Third, political factors are less important to the health services than during

[5] Preliminary analysis of data collected by the Shanghai Medical University during 1993.

[6] A preliminary analysis of a survey carried out by the School of Public Health of the Shanghai Medical University of a sample of 38 village health workers in three poor counties show that they derived over 55% of their income from agriculture and other activities, over 35% from user fees and profits from drug sales, and less than 10% from payments for preventive work and salaries (personal communication by Zhan Shao-kang).

the 1970s. One of the most important reasons for this is the shift to household agricultural production, which has meant that people no longer have to participate in mass health campaigns without pay. In addition, there has been a reaction against the intensive political mobilization that took place during the Cultural Revolution. Barefoot doctors used to be answerable to local political leaders, but rural doctors are now almost entirely free from supervision. The same is true, although to a lesser extent, of staff in the higher levels in the health service.

9.2.3. Summary of the main problems in the health sector

A number of problems have come to prominence over the past few years. The urban areas have experienced rapid increases in medical costs. Between 1980 and 1988, real expenditure per enrolled member grew by 9 per cent a year for the public service medical scheme and 5 per cent a year for labour insurance (Tang *et al.* 1994). This is due partly to the ageing of the population, but also to a system of payment which encourages hospitals to use sophisticated equipment and to sell a high volume of drugs. Rich rural areas, which tend to be in good communication with a city, have also experienced increases in health expenditure. For example, one county recently reported that its co-operative health care scheme had collapsed as a result of rapid rises in claims for hospital care.[7]

The dominant problems in the poor areas are the inability of people to pay for the health care they need, and the financial difficulties of service providers. Most residents of poor counties have easy access to a village health worker; for example, Tang *et al.* (1994) found similar numbers of outpatient visits per capita in rich and poor areas. However, the poor are less likely to consult a qualified doctor at township or county level when they fall ill and many find it difficult to purchase a full course of drugs (Croll 1994; Tang *et al.* 1994). This is because charges have risen faster than inflation, while at the same time the collapse of the co-operative medical schemes has meant that peasants are no longer reimbursed for a portion of their medical costs.

Many people cannot afford inpatient treatment. This is illustrated by a household survey which found that 45 per cent of people referred to a hospital or health centre in the poor counties were not admitted because of its cost (Tang *et al.* 1994).

Many health centres in poor areas are run down and poorly equipped. Their government grants no longer fund even their salary costs; however, they are under pressure to maintain staffing levels. A recent study of health centres in three poor counties found that they had cut spending on maintenance and

---

[7] Report from Yuhang County to a workshop on the management of CHCSs held in Shanghai, September 1993.

consumable inputs in order to pay their staff (Gu *et al.* 1995*b*). Many health centres in poor townships provide fewer services than during the 1970s because they have lost qualified personnel (Gu *et al.* 1995*a*).

In many poor villages, the local health workers have become private healers and drug sellers. Often they cannot afford equipment. Most of them earn much more money from treating patients and providing them with drugs than from preventive work. The preventive programmes have deteriorated in some poor areas. For example, in one poor county, immunization levels fell from 85 to below 50 per cent between 1989 and 1992 (Tang *et al.* 1995*b*). The programmes to prevent schistosomiasis and treat tuberculosis have also become less effective in some areas.

9.3. Co-operative Health Care Schemes (CHCSs)

The response of the MoPH to the financial problems of the rural health services has been to encourage townships and villages to replace the collapsed co-operative medical schemes with co-operative health care schemes (CHCSs).[8] The transition from a collective to a market economy, it was first thought, made it necessary for the health sector to replace schemes financed out of collective funds with voluntary medical insurance.

The government aims to have 70 per cent of the rural population enrolled in a scheme by the year 2000 (MoPH 1991). However, by 1994 only 7 per cent of villages were covered by a CHCS (Bloom *et al.* 1995). The slow expansion of coverage, coupled with the fact that the majority of successful CHCSs could not be accurately characterized as 'voluntary insurance', suggest that the policy was based on an overly simplistic view of the functioning of the market for health care services (Evans 1984; Hsiao 1994). In particular, government has to ensure that health services are adequately funded and that they provide the population with access to an appropriate mix of safe and effective services.

9.3.1. What are CHCSs?

CHCSs are third-party payers; that is to say, they collect money and disburse it directly to health service providers or to service users as reimbursement for medical care payments. They share a number of characteristics (Tang *et al.* 1994; Feng *et al.* 1995). They are organized on a not-for-profit basis and most are managed by township or village-level committees. They derive revenue from several sources including household contributions and grants from

---

[8] There is no commonly accepted terminology for the wide variety of schemes that have emerged over the past decade. Tang *et al.* (1994) advocate the use of the term 'co-operative health care scheme' to distinguish them from the co-operative medical schemes of the pre-reform era.

township governments or village welfare funds. Most cover both outpatient and inpatient care but some cover only inpatient treatment. Some schemes provide free services to their members, but mostly they reimburse members for the money they spend on medical care. Members can generally claim only a portion of their costs, and there is usually a ceiling beyond which the scheme will not pay.

9.3.2. Sources of finance for CHCSs

Voluntary versus compulsory household contributions

Membership of a CHCS is voluntary in law. In practice, however, most schemes have an element of compulsion, in the form of pressure by local political leaders. This is illustrated by Tang *et al.* (1994), who found that, in more than three-fifths of villages with a scheme, over 90 per cent of the population was enrolled. One would expect to find more villages where a smaller proportion were members, if households could decide each year whether they wished to contribute. The success of a scheme appears to depend on the ability of local leaders to ensure that people join and remain in it for several years. Eklund and Stavem (1990) reported a similar finding in Guinea Bissau.

A number of explanations have been put forward as to why voluntary insurance has not established itself as a means of financing health services in most industrialized countries (Belsley 1994). One is so-called 'selection bias'—the preferences of healthy people not to pay for coverage, and of the aged and sick to do so. Another is the resistance by better-off households to membership of a scheme in which contribution size is linked to household income. A third is the inability of the poor to pay the full cost of their care. These factors may have retarded the growth of voluntary schemes in rural China. Contributions to CHCSs will continue to require an element of compulsion in future. Their success will depend on the commitment of local leaders to the provision of health services and on the trust of the population in the ability of these leaders to provide a reasonable service.

Should CHCSs be regarded as social insurance?

Contributions to local health prepayment schemes could, in theory, be set at a level that spreads the average cost of medical care over an average contributor's life cycle. This is the principle underlying the design of social security. It is difficult in China to persuade peasants to make larger contributions than the value of the benefits they expect to receive during the following year. Household contributions usually account for less than half of the cost of local health services in areas with a CHCS; the rest is financed out of contributions by village welfare funds, township governments, and the county health bureau. This is hardly surprising in a country that has undergone major upheavals, and where people cannot be certain that local governments will honour their commitments. This is one reason why most successful CHCSs complement household contributions with funds derived from other sources. Similar considerations apply to other countries undergoing major economic and political change, where it could take years to create confidence in social insurance institutions.

General taxes or earmarked contributions

As outlined above, household contributions to a CHCS are not simply voluntary insurance premiums or social security contributions. They are a form of earmarked quasi-taxation, or community financing. They are not part of a formal tax system, and contributions are not required by law. However, they are collected by township governments or village committees, and peasants are under pressure to contribute. The money collected is paid into a special fund in exchange for entitlements to specific services. The reason for this is linked to general considerations with regard to local government finance.

The national leadership has been unwilling to take the political risk of imposing high enough taxes on peasants to replace the revenue lost when the communes were dissolved (Shue 1984, Kelliher 1992). Townships and villages have responded by introducing levies to finance local services, hoping that peasants will be more willing to pay contributions earmarked for specific activities. These revenues are called 'extra-budgetary' because there are no legal sanctions for non-payment and the funds are managed separately from government revenue. In urging township governments to include CHCSs in their portfolio of levies, the MoPH is acting as an advocate for the local health services, since the national government has no direct influence on the use of extra-budgetary revenue.

The number of non-tax levies on peasant households proliferated during the early 1990s, and there has been serious resistance to paying them in some parts of the country. One reason is that some township governments do not provide value for money to the population. In mid-1993, the State Council made it illegal to impose levies of more than 5 per cent of peasant income. This underlines the links between the attempt to finance health through CHCSs and the effort to establish effective local governments.

In the context of the reform of local tax systems, it may be necessary to reassess the role of earmarked contributions. Although it may be easier to persuade peasants to pay contributions that are directly linked to specific services, international experience suggests such contributions create high administrative costs, reduce government's freedom to adjust resource allocation, and make it difficult to link the size of contributions to ability to pay (McCleary 1989).

Inter-regional inequalities in local government finance

The system of inter-provincial and inter-county fiscal transfers has ensured that all counties have basic levels of government service (World Bank 1989). However, the radical devolution of financial management has made it difficult to increase the amounts of money transferred between rich and poor regions, in spite of the growing inter-regional inequalities (Zuo 1997).

Governments in poor counties face considerable financial difficulties which have been exacerbated by the rapid salary increases.[9] The growing difference between public sector pay and average rural incomes in these areas has diminished the capacity of local governments to fund their budgets out of local tax revenue. According to Zuo (1995), a number of localities are trapped in the situation called 'Chi Fan Cai Zhen' (finance for living only), which means that the government budgets pay for little more than salaries. China needs to develop new models to ensure that basic public services are adequately funded in poor areas.

The rapid growth of non-agricultural rural enterprises has provided a major new source of revenue for township governments (Song and Du 1990). These enterprises pay management fees and a share of profits to the government that owns them, in addition to paying taxes. The importance of this source of extra-budgetary revenue is illustrated by the finding of Tang *et al.* (1994) that townships with CHCSs had higher levels of non-agricultural output than townships without them, in spite of the fact that average household incomes were similar.

The growth of non-agricultural enterprises has been much more rapid in the more developed parts of the country, where it may be possible fully to finance rural health and other services through a combination of user charges, household contributions, and allocations out of other sources of extra-budgetary revenue. In time, the extra-budgetary sources of revenue may evolve into a formal system of local taxation and/or social insurance.[10]

In areas that do not have substantial non-agricultural production, it may not be possible to finance basic services solely out of local resources. In that case, higher levels of government will have to channel additional funds to health and other services. China has established special anti-poverty programmes. Most of the funds are transferred to poor counties as low interest loans to be invested by local governments. Policy-makers in the health sector have begun to ask whether anti-poverty money should be spent on basic

---

9 For example, Gu *et al.* (1995*b*) report that the government of Donglan, a poor county in Guangxi Province, had to draw funds from the anti-poverty programme in order to pay its salary bills during 1992.

10 At a workshop in Suzhou City in December 1994, a report from Jiangsu Province stated that some joint ventures (with foreign partners) were no longer willing to transfer funds to local governments on an informal basis. This suggests the need in future to develop a formal taxation system.

health services. This would mitigate some of the short-term problems of rural health finance and prevent a damaging deterioration of basic services in very poor areas. However, in the longer term it would be impossible to sustain adequate levels of funding unless development led to improvements in local tax capacity or anti-poverty funding became institutionalized as part of a fiscal system which transfers substantial amounts to poor regions.[11] Local governments in the richer parts of the country are likely to resist substantial increases in inter-regional redistribution.

The second potential source of funds is the reallocation of the government health budget. National and provincial levels do not provide much money to the counties, and the counties transfer very little to townships or villages. The major exception is government funding of preventive programmes. All three levels could provide additional money for basic health services. However, this would have to be funded out of an increase in health budgets or by cuts in government grants to hospitals.

9.3.3. The relationship between CHCSs and health service providers

The pre-reform rural health services operated in a quasi-military manner which combined a tightly organized bureaucracy with political mobilization. For example, the preventive programmes were planned centrally and implemented locally, with technical leadership from the health bureaucracy and political backing from the Communist Party.[12] This system was extraordinarily successful in meeting the basic needs of the population using semi-skilled front-line health workers who performed clearly defined tasks under close supervision.

China is seeking an alternative to the bureaucratic/political model for inducing health service providers to deliver an appropriate mix of preventive and curative services at an affordable cost. Among the issues that it needs to address are the financial incentives for health workers, the planning and regulatory framework, and the mechanisms for making providers of health services accountable to the community.

Systems of payment and economic incentives

Prior to the economic reforms, government health workers brought their salary with them when assigned to a new facility. It is argued that this en-

---

[11] There are parallels between the re-thinking of the role of anti-poverty programmes in China and the increasing willingness of international donors to support the operating costs of basic health services in very poor countries (Smithson 1994; World Bank 1993).

[12] As in every other sector, detailed guidelines were formulated and quantitative targets were set; local administrative and political leaders were responsible for ensuring that targets were met.

couraged high levels of employment and low productivity, as in other sectors (Yu 1992). However, bureaucratic and political controls counterbalanced the economic signals, and it is generally acknowledged that the services were cost-effective.

Since 1980, health workers have become more responsive to economic incentives. This reflects a general change in social attitudes as well as a decrease in the influence of political and administrative controls. This has contributed to a shift in the balance of services in favour of increasingly expensive curative care.[13]

The design of the health insurance schemes for formal sector workers, in which beneficiaries are entitled to health care that is paid for largely by their employers on a fee-for-service basis, has contributed to increases in medical costs as a result of 'moral hazard' (Pauly 1986); neither users nor providers of services have an incentive to limit expenditure.

Most CHCSs have emulated the design of the work-related schemes except that patients are reimbursed directly and for only part of their costs. These schemes have experienced rapid increases in the value of claims and in some cases this has led to their collapse.[14] The most common response to this by CHCSs has been to lower the proportion of costs they reimburse (Cretin *et al.* 1990). This relieves financial pressures on them by shifting the burden to the patients. However, it achieves this by diminishing the value of the scheme to its members, while ignoring the reasons for the cost increase. China needs to follow the lead of most advanced market economies and shift its focus from measures aimed at decreasing demand for services, to those that influence provider behaviour.

Experiments are under way with alternatives to fee-for-service payment. In some counties rural doctors are paid a salary by their village or the township health centre. A number of provinces have introduced child health schemes in which parents pay a fixed sum to the health service for a full course of immunization for a child (Zi 1990). The most interesting innovations concern the design of payment mechanisms which reward good-quality work. For example, the immunization schemes include the imposition of a cash penalty if a child develops one of the diseases against which it should have been immunized. There have also been attempts to link the size of bonuses for health centre employees to the achievement of performance targets. The design of systems of payment that encourage appropriate patterns of service delivery is an important area for future work.

[13] The increases in cost apply even to the village health stations that used only a small number of drugs during the 1970s. Rural health workers can now order anything they wish except narcotics and major tranquillizers. The profits they earn from drug sales are an important source of income. This has led to over-use of powerful (and expensive) antibiotics which can have serious side-effects, and of tonics and vitamins which do neither harm nor good. On the other hand, in some areas there has been a decrease in village-level preventive work.

[14] For example, the collapse of the schemes in Yuhang and Penan Counties was reported to a workshop for managers of CHCSs in Shanghai in September 1993.

The planning and regulatory framework

In order to make the best use of health care technology, people must trust health workers to act in their patients' best interest (Arrow 1963). The agency function of health workers is an important reason for the complex regulatory systems in the health sectors of most advanced market economies. The freedom of health workers in those countries to respond to economic incentives is limited by a web of controls enforced by professional organizations, regulatory bodies of the state, and the legal system (Luft 1983). Health workers also function within a cultural, political, and professional environment which ensures that they balance their well-being against that of their patients and society. China has not made much progress in establishing an effective regulatory system to replace the previous reliance on bureaucratic and political controls.

Under the command economy, the rural health services had an impressive information system whereby public health programmes defined indicators of service delivery; resource use was documented in county, provincial, and national plans; and regular reports were transmitted up the administrative system to enable them to assess implementation.[15] The performance of health service providers was monitored by higher levels in the government service and local political cadres.

Although the health services are still well managed in many parts of the country, supervisory relationships and data flows have been disrupted in other areas. Many county health bureaux do not have reliable information about the population's health or the activities of health service providers. Budgets submitted to them by hospitals and health centres under-report revenue generation, and village health workers do not make any financial reports in most areas. One of the most important steps towards a better regulated system would be the establishment of reliable reporting systems.

The problems that have arisen with the cost and quality of services demonstrate that the shift from the command economy to market socialism has not eliminated the need for social organization of the health sector. However, the weakness of the regulatory system is illustrated by the almost total lack of legal constraints on the sale of drugs. Even village health workers can sell any drug except narcotics and anti-psychotic tranquillizers, and they routinely prescribe dangerous antibiotics that are available only from hospital specialists in other countries. A regulatory framework needs to be established.

The establishment of legal controls has a limited effect on the behaviour of health service providers unless adherence to them is enforced. This is illustrated with regard to township health centres, whose contracts often stipulate the services to be provided. In practice, only the financial provisions are

---

[15] There are doubts about the accuracy of some data because local authorities may have exaggerated their achievement of targets.This is illustrated by the saying: 'The cadre makes the information and the information makes the cadre.'

routinely monitored because township governments do not have the capacity to assess the quality of health services and there is no political pressure on them to do so.

Another reason for the inadequate regulation of rural health services in poor areas is that county health bureaux and township health centres are under serious financial pressure. In many areas they provide almost no in-service training courses for village health workers, and they allocate little money for supervisory visits. Furthermore, the personnel responsible for monitoring preventive and curative services spend an increasing proportion of their time providing clinical services as a way of supplementing their department's income.

Making health services answerable to the population

Another reason for the slow spread of CHCSs has been a lack of confidence that they will meet the population's needs. In some schemes families of powerful individuals make larger claims for reimbursement than other members, and in others there has been a conflict about the allocation of funds between increasing health worker income and reimbursing patients for medical care.[16] Measures are needed to make local health services answerable to the population.

The management committees of many CHCSs include representatives of peasant committees, women's groups and local health workers, as well as senior administrators from township government and village committees. However, little is known about how the committees are selected and in whose interest they function. The government has recently enacted an Organic Law of Villagers Committees aimed at encouraging community participation in village management (O'Brien 1994). It is too early to determine whether this will make local services more accountable to the community.

9.4. Towards a Strategy for Rural Health Finance

During the period of the command economy, China's rural health services provided widespread access to preventive services and curative care. The transition to a market economy has revealed the many factors that influence the health sector. For example, the replacement of communes by townships has removed an important source of finance; the partial liberalization of the labour market has made it more difficult for poor rural areas to retain qualified health workers; and the privatization of village health workers is transforming barefoot doctors (leaders of public health programmes and

---

16 Presentation to a workshop of CHCSs held in Shanghai during September 1993.

providers of basic curative care) into rural doctors (semi-skilled healers and drug sellers).

The almost exclusive focus of government strategies on the establishment of new sources of revenue has proved to be too narrow an approach for adapting the rural health services to the market economy. It has become apparent that an unregulated market is neither a feasible nor a desirable alternative to the bureaucratic/political model of organization of health services. The state and/or other social organizations need to ensure that everyone has access to care and that health facilities provide an appropriate mix of safe and effective services.

China's experience of the adaptation of its rural health services to economic and institutional change is relevant to other countries. For example, many ex-colonies have state-financed health services provided by a centralized government bureaucracy. As in China, the health services in a number of these countries are experiencing constrained public finances, diminished control by government over services in the periphery, changes in public sector pay, and an altered relationship between public and private sectors.

One must be careful when comparing China with other parts of the world. For example, there is much greater inequality, and political and administrative structures tend to be weaker, in many countries of sub-Saharan Africa. None the less, there are parallels between the semi-privatization of health services in China's poor rural areas and the situation in much of rural Africa, where people have to pay for services and government health workers supplement their income by charging fees and selling drugs (in practice, if not in law).[17] In both areas, it will be necessary to re-establish suitable and appropriate systems of rural health finance and mechanisms for regulating the behaviour of health service providers.

9.4.1. Sources of finance

The immediate cause of the financial problems of China's rural health services is that local governments have not been able to collect enough tax to fund increases in public sector pay and, at the same time, compensate for the revenue lost because townships no longer retain a share of agricultural production. As in other countries, local governments in poor areas of China find it difficult to raise revenue from peasants. They also have trouble funding services whose cost includes relatively high salaries for skilled workers.

---

[17] In many African countries government salaries have fallen to very low levels. Health workers supplement their income by seeing private patients after hours, accepting bribes to give preferential treatment, or selling drugs which should be provided free of charge. Many of these revenue-generating activities are illegal and unregulated. However, they provide an essential source of income without which government health workers would not be able to survive. See Able Smith and Rawal (1992) for a description of the Tanzanian situation.

China's rural health services illustrate that a high proportion of health expenditure can be generated from user charges. However, as in other countries, these charges have created difficulties for the poor, who often cannot pay for a consultation with a doctor, a full course of drugs, or inpatient care. This highlights the need to keep charges low and/or to provide a safety net for the poor, particularly when, as in China, income inequalities are growing. The high level of dependence on user charges has also contributed to an increase in inter-regional differences in services, because facilities in poor areas have found it difficult to generate enough money.

The successful CHCSs illustrate that workable systems of health finance can include a combination of sources, such as user charges, general tax revenue, and local quasi-taxes (earmarked household contributions and other 'extra-budgetary' sources of revenue). The concept of quasi-taxation underlines the informal nature of many activities at township and village levels. Because of the lack of a clearly defined legal framework, township governments and village administrations bear some similarity to what are called 'community organizations' in other countries.

CHCSs are a transitional form, reflecting the informal nature of local government. The intention is that over time they will be integrated into a reformed system of finance and administration of local services. It is impossible to anticipate whether the future system of health finance will resemble tax funded services or social health insurance. The establishment of similar schemes in other countries should also be viewed in the context of the institutional development process. Their structure will depend upon the legal and administrative status of local governments and community organizations.

Most successful CHCSs are in areas experiencing rapid economic growth, where local governments generate substantial revenues from tax and quasi-tax. It has been much more difficult to finance health and other services in poor areas, where households are less able to pay levies and where governments can barely pay their salary bills. National or provincial governments will have to subsidize health services in these areas. A number of countries have experienced similar difficulties in funding services in poor localities after devolving responsibility for service delivery without transferring adequate sources of revenue (Bird and Wallich 1993; Cornia and Stewart 1990).

9.4.2. Planning, monitoring, and regulation of service delivery

China's strategy for rural health finance does not adequately take into account the influence of the system of finance on the behaviour of health service providers. There has been a shift towards an increasingly costly style of curative care as a result of a system of payment that discriminates against preventive services and basic curative care and an increased ability of health workers to respond to financial incentives.

Basic health services have deteriorated in some poor areas, largely as a result of financial problems. In addition, fragile administrative and political structures have been weakened by economic problems (Wang and Bai 1991). Furthermore, some local leaders have responded to the diminished influence of higher levels of government by acting in their own interest and neglecting the needs of the population. Village health workers in these areas tend to be less well trained, which, coupled with the strong incentives for them to concentrate on money-earning activities, makes the lack of supervision particularly undesirable.

Other developing countries face similar problems with inadequate regulation of the health sector. Many of them have deployed large numbers of semi-skilled health workers who were trained to function effectively in a hierarchical management system. Subsequently, their public health services have experienced economic problems, and, as a result, monitoring and supervisory systems have become weaker and health workers have had to supplement their government salaries by selling drugs or charging for services. A virtually unregulated (legal or illegal) private sector is emerging in many developing countries, particularly in sub-Saharan Africa.

9.4.3. The way forward

The experience of poor areas of China suggests that unregulated, poorly trained rural health workers do not provide a safe, effective service. It is difficult to define the form that an effective regulatory and incentive system should take. However, it is possible to identify some of its characteristics. First, preventive programmes need to be adequately funded and properly managed to ensure high levels of coverage.

Second, health workers need opportunities to earn an adequate living without selling large amounts of drugs. This may require a return to government-funded public sector salaries, or it may require local payments that reflect average incomes in the locality. In addition, it may be possible to link pay to the volume of work (for example the number of patients in a catchment area) and to measures of performance (such as the level of immunization and the hours that the health facility is open). In any case, the payment of health workers must be linked to a clear definition of the role they are expected to play. In some areas, it may not be possible to provide an adequate income for everyone currently employed by the health sector.

Third, a regulatory framework needs to be defined that establishes clear performance guidelines and specifies sanctions for failing to meet them. It is difficult to enforce regulations where administrative systems are weak and local leaders do not care about basic health services. The system will have to combine supervision by government employees, the establishment of professional regulatory bodies, and the creation of institutions that make local health service providers answerable to the population.

The principal message of the China case study is that rural health finance is strongly influenced by changes elsewhere in the health sector and in a country's economic, administrative, and regulatory system. It illustrates the close links between the funding of rural health services and the system of local government finance. It also demonstrates the need for effective governmental and community structures to monitor the behaviour of health workers.

The re-establishment of effective, low-cost, services in poor areas of China must take place in the context of a broader effort to create functioning township governments and to ensure that local services are accountable to the population. The same considerations apply to other countries, where strategies for financing rural health services must take into account the administrative and regulatory environment within which they are expected to operate.

The problems of rural health services also cannot be addressed in isolation from the rest of the health sector. The rapid growth of China's urban health services has had a negative effect on health services for the poor by attracting the best personnel out of the rural areas and by contributing to a change in attitudes to health care. The style of services provided to those covered by work-related insurance schemes is becoming the standard to which people living in neighbouring rural areas aspire.[18] This has contributed to a generalized increase in the cost of medical care.

There is a widening gulf between the sophisticated facilities that serve members of work-related insurance schemes and the disadvantaged health services in poor rural areas. A national strategy for slowing down this trend would have to include the reform of work-related health insurance schemes, to control costs and encourage the development of a cost-effective style of service, and the reallocation of public sector funds in favour of services for those not covered by insurance. It will be difficult to prevent further deterioration of health services in poor areas unless these measures are taken. The same applies to other countries where strategies for meeting the health care needs of the poor must include reforms in the financing of services used by the relatively privileged. The importance of this issue is related to the degree of inequality between a country's regions and social groups.

There is an increasing international interest in options for health sector reform, and many low and middle-income countries are considering alternative ways of organizing their health services. There is a danger that some of them will import strategies without adequately adapting them to the local

[18] There are interesting parallels with Latin America, where social security health schemes for formal sector workers have institutionalized inequalities by establishing an entitlement to a sophisticated style of health care for a minority of the population. In many Latin American countries the cost of care provided by such schemes has increased over time, and it has been difficult to extend coverage to other population groups (Mesa-Lago 1991; Ugalde 1985).

situation. They also may ignore the need to phase health sector reforms to take into account parallel changes in the rest of the economy. Poorly designed restructuring programmes can seriously damage rural health services. The lesson from China is that a reform strategy should be based on a thorough situation analysis that takes into account the economic and institutional context. This improves the chances that sectoral reforms will contribute to the establishment of adequately funded rural health services capable of meeting the population's needs.

References

Abel Smith, B. and Dua, A. (1988) 'Community financing in developing countries: the potential for the health sector', *Health Policy and Planning*, 3(2): 95–108.
—— and Rawal, P. (1992) 'Can the poor afford "free" health services? A case study of Tanzania', *Health Policy and Planning*, 7(4): 329–41.
Ahmad, E. and Hussain, A. (1991), 'Social security in China: a historical perspective', in E. Ahmad, J. Drèze, J. Hills, and A. Sen (eds.), *Social Security in Developing Countries*, Clarendon Press, Oxford.
Arrow, K. (1963) 'Uncertainty and the welfare economics of medical care', *American Economic Review*, 53(5): 941–73.
Belsley, P. (1994) 'The demand for health care and health insurance', in A. Mcguire, P. Fenn, and K. Mayhew (eds.), *Providing Health Care: The Economics of Alternative Systems of Finance and Delivery*, Oxford University Press, Oxford.
Bird, R. and Wallich, C. (1993) 'Fiscal decentralization and intergovernmental relations in transition economies', Policy Research Department Working Paper WPS 1122, World Bank.
Bloom, G. (1991) 'Managing health sector development: markets and institutional reform', in C. Colclough and J. Manor (eds.) *States or Markets? Neo-Liberalism and the Development Policy Debate*, Oxford University Press, Oxford.
—— Tang, S., and Gu, X. (1995) 'Financing rural health services in China in the context of economic reform', *Journal of International Development*, 7(3): 423–41.
Burgess, R. and Stern, N. (1991), 'Social security in developing countries: what, why, who and how?' in E. Ahmad, J. Drèze, J. Hills, and A. Sen (eds.), *Social Security in Developing Countries*, Clarendon Press, Oxford.
Byrd, W. and Gelb. A. (1990), 'Why industrialize? The incentives for rural community governments', in W. Byrd and Q. Lin (eds.), *China's Rural Industry: Structure, Development, and Reform*, Oxford University Press, Oxford.
Cornia, G. A., and Stewart, F. (1990), 'The fiscal system, adjustment, and the poor', *Innocenti Occasional Papers*, Report no. 11.
Creese, A. (1991), 'User charges for health care', *Health Policy and Planning*, 6(4): 309–19.
Cretin, S., *et al.* (1990) 'Modelling the effect of insurance on health expenditures in the People's Republic of China', *Health Services Research*, 25(4): 667–85.
Croll, E. (1994). *From Heaven to Earth: Images and Experiences of Development in China*, London: Routledge.

Eklund, P. and Stavem, K. (1990) *Prepaid Financing of Primary Health Care in Guinea Bissau: An Assessment of 18 Village Health Posts*, Africa Technical Department, World Bank, Washington, DC.

Evans, R. G. (1984) *Strained Mercy: The Economics of Canadian Health Care*, Butterworth, Toronto.

Feng, X., Tang, S., Bloom, G., Segall, M., and Gu, X. (1995) 'Cooperative medical schemes in contemporary rural China', *Social Science and Medicine*, 41(8): 111-18.

Gu, X. Y., Bloom, G., Tang, S., and Lucas, H. (1995*a*) 'Financing health services in poor rural China: a strategy for health sector reform', IDS Working Paper no. 17, Institute of Development Studies, Brighton.

———————(eds.) (1995*b*) 'Health expenditure and finance in three poor counties of China', IDS Working Paper no. 21, Institute of Development Studies, Brighton.

Howes, S. and Hussain, A. (1994), *Regional Growth and Inequality in Rural China*, Development Economics Research Programme, London School of Economics EF no. 11.

Hsiao, W. (1994), 'Marketization: the illusory magic pill', *Health Economics*, 6(3): 351-8.

Hussain, A. (1990) *The Chinese Enterprise Reforms*, Development Economics Research Programme, London School of Economics CP no. 5.

—— and Stern, N. (1992) *Economic Reforms and Public Finance in China*, Development Economics Research Programme, London School of Economics CP no. 23.

Kelliher, D. (1992) *Peasant Power in China*, Yale University Press, New Haven, Conn.

Kutzin, J. (1995), 'Experience with organizational and financing reform of the health sector', SHS Paper no. 8, World Health Organization, Geneva.

Luft, H. S. (1983) 'Economic incentives and clinical decisions', *The New Health Care for Profit*, Institute of Medicine/National Academy Press, Washington, DC.

McCleary, W. (1989), 'Earmarking government revenues: does it work?' Policy, Planning and Research Working Paper no. WPS 322, World Bank, Washington, DC.

Mesa-Lago, C. (1991) 'Social security in Latin America and the Caribbean: a comparative assessment', in E. Ahmad, J. Drèze, J. Hills, and A. Sen (eds.) *Social Security in Developing Countries*, Clarendon Press, Oxford.

MoPH (Ministry of Public Health), People's Republic of China (1991) 'The eighth five-year plan and targets for the year 2000 for China's health services' (abstract), *Chinese Public Health Management*, 5: 257-61

Normand, C. and Weber, A. (1994) *Social Health Insurance*, World Health Organisation, Geneva.

O'Brien, K. (1994) 'Implementing political reform in China's villages', *Australian Journal of Chinese Affairs*, 32: 33-59.

Pauly, M. (1986) 'Taxation, health insurance and market failure in the medical economy', *Journal of Economic Literature*, 24: 629-75.

Prescott, N. and Jamison, D. (1984) 'Health sector finance in China', *World Health Statistical Quarterly*, 37(4): 387-402.

Riskin, C. (1987) *China's Political Economy*, Oxford University Press, Oxford.

Ron, A., Abel Smith, B., and Tamburi, G. (1990) *Health Insurance in Developing Countries*, ILO, Geneva.

Shue, V. (1984) 'The fate of the commune', *Modern China*, 10(3): 259-83.

Sidel, V. and Sidel, R. (1973) *Serve the People: Observations on Medicine in the People's Republic of China*, Josiah Macy Jr Foundation, New York.

Smithson, P. (1994) 'Health finance and sustainability', Save the Children Fund Working Paper no. 10, London.

Song, L., and Du, H. (1990) 'The role of township governments in rural industrialization', in W. Byrd and Q. Liu (eds.), *China's Rural Industry: Structure, Development and Reform*, Oxford University Press, Oxford.

State Statistical Bureau of the People's Republic of China (SSB) (1993) *China Statistical Yearbook 1993*, China Statistical Information Consultancy Center, Beijing.

Tang, S., Bloom, G., Feng, X., Lucas, H., Gu, X. and Segall, M. (1994) 'Financing rural health services in China: adapting to economic reform', IDS Research Report no. 26, Institute of Development Studies, Brighton.

Ugalde, A. (1985) 'The integration of health care programs into a national health service', in C. Mesa-Lago (ed), *The Crisis of Social Security and Health Care*, Latin American Monograph and Document Series no. 9, Center for Latin American Studies, University of Pittsburgh.

Wang, X. and Bai, N. (1991) *The Poverty of Plenty*, Macmillan, London

World Bank (1987), *Financing Health Services in Developing Countries: An Agenda for Reform*, World Bank, Washington, DC.

——(1989) *China: Revenue Mobilisation and Tax Policy Issues and Options*, Report no. 7605–CHA, Country Operations Division, China Department, Asia Region, World Bank, Washington, DC.

——(1990) *Long-Term Issues and Options in the Health Transition*, Report no. 7965–CHA, Environment, Human Resources, and Urban Development Division, Asia Country Department III, World Bank, Washington, DC.

——(1992) *China: Strategies for Reducing Poverty in the 1990s*, World Bank, Washington, DC.

——(1993) *World Development Report: Investing in Health*, Oxford University Press, Oxford.

Xu, S. (1985) 'Health statistics of the People's Republic of China', in S. Halstead *et al.* (eds.), *Good Health at Low Cost*, Rockefeller Foundation, New York.

Yu, D. (1992) 'Changes in health care financing and health status: the case of China in the 1980s', *Innocenti Occasional Papers*, Economic Policy Series no. 34.

Zhan, S. (1997), 'Drug use in rural health care', *IDS Bulletin*, 28(1): 66–70.

Zi, W. (1990), 'Financial inducement for improving the efficacy of immunization', *World Health Forum*, 11: 173–8.

Zuo, X. (1995) 'Financing local services in poor townships', *IDS Bulletin*, 28(1): 81–91.

PART V

Improving Efficiency

10

Improving the Efficiency of Public Sector Health Services in Developing Countries: Bureaucratic versus Market Approaches

ANNE MILLS

10.1. Introduction

There is widespread concern over the efficiency of public sector health services in developing countries. To some the main problem is allocative efficiency: the distribution of resources between different health interventions and the over-provision of less cost-effective interventions. To others the main problem is technical efficiency: for example the widespread waste of resources because of poor purchasing and distribution systems and overstaffing.

The purpose of this paper is to raise the question of the best means of remedying the widely acknowledged inefficiencies of the public health systems in developing countries, and in particular to ask whether improvement is best pursued by a continuation and reinforcing of attempts to improve government policy-making, planning, and management structures relating to public provision, or whether there is value in market-oriented reforms that retain public financing but encourage competition between providers. The latter option draws on current reforms in developed countries, particularly in Western Europe, which seek to create quasi-markets/provider markets in health care in order to harness the benefits to be expected from competition (Le Grand

I thank my colleagues for their assistance in developing the ideas in this paper. An early draft of the paper was presented at a meeting of the UK Health Economists Study Group and benefited from discussion there. The discussion on contracting owes much to the work of Jonny Broomberg, including the details of arrangements in South Africa. The Health Economics and Financing Programme is supported by the Overseas Development Administration.

and Bartlett 1993). These reforms are being reflected in some of the recent thinking of agencies such as the World Bank and the Overseas Development Agency (ODA).[1]

This paper takes for granted the desirability of substantial public finance, and does not debate this.[2] It rather asks the question, given the substantial public finance that exists for health care in many developing countries, is this most efficiently employed in financing a public health bureaucracy, or are there arguments in favour of a pro-competition strategy? The main concern of the paper is with how to improve efficiency, though equity concerns are not completely ignored. In terms of efficiency, the concern is as much with how to use existing resources to greater effect as with simple cost savings.[3]

10.2. The Size of the Problem

Before addressing the question of the inefficiency of health provision, it is important to consider the objectives that governments seek to achieve in the health sector since these should influence the means they adopt (Culyer 1992; Williams 1993). Two distinct ethical principles can be distinguished. In the first, access to health care is considered a right of citizenship which should not depend on individual income or wealth, and emphasis is placed on reducing health inequalities. In the second, access to health care is considered to be essentially similar to access to other good things of life which are acquired through work or inheritance, and less emphasis is placed on the government's role in improving equity. The first view is broadly held in Europe and in many developing countries which it has influenced. The second view is more characteristic of the US health system and of countries where the public sector has a more residual role, for example charging fees for all except indigents.

---

[1] A recent internal donor document stated that 'The European donors appear to be thinking concretely about whether the [health] reforms being developed in their own countries are relevant to, or could be adapted to support, the reform agendas of their partners in developing countries.' The *World Development Report 1993* states that 'In most circumstances . . . the primary objective of public policy should be to promote competition among providers—including between the public and private sectors (when there are public providers). . . . Competition should increase consumer choice and satisfaction and drive down costs by increasing efficiency. Government supply in a competitive setting may improve quality or control costs, but non-competitive public provision of health services is likely to be inefficient or of low quality' (World Bank 1993*a*).

[2] The virtues of public finance are hotly disputed. Birdsall and James (1993), for example, argue that tax finance (and public provision) should be retained exclusively for public and quasi-public goods targeted at lower-income groups; the bulk of health care would be funded by mandatory insurance, subsidized if necessary for low-income groups, and with care provided by the private sector. Others (e.g. World Bank 1993*a*) note some of the efficiency and equity problems of this approach.

[3] Efficiency is considered to have increased if more output is gained with the same resources, or a given output is produced with fewer resources. Only the latter situation results in cost savings. In both cases it is assumed that quality is held constant.

Despite the differences that these views imply in the objectives and strategies of health systems in different countries, international health policy generally takes it for granted that the common objective of health systems is to maximize health status, given the resources available (World Bank 1993*a*).[4] In examining the efficiency of public provision of health care, this paper thus takes as its starting point three dimensions of efficiency. The first is cost effectiveness: to select those interventions which improve health at least cost, or which maximize health gain for a given budget. The second is technical efficiency, where maximum possible output is obtained from a given quantity of inputs, or a given output is achieved with minimum inputs.[5] The third is operating efficiency, where the least-cost combination of inputs is used to produce given outputs.[6]

The question of the extent of inefficiency in the public health sector should ideally be addressed in terms of health outcome: to what extent does public sector health expenditure achieve the maximum potential improvement in health? While there have been a few interesting studies which suggest that some countries perform much better than others (Halstead *et al.* 1985; Cumper 1984), health status and expenditure data on developing countries are too poor to draw firm conclusions for particular countries. Hence most arguments on the inefficiency of the public sector rely on proxy indicators.

The first argument is that public health systems provide low coverage of those in greatest need, particularly the rural poor. This is assumed to be inefficient because it is argued that some of the most cost-effective measures (e.g. immunization, ante-natal and post-natal care, treatment of common infectious diseases) are those that improve the health of those with the worst health status, namely the poor.

The second argument is that service provision is biased towards hospitals. For example, hospitals may absorb 50–60 per cent of current government health sector, 60–80 per cent of government health facility expenditure, and around 70 per cent of district expenditure (Mills 1990). Within hospital expenditure, the lion's share is often absorbed by central and general hospitals, leaving district hospitals with the smallest share. However, three qualifications must be made. First, it is difficult to set a norm for the share of health expenditure that should pass through hospitals; hospitals often provide substantial primary care to local, densely populated urban areas (and there is scanty but mixed evidence on whether this is more expensive than if such care were provided by community-based facilities). Second, much of the care provided by central and general hospitals is in fact what the World

---

[4] This may be contrasted with the libertarian approach, which implies that objectives should be more concerned with satisfying individual preferences (e.g. permitting individuals to choose not to improve their health).

[5] That is, the facility is operating on the production possibility frontier.

[6] A fourth dimension of efficiency, that of achieving the desirable overall level of output of the health sector, is not considered here.

Bank defines as 'essential clinical care': i.e. many of these hospitals are misnamed.

The third argument is related to the first two, namely that the mix of interventions financed and provided by the public sector is highly inefficient. This argument is a particular feature of the 1993 *World Development Report* (World Bank 1993*a*), and draws on a large study of the cost effectiveness of interventions against the major diseases in developing countries which has produced 'league tables' ranking interventions and programmes in terms of cost per DALY (disability-adjusted life year)[7] (Jamison *et al.* 1993). The results of the ranking, when compared with the 'global burden of disease',[8] indicate the extent to which it is possible to reduce the disease burden by devoting increased resources to the most cost-effective measures. For example, the 1993 *World Development Report* argues that implementing a basic public health package of interventions and a package of essential clinical services would eliminate 32 per cent of the DALYs lost in low-income countries, and 15 per cent in middle-income countries (assuming 100 per cent coverage). While there is considerable scope for challenging the details of the calculations, it is difficult to quarrel with the basic conclusion of misallocated resources; indeed, this point has been made frequently in the past and was a prime reason for the primary health care emphasis of international health policy in the 1970s and 1980s.

The fourth argument is that publicly provided services are highly inefficient (in terms of both technical and operating efficiency) in their use of inputs. Rigorous proof of this is difficult to supply since work has only recently begun on estimating production and cost functions for health facilities and, as in developed country studies, it is difficult to account for quality and case-mix variations in the estimates (Barnum and Kutzin 1993). A recent study by Wouters, however, was able to assess both technical and economic efficiency in a sample of health facilities in Nigeria (Wouters 1993). She concluded that many public (and also private) facilities were not operating at full technical capacity, and that public facilities were not using cost-minimizing combinations of health workers. Cost accounting studies commonly show wide variation in the unit costs of similar types of facility, providing evidence that strongly suggests inefficiency (e.g. Berman 1993; Bloom and Segall 1993; Gilson 1992; Koita and Brunet-Jailly 1989; Mills 1993; Purohit and Rai 1992).

Further evidence comes from input-specific studies. Two inputs cause particular concern: staff numbers and use, and drugs. Studies often show extremely low productivity of staff in the public sector (World Bank 1993*b*; Berman 1993; Lewis *et al.* 1991), together with a gross lack of the comple-

[7] DALY is a measure combining mortality and disability reductions resulting from interventions, and incorporating age weights, disability weights, and discounting.

[8] The number of DALYs lost as a result of all deaths and disability arising in 1990, classified by 109 disease categories, age, sex, and 8 geographical regions.

mentary resources that would enable them to practise. For example, a study in Uganda indicated that health personnel could be reduced by 30 per cent without affecting the quantity or quality of services (Republic of Uganda 1991). The work of the Drug Action Programme in WHO has documented the inefficiency of many public drug supply and distribution systems (Foster 1993). Waste occurs through buying unnecessarily costly drugs in inefficient ways; through distribution systems which favour hospitals, neglect peripheral services and lead to leakages; through poor prescribing of the wrong drugs, in wrong dosages, and in excessive numbers; and through poor patient compliance.

Studies are beginning to show widespread problems, at least in the poorest countries, in the quality of care provided. For example, a study of dispensary care in a region in Tanzania showed that many facilities fell below the standard that might reasonably be expected in the circumstances of low-income countries, in terms of both structural quality (availability of necessary inputs) and process quality (standards of patient care, such as history taking and drug prescribing) (Gilson 1992). Studies of hospital quality are more difficult to do: however, findings are likely to be similar (as a study in Papua New Guinea indicates—Thomason and Edwards 1991).

There is thus ample evidence of the inefficiency, in terms of all three types, of publicly provided health services. None the less, the evidence is by no means conclusive. In the first place, it relies on what is still a relatively small number of country-specific studies, and the evidence of greatest inefficiency comes from the poorest countries in Africa, making it difficult to know to what extent the conclusions can be generalized. In the second place, there are also examples of 'highly efficient public health centres and district hospitals' (World Bank 1993*a*): the Bank quotes the examples of Chile, China, Sri Lanka and Zimbabwe. In the third place, conclusive evidence is lacking, at least in the poorest countries, that non-public services necessarily perform any better (see Chapter 4 above). For example, the Tanzanian study referred to above found that mission facilities were not consistently better than government dispensaries, and for certain services (e.g. ante-natal care) tended to perform worse (Gilson 1992).

Before considering the scope for improving efficiency, it is important to explore the explanations for observed inefficiencies. In terms of non-cost-effective allocation of resources, there are four main explanations commonly offered. First is the dominance of the medical profession in health decision-making in most countries, and the incentive structures and status concerns that favour hospital practice and medical specialization. These priorities tend to be reflected in consumer preferences, though in addition poor, remote populations lack the political voice to bring their needs to the notice of the government. Second is the difficulty that all governments face in making policies on the basis of technical analysis: the policy-making process is often weak, and most ministries of health lack information on both costs and effectiveness. Third, donor interventions have not in the past necessarily promoted a cost-effective mix of interventions. For example, a good part of the hospital infrastructure in the poorest countries has been financed by donors, with some investments taking place even quite recently. Fourth, it has been argued that public choice theory explains much of the misallocation: that more influential consumer and producer groups are able to divert resources to the costly overprovision of services that predominantly benefit upper-income groups and have a much lower social rate of return, at the expense of providing basic services to the poor (Birdsall and James 1993). However, in the poorer countries such overprovision is relative: even hospitals lack adequate revenue to function properly.

In terms of low technical and operating efficiency, many of the explanations lie in the nature of public bureaucracies and the lack of incentives they provide for efficient resource use. Decision-making is usually highly centralized, and planning and management structures are often weak. Government regulations impede action to improve efficiency (e.g. adjust staff numbers to local workloads), and the ministry of health, even if it wishes to, has very limited ability to introduce greater flexibility on its own authority. The health management cadre is dominated by medically trained staff, who have little management training and are supported by relatively poorly educated administrators.

Other explanations lie in the pervasive influence of lack of resources. Where government salaries suffice for only part of the month, as in some of the poorest African countries, it is not surprising that staff are poorly motivated, public resources get diverted to private use and utilization levels are low. Many of the government procedures that are considered to be inefficient and irrational, such as withholding budgets at the start of the year and issuing supplementary budgets through the year, can be shown to be highly rational given the financial uncertainties facing governments (Caiden and Wildavsky 1974). The poorest countries are also dependent on donor funds; and efficiency has suffered from donor preferences for highly visible, 'vertical' programmes[9] which have done little to help build capacity (World Bank 1993*b*; Save the Children Fund 1993).

Some of the reasons for technical and operating inefficiency are well documented in the detailed studies of hospital costs in developing countries. Trisolini *et al.* (1992) demonstrate, for the main hospital in St Lucia, that only 20 per cent of costs were within the control of the hospital, and there was no control over staff costs. There were no responsibility centres within the hospital, and hence few means to either find out about or control resource use. Similar deficiencies are found in public hospitals in many other countries (Mills 1993; Lewis *et al.* 1991; Barnum and Kutzin 1993).

---

[9] Vertical programmes are those that have their own management structure and funding, with services delivered separately and not integrated with other primary-level activities.

10.3. Bureaucratic Approaches and Evidence of their Success

There have been many programmes designed to tackle the weaknesses of publicly provided health care. The problem is not to list them but to assess their success, since reforms are frequently described as if their mere existence is proof that they are effective. Many evaluations are done with a medical or epidemiological focus, to demonstrate improved health care or improved health status, but the impact of structural and procedural changes on efficiency or cost savings are not documented.[10] Monitoring tends to be limited to the time period of an externally funded project and not to continue after the project has finished, so the sustainability of reforms is hard to assess. Four approaches to reform are considered here—structural changes, financing changes, improvements in the policy process, and management system improvements—with a focus on whether they have created, or are likely to create, improvements in efficiency and cost savings.

10.3.1. Structural changes

A number of structural changes have been proposed to improve efficiency, the most common being decentralization of planning and management, usually to the 'district' level (Mills *et al.* 1990). Some measure of decentralization is likely to be a prerequisite for improved efficiency, since it is the first step in informing local managers of the resource consequences of their actions, and in giving them some ability and incentive to improve their performance. However, despite fairly substantial experience of the implementation of decentralization policies, it is still not clear precisely what actions and conditions are necessary for decentralization to be a success (Mogedal *et al.* 1995). Nor is it clear that structural change will necessarily result in changes in the way that organizations behave. Governments are often reluctant to hand over sufficient responsibility, particularly budgetary authority. Control over staff is also often retained at the national level. Decentralization can blur lines of authority, for example when district managers have responsibility both to a local chief officer and to the national ministry of health. Furthermore, decentralization requires investment in the strengthening of local management levels and improvement of information systems. Whether this,

[10] In the two recent reviews of developing country health policies (World Bank 1993*a*, *b*), it is remarkable how many reforms are proposed, but how little detailed evidence can be put forward on the impact of past reforms in terms of quantitative measures of efficiency or equity. Similarly, the book by Barnum and Kutzin (1993) documents very fully low levels of hospital efficiency, but its suggestions on remedies lack any actual evidence of the success of reform strategies.

plus the transaction costs involved in maintaining the new management structures, are outweighed by efficiency gains is not a question that appears yet to have been addressed.

Other structural changes proposed include reorganizing of ministries of health in order to separate the management of the health service from the running of the ministry of health; giving a greater degree of autonomy to large public hospitals; and setting up management boards for health facilities and districts. There has been little reported experience of the success of these strategies. The second strategy is currently in fashion as a way of forcing some of the most inefficient parts of the health system, large tertiary hospitals, to improve their performance. It is reported that this change in Tunisia has led to some gains in efficiency (World Bank 1993*a*). Similar reforms in several African countries (e.g. Kenya, Uganda, Zambia, and South Africa) are as yet at a rather early stage to be evaluated. Again, as with general decentralization policies, there is no evidence on whether implementation costs would outweigh cost savings.

A much more radical way of enforcing cost savings is essentially to divest the public sector of the tertiary facilities, either by giving them independent status within the public sector and requiring them to raise their own income, or by shifting them into the private sector.[11] Under this approach, if it is to lead to cost savings, subsidized treatment would need to be denied to patients with low-priority conditions who would before have got free or subsidized care.

A number of implications follow. First, the health system would become increasingly inequitable, since those who had insurance or could afford to pay the fees would still have access. It is also highly likely that those with political influence would continue to have access. Whether equity is improved in other ways would depend on the government's ability to shift at least some of the cost savings to improve public health and essential clinical services in areas poorly provided for. Second, tertiary hospitals are often the only hospital for large urban populations. Either patients have to be given access selectively (which would require establishing those procedures to which they are entitled, and corresponding subsidies, information systems, and monitoring), or new, lower-level facilities would have to be constructed.

The scope for cost savings from reducing public expenditure on tertiary care would seem to be considerable, given its relatively high share of total public expenditure.[12] Even if it is assumed that as much as half of current

[11] In Uruguay, for example, social insurance funding has been used to establish high-technology institutes in the private sector (Marquez 1990). In Malaysia, the specialist MOH cardiology facility has been made autonomous and is required to raise its own revenue: those who are referred there and cannot pay must seek a government subsidy and join a waiting list for admission.

[12] The *World Development Report* states that 'Tertiary hospitals alone may consume 30–50% of the health budget' (World Bank 1993*a*).

tertiary expenditure is for care that is known to be cost-effective (e.g. out-patient care; standard acute surgery), the sums that might be saved are not negligible. Two cautionary notes should, however, be sounded. First, there is little evidence that governments are likely to be able substantially to shift the costs of access to tertiary care to users in countries where only a small pro-portion of the population is insured. Denying access is politically difficult (especially since these facilities are often in the capital city) and considerable subsidies are likely to remain. Second, if the management of such facilities is handed over to independent boards or to the private sector, they may pay higher salaries and/or take the facility up-market, raising the costs above their previous level. Hence the cost of care for publicly subsidized patients may actually increase, though the quality may be better.

In a number of Latin American countries, cost savings have been sought by amalgamating the separate health services of the ministry of health and social security funds, in order to reduce duplication.[13] Marquez (1990) comments that substantial savings and expansion of coverage have resulted. Such re-forms reflect the emphasis placed until recently on rationalization, integration, and co-ordination. Such values are being challenged by pro-competition policies (see below).

Recommendations are increasingly being made for ministries of health to make greater use of non-government organizations (NGOs) to deliver ser-vices for low-income groups, through subsidies. For example, mission health services have been advocated as models of quality of care and cost recovery for government facilities (Vogel 1987) and as providing the advantage of overseas income (World Bank 1993*b*). The advantages of the not-for-profit sector more generally have also been emphasized (Fiedler 1990). In efficiency terms, the value of expanded use of NGO providers depends on two con-ditions: that they provide services of a given quality at lower cost (net of user fees) than the government, and/or that they are able to subsidize that cost from local or overseas charitable income. Despite the above assertions, there is little hard evidence of consistently better cost performance by missions than by government (Bennett 1991), though their fee collection performance is probably better. In a number of countries missions are finding it increasingly difficult to maintain their overseas income, and some are in serious financial difficulties. As they become more dependent on government subsidies, they may themselves become more like government bureaucracies; and if govern-ment facilities can be given greater ability to manage their own affairs through decentralization, they may gain some of the advantages of flexibility that missions now have. However, lack of evidence on current behaviour makes it difficult to make firm predictions. Other parts of the NGO health sector have been little studied.

---

[13] e.g. in Brazil, Nicaragua, and Panama.

10.3.2. Financing changes

While the desirability of user fees as a means of shaping consumer behaviour
is much debated (Gilson 1987*a*; McPake 1993), there is less controversy over
the value of providing a facility with additional revenue. As long as the local
level is permitted to retain all or most of the income and the cost of collecting
the fee is not out of proportion to the income raised, fee revenue can enhance
technical efficiency by financing complementary inputs such as drugs and
maintenance, and providing a supplement to staff salaries (Marquez 1990;
Barnum and Kutzin 1993). Improved quality should then reduce welfare
losses from the imposition of fees, produce higher utilization levels, and thus
make better use of existing capacity. For example, in a study of hospital fees
in the Dominican Republic, user fee income was argued to be important in
enhancing effectiveness, productivity, and staff morale (Lewis 1993). The
experience of the Bamako Initiative has demonstrated that by charging
modest fees it is possible to support primary health services in a number of
countries and improve their quality (McPake and Hanson 1993).[14] Fees can
also be used to encourage users to attend the local facility by exempting fees
at higher levels for referred patients, or by fees graduated by level of facility
(Abel-Smith and Creese 1989). There is little evidence of how well such
'bypass' fees work in practice and some evidence of problems: fees at the
hospital level may not be high enough to discourage excessive use; or even, as
in some Bamako Initiative countries, fees may be charged at the primary level
but not further up the system.

10.3.3. Improvements in the policy process

The main current proposal for improving the process of policy-making is that
made in the 1993 *World Development Report*: to make policy-makers aware
of the burden of disease, the relative cost effectiveness of means of reducing
it, and the need to define 'packages' of essential interventions which are publicly financed. While the analysis was initially in global terms, country-specific
studies are now being carried out, for example in Uganda, Mexico, Thailand
and Kenya.

  There are two main reasons for doubting that this strategy on its own
(without structural changes) will have a major impact on efficiency. First, cost
effectiveness analysis represents merely a means of improving the information
available to policy-makers. It is likely to be only one factor that they will take
into account in setting policies. While there is discussion on how to translate

---

[14] The authors accept that the Initiative has not solved the problem of financial access for the
poorest.

the results of the analysis into health care provision and provider behaviour, no firm recommendations on how to do this have yet emerged.[15] Indeed, it is not nearly as simple as current analyses suggest. For example, for many clinical interventions cost effectiveness may vary enormously depending on the characteristics of the patient: a procedure may be cost-effective for a healthy adult in middle age, but not for an elderly person with multiple pathologies. Second, data on the cost effectiveness of different interventions are largely unavailable for any specific country. Heavy reliance will thus have to be placed on general international experience and studies from a wide variety of countries. Policy-makers may then doubt the relevance of the analysis to their own country circumstances.

Cost effectiveness analysis will lead to improvements in efficiency if the public sector provides more interventions of high cost effectiveness to more people and fewer interventions of low cost effectiveness. Whether it leads to cost-savings will depend on where the cut-off point is located. It is conceivable that total expenditure could remain the same but its make-up in terms of interventions could be changed. In some of the poorest countries, the World Bank accepts that providing access for 100 per cent of the population to a minimum package of essential services would require an increase in expenditure (World Bank 1993*a*).

10.3.4. Management system improvements

Most of the measures to improve the efficiency of publicly provided health care fall under the general heading of management system improvements. They include improving planning and budgeting systems at all levels; improving information systems including information on costs; improving financial management and accounting systems; improving management of inputs such as staff, essential drugs and other supplies, transport, and buildings and equipment; imposing controls on the supply of expensive technology including highly trained staff; creating and expanding of management cadres for hospitals and health authorities; introducing management training for all health professionals involved in management; and initiating quality assurance programmes. This list is too long to deal with here; hence the discussion confines itself to those measures on which there is at least some evidence of whether they have led, or are likely to lead, to cost savings or improved efficiency.

There has been much emphasis over a number of years on improving planning procedures, including building up planning units in ministries of

---

[15] Those strategies currently being suggested are improving the training of health workers, controlling the purchase of technology, designing reimbursement policies, and educating consumers.

health and introducing programme budgeting; however, there is little evidence that they have had much influence on resource allocation except as managers of the development programme (Kalumba and Freund 1989; Issaka-Tinorgah and Waddington 1993). Their strategic planning function has largely been confined to writing plans, which have had little impact on actual decisions (Cumper 1991). There is often a considerable gap between stated policies, for example commitment to primary and preventive care, and actual resource allocation patterns (Gilson 1987; Bloom and Segall 1993). One of the few evaluations of planning reforms, in the ministry of health in Ghana, suggests that the reforms were far too ambitious, introducing too much change at once, placing too many demands on untrained staff, and assuming that forward planning was of value when in reality staff worked in a highly uncertain financial environment, where even approved budgets were not honoured (Issaka-Tinorgah and Waddington 1993). Reforms should rather have been more modest, acknowledging political and economic realities and recognizing the need for training.

Staffing inefficiencies can be approached in three ways: through control of the numbers in training; changes in the numbers and mix of staff employed; and improved control of staff including the provision of incentives for improved performance and increasing ability to dismiss excess or incompetent workers. Although many countries already have, or soon will have, an oversupply of physicians (Abel-Smith 1986), there seems to have been little success in controlling the numbers trained, at least in Latin America (Marquez 1990). Given the scope in the health sector for supply-induced demand, and the difficulty of changing expectations about public sector employment, the problem of excess supply may well persist.

Excess supply encourages overstaffing of hospitals. For example, in a study in a hospital in the Dominican Republic (Lewis *et al.* 1991), only 12 per cent of contracted physician time could be accounted for by patient care activities, indicating serious underutilization of available manpower and misallocation of resources (79 per cent of the hospital's budget was allocated to personnel). Hospital directors had virtually no control over staff assigned to the hospital. The solutions were seen to be greater autonomy for hospital managers and physican payment that was linked to productivity. The potential for altering physician employment and payment methods in the context of oversupply is suggested by the experience of PROSALUD in Bolivia. This externally supported network of clinics with non-profit management is reported to have reduced staff costs substantially by employing fewer staff, increasing flexibility in job allocations, keeping wages down but offering a guaranteed salary, and paying a bonus linked to the clinic's revenue performance (Fiedler 1990, 1991; Gish 1991).

The problem of oversupply of doctors contributes to an inappropriate staff mix, especially in countries where female labour force participation (and hence the number of nurses) is low. Many countries in Africa have shown that it is possible to provide services of adequate quality with paramedical staff; however, where doctors are in excess supply there is considerable opposition to such substitution. Again, increasing local management authority to hire and fire and give incentives for good performance seems to offer the greatest potential for improving efficiency (and would require the implementation of decentralization policies).

In terms of other inputs, greatest emphasis has been placed on improving the efficiency of the supply and use of drugs. It is generally accepted that it is possible to reduce procurement costs by competitive tendering and adherence to an essential drug list (Ross-Degnan *et al.* 1992)—the World Bank (1993*a*) suggests by 40–60 per cent. Given that pharmaceuticals account for 10–30 per cent of recurrent public spending on health, this implies savings of around 5–15 per cent. These are most difficult to achieve where doctors have the power to oppose generic prescribing and essential drugs lists and where there is a powerful local pharmaceutical industry (Marquez 1990). Distribution systems seem harder to reform and the means of efficiency improvements are more controversial: a review of the distribution and use of pharmaceuticals in developing countries concluded that 'the public sector can be made to work' (Foster 1993). Others, however, disagree, arguing that none of the strategies to improve public sector distribution systems have been particularly success-ful (Vogel and Stephens 1989). Even advocates of government-run essential drugs systems accept that little evidence is available of success in improving public sector prescribing practices (Ross-Degnan *et al.* 1992).[16]

In summary, there is little doubt that there is considerable potential for health services, especially hospitals, to improve technical and operational efficiency. In hospitals, the following examples indicate that the management reforms necessary to increase efficiency are often fairly obvious and do not re-quire sophisticated approaches. In Malawi, a hospital cost analysis indicated that, in all six hospitals studied, there was a high degree of awareness among district health officers of the need for control of resource use, and some successes in ensuring that resources were used effectively (Mills 1993). However, reforms seemed to depend on the interest and energy of the senior staff, especially the district health officer, who had many responsibilities and who rarely stayed for more than two or three years. One of the greatest needs therefore was to establish a cadre of hospital managers with sufficient authority to control resource use. Similar conclusions have been reached in Papua New Guinea (Thomason and Edwards 1991). In other countries low utilization may be a major source of inefficiency, and requires that greater attention be paid to improving aspects of performance that users value. For example, the introduction of payment to finance an essential drugs supply,

---

[16] Though private prescribing is as bad or worse, and is likely to be more difficult to reform because of the financial interest which private prescribers have in prescribing the more expensive drugs.

and tight management and financial control, can be sufficient to have a substantial effect on utilization without major additional external resources (Unger *et al.* 1990). In Indonesia, it has been argued that adding a specialist and surgical services to lower-level hospitals would greatly boost use (Barnum and Kutzin 1993).

What is not understood, however, are the influences leading ministries to introduce sustained reform, and the means to inculcate a managerial culture and capacity that gives priority to improved resource use.

10.3.5. Relative attractiveness of different approaches to reform

Given an aim of raising the resources available to the health sector, the question can be asked whether improvements in efficiency and user fees are complements or substitutes. Reforms that increase technical and allocative efficiency make existing resources go further, and mean that more interventions and services can be provided within a given budget. These reforms are desirable regardless of the policy on user fees. Indeed, it is preferable to improve technical and operating efficiency before requiring users to pay, so they do not subsidize inefficient services. User fees, as discussed above, may enhance technical efficiency by ensuring adequate funding of inputs. Their effect on allocative efficiency is more complex, and depends both on the structure of the fee system and on the response of users. If the fee system is structured in a way that provides incentives to use cost-effective care (e.g. if it exempts or highly subsidizes services with quasi-public good characteristics or externalities; or if it encourages use of the lowest appropriate level of care), then user fees can complement supply-side reforms. However, even very low fees may deter needy users unless an effective exemptions system is in place. There is very little evidence on whether public health services can operate such systems well.

An issue that has barely begun to be addressed is the possible trade-off between cost reduction and quality, and whether different approaches to reform have different implications for this trade-off. Quality in health care is peculiarly difficult to assess, given the ill-defined nature of the production function. It is difficult to specify what health care procedures constitute care of adequate quality, let alone to monitor whether they are carried out and have a positive impact on health. The few studies that have so far been done tend to indicate a lack of correlation between unit cost and quality at health centre level; that is, low-cost centres are as likely to deliver care of adequate quality as high-cost centres (Gilson 1992). Thus, there is likely to be considerable scope in practice for improving technical efficiency without harming (or even in the process enhancing) quality. However, there is a danger that reforms introduced in order to provide incentives for increased productivity such as performance-based pay, and to increase the resources available to facilities such as user fees, may threaten quality. For example, quality may be reduced if strict cost control accompanies incentives to increase throughput, and if user fee policy generates strong incentives to oversupply certain drugs or technologies in order to increase hospital income (as is the case in China: see Bumgarner 1992).

This review has highlighted not only the lack of evidence on the impact of reforms, but also the lack of attention paid to the factors that determine whether a particular reform is implemented successfully, and which means of implementation are most likely to enhance the chances of success. In particular, it is important to consider how all those who will affect the success of reform, such as politicians, managers, health professionals, and communities, can be encouraged to develop and support reforms, and carry them through. It seems that many of the approaches to improving management processes may do little to change the incentives facing managers and health workers, and hence are unlikely to have a dramatic impact on efficiency. This concern is leading some to advocate much more radical structural changes, particularly a greater reliance on market mechanisms and the private sector.

10.4. Market Approaches

Market approaches are taken here to be reforms that aim to introduce competitive pressures into public health services. The starting point for the discussion is some of the European health reforms that aim to introduce competition. The reforms of most potential relevance to developing countries are those relating to provider (or quasi-, or internal) markets.[17] These can be considered to take two main forms (Brazier *et al.* 1990). Provider markets involve the separation of responsibility for financing care from the responsibility for providing it. A statutory purchasing authority provides care by a combination of contracting with other agencies (public only or private as well) and direct provision. In the variant of provider markets with consumer choice, emphasis is placed on the consumer selecting either the purchasing agency (who contracts with providers to supply the required health care) or the provider (who is rewarded for a higher workload by increased funding from a passive purchaser).

Proponents of provider markets argue that they will generate both substantial increases in efficiency and increased consumer choice and influence over health services. The means by which these beneficial outcomes are considered to occur are twofold (Broomberg 1994). First, it is argued that provider markets will give rise to competition among providers for contracts, and that competition will enhance efficiency on the supply side. The concern that there

---

[17] The terminology is confusing. See Broomberg (1994) for an explanation of the various terms and how they differ.

will be too few providers in many geographical areas to ensure competition is
countered by the argument that markets need only be contestable for incentives for efficiency to be created (Baumol *et al.* 1988). Second, the replacement
of direct management by contractual relationships between purchasers and
providers is argued to promote increased transparency of prices, quantities,
and quality in trading, as well as managerial decentralization, both of which
will also enhance efficiency. Proponents of market reforms recognize that
they come at a cost, in the form of transaction costs, but consider that the
gains in efficiency will outweigh the costs involved in setting up and maintaining markets.

So far, it appears that the jury is still out on whether the gains that can be
argued in theory to arise are in fact realized in practice (Le Grand and Bartlett
1993; Roberts 1993; Robinson and Le Grand 1994). The theoretical and
empirical arguments in the developed country context will not be debated
here; rather, the concern is to explore whether there are some aspects of the
reforms that are relevant in a developing country context, or whether there
are particular features that render them irrelevant or harmful. It should be
noted that the essential feature of the reforms is competition: reforms such as
giving self-managing status to large hospitals are not regarded here as
market-oriented reforms unless there is competition for funding and/or
patients.

To achieve the ideal outcome of a quasi-market, namely efficiency, provision of choice, and responsiveness to consumers, it is argued that there must
be competition on both the purchaser and provider side (Bartlett and Le
Grand 1993), though there is some debate as to whether competition on the
purchaser side is as important as competition on the provider side. This
section first considers briefly the feasibility of the consumer choice model,
involving competition on the purchasing side, before turning to the supply
side and providers.

10.4.1. Competition on the purchasing side

Consumer-led competition can be encouraged in two ways: by allowing consumers to select one of a number of competing purchasers, such as insurance
agencies or health maintenance organizations, who will act on their behalf, or
by allowing them to select their provider directly.[18] The former option will
entail particular difficulties in virtually all developing countries. A universal

---

[18] A common feature of most developing countries is that consumers already have considerable choice because of the extent of private provision (ranging from traditional practitioners,
through drug stores, to modern medical practitioners). However, the ability to exercise choice is
for most people severely limited by income. The concern here is the ability of those whose
financial access to health care is facilitated by the state to exercise choice as to where they can
obtain care.

feature is a large proportion of the population who are not within the formal employment sector, and whose cash incomes are very low. Giving them choice of purchaser would require large state subsidies and entail problems of identifying who required subsidies.[19] A further feature of developing countries is a lack of large financial institutions which could act as competing purchasers. Moreover, there would be major problems in preventing them discriminating in favour of low-risk groups, thus encouraging adverse selection.[20] Competition among purchasers may be an option in some of the urban areas of the richer countries for those in formal employment, and might help to overcome some of the entrenched inefficiencies of social insurance systems.[21] But it seems unlikely to be a solution to meet the health care needs of the majority of the consumers of public health services.

Encouraging providers (either public providers only, or public and private) to compete for consumers requires a system for rewarding providers who attract more custom, and hence for paying them for providing care to identifiable consumers. It generally requires public providers to charge cost-covering fees. It is not infrequently argued by pro-competition economists that at present there is unfair competition in developing countries, which hampers the development of the private medical sector, because public services are provided free (or are highly subsidized). Hence charging fees in the public sector is argued to be necessary to promote competition.

However, the problem of enabling consumers to pay cost-covering fees is unresolved. Two solutions are commonly put forward: insurance and exemptions. Insurance is only just now reaching a high proportion of the population in the richer developing countries; for most, it covers only a small proportion of public sector clients most of whom are not in formal employment. The requirements for paying premiums and identifying the insured are hard for low-income countries to satisfy for most of the current users of public health services.

Exemptions schemes encounter three main problems. First, although they are frequently seen as the solution to the equity problems of user fees, there is very little evidence of the extent to which they are effective in protecting the poor (and making the richer groups pay). There is cause for concern that exemptions may be poorly targeted (for example, civil servants often make up a large proportion of the exempt), that they may be stigmatizing and hence underclaimed, and that objective measures of poverty are unavailable,

[19] A feasibility study of a local health maintenance organization in a rural parish in Jamaica showed that the scheme was not financially viable, partly because the contribution the Ministry of Health was prepared to pay for indigents was well below the level of voluntary insurance premia and inadequate to cover the likely cost of services (Abel-Smith 1989).

[20] Adverse selection can occur when insurers avoid giving cover to higher-risk patient groups. In this case it arises when insurers are not adequately compensated for the higher costs of care for these groups (and thus have an incentive not to enrol them).

[21] For example, there is considerable interest in parts of Latin America in competing health maintenance organizations (Tollman *et al.* 1990).

providing scope for more subjective factors to influence decisions. Second, in most poor countries the great majority of public facility users would be exempted according to any reasonable definition of poverty:[22] hence there are serious questions as to whether the administrative cost of such fees would be worth the revenue raised. Third, there would need to be a system whereby the purchaser covered the costs of care of those who are exempt or partially exempt. In this context, the possibility of health care vouchers is often mentioned, whereby the provider would collect the vouchers from patients and then claim reimbursement from the purchaser. However, if these are not available to everyone (which seems likely), they also entail the problems of targeting the needy as well as controlling their issue and use. For example, vouchers are issued in Taiwan for the insured to take to obtain medical treatment, and are then used by the facilities to claim payment. There is a major problem in that the facilities collude with the insured to claim unnecessary treatment.[23]

A final concern with the model where consumers choose providers directly is people's ability to behave as informed consumers. In developing countries, large proportions of the population are uneducated or poorly educated, have limited access to sources of information such as the mass media and newspapers, and are distant from providers in terms of socioeconomic status and educational level. If the UK prefers purchasers to act as informed consumers on behalf of individuals, there is even more of a case to be made for this in developing countries.

Whether the purchaser role can, or should, involve competition between purchasers is debatable. Given the paucity of institutions that could act as competing purchasers in many developing countries and the dangers of adverse selection, it may be that the most desirable and feasible option is to have monopoly purchasers, with the responsibility of assessing the needs of their local population and then contracting with public or private sector facilities, either selectively (for particular services) or for the whole range of required services.

10.4.2. Provider competition

A wide diversity of market approaches is possible.

1. A comprehensive provider market could be established, incorporating both public and private facilities, organizationally quite separate from purchasers.
2. In underserved, low-income rural areas, existing or new private

---

[22] In Jamaica, for example, by no means one of the poorest countries, it was estimated that the poor who would have to be exempted from fees amounted to 50% of the population, and the near-poor, who would have to be subsidized, to a further 30% (Abel-Smith and Creese 1989).

[23] Cheng-Lan Su, personal communication.

providers could be given the opportunity to bid to build and provide primary and secondary level services for the general public.

3. In urban areas with an established private sector, contracts could be agreed for a variety of different types of care, ranging from primary care to whole hospitals, particular types of patient care, and particular diagnostic procedures.
4. Public facilities could be offered to private sector entities to run on a long-term lease, involving temporary transfer of ownership.
5. Management contracts could be offered to the private sector to run public facilities (without temporary transfer of ownership).
6. Contracting out of non-clinical services in public hospitals could be encouraged.
7. Delivery of disease control activities could be contracted out (e.g. residual spraying, immunization).

A limited amount of contracting exists already in developing countries. The most common arrangement is of contracting for non-clinical services. For example, there is some contracting out of laundry services in India, Sri Lanka, Indonesia, Bangladesh, Pakistan, Malaysia, Mexico, Thailand and Zimbabwe; of security services in Malaysia and Sri Lanka; of laboratory services in Nigeria; of the maintenance of large equipment in Venezuela and Zimbabwe; and of billing insurance agencies in Zimbabwe (Bennett and Mills 1991; McPake and Ngalande-Banda 1994; Ellis and Chawla 1993; World Bank 1993*a*, *b*). However, information on these arrangements appears to be anecdotal, and there has been little careful evaluation of their success.[24] It is reported that a large public hospital in Tunisia has fully contracted out all food, cleaning, and security functions, and now obtains services of much higher quality, at similar or even lower unit cost (World Bank 1993*a*); that contracting out all cleaning and portering services in the three public hospitals in Kingston, Jamaica, saved half the budget and improved the standard of services (Abel-Smith 1989); and that, because only two companies were available to bid for a catering contract in Lesotho, the supplier was able to charge more than competitive rates (Bennett 1991). In all these cases, however, very limited details are available.

Contracting of clinical services is generally considered to be less common (McPake and Ngalande-Banda 1994). However, this depends partly on what is defined as contracting. Many African countries provide a substantial subsidy to mission health services which are major suppliers of services to the general population (e.g. in Rwanda, Zimbabwe, Malawi, Swaziland, Ghana, Tanzania). While in the past the mission services simply provided their accustomed facilities, increasingly they are taking on additional responsibilities in return for the subsidy, for example to act as district-designated hospitals and

---

[24] Research is currently under way, supported by the Health Economics and Financing Programme and the ODA, to evaluate contracting arrangements in Thailand, Papua New Guinea, Mexico, and South Africa.

to supervise lower-level facilities in the district, and to help implement nation-wide programmes such as those for immunization or TB treatment. Similarly, hospitals run by industrial or agricultural enterprises may provide treatment for the local population in return for a subsidy—for example mine hospitals (McPake and Hongoro 1993). These are however incipient forms of contracting: there is usually no obvious competition in the awarding of the contract, and governments are only slowly becoming aware of the possibility of specifying the services to be delivered in return for the subsidy, and of monitoring performance.

South Africa provides an unusual example of quite extensive contracting for hospital care (Broomberg 1994). In 1989, 15.5 per cent of total hospital beds, and 53 per cent of privately owned beds, were under some form of contracting arrangement. One for-profit company runs 23 hospitals; the majority of these are providing long-stay care, but three in rural areas are functioning as local district hospitals providing a normal range of acute inpatient care as well as outpatient services. Other contracting arrangements are more similar to those in other parts of Africa: NGO hospitals receiving a global budget to cover the care of non-private patients.

Other examples of contracting are available from the social insurance sector. Again, most of these are not good examples of contracting, in the sense that competition is not an explicit (and often not even an implicit) aim, and payment systems provide no incentive to cost control. For example, in Brazil the federal government has contracted, through the social security programme, for more than 80 per cent of all private hospital beds (Rodrigues 1989). The history of the arrangement demonstrates the cost control problems created by fee-for-service payments, and the difficulties of changing behaviour through a new case-based prospective payment mechanism.

The one arrangement that appears to have competition as a prime objective is the new social insurance system in Thailand. The social security office contracts with hospitals (public or private) to provide comprehensive care in return for an annual capitation fee. The hospital is chosen annually by the employer, and must make adequate arrangements for specialist and outpatient care (often contracting itself with primary and specialist facilities to ensure this).[25]

10.4.3. Conditions in developing countries likely to affect the success of market mechanisms

Given the lack of experience with contracting in developing countries, the discussion of its relevance to such countries must inevitably be speculative.

[25] In the first year of the scheme, health care utilization rates were very low, it is believed because the hospitals chosen by employers were not accessible for employees. There are plans to move towards employees selecting their preferred provider.

Concerns surround three main areas: the market structure; issues surrounding managing contracts; and wider effects on the whole health system.

Market structure

An obvious problem in developing countries is that they are often characterized by lack of health facilities, and difficulties of physical access further limit services available within a specific geographical area. Thus, in many rural areas there is an obvious lack of competition for particular types of medical care, and contracting for clinical care seems to make little sense.

However, points can be made against this view. First, in rural areas where only one facility is adequate to service the local population, the contracting arrangement could involve a management contract for an existing publicly owned facility, or for leasing the building. Where a facility does not exist, the contract could involve the private sector building and then operating the facility.[26] The question then is whether private companies exist (or might exist) that would be interested in such contracts. In countries like South Africa, where there is already substantial private sector experience in running hospitals, and where private hospitals, having grown very rapidly, are facing financial difficulties (Price 1994), or Thailand, where the private sector is heading towards an oversupply of hospital beds in Bangkok, the public sector market has certain attractions. In other countries at an earlier stage of the private hospital boom, it may be that opportunities in the private sector are as yet too profitable for the private sector to be interested in government contracts.

Second, in large urban areas there may already be sufficient facilities to provide competition, or at least to ensure contestability. For example, private services, whether hospitals, nursing homes, or diagnostic facilities, have been growing fast in many capital cities, particularly with the perceived decline in public sector services. Against the contestability argument are constraints on market entry, particularly those relating to government regulations (though regulations are being eased in a number of countries—see Bennett and Mills 1991), the ease with which capital can be raised, and the acknowledged problems in all countries of the significant sunk costs and asset specificity associated with health care provision (Roberts 1993). An established large hospital may be able to deter competitors from entering the market and making supra-normal profits unless demand is growing very fast.

Such problems, however, are likely to be less significant for primary care than for hospitals. Private providers abound in the urban areas of many cities, and require little to practise except a building and minor equipment. It seems

[26] This was the arrangement in two of the three contracts for local acute hospital care in South Africa; in the third the government had already built the hospital, but decided to contract a private company to run it.

surprising, therefore, that there has been virtually no consideration of primary care contracting. The reason may be that there is assumed to be a stronger case for direct public provision of primary care than for hospitals because of arguments relating to externalities. However, public urban health centres are often in short supply, underused if quality is poor, and less popular than private clinics (Yesudian 1994; Pannarunothai 1993): hence there is likely to be considerable scope for competitive contracting for primary care facilities in many cities.

A major concern in developing countries is likely to be the quality of the private sector. Will firms and medical practitioners look for an opportunity to make a quick profit, or are there reputable firms that have a long-term interest in the sector? It should be emphasized that it is by no means clear that the existing private sector is necessarily efficient (Wouters 1993; Bennett 1991), whatever the claims made on its behalf (World Bank 1993b). Hence the process of managing any contract is likely to be vital. Partly because of concern over quality and motivation in the private for-profit sector, NGOs (especially missions) are frequently mentioned in terms of their potential for supplying services on behalf of the public sector. Whether they are likely to be interested in competitive tendering still has to be established, and it is possible that their motivations may not be sufficiently financial to provide the incentive to efficiency that contracting seeks to provide.

On the purchaser side, there are also a number of concerns. Prime among them must be the competence of the public sector to act as an efficient purchaser. The managerial problems that result in inefficient publicly provided health services are also likely to result in poor regulatory performance, and in the possibility of regulatory capture (Bennett *et al.* 1994) or at worst corruption. It follows that there are also concerns as to whether the purchaser's aim will be to maximize the welfare of users. These concerns are greater when it is taken into account that the purchaser may be not the national ministry of health, but a regional or provincial authority. A weak purchaser may permit providers to behave more opportunistically than they otherwise would.

Another factor that may undermine the ability of the health authority to act as an efficient purchaser is the pervasive uncertainty about resources which is characteristic of many developing countries. This may have a number of consequences that affect the market, and particularly may make all concerned highly risk-averse. Health authorities may be unwilling to enter into long-term contracts, while providers may be unwilling to agree a short-term contract. Health authorities may be unwilling to pay an adequate price, and thus there may be no takers for the contract.

Managing contracts

There must be severe questions concerning the ability of many governments to negotiate and manage contracts. Governments are generally inexperienced in contract design and management. There are even concerns in several countries about the ability of the government tender board to manage contracts for non-clinical services. There is a danger that poorly designed contracts will distribute all or most of the risk to the purchaser, and reduce the incentive for efficient provision. For example, the two existing South African contracts that involve the purchaser building and then running an acute hospital appear to be highly advantageous to the provider, since they guarantee payment for a minimum occupancy level and the contract period is long (Broomberg 1994).

Information systems are usually very weak, on both cost and quality. While it is assumed here that contracting is likely to be selective, purchasers still need to know enough about their own cost structures to judge whether a service is worth putting out to contract, and whether the contract price is reasonable. This was a problem, for example, with contracting for non-clinical services in Lesotho (Bennett 1991). Thus, the contractor may be better informed than the purchaser about the risks involved, permitting the former to profit at the expense of the latter. However, it is also possible that potential contractors have equally poor information systems, and are ill-equipped to take on the contracts.[27] Weak information systems imply that the transactions costs of establishing and monitoring contracts may be relatively high.

A final problem in specifying and managing contracts may be user fees. For example, in the case of a contract with a mine hospital in Zimbabwe, a government clerk was placed in the hospital with the responsibility of certifying who was eligible to be given free care; in practice, however, everyone received free care (McPake and Hongoro 1993). In the re-negotiation of the contract, the government wishes the hospital to ensure payment by those who should pay (particularly those who belong to medical aid schemes and higher-income groups). The hospital, not surprisingly, is unwilling to be faced with the task of collecting payment and risking bad debts. In all three of the contracted district hospitals in South Africa, a government cashier sits in the hospital and collects fees. Governments may not find it possible to shift the risks associated with collecting fees to the contractor.

Wider effects on the health system

In assessing whether the benefits of contracting are likely to outweigh the costs, account must be taken of the effects on the health system as a whole. There are a number of concerns.

---

27 For example, a well-known international firm of management accountants took on a contract to help improve the management and financial control of a large teaching hospital in Africa. Despite their general expertise, they were ill-prepared for the particular complexities of sophisticated hospitals: particularly the power that specialists had over resource allocation. If well-known firms can misjudge the difficulties, so may smaller, local firms (personal communication).

First, where a reasonably elastic supply of human and physical resources to the health system does not exist, there is a strong danger that prices and salaries will increase, and the contracted service will benefit at the expense of public providers. In a number of countries, the public sector already faces severe competition from the private sector for trained staff. However, to the extent that many countries have an excess supply of professionals (particularly doctors), the problems are lessened though they may still be manifest in high staff turnover.

Second, contracting may lock the government into contracts that have to be paid regardless of their financial circumstances. This is likely to be a major problem in the poorest countries, which can afford to fund few services at a reasonable level. Thus, an area with a contract may be protected at the expense of other areas with publicly provided services. However, it can also be a problem in richer countries. For example, in the case of the mine hospital referred to earlier, the district population benefited from a much higher level of expenditure than that available for other districts in the same province (McPake and Hongoro 1993). Equity problems may also arise, given the likely problems in terminating a contract: the government may not be an effective negotiator when faced with the threat of a contractor pulling out; hence there may be a tendency over time for contracted services to benefit at the expense of public provision.

Finally, where contracting for hospital care is introduced in urban areas where facilities are plentiful, as in the case of the social insurance system in Thailand, there is a danger that competition may distort the behaviour of public hospitals, encouraging them to concentrate on services where they are in competition with the private sector rather than on those that provide greatest health benefit to the local population (Saltman and Otter 1992).

10.4.4. Design of contracting systems

It may seem, from the above catalogue of problems, that market mechanisms to encourage efficiency in the public sector are of no value. However, there are likely to be some forms of contracting which may be useful in some circumstances. This section is a preliminary attempt to identify the forms and circumstances.

In terms of the approach to provider markets, it seems highly unlikely that any developing country would be in a position to implement a nationwide system such as that in the UK. Of relevance are likely to be contracts with private sector firms to run public facilities, selective contracting in urban areas for specific clinical services and for primary care, and contracting of non-clinical services in hospitals and for specific public health measures such as environmental health services.

Management contracts, to work well, should give the contractor control over all resources used in the hospital, including staff. Contracts that leave staff employment in the hands of the government are unlikely to be effective in improving efficiency where a major source of inefficiency is staff numbers and working practices.[28] The source of competitive pressure would have to be the threat that the contract would not be renewed. This threat may be more plausible if the hospital building is government-owned (despite the danger that the operator may run down the capital stock). The problem of shortage of government funds for construction may be overcome if donors are willing to provide capital for district hospitals.

It would be desirable for the contract to involve not only the provision of hospital services, but also the running of and support to district primary care services. Otherwise the hospital, especially if paid on a per-day basis, may have a financial interest in getting patients into the hospital rather than keeping them out of it. Moreover, integration would enable hospital-based expertise to be shared with the community services and would avoid the inefficiency inherent in a situation where community services have to be supported from a separate centre.

Selective contracting in urban areas may provide the opportunity for private hospitals with excess capacity to offer their services to the public sector at discounted prices. However, it is important that there be actual competition or the threat of competition, and that the choice of services should be governed by consideration of cost effectiveness. In many rapidly developing countries there is at present a boom in medical technology, and probably excess capacity in diagnostic equipment in the private sector (Nittaramphong and Tsangcharoensathien 1994). Contracting should not be the means of giving public sector patients excessive access. Contracting for non-clinical and primary care services are likely to be the easiest to implement, at least in those countries with a reasonably sized private sector.

The most difficult questions are likely to arise over the design of contracts. The contract must provide for a reasonable distribution of the risk between purchaser and provider. Poor information systems are likely to make case-based payment systems difficult to implement in many countries, and providers (except possibly NGOs) may be unwilling to accept block contracts.[29] Fee-for-service systems are generally accepted to have undesirable effects (World Bank 1993a). The different objectives of purchaser and provider may best be accommodated by some form of cost and volume contract, or by the less undesirable form of fee-for-service where there is a standard charge per day.

Monitoring of quality, especially where there is doubt over the ethical behaviour of the private sector, is likely to be vital. It is clear that existing

[28] This problem is seen in some of the South African contracts where the contractor employs only the adminstrative staff.

[29] These provide a lump-sum payment in return for which the provider treats all patients who turn up.

contractual arrangements for clinical services involve virtually no monitoring of quality. McPake and Hongoro (1993) argue that, where the contract provides an incentive to minimize services per day (as for example in a fee-per-day payment), any tendency to reduce quality can be monitored through checking whether necessary physical inputs are provided. However, there are other aspects of the performance of the contract that this approach to monitoring would miss. For example, adverse selection may be a problem when the contract cannot easily be designed to ensure that providers have no incentive to avoid particularly high-cost patients, and moral hazard may occur when providers can take advantage of the agreement reached to put fewer resources into the contract. Given the poor information systems in developing countries, the best approach may be carefully selecting contractors, building up a long-term relationship with providers, and monitoring the physical resources provided.

10.5. Conclusion

Positions are already beginning to be taken on the value of market approaches to improving the efficiency of the public health sector in developing countries. The World Bank, for example, argues that,

for some services provided by the public sector, the system of provision is so grossly inefficient that it is unlikely to be cost-effective no matter what interventions the system tries to provide. Such inefficiencies have been criticized so clearly and for so long that it is evident that they will only be overcome by radical changes in the organization of health care—such as a shift in the government's role from providing care to financing care and stimulating competition among providers. (World Bank 1993*a*)

The Chief Health Advisor of the British Overseas Development Administration is quoted as saying that 'dividing investors from providers creates friction, but in the long term leads to more effective use of resources' (Dean 1994).

However, such policy prescriptions are being advanced in an almost total lack of knowledge on whether these solutions are likely to be any better than the systems they are intended to replace. Moreover, it is not clear that it will be any easier to develop government capacity to negotiate and monitor contracts and regulate the private sector than to improve the efficiency of public providers. There is also a potential contradiction between the emphases of the *World Development Report 1993* on funding only interventions that are cost-effective and making greater use of the private sector, since the latter's actions are likely to be less easy to influence.

Despite the remarkable lack of evaluation of the impact on efficiency of reforms to public provision, there are sufficient examples to indicate that it is possible to make improvements. The evidence suggests that technical efficiency is best promoted by a combination of decentralization and strengthening of local management capacity which provides both the incentive to improve efficiency and the means of so doing. Such action would also help to improve operating efficiency, but more substantial improvements may require national-level policies to change, for example professionally set staffing norms. Means to improve allocative efficiency are less clear, not least because it requires a greater degree of political direction and clear decisions on what the public sector can and cannot provide.

Both bureaucratic and market reforms would appear to demand decentralization. An important question for further investigation is the extent to which this will on its own enhance efficiency, by changing the incentives faced by managers and health workers, without needing the introduction of the administrative and organizational complexities required to create and maintain competition. Furthermore, since countries differ greatly in the potential for reforming the public sector and in the extent of private sector activity, further investigation needs to define more clearly the country and market characteristics that can guide decisions on which approach is the most desirable and for which services. Finally, greater effort needs to go into monitoring the consequences of reform for efficiency (and equity), and in comparing efficiency gains with the costs of bringing them about.

References

Abel-Smith, B. (1986). 'The world economic crisis. Part 2: health manpower out of balance', *Health Policy and Planning*, 1(4): 309–16.
—— (1989). 'Jamaica', in B. Abel-Smith and A. Creese (eds.), *Recurrent Costs in the Health Sector: Problems and Policy Options in Three Countries*. World Health Organization, Geneva.
—— and Creese, A. (eds.) (1989). *Recurrent Costs in the Health Sector: Problems and Policy Options in Three Countries*. World Health Organization, Geneva.
Barnum, H. and Kutzin, J. (1993). *Public Hospitals in Developing Countries: Resource Use, Cost, Financing*. Johns Hopkins University Press, Baltimore.
Bartlett, W. and Le Grand, J. (1993). 'The theory of quasi-markets', in J. Le Grand and W. Bartlett (eds.), *Quasi-markets and Social Policy*. Macmillan, Basingstoke.
Baumol, W. J., Panzar, J. C., and Willig, R. D. (1988). *Contestable Markets and the Theory of Industry Structure*. Harcourt Brace Jovanovich, New York.
Bennett, S. (1991). *The Mystique of Markets: Public and Private Health Care in Developing Countries*, PHP Departmental publication no. 4, LSHTM, London.
—— and Mills, A. (1991). *The Public/Private Mix in National Health Systems and the Role of Ministries of Health*. WHO/SHS/NHP/91.2, World Health Organisation, Geneva.
—— *et al.* (1994) 'Carrot and stick: state mechanisms to influence private provider behaviour'. *Health Policy and Planning*, 9(1): 1–13.
Berman, P. (1993). 'The productivity of manpower and supplies in rural Java', in A.

Mills and K. Lee (eds.), *Health Economics Research in Developing Countries*. Oxford University Press, Oxford.

Birdsall, N. and James, E. (1993). 'Health government and the poor: the case for the private sector', in J. N. Gribble and S. H. Preston (eds.), *The Epidemiological Transition: Policy and Planning Implications for Developing Countries*. National Academy Press, Washington, DC.

Bloom, G. and Segall, M. (1993). *Expenditure and Financing of the Health Sector in Kenya*, Commissioned Study no. 9, Institute of Development Studies, Brighton.

Brazier, J., Hutton, J., and Jeavons, R. (1990). 'Evaluating the reform of the NHS', in A. J. Culyer, A. K. Maynard, and J. W. Posnett (eds.), *Competition in Health Care: Reforming the NHS*. Macmillan, Basingstoke.

Broomberg, J. (1994). *Managing the Health Care Market in Developing Countries*. Departmental Publication no. 11, Health Policy Unit, London School of Hygiene and Tropical Medicine (forthcoming).

Bumgarner, J. R. (1992). *China: Long Term Issues and Options in the Health Transition*. World Bank, Washington, DC.

Caiden, N. S. and Wildavsky, A. (1974). *Planning and Budgeting in Poor Countries*. Transactions Books, New Brunswick, NJ, and London.

Culyer, A. J. (1992). 'The morality of efficiency in health care: some uncomfortable implications'. *Health Economics*, 1(1): 7–18.

Cumper, G. E. (1984). *Determinants of Health Levels in Developing Countries*. Research Studies Press, Letchworth, Herts.

—— (1991). *The Evaluation of National Health Systems*. Oxford University Press, Oxford.

Dean, M. (1994). 'Redirecting British foreign aid'. *Lancet* no. 343 (1 January): 45.

Ellis, R. P. and Chawla, M. (1993). 'Public and private interactions in the health sector in developing countries. Phase 1: Review of concepts and literature, and preliminary fieldwork design'. Health Financing and Sustainability Project, ABT Associates, Bethesda, Md.

Fiedler, J. L. (1990). 'Organizational development and privatization: a Bolivian success story'. *International Journal of Health Planning and Management*, 5(3): 167–86.

—— (1991). 'Organizational development and privatization: a Bolivian success story—a rejoinder'. *International Journal of Health Planning and Management*, 6(2): 157–60.

Foster, S. (1993). 'Economic aspects of the production and use of pharmaceuticals in developing countries', in A. Mills and K. Lee (eds.), *Health Economics Research in Developing Countries*. Oxford University Press, Oxford.

Gilson, L. (1987a). *Government Health Care Charges: Is Equity Being Abandoned?* EPC Publication no. 15, LSHTM, London.

—— (1987b). 'Swaziland: health sector financing and expenditure'. *Health Policy and Planning*, 2(1): 32–43.

—— (1992). 'Value for money? The efficiency of primary health units in Tanzania'. Ph.D. thesis, University of London.

Gish, O. (1991). 'Organizational development and privatization: A Bolivian success story—a comment'. *International Journal of Health Planning and Management*, 6(2): 155–6.

Halstead, S. B., Walsh, J., and Warren, K. S. (eds.) (1985). *Good Health at Low Cost*. Rockefeller Foundation, New York.

Issaka-Tinorgah, A. and Waddington, C. (1993). 'Encouraging efficiency through programme and functional budgeting: lessons from experience in Ghana and the Gambia', in A. Mills and K. Lee (eds.), *Health Economics Research in Developing Countries*. Oxford University Press, Oxford.

Jamison, D. T. *et al.* (1993). *Disease Control Priorities in Developing Countries*. Oxford University Press, Oxford.

Kalumba, K. and Freund, P. (1989). 'The eclipse of idealism: health planning in Zambia'. *Health Policy and Planning*, 4(3): 219–28.

Koita, A. and Brunet-Jailly, J. (1989). 'Mali', in B. Abel-Smith and A. Creese (eds.), *Recurrent Costs in the Health Sector: Problems and Policy Options in Three Countries*. World Health Organization, Geneva.

Le Grand, J. and Bartlett, W. (eds.) (1993). *Quasi-markets and Social Policy*. Macmillan, Basingstoke.

Lewis, M. (1993). 'A study of hospital fees in the Dominican Republic', in A. Mills and K. Lee (eds.), *Health Economics Research in Developing Countries*. Oxford University Press, Oxford.

—— Sulvetta, M. B., and La Forgia, G. M. (1991). 'Productivity and quality of public hospital medical staff: a Dominican case study'. *International Journal of Health Planning and Management*, 6: 287–308.

Marquez, P. (1990). 'Containing health costs in the Americas'. *Health Policy and Planning*, 5(4): 299–315.

McPake, B. (1993). 'User charges for health services in developing countries: a review of the economic literature'. *Social Science and Medicine*, 36(11): 1397–1405.

—— and Hanson, K. (1993). 'The Bamako Initiative: where is it going?' *Health Policy and Planning*, 8(3): 267–74.

—— and Hongoro, C. (1993). 'Contracting out in Zimbabwe: a case-study of a contract between Wankie Colliery hospital and the Ministry of Health'. *Health Economics and Financing Programme*, LSHTM, London.

—— and Ngalande-Banda, E. (1994). 'Contracting out of health services in developing countries'. *Health Policy and Planning*, 9(1): 25–30.

Mills, A. (1990) 'The economics of hospitals in developing countries. Part 1: expenditure patterns'. *Health Policy and Planning*, 5(2): 107–17.

—— (1993). 'The cost of the district hospital: a case-study from Malawi'. *WHO Bulletin*, 71(3/4): 329–39.

—— *et al.* (1990). *Health System Decentralisation: Concepts, Issues and Country Experience*. World Health Organisation, Geneva.

Mogedal, S., Steen, S., and Mpelumbe, G. (1995), 'Health sector reform and organizational issues: lessons from selected African countries', *Journal of International Development*, 7(3): 349–68.

Nittaramphong, S. and Tsangcharoensathien, V. (1994). 'Thailand: private health care out of control?' *Health Policy and Planning*, 9(1): 31–40.

Pannarunothai, S. (1993). 'Equity in health: the need for and the use of public and private health services in an urban area in Thailand'. Ph.D. thesis, London School of Hygiene and Tropical Medicine, London.

Price, M. (1994). 'The impact of political transformation in South Africa on public/private mix policy debates'. *Health Policy and Planning*, 9(1): 50–62.

Purohit, B. C. and Rai, V. (1992). 'Operating efficiency in inpatient care: an exploratory analysis of teaching hospitals in Rajastan, India'. *International Journal of Health Planning and Management*, 7: 149–62.

Republic of Uganda (1991). *National Health Personnel Study*. Ministry of Health, Kampala.

Roberts, J. (1993). 'Managing markets'. *Journal of Public Health Medicine*, 15(4): 305–10.

Robinson, R. and Le Grand, J. (eds.) (1994). *Evaluating NHS Reforms*. King's Fund Institute, London.

Rodrigues, J. (1989). 'Hospital utilisation and reimbursement method in Brazil'. *International Journal of Health Planning and Management*, 4: 3–15.

Ross-Degnan, D. *et al.* (1992). 'A strategy for promoting improved pharmaceutical use: the international network for rational use of drugs'. *Social Science and Medicine*, 35(11): 1329–41.

Saltman, R. B. and Otter, C. V. (1992). *Planned Markets and Public Competition*. Open University Press, Buckingham.

Save the Children Fund (SCF) (1993). *Investing in Health. World Development Report 1993: The SCF perspective.* SCF, London.

Thomason, J. and Edwards, K. (1991). 'Using indicators to assess quality of hospital services in Papua New Guinea'. *International Journal of Health Planning and Management*, 6: 309–24.

Tollman, S., Schopper, D., and Torres, A. (1990). 'Health maintenance organisations in developing countries: what can we expect'. *Health Policy and Planning*, 5(2): 149–60.

Trisolini, M. G. *et al.* (1992). 'Methods for cost analysis, cost recovery and cost control for a public hospital in a developing country: Victoria Hospital, St Lucia'. *International Journal of Health Planning and Management*, 7: 103–32.

Unger, J.-P., Mbaye, A., and Diao, M. (1990). 'From Bamako to Kolda: a case-study of medicines and the financing of district health services'. *Health Policy and Planning*, 5(4): 367–77.

Vogel, R. J. (1987). *Cost Recovery in the Health Care Sector: A Synopsis of Selected Country Studies in West Africa*. World Bank, Washington, DC.

—— and Stephens, B. (1989). 'Availability of pharmaceuticals in sub-Saharan Africa: roles of the public, private and church mission sectors'. *Social Science and Medicine*, 29(4): 479–86.

Williams, A. (1993). 'Priorities and research strategy in health economics for the 1990s'. *Health Economics*, 2(4): 295–302.

World Bank (1993*a*). *World Development Report 1993: Investing in Health*. World Bank, Washington, DC.

—— (1993*b*). 'Better health in Africa'. Draft, Africa Technical Department, World Bank, March 1993.

Wouters, A. (1993). 'The cost and efficiency of public and private health facilities in Ogun State, Nigeria'. *Health Economics*, 2(1): 31–42.

Yesudian, C. A. K. (1994). 'Behaviour of the private sector in the health market in Bombay'. *Health Policy and Planning*, 9(1): 72–80.

11

Improving the Cost Effectiveness of Education Systems: An Assessment, and an Illustration from South Africa

CHRISTOPHER COLCLOUGH

11.1. Introduction

It is widely agreed that the present disposition of resources in the education sector in developing countries is both inequitable and inefficient. Inequity is best illustrated in the case of Africa, where one-fifth of total public educational spending provides higher education for only 2 per cent of the age group. On the other hand, primary schooling captures less than half of all education expenditures even though it is the only part of the system that most people have the chance to join. While those who succeed in gaining access to the tertiary levels of education are disproportionately the progeny of the richer groups in society, large numbers of children from poorer families do not enrol at the base of the system (for a range of demand-side as well as supply-side reasons), and many more have access to primary schooling of only very poor quality.

This distribution of educational resources is not only inequitable, but also inefficient, because in most developing countries expenditures upon primary schooling are associated with greater social returns than those at higher levels. Efficiency losses are increased by the fact that almost two-thirds of those not enrolled in primary school are girls, for whom the social productivity of primary schooling is greater than for boys (partly, but not only, because of their relatively greater underenrolment).

Internal efficiency in education is also low in many countries, particularly at primary level. High rates of repetition and drop-out often imply that it takes twice as long (and therefore costs twice as much) as it should to produce a school-completer. Not all educational expenditures on those who leave early are wasted. However, in many countries children attend schools with insufficient materials provision for learning to proceed adequately, and those who leave school illiterate are unlikely to retain lasting benefits. Internal efficiency is, therefore, a positive function of school expenditures: it becomes worse as per capita resources for schooling decline.

Much of the recent debate about how to change these circumstances has focused upon ways and means of passing more of the costs of education—mainly, but not only, at tertiary levels—to its recipients, thereby liberating more state resources to expand access and improve the quality of education lower down the system.[1] In this literature, the opportunities available to reduce the costs of schooling, so as to reallocate existing resources within the system, have tended to be ignored. Partly, this reflects the fact that government spending on education has already been severely reduced, in per capita terms, in most of the developing countries affected by recession during the 1980s. In these cases, where declines in the quality of educational services have been widespread, it might seem obvious that securing further savings from reductions in unit expenditures would be unwise. However, declines in public expenditures per pupil have occurred in unplanned and unsystematic ways, such that school quality has often been reduced unnecessarily sharply. This paper examines the potential for a more focused approach, which would allow resources to be concentrated on those aspects of educational provision that are essential to preserve the quality of schooling. The opportunities are assessed on the basis of internationally available evidence, and they are illustrated in the particular case of South Africa, where cost reduction measures in the more privileged parts of the educational system have become vital, if the policy aims of the new democratic government are to be achieved.

11.2. Cost Reduction and the Idea of an Educational Production Function

The idea that there is a determinate relationship between inputs to the production process and the outputs that subsequently emerge has long been central to microeconomic analysis. If a firm's production possibilities are governed by certain technical relationships between different factors of production, the production function describes the maximum feasible output obtainable from alternative combinations of these inputs. Thus, knowledge of the prices of these inputs can lead to a fairly easy determination of the minimum cost combination of inputs necessary for the production of any given level of output. Production functions are powerful analytic tools which have been applied to the analysis of most forms of economic production.

---

[1] See e.g. Mingat and Tan (1986), Jimenez (1987), World Bank (1986). For critiques, see Colclough (1996), and Ch. 3 above.

Since the mid-1960s, they have also been widely used in the economic analysis of education—albeit mainly in the literature on education in industrialized market economies.

The application of this idea to education is, however, more hazardous than with other forms of production. While it may be reasonable to assume that managers of firms in some sense 'know' the shape and characteristics of the production function that they face in their industry, this is not the case with educational managers. Moreover, the inputs to the schooling process are much less homogeneous (teachers, goals, pupils) than in industry (where labour usually faces more defined tasks than do teachers in schools), and the characteristics of the outputs (more schooled pupils) cannot be unambiguously compared with earlier inputs for 'value added' purposes. As a result of these differences, some authors have dismissed the possibility that attempts to investigate the education production function will ever produce sensible results (Bowles and Levin 1968; Levin 1976).

This has not deterred researchers from seeking evidence for production relationships within the schooling process. (Hanushek (1986) reviews 144 such studies, and Fuller (1987) summarizes the results of 60 empirical studies conducted in developing countries.) However, reflecting the above difficulties, the main aim of this literature has been to identify the most important factors influencing school outcomes, rather than to specify fully the technical form of the production function in education. Accordingly, knowledge of the minimum cost combinations of inputs to education that would be required to achieve given outputs remains somewhat elusive.

For the same reasons, the diagnosis of economic inefficiency within the schooling process is less clear-cut than in other sectors. Although the conceptual framework within which efficiency can be assessed is the same, evidence for its occasion is more indirect than elsewhere. It is usual to distinguish two kinds of efficiency. Economic efficiency refers to achieving, with respect to a particular set of outputs, an optimal mix of inputs, given their respective prices and the nature of the production function. Technical efficiency, on the other hand, refers to the ways in which these inputs are used in production, and is achieved when output is maximized (given the choice of input mix), i.e. when the firm, or industry, is operating on its production frontier.

In education these distinctions are also important. We wish to know, for example, whether, in a particular price–wage context, the school system is characterized by optimal pupil–teacher ratios, trained teachers, schoolbooks per child, and so on. Having some notion of what constitutes economic efficiency is thus important to achieving effective policy choice. Technical efficiency is also important. We wish to know the most effective ways for teachers to use the various technologies available to them, and how to organize schools, classrooms and lessons in order to maximize their effectiveness.

A major problem, however, which confronts all attempts to estimate the education production function—and thus to diagnose best practice techniques—is that many potentially important variables cannot be adequately measured. The innate abilities of different groups of students are usually unmeasured, as are the qualitative differences between schools and programmes. Equally, teachers with the same measured attributes and qualifications may have very different teaching styles and techniques, which may have a significant impact upon the achievement of their pupils. Thus, as Murnane and Nelson (1984) argue, the possibility of there being significant skill differences between teachers with similar qualifications undermines the ability of the production function approach to establish objective indicators of desirable school inputs and of their optimal combination.

An equally important problem is that the objectives of schools also differ. Even if examination results are, in general, an efficient proxy for the most valued outputs of schools, both their average value and their distribution are likely to be judged separately important. Thus, minimizing the standard deviation of examination results among final-year classes may, to some extent, be competitive with the goal of achieving the highest average results, and these goals may be differently emphasized among schools. Accordingly (as argued by Brown and Saks 1975), studies that exclude consideration of the distribution of examination results among pupils may be measuring the output variable incorrectly, and thus may produce biased estimates of the relative importance of different input variables to the schooling process.

For all of these reasons, obtaining indications of the existence of inefficiencies in education are less than straightforward. If, as some would argue, schools are inherently inefficient, owing to the absence of incentives for teachers to minimize costs, or to their lack of knowledge of how best to maximize their output (however defined), this provides added difficulties for gaining insights about how to make schooling more cost effective on the basis of cross-section data from different schools.

A final point is that most of the extant studies of education which adopt a strict production function approach have been conducted in the countries of Europe and North America. The research in developing countries has focused mainly on testing Coleman's hypothesis (Coleman *et al.* 1966) that schools make little difference to student achievement. Accordingly, as Fuller concludes (1987: 275), the relative magnitude of the effects arising from different school factors has been explored only rarely in developing countries. Since education systems in developed countries are uniformly better resourced, with a higher quality of both inputs and outputs than their counterparts in the nations of the South, it is by no means certain that evidence from the former on the relative importance of teacher training, or of expenditures on teaching materials, is of much help for countries in the South, where teachers may, on average, have spent only half as long in school, and where real per-pupil expenditures on materials may be only 3–5 per cent of their levels in developed market economies.

This, then, appears to provide support for the view that, while attempts to reduce the cost of education in northern countries are worthwhile, in many countries of the South, resources are already so meagre and thinly spread that attempts to reduce the costs of schooling further are more likely to undermine the efficacy of the schools than to improve the effectiveness of resource use. At the least, evidence for the viability of efficiency reforms needs to be based upon evidence gleaned from their effectiveness in developing, rather than developed, countries, and in such comparisons the potential negative impact upon the quality of schooling needs to be directly confronted.

11.3. A Framework for Examining the Role of Cost Reduction in Developing Country Education Systems[2]

The main aim of cost reduction strategies in the education sector of developing countries is to generate efficiency savings which can be used either to increase enrolments, or educational quality elsewhere in the system. This is not, of course, the only way of securing enhanced enrolments or quality, as indicated below. It can be shown[3] that

$$GER \equiv x/ac, \qquad (1)$$

where GER = the gross enrolment ratio, i.e. the total enrolments at a given level of education as a percentage of the population in the relevant school age group, x = the proportion of GNP spent on schooling, c = average unit costs as a proportion of per capita income, and a = the proportion of the population of school-going age.

The most direct way of increasing enrolments is obviously by increasing expenditures on education. The above equation implies that increases in the proportion of national income allocated to any level of education would increase the GER by the same proportionate amount, provided that unit costs, and the number of people eligible to attend, remained unchanged. It also implies that, for given levels of expenditure, reductions both in unit costs and in the proportion of the population eligible to attend school (e.g. by reductions in the rate of population growth) would increase the proportion of children enrolled.

It is useful also to distinguish between those expenditures incurred by the state and by private households. Thus, the proportion of GNP spent on any

---

[2] A more extensive discussion of some of the material presented here and in the next section of this paper can be found in Colclough with Lewin (1993: chs. 2 and 4).

[3] Let E = enrolments, X = recurrent expenditures made by society on schooling, C = the recurrent cost per pupil, Y = GNP, x = the proportion of GNP spent on schooling, c = unit costs as a proportion of per capita income, and a = the proportion of the population of school age. Now, $E \equiv X/C \equiv xY/c(Y/P) \equiv xP/c$. Thus, $E/P \equiv x/c$, and, since $GER \equiv E/aP$, then $GER \equiv x/ac$.

level of schooling (x) comprises expenditures by government (x_g) and by the private sector (x_p). Similarly, for expenditures per pupil, total unit costs (c) comprise those provided by the government (c_g)—e.g. the per-pupil costs of teachers, learning materials, etc.—and those provided by households (c_p)— e.g. the per-pupil costs of school fees, uniforms, school exercise books, and other privately financed schooling costs. So, the first equation can be extended, as follows:

$$GER \equiv (x_g + x_p) / a(c_g + c_p). \tag{2}$$

This second equation recognizes that there are always some direct costs of schooling that are met by private households, in addition to those that are met by the state. Thus, if public expenditures on schooling increase, the impact upon the GER will depend, *ceteris paribus*, upon the extent to which private and public expenditures are substitutes. In order to increase enrolments (or to improve school quality), governments may, therefore, be able to choose either to enhance public inputs to schooling, or to raise more monies from the private household sector via cost recovery or other approaches. On the other hand, if these two categories of expenditure are required in fixed proportions (which, in the context of a given legislative framework for education, may often be the case), enhanced public expenditures on schooling will increase the GER *only if* private expenditures also rise.

The denominator of the equation indicates that cost reduction strategies by government may also bring some unexpected consequences for private expenditures. For example, in circumstances where the mix of expenditure items funded by government and households remained unchanged, if c_g fell, c_p would also need to fall by an exactly similar proportion if an increase in GER were to be achieved with no increase in private expenditures on schooling (x_p). And, in those circumstances, if x_p did not rise—or if it rose insufficiently—then x_g would have to fall below its previous level, and the opportunity to increase GER to the extent promised by the reductions in publicly financed unit costs would be frustrated.

Some types of educational reform are, in principle, capable of reducing unit expenditures for both the state and private households at the same time, but whether they do so in practice is a different matter. For example, the financial savings arising from reductions in the real value of teachers' salaries, in the length of the school year, in the teacher–pupil ratio—i.e. those reforms that affect the general structure of the system and its cost parameters—are, in practice, likely to be much smaller for private households than for the state. This is because in most countries these two parties pay for different items, with the government generally funding teachers' salaries, and households contributing to other items of recurrent expenditure such as textbooks, materials, sports items, etc. Thus, unless deliberately designed otherwise, policies to reduce public expenditures per pupil are likely to leave privately incurred unit costs either unchanged or possibly even higher than they were before.[4] In these circumstances, as equation (2) makes clear, if the demand response were such that households were unwilling to increase the proportion of their income that they devote to schooling, the net result of cost reduction by the state would be to reduce x_g rather than to increase the GER. Accordingly, even if publicly financed unit costs can be reduced, increased enrolments are likely to require higher private spending on education. Consideration of the demand side therefore is a prerequisite for effective policy design.

I argued above that the selection of the most promising strategies to achieve reductions in the costs of schooling in developing countries need to be informed primarily by research conducted on education systems in those countries, rather than in those in the North. Some discussion of the main lessons from such research now follows, together with an indication of the most likely areas where savings in educational costs might be sought in developing countries.

11.4. Cost Reduction in Education Systems in Developing Countries

Many developing countries cannot easily increase the proportion of public expenditures going to education in current economic circumstances. However, they do have the option of seeking improvements in the efficiency with which resources are used, thereby allowing increased output for given levels of cost.[5] The two items that dominate the determination of the unit costs of education are the earnings of teachers and the size of the teacher–pupil ratio. Since salary costs typically account for around 90 per cent of recurrent expenditures, it is sensible to begin with some discussion of teachers' earnings.

11.4.1. The average earnings of teachers

In many early analyses of the growing costs of education in the South, it was argued that the levels of teachers' salaries were problematic, and that they should be reduced as part of a strategy to reduce unit educational

---

[4] This would obviously be so in the case of reducing state subsidies to private schools, or of reforms that were designed to shift direct costs from the public to the private sector (e.g. meal, tuition, or boarding charges). The latter reduce unit costs to government, but raise them, by an equivalent amount, to households.

[5] There is, of course, a problem caused by the fact that both the quantity and the quality of educational provision are critical variables in establishing the 'value' of the product delivered by the schools. Thus, measures to reduce costs may often reduce quality and, therefore, the value of the product. This trade-off needs to be confronted in assessing the extent to which particular reform measures can improve the efficiency of schooling.

costs.[6] Teachers' earnings had increased rapidly from the mid-1960s onwards, often as a result of upgrading the average qualifications of teachers (to which salaries were often explicitly linked), and of a particularly rapid expansion of tertiary facilities, staffed by very high-cost personnel, which thereby caused the average cost to rise. More recently, however, real wages have fallen considerably in most low-income and adjusting countries following the sharp devaluations of the 1980s, and particularly so in sub-Saharan Africa, where on average they were halved over 1970–85 (see Colclough 1990). Teachers fared slightly worse than other groups over that period. Staff morale is widely reported to be so low now that further declines would be counterproductive. In many countries of the South, the important question is how salaries can be increased, rather than further reduced.

The average earnings of teachers can be affected by means other than salary decline. Although there is good evidence from a range of countries that teacher quality, defined in various ways, has a positive impact upon student achievement (Fuller 1987: 280–3), there exist possibilities of changing the structure of the profession towards a more intensive use of lower-cost personnel. A number of countries, including Senegal and Colombia, have utilized 'assistant teachers' to take on those classroom tasks, such as supervising pupils during periods of self-study, which do not strictly need full teaching skills or qualifications. The redeployment of staff to reduce overheads may also be possible. In Ghana, the number of non-teaching staff in schools was reduced by 8,500 persons in 1986. Two years later, in Senegal, 1,260 administrators were redeployed to teaching jobs as part of that country's educational reforms (Mondon and Thelot 1989), which secured a 10 per cent increase in the teaching force at primary level with no net additions to recurrent costs.

11.4.2. Teacher–pupil ratios

Using teachers more intensively, without commensurate increases in earnings, is a further possibility for reducing unit costs. In the mid-1980s, about half of the sub-Saharan African countries for which data are available had pupil–teacher ratios of 37 or less at primary level and 23 or less at secondary level (UNESCO 1989). Since salaries account for around 90 per cent of recurrent costs, a 20 per cent increase in these ratios—from, say, 35 to 42 at primary level and from 23 to 28 at secondary level—would bring an almost exactly similar budgetary saving.

The most obvious way to decrease teacher–pupil ratios is to increase the size of classes. Available evidence from developing countries suggests that increases in class size to around 40 pupils at primary level have little negative

---

[6] See e.g. Jolly (1968), who sets the particular problem of teacher remuneration in the broader context of rising wages and salaries throughout the economy. Also see Hallak (1972: 117 ff.) and UNECA (1978).

impact upon the cognitive achievements of pupils (Thorndike 1973; Simmons and Alexander 1980; Fuller 1987).[7] Here, then, there appears to be significant scope for reductions in unit costs. Whatever the reported average figure for class-size at national level, however, there is always a wide dispersion around the mean. Obviously, attempts to raise class-size should focus upon those schools with the smallest number of children per class, while reducing, wherever possible, the number of overcrowded classes. Often, low population density in rural areas—or, indeed, low demand for schooling by consequence of low quality—prevent easy increases in class-size, whereas overcrowding is a frequent problem in urban centres. School mapping, and the rationalization of facilities, can help to tackle this. But in some countries the geographical distribution of the population of school age does present an important constraint on the potential effectiveness of these measures.

A rather different way of increasing teacher–pupil ratios is to introduce some form of multiple shift schooling. Under such systems, two or more entirely separate groups of pupils can be accommodated for regular teaching during the same term, week, or day in the same school. The most common of such approaches involves one group of pupils attending in the mornings and a second group using the same facilities in the afternoons. But there are other variants. Whether teachers' salary costs are reduced by multiple shift approaches depends upon the particular system used. If each shift required a different set of teachers (as in Singapore) or, alternatively, if teachers taking two shifts were paid for their additional work *pro rata*, salary costs would be reduced only to the extent that two shifts reduced the number of teaching hours per pupil, and thus the number of teachers required. Again, if teachers were paid more for two sessions than for one, but at a lower hourly rate (as in Senegal in the late 1980s, where those teaching the second shift received a 25 per cent supplement to their basic salaries for a 48 per cent increase in hours worked), savings in the number of teachers and increased savings in the salary bill could be achieved.

As regards recurrent costs more generally, double-shift schooling also usually achieves economies in the employment of clerks, cleaners, and maintenance and security workers. These and other recurrent costs are not halved by double-shift methods, since the more heavy use of plant involves higher maintenance expenditure than in the case of single-shift arrangements. Nevertheless, savings here can still be significant.

The most substantial source of cost reductions from double-shift teaching is in the area of capital costs. Here, major savings in the costs of land, equipment, libraries, laboratories, and classrooms can be made. For example, Zambia's extensive use of double- and triple-shifts allowed its capital costs at primary level to be almost halved (Bray 1989: 32). In Jamaica and Malaysia,

---

[7] It is interesting to note that this is also one of the main findings from production function studies conducted in industrialized countries: class size appears to have no significant impact upon student performance (Hanushek 1987: 41).

also, savings in capital costs of 32 and 25 per cent, respectively, were obtained.

Of course, there are also costs of double-shifting. Parents have to look after their children during the shift that they do not attend, the costs of which, in the market place, may be substantial. Tutors are sometimes privately retained in order to compensate for the short day that double-shifts usually imply. There is also a range of risks to the quality of schooling which double-shift methods bring: the school is usually more tense and hurried as both breaks and teaching time are reduced; teachers, particularly those who have already taught a morning session, may often be tired and therefore able to offer only an impeded service; preparation and marking time is squeezed; and management costs and inefficiencies rise, the more difficult the conditions become.

Nevertheless these, and other problems are not decisive. There is, in fact, very little concrete evidence to suggest that double-shifts (and their associated reduced learning time inputs) have any significant impact upon the cognitive achievements of children. Early studies in Malaysia (Beebout 1972) and Chile (Farrell and Schiefelbein 1974) found no significant association between the level of academic performance and the number of shifts in which a school was daily utilized. In the case of Senegal, double-shifting allowed an 11 per cent increase in enrolments with only a 2 per cent increase in the teaching force by 1988. An evaluation of the experience in 1989 showed, on the basis of language and mathematics tests, that the move to double-shift teaching had not been associated with a reduction in school quality.

With or without multiple shifts, shortening the school year or day provides a further means of using teachers more intensively. Teaching days vary from 158 per year in Ghana to 220 in Korea. Since daily teaching hours also vary, the range of instructional time made available between different countries probably differs by a factor of two. In some countries, therefore, there may be scope to increase the annual teaching load without a commensurate increase in costs. Alternatively, shortening the school year, while maintaining the average teaching time per teacher, would save costs, although the available evidence suggests that student achievement would be negatively affected by sharp reductions in institutional time (Arriagada 1981; Heyneman and Loxley 1983).

11.4.3. Improving internal efficiency

The counterpart to using teachers more intensively is achieving a more effective use of pupil time. The costs per graduate from each level of the school system are increased the longer it takes the average child to graduate. Reductions in this average time span—by reducing the incidence of early leaving and repetition of grades—thereby reduce total costs per graduate.

In all systems there are defined points at which children leave school. In most developing countries, such leaving points include the end of the primary, lower secondary, senior secondary, and tertiary cycles. Children who leave school at points other than these are often described as 'drop-outs'. Yet whether their 'drop-out' is indeed more wasteful than that of children leaving at one of the established exit points is debatable. It is only so if the benefits of schooling accrue not on a *pro rata* basis for each year attended, but are more than proportionately bunched at the end of each particular cycle. This may be plausible for some—but by no means all—curricula, particularly so for skills which, like literacy and numeracy, take several years to acquire.

In 25 low-income countries of sub-Saharan Africa (SSA), 13 per cent of primary school pupils and 10 per cent of secondary school pupils were repeaters in 1983 (World Bank 1988: 136). But the range across countries was wide—from one-third of primary school pupils in Mali, Togo, and Central African Republic and over one-fifth in Benin, Guinea-Bissau, Guinea, and Mozambique, to close to zero in Tanzania, Zimbabwe, Ghana, and Zambia, where policies of automatic promotion prevailed. This range demonstrates the opportunity: primary enrolments could have been increased by over 20 per cent in six of the first seven African countries mentioned above, simply by abolishing repetition.[8] Furthermore, in the average SSA country this reform would be capable of pushing enrolment ratios up from their present two-thirds to around three-quarters without any increase in educational costs. Although some small level of repetition allows slow learners with special problems to be helped, in many countries repetition rates far exceed these levels. Reducing them could generate substantial savings, without commensurate costs to the quality of schooling being incurred.

This is not to imply that introducing improved repetition rates is straightforward. Often such rates are high because the curricular demands placed upon children are too great in comparison with their needs and capacities. Alternatively, they may reflect the poor quality of schooling, and be reducible only where resources available to the schools are increased, to help children to learn more effectively. Here, reducing rates of repetition would deliver smaller net savings than might first appear. However, they could remain significant: rates of repetition approaching 30 per cent allow the possibility of substantially increased expenditures per pupil if these rates could be brought down to more tolerable levels.

11.4.4. Capital costs

Capital expenditures on education in low-income and adjusting countries fell during the 1980s—much more sharply than recurrent expenditures on

---

[8] These countries comprise all those with gross repetition rates in excess of 20%, with the exception of Togo, where the primary gross enrolment ratio already exceeds 100%.

education in real terms. But this was primarily a function of budgetary constraints, and only rarely because of savings in capital costs. Comparative data on construction costs in education are scanty and unreliable. However, the experience of a number of countries demonstrates that, by using local rather than imported materials, and by using low-cost, low-maintenance construction technology, considerable savings can be made. For example, as a result of these kinds of innovation, together with increasing the involvement of local communities in construction work, Senegal reduced capital costs by 40 per cent—albeit from a very high base—after 1985. Recurrent maintenance costs were also reduced.

11.4.5. Boarding versus day schools

Evidence from Malawi showed that the annualized capital and recurrent costs per pupil of boarding schools were more than twice as high as those of day schools, while for Somalia the differential appeared to be as great as 3.5 times (World Bank 1988: 60). Ironically, boarding is particularly prevalent in the countries that can afford it least. Thus, quite a high proportion of the most educationally disadvantaged countries provide boarding facilities for a significant proportion of secondary students. The main reason is that, where a fairly small proportion of primary leavers continue on to secondary school, it is frequently not possible to provide cost-effective day schools in rural areas. Boarding is therefore necessary if children from rural households are to gain access to secondary school. To some extent, then, high secondary costs in poorer countries are an inevitable consequence of their lower secondary enrolment ratios. While this situation cannot be changed overnight, care is needed to reduce dependence upon boarding as secondary education expands and as day provision becomes increasingly viable.

11.4.6. Non-formal delivery systems

Non-formal education can be cheap, but the extent to which it is cost effective is an unresolved matter. At lower levels of schooling 'basic education' was for many years advocated as a cheaper, lower-cost alternative for those whom the formal system had passed by. It was believed—by the World Bank and other agencies (World Bank 1974)—that many developing countries with low primary enrolment ratios were too poor to secure universal access to primary schooling. Aid agencies would therefore support shorter, cheaper alternatives, which focused upon providing skills that would be useful to rural populations. The idea was to concentrate upon those aspects of the primary curriculum that led to the formation of economically useful skills—such as literacy and numeracy—and to add others which might support productive self-employment in primarily rural communities. Thus, rather than placing emphasis upon helping developing countries to universalize existing primary systems, it was believed to be more functional and cost effective to provide a specially designed programme which would improve equity by giving some education to those presently excluded and, hopefully, deliver somewhat higher returns, for the investments made, than would conventional primary schooling.

These initiatives, although well-intentioned, were mistaken. The great weakness of education programmes set up in parallel with, and using different curricula from, primary schooling is that their graduates are unlikely to be able—no matter how well they have performed—subsequently to progress through to secondary or higher levels of education. Thus, the proposed reforms could easily have become mechanisms for legitimizing existing inequalities in society, rather than the means for their mitigation. Equally, they appeared to ignore some important lessons from history. For example, the main reason for the eventual failure of the Gandhian basic education movement in India—which is the world's largest experiment to date with parallel primary systems—was precisely that parents were not prepared to continue to support a movement which, notwithstanding the laudability of its stated aims, militated against the possibility of their sons or daughters gaining access to higher levels of formal education, and thus to the potential economic rewards which that allowed (Sinclair with Lillis 1980).

The costs of attempting to replicate the teaching of the schools using distance teaching methods usually appear high. But at tertiary level the evidence for positive net savings accruing from this kind of non-formal education are stronger. One comprehensive review of the evidence concludes that this is mainly because, the more advanced is an educational course, the more the teachers working on it are paid (Perraton 1982: 22–3). Because staff salaries are such a large item in most educational budgets, the total cost of more advanced courses is largely a reflection of these higher salaries. Thus, since distance teaching mainly saves salary costs, and since many of the other (materials and equipment) costs of distance education are the same regardless of the level at which the course is offered, it is much easier for distance-teaching costs to appear favourable when compared with those of higher education than with those at lower educational levels. Here, then, lower costs per graduate can be expected, and significant economies can be gained.

11.4.7. Education with production

Another approach to reducing the costs of schooling and increasing its 'relevance' for the majority of pupils is the introduction of production activities into the schools. The idea behind such schemes is to provide pupils with vocational skills which may prove useful to them in later life, and to produce items for sale, the revenues from which can contribute to the running costs of the school.

Experience with such initiatives is now very large. But few of them have been a clear success. Students and parents often oppose the allocation of time to production activities if this is seen to damage performance in competitive examinations which give access to modern sector jobs. The quality of products made in schools is often lower than those with which they compete. Marketing is often a significant problem (Gustafsson 1988). A related point is that efficiency is often lower than in commercial production. These activities in the schools therefore require subsidy (directly or through discounting teacher costs), or protection. Finally, too much emphasis on production may lead to the subordination of learning to repetitive manufacturing tasks which allow little coherent skill acquisition.

Nevertheless, under some circumstances production can make a modest but significant contribution to the costs of schooling (see Komba and Temu 1987; Bray with Lillis 1988). This tends to be in circumstances where the schools are led by forceful persons committed to the ideas of vocationalism or community service. Advocates of such policies argue that students, particularly at secondary level, have an obligation to contribute to the administration, maintenance, and development of the schools from which they benefit, and that the expression of this obligation brings educational as well as financial benefits. In the longer run, however, linking education with production often proves difficult to sustain in situations where selection pressures retain a dominant influence over the curriculum. This was one of the main reasons for the failure of the experiments with 'relevant' secondary schooling in Botswana in the late 1970s (van Rensburg 1974; Colclough and McCarthy 1980: ch. 8; Gustafsson 1987).

Thus, the ideas behind attempts to bring not only skill formation, but also productive work into the classroom may seem attractive. But they usually bring few net benefits in revenue terms, and employers complain that skills are not adequately acquired. They may, however, be separately desirable, as means of inculcating values which society wishes to promote.

11.4.8. Length of the school cycle

An alternative means of reducing the recurrent costs of schooling is, of course, to reduce the length of the school cycle. In terms of the notation of equation (2), this reform reduces the value of a, rather than that of c_g or c_p. This is because, the longer are the primary, secondary, and tertiary cycles of education, the greater is the proportion of the population who will be eligible to attend. It is, therefore, important to assess whether the existing length of each cycle is pedagogically appropriate, since reductions could generate substantial resources to improve the quantity or quality of schooling. The most common cycle length at both primary and secondary levels is six years. But there is great variation between countries. Similarly, higher education ranges from two to six or more years, with a wide variety of patterns at degree and sub-degree levels. It appears, at least for primary schooling, that excessive length leads to lower internal efficiency. In longer cycles, pupil motivation tends to be lower in the middle grades, and repetition rates higher. Furthermore, the propensity to drop out of school is positively related to previous repetition.

The relationship between the length of school cycles and the cognitive achievements of pupils is not well documented. There is, however, some recent evidence that, at least in science subjects, those countries with longer cycles do not have significantly higher student achievement (Postlethwaite and Wiley 1991). This does not, of course, imply that cycles can always be shortened with impunity. However, there are some countries where the opportunities to achieve economies in this area are fairly obvious, while others have already implemented these kinds of reform. For example, until the late 1980s, Ghana had a pre-university cycle which—owing to the existence of 'second chance' secondary schools called middle schools, where students who had failed their entrance test to secondary school could register and try again in successive years—for many students lasted for up to 17 years. This was reduced to a maximum of 13 years as part of Ghana's recent educational reforms, thereby achieving significant recurrent savings which were reallocated to primary schooling.

In summary, the range of reforms discussed above provides some promising avenues for securing efficiency savings in most developing countries. Some of them involve reorganizing existing practice in ways that would be more effective from an educational viewpoint, and in that sense they have few, if any, associated costs. But most of them are not costless, and their implementation requires careful weighing of their negative effects against the financial benefits to be gained—most usually for the purpose of improving the quality/quantity of primary school places. Their combined impact is difficult to estimate, and depends entirely upon local circumstances. However, simulations for more than 100 countries show that savings of up to 25 per cent of public recurrent education budgets would often be possible, arising from a mix of double-shifting, increases in class-size, the introduction of teacher-helpers, and moves towards automatic promotion (see Colclough with Lewin 1993: chs. 5, 6). In what follows, I ask whether any or all of these reforms are likely to be relevant in helping South Africa to improve educational provision in the post-transition period. The discussion elucidates the nature of the choice that is being faced in that country between cost-shifting and cost-saving approaches to educational restructuring.

11.5. Possible Financing Reforms for Schooling in the New South Africa: Cost-Saving versus Cost-Shifting Approaches

The ways in which the financing of education in South Africa might be reformed has been high on the agenda of questions being faced by the new government in that country. Decades of inequality in the provision of education have led to a highly differentiated system, with far greater educational resources being made available to Whites than to Blacks. The former have historically received a standard of education similar to that available in industrialized countries, whereas education for the latter has usually been of very poor quality, characterized by overcrowded classrooms, high drop-out rates, and insufficient and poorly qualified teachers. The Government of National Unity, led by the African National Congress (ANC), is committed to the provision of a ten-year basic primary cycle which is to be compulsory and free (ANC 1994: 10; Government of South Africa 1995: 73–8). This implies expanding access to cover those presently out of school, and substantially upgrading the quality of schooling over the medium term. The costs of these changes will be substantial, and will not be able to be financed simply by expanding public expenditure on education, since the education budget is already large by international standards. The remainder of this paper examines the prospects for generating additional resources for education by reforming the ways in which the school system is presently financed, paying particular attention to the potential use of some of the efficiency reforms discussed earlier. Not all of them are applicable. But it will be shown that securing changes in teacher–pupil ratios and average teacher earnings, and improvements to internal efficiency, appear particularly promising in the South African context. It will also be shown that cost-shifting approaches could be used in tandem with these reforms, in order to help equalize public subsidies across both high-cost and lower-cost schools.

11.5.1. The costs of education in South Africa

Table 11.1 summarizes trends in education financing by the public sector since the late 1980s, and compares this with both total public spending and GDP. It can be seen that public spending as a whole increased substantially in the late 1980s, rising to slightly more than one-third the value of GDP by 1992/3. Education spending increased even more rapidly—by 27 per cent in real terms over the years 1987/8–1992/3—and amounted, by the latter year, to almost one quarter of public spending, and about 7 per cent of GDP. Both of these ratios placed South Africa comfortably within the top 10 per cent of low and middle-income countries ranked according to education spending by the state (UNDP 1993: 164–5), which itself suggests the difficulties inherent in

TABLE 11.1 Public expenditures on education, 1987/8–1995/6 (millions of rands)

	1987/8	1988/9	1989/90	1990/1	1991/2	1992/3	1993/4	1994/5	1995/6 (forecast)	Notes for 1995/6 estimates
Public expenditure on education	9920	11362	13654	16977	19882	24398	27263	29391	32213	Source: Budget Review
Total public expenditure	50075	60027	72707	87989	97588	120805	134980	139855	153088	Source: Budget Review
% of GDP	29.2	29.0	30.1	32.4	30.5	34.7	34.1	31.4	30.7	
Total public expenditure less interest	43284	51945	61973	76036	83355	102608	111574	116198	124703	Source: Budget Review
% of GDP	25.3	25.1	25.7	28.0	26.0	29.5	28.2	26.1	25.0	
GDP at market prices	171309	206888	241599	271811	320226	347785	395442	444982[a]	498380	Projected at 12% nominal growth
Public expenditure on education as % of GDP	5.8	5.5	5.7	6.3	6.2	7.0	6.9	6.6	6.5	
Public expenditure on education: as % of total public expenditure	19.8	18.9	18.8	19.3	20.4	20.2	20.2	21.0	21.0	
as % of total public expenditure less interest	22.9	21.9	22.0	22.3	23.9	23.8	24.4	25.3	25.8	
Consumer price index (1990 = 100)	69.8	78.7	90.6	103.5	119.7	134.3	147.4	160.7	176.6	Assumes 9.9% inflation 1994/5–1995/6
Public expenditure on education in 1990 prices	14215	14431	15075	16411	16611	18160	18496	18289	18241	
% increase		1.5	4.5	8.9	1.2	9.3	1.8	-1.1	-0.3	

[a] Includes author's projection for first quarter of 1995.

Sources: *Expenditure figures in current prices*: 1987/8–1993/4, Buckland and Fielden (1994: app. II (by A. Donaldson)); 1994/5–1995/6, Department of Finance, *Budget Review*, March 1995: table 5 and s. 4.3.3. *GDP at market prices*: South African Reserve Bank (1993 and 1995: table S-95) (note: earlier published series corrected from 1991/2 onwards). *CPI*: South African Reserve Bank (1995: table S-120) (provisional figures for February and March 1995 used, as reported by CSO).

seeking further substantial increases in the proportionate importance of such expenditures.

After 1992/3, however, the budgetary stance changed. The real value of public expenditure as a whole fell over succeeding years, and it can be seen from the table that education spending remained constant in real terms. The budgeted figures for 1995/6 (the first full year of the new democratic government) implied a slight fall in real spending on education, which again constrained the education budget to the levels of expenditure first attained in 1992/3. Without begging questions about the merits of the budgetary stance adopted by the new government, the tight approach to budgetary allocations in education compounds the difficulties raised by the need to restructure and expand the school system: with population growth at around 2 per cent per year, and enrolment growth much faster than this, at perhaps 4 per cent per year, publicly provided resources per pupil declined by about 12 per cent over 1992/3–1995/6, creating severe problems for the effective running of the existing system, and constraining the possibilities for reform.

The question arises as to why, if historic allocations to education have been large by international standards, the available resources for education should be judged to be inadequate. The answer is, of course, that South Africa is no ordinary case. There has been a heavy bias in the allocation of educational resources (as in other sectors), towards a minority of the population. By consequence, South Africa does not have the depth of human resources availability which would otherwise be expected on the basis of its proportionate allocations to education in recent years. Nor does it have an education system which generally reflects such resourcing. Capital and human resources in education are strongly concentrated in the ex-tricameral schools (i.e. schools previously reserved for the white, Asian, and coloured populations) and in the historically white universities. The costs of running these institutions reflect this history; for example, the ex-tricameral department schools have, in recent years, accounted for about one-fifth of the total school enrolments up to middle secondary level, yet their costs have absorbed almost one-half of total expenditures on schooling up to that level. Thus, in the context of a severely constrained budget, educational improvements for the majority of the population will depend initially upon the speed and extent to which a redistribution of capital and human resources within the education system, and in the annual budgets that support any given distribution, can occur.

11.5.2. Options for the future

The quality of schooling that is provided almost always affects the resources it requires, so there is no single, or straightforward, estimate which can be made of the costs of universal provision. Estimates of such costs are predicated upon the provision of a service of a particular quality being made available, and thus require the resolution of the trade-off between what may be pedagogically desirable and what proportion of its resources a society believes should be allocated to schooling. In cases where, as in South Africa, the provision of a school system for all children, of a standard similar to that in industrial countries, would absorb an untenably high proportion of GNP, the costs of alternative measures to enhance school quality have to be compared with their likely relative effectiveness, in order to decide which should be adopted for implementation.

In what follows, a framework is provided within which the appropriate levels of resourcing the school system can be judged. The cost-impact of a range of different reforms to the school system are examined which could expand its capacity sufficiently to be able to provide ten years of schooling for all children, and would considerably improve the quality of schooling available to the majority of the population. The purpose of this is to explore the cost and resource impact of some important policy alternatives, rather than to advocate a particular set of policy reforms. Only by making their relative costs explicit can rational choice of reforms be facilitated.

It should be noted that, since the costs of education are a direct function of the quality of service provided, the notion of 'free and compulsory' education is constrained in important ways. On the one hand, a commitment to providing free schooling for all children presupposes the idea of a certain minimally acceptable quality of schooling which would be made available to all. But on the other hand, some idea of a maximum affordable quality of schooling is also likely to be implied. In cases where families wish to avail themselves of a higher quality of schooling than that, the supplementation of public funds by private resources may be required. In that sense, then, the South African state is likely not to be able to guarantee to provide fee-free schooling at levels of quality beyond those that are deemed affordable for all.

No official figures had been published by 1995 for expenditure on different categories of schools. However, an educational expenditure survey was conducted by the Development Bank for the year 1991/2, which provides the most comprehensive data source for expenditure between different parts of the system. Although 1995 saw a promising beginning to the enrolment of children in schools from which they had been previously barred, the broad dimensions of inequality had not changed significantly over the intervening years. Accordingly, the use of costs and parameters based upon 1991/2 data still provides a useful framework to analyse the resource implications of achieving universal provision of schooling of an acceptable quality.

Table 11.2 sets out the public sector costs, and financing possibilities, of ten years of free and compulsory schooling, based upon 1991/2 data. The first five rows of the table summarize a number of important dimensions of inequality for the primary and junior secondary school systems in each of the tricameral departments (i.e. those historically serving Whites, Indians, and Coloureds, respectively) and in the departments serving the African population for

Christopher Colclough

TABLE 11.2   Public sector costs and financing of 10 years o

	Total recurrent expenditure (R'000)	Increment to recurrent expenditure (R'000) (Reforms only)	Personne! costs (R'000)
	(1)	(2)	(3)
Costs and parameters 1991/2			
House of Assembly (Whites)	2,980,087		2,681,0:
House of Delegates (Indians)	633,013		597,1:
House of Representatives (Coloureds)	1,880,230		1,690,2(
Subtotal	5,493,330		
African departments	6,655,054		6,131,3:
TOTAL	12,148,384		
Additional costs of upgrading formerly African schools			
Enrolment of children presently out of school	7,507,987	852,933	6,909,1:
Reduce pupil–teacher ratio to 40 (primary) and 35 (junior secondary)	10,199,178	2,691,191	9,602,8
Increase materials expenditure per pupil	10,795,525	596,347	9,602,8
Upgrade teachers to M+3	11,329,120	533,595	10,136,4
TOTAL ADDITIONAL COSTS, FORMER AFRICAN SCHOOLS		4,674,066	
Efficiency reforms to reduce costs			
1. Automatic promotion in formerly African schools	1u,384,412	–944,707	9,291,7
2. Equalize per capita subsidy at R1,370 financed by, in formerly non-African schools:			
P/T ratio of, say 33 (primary) and 25 (junior secondary)	3,699,849	–1,793,481	3,174,9
Materials per pupil of R150 (primary) and R300 (junior secondary)	3,512,327	–187,522	3,174,9
Average personnel costs per teacher R45,000 (primary), R55,500 (junior secondary)	3,168,204	–344,123	2,830,8
Increased parental contributions	2,443,062	–725,142	
Subtotal savings (formerly non-African schools)		–3,050,268	
TOTAL SAVINGS		–3,994,975	
Net additional costs of programme			
(total extra cost in African schools minus total savings)		679,091	
TOTAL COSTS OF PROGRAMME	12,827,475		

Notes and assumptions: see text.
Sources for data in costs and parameters 1991/2, columns (1)–(7): Buckland and Fielden (1994: table 3.12, and app. tables IVb and Vc).

1991/2. The differences in state funding (column (1)) and in publicly financed costs per pupil (col. (8)) illustrate the extreme inequalities in the provision of resources to the different systems. It can be seen from column (8) that four times as much was spent by the government upon primary and junior secondary schooling for the average white child than upon that for African children. Unit cost differentials for Indian and Coloured children, compared with Africans, were about 3:1. The major cause of these sharp differences in costs per pupil were the enormous differences in pupil–teacher ratios between schools serving the African population and other schools. House of Assembly schools, serving mainly the white population, were the most privileged, with ree and compulsory schooling in South Africa, 1991–2

Materials and other recurrent support costs (R'000)	Pupils	Teachers	Pupil–teacher (P/T) ratio	Average unit costs per pupil	Average personnel costs per teacher	Personnel costs as % of total recurrent	Average materials and other recurrent support costs	
							Per teacher	Per pupil
4)	(5)	(6)	(7)	(8)	(9)	(10)	(11)	(12)
299,057	770,618	45,504	16.9	3 867	58,919	89.96	6,572	388
35,839	211,751	10,155	20.9	2,989	58,806	94.34	3,529	169
190,024	800,888	36,015	22.2	2,348	46,931	89.89	5,276	237
523,682	7,414,773	136,307	54.4	898	44,982	92.13	3,842	71
598,831	8,267,473	152,816	54.1	908	45,212	92.02	3,919	72
596,347	8,267,473	213,438	38.7	1,234	44,991	94.15	2,794	72
,192,693	8,267,473	213,438	38.7	1,306	44,991	88.95	5,588	144
,192,693	8,267,473	213,438	38.7	1,370	47,491	89.47	5,588	144
,092,678	7,578,517	195,652	38.7	1,370	47,491	89.48	5,585	144
524,920	1,783,257	58,557	30.5	2,075	54,219	85.81	8,964	294
337,398	1,783,257	58,557	30.5	1,970	54,219	90.39	5,762	189
337,398	1,783,257	58,557	30.5	1,777 1,370	48,343	89.35	5,762	189

only 17 pupils per teacher (col. (7)). African schools, on the other hand, had an average of 54 pupils per teacher in the primary and junior secondary systems—more than three times as many. The contrast with the other tricameral departments was also as great, where pupil–teacher ratios of around 20–22 held. Since teacher costs account for about 90 per cent of recurrent spending on the school system (col. (10)), sharp unit cost differentials between African and other departments were an inevitable consequence of these differences in relative teacher complements.

In addition, teachers were better qualified in the tricameral departments, as reflected by the differences in average personnel costs shown in column (9). Cost differentials for teachers' salaries were in fact higher than suggested by these data, since support personnel—who on average are paid less than

teachers—were proportionately more numerous in the tricameral departments, and their earnings are not separated out here. Provision for materials
and other support costs, too, were highly maldistributed: although the proportion of recurrent expenditure devoted to these items did not vary greatly
between departments (col. (10)), their value per pupil differed by a factor of
more than five as between white and African schools (col. (12)), owing to the
large differences in public expenditures per student between them.

The middle section of the table investigates the costs of introducing a series
of reforms for the purpose of up-grading the quantity and quality of schooling available to African children. A minimum estimate for the number of
children in the primary age group who were out of school in 1991 is some
850,000—about 10 per cent of the African school-age population.[9] The first
row of this section of the table indicates that the additional cost of enrolling
these children (the overwhelming majority of whom were African) at the unit
cost levels then pertaining in the African departments would have amounted
to about R853 million (col. (2)).

Each of the reforms shown in the table are incremental, thereby indicating
the cumulative increase in costs arising from continual improvements to the
system.[10] Thus, the second row in the middle section of the table shows the
additional costs arising from reducing the pupil–teacher ratio in the erstwhile
African primary system from present levels of 58:1 to 40:1, and in the junior
secondary system from 45:1 to 35:1, for the enhanced number of students that
would arise from an elimination of under-enrolment. This reform would increase the number of teachers required in the erstwhile African schools by 40
per cent, and would increase the recurrent costs of this sector by about R2.7
billion (col. (2)).

The target pupil–teacher ratio for primary schooling reflects ANC policy to
reduce class size to a maximum of 40 pupils throughout the primary system
(ANC 1994: 100). What then would such a reform do for class size in the ex-
African departments? The provision of a pupil–teacher ratio of 40:1 would
not be sufficient, on its own, to guarantee an average class size of 40. This is
because many head teachers spend most of their time on administrative and
managerial duties. Additionally, in the upper grades there are often specialist
teachers whose presence tends to push the teacher–class ratio above 1:1. If we
assume that 10 per cent of teachers are accounted for as heads, or as special

---

[9] This has been calculated on the basis of data in DBSA (1993) and CSS (1992). See Colclough
(1994).

[10] It should be noted that Table 11.2 is an aggregation of two analyses which were performed
for primary schooling (7 years) and junior secondary schooling (3 years) separately. Thus, the
pupil–teacher ratio for the African departments of 54.4 shown in the table is a weighted average
of the ratios for primary schooling of 57.6 and for junior secondary schooling of 44.9, which held
in 1991/2. The impact of introducing each of the reforms was also examined separately for the
two school cycles, because the cost parameters at junior secondary level are significantly different
from those at primary, leading to substantially larger unit costs in the former. The impact of the
reforms shown in the table is again the aggregation of the results of the two separate analyses.

subject teachers, an average class size of 40 would then require (with a pupil–teacher ratio of 40:1) 20 per cent of primary school pupils to be enrolled in double-session teaching arrangements (whereby one teacher would be responsible for two classes in separate shifts). To the extent that more than 10 per cent of teachers were accounted for in these ways, the extent of double-shifting would have to be greater in order for a pupil–teacher ratio of 40:1 to deliver an average class size of 40. Furthermore, the difficulties involved in achieving a *maximum* class size of 40 are much greater than those of achieving an *average* value of this amount. To the extent that population densities in some areas prevented class size from reaching 40, the requirement for teachers would again increase beyond that implied by the 40:1 ratio, in order to restrict class size to a maximum of 40 in other parts of the country. All in all, the above considerations seem to imply that a reduction in the pupil–teacher ratio to 40:1 at primary level is unlikely to enable a maximum class size of 40 to be achieved without perhaps one-quarter of primary school pupils being taught under double-session arrangements.

In order to avoid these consequences—i.e. to accommodate all primary pupils in single-shift classes of, on average, 40 children—the primary pupil–teacher ratio would need to be reduced to around 35:1. This would increase the teachers required by a further 22,776, which, in turn, would imply additional personnel costs of R966.5 million, over and above those shown in column (2) of the table. Clearly, the costs of reducing the pupil–teacher ratio are high. Whether a target for this ratio lower than 40:1 at primary level should be selected depends upon a comparison of the likely budgetary costs, as set out above, with a judgement—based upon social and pedagogic considerations—about the proportion of the pupil population which could be tolerably accommodated in double-shift arrangements.

For the purpose of demonstrating the net effect of reducing the pupil–teacher ratio, it was assumed above that the cost of recurrent materials per pupil remained unchanged (which, in turn, implied a sharp and undesirable fall in the materials support per teacher in the formerly African schools, by about 30 per cent—see col. (11)). Accordingly, the next row in the table investigates the impact of doubling the expenditure on materials per student to R144 (col. (12)), thereby achieving similar levels to those characterizing schools in the House of Delegates in 1991. The cost of this would be a relatively modest R596 million (col. (2)), and represents one of the most cost effective means of improving learning outcomes for the pupils enrolled.

An early priority for educational policy will be the task of upgrading the training qualifications of the teaching force. The next row of the table provides an estimate of the additional salary costs consequent upon upgrading all the teachers in schools serviced by the former African departments to matriculation plus three years of teacher training (M+3) levels of qualification. It appears that approximately half of the teaching force in these schools required such upgrading and that the salary impact would be approximately

R5000 per teacher in 1991/2 prices (see Buckland and Fielden 1994: 44). Again, it can be seen that the cost impact of this—at about R530 million (col. (2))—is far less than that involved in reducing the pupil–teacher ratio, although the direct costs of providing the upgrade training are excluded from this calculation.

It can be seen (col. (2)) that the additional recurrent costs of all of these reforms taken together would amount to some R4.674 billion—equivalent to about 40 per cent of recurrent expenditure on primary and junior secondary schooling in 1991/2, and to some 23 per cent of total recurrent expenditure on education at that time. These amounts are substantial, and could not be financed simply by allowing the recurrent budget to rise, for reasons indicated earlier. They comprise, however, a 'mimimum' list of required improvements to the African education system, if the electoral commitments of the ANC are to be delivered over the next few years. Accordingly, the question arises as to whether any efficiency reforms are available which could reduce the net financial impact of these improvements in the schooling available to African children.

One of the more promising possibilities concerns savings that may accrue from the reduction of rates of repetition. It appears that, over the whole 12-year school cycle, the average African school-completer has typically taken one year longer to progress through the system than pupils in the extricameral schools (Buckland and Fielden 1994: 41). This provides proxy evidence for the fact that repetition rates in the latter schools may be lower by some 8 percentage points than those in ex-African schools. This evidence is only proxy, in that it may well be that rates of drop-out followed by subsequent re-entry are higher among African children. If so, this would tend to increase the age dispersion of these pupils relative to other groups. Nevertheless, there is other evidence to show that repetition has been higher among African children. Accordingly, the first row of the last section of the table indicates the savings accruing from the introduction of 'automatic promotion' for these groups. It should be noted, first, that these estimates equalize the average rates of repetition as between ex-African and all other schools; thus, they are compatible with some minimal rates of repetition continuing in future. Second, the reasons for repetition rates being high in the past are essentially to do with the interaction between curricular demands on the one hand, and very low levels of resourcing in ex-African schools on the other. The qualitative improvements implied by the reforms discussed above could do much to facilitate reductions in rates of repetition without adverse consequences being incurred for the quality and efficiency of learning. It can be seen that the potential savings are significant. The table shows that the drop in rates of repetition would imply a reduction in the size of the student body of almost 700,000 pupils (col. (5)), and annual savings of over R900 million in 1991/2 prices.

A second important set of savings is available as a consequence of a move

towards equalizing the publicly provided resources available to the historically white and the historically black schools. There are a number of different
ways in which this could be done. One approach would be to equalize the per
capita subsidy for non-salary expenditures. But, as can be seen from the
table, since only R317 of the 1991/2 unit cost differential of R2,969 between
ex-HoA and ex-African schools arose from non-salary expenditure differences
(compare col. (8) with col. (12)), the potential for achieving more equitable
resource allocation via these means is very limited. An alternative would be
to move teaching staff from the presently high-cost to the low-cost sectors,
and vice versa. This alone, however, would not bring budgetary relief, and
major personnel shifts would in practice prove to be extremely difficult owing
to the present residential distribution of the population. The only practical
way of achieving an equitable distribution of public resources will be by
moving towards the provision of equal per capita subsidies—and ultimately
to a distribution of subsidies strongly skewed towards the poorest communities—throughout the school system, for all children, irrespective of
race.

The impact of this reform is shown in the table. It is a simple matter to
calculate, from the first four rows of the table, the savings to the public sector
that would arise from reducing per capita subsidies to primary schooling to
any given amount. This can be done by multiplying the pupil numbers shown
in col. (5) by the difference between the unit costs shown in col. (8) and the
target values selected. It will be noted that the reforms to improve the quality
and quantity of schooling for African children illustrated in the table have the
effect of increasing the unit costs in these schools from R898 to R1,370.
Accordingly, I show the savings to the public budget that would accrue from
equalizing the per capita subsidy across all schools at R1,370 per annum. It
can be seen from column (2) that this generates very significant savings of R3
billion in 1991/2 prices which, together with those arising from the reduction
in rates of repetition, would reduce the net additional costs of the whole programme to about R679 million per year—equivalent to a relatively modest 3
per cent increment to total recurrent spending on education in 1991/2.[11] This,
then, implies that ten years' free and compulsory schooling could be achieved
with only a modest addition to budgetary resources, providing that a strong
and consistent approach to reform is adopted throughout the system.

---

[11] It should be noted that the direct costs of training the extra 78,000 teachers needed for the
school expansion and reductions in pupil–teacher ratios are not included in these calculations.
Also excluded are the direct costs of upgrading the teachers among the existing teaching
force, and the costs of additional classrooms needed both to meet the shortages of school facilities
which have built up in recent years and to accommodate those presently out of school. Each
of these costs is 'once-for-all', in the sense that it does not represent a continuing burden on the
recurrent budget. The capital costs of school construction were intended to be met out of the
reconstruction and development programme (RDP), which was financed from extra-budgetary
resources.

There are, of course, a range of ways in which the introduction of equal per capita subsidies could be pursued, each of which may have different implications for the quality of schooling available in the erstwhile privileged sector. One approach would be to expand the enrolments and desegregate the latter schools, imposing the same cost parameters (teacher–pupil ratios, class size, materials support, etc.) throughout the system. This would result in a more equitable distribution of inputs, but would sharply reduce the quality of schooling in the erstwhile privileged sector. Although this has already partly occurred, by consequence of African children now being allowed to enrol at any government or aided school, the extent of redistribution was, by end-1995, still limited.

A more pragmatic approach, which would be compatible with the provisions of the South African Schools Bill 1996, would simply be to cut state spending on the higher-cost schools, and allow parental contributions to make up the financial deficit, as determined by each school and its governing body. The solution adopted in each school would depend upon parental incomes and wishes. The likely outcome of this policy would be a decrease in average cost parameters in the erstwhile privileged sector to levels below those associated with earlier times, but higher than costs obtaining throughout the rest of the system. One possible set of implications of this policy are illustrated in Table 11.2, where increases in average pupil–teacher ratios, together with some reductions in materials support and in average teacher costs, could cover a significant proportion of the financial gap caused by the reduced levels of state funding. These changes would reduce unit costs in the erstwhile privileged sector from recent levels of R3,000 per pupil to around R1,780 (col. (8)). This would imply an increase in parental contributions in these schools of, in 1991/2 prices, around R400 per pupil per year (the difference between the state subsidy available to all and the somewhat higher unit cost of schooling in the ex-tricameral schools)—a relatively easily affordable sum. Alternatively, some further reduction in unit costs could be achieved if average teacher costs in the erstwhile privileged sector were reduced to levels obtaining in the rest of the system. If this were achieved, the remainder required from increased parental contributions would fall to around R200 per pupil.[12]

11.6. Conclusion

South Africa presents a typical case of an African school system that is in great need of qualitative improvement and quantitative expansion. Temporary increases in state spending on education are possible, but are unlikely to

---

[12] Average personnel costs per teacher of R47,491 would imply unit costs, post-reform, in the ex-tricameral schools of R1,560 p.a.—i.e. parents would face average fees of approximately R200 per pupil per year.

provide a long-term solution. Efficiency reforms within the formerly African school system seem able to produce some useful financial savings: double-shifting might be capable of saving about R1 billion, but a more modest amount of double-shifting, involving, say, 10–15 per cent of pupils, would imply savings of about half that amount; and reductions in repetition could save about R950 million, on an annual basis. Nevertheless, the likely cost of the quantitative and qualitative improvements required for African schooling far outweighs these magnitudes.

This paper has shown, however, that efficiency reforms focused upon the formerly privileged sector of schooling would be capable of financing most of the remaining shortfall. The power of increases in pupil–teacher ratios to reduce the costs of schooling in the former tricameral schools is considerable: if these were increased to around 40:1 (which, as argued in the first part of this paper, could be achieved without bringing disastrous consequences for the quality of schooling), the greater part of the costs of improving facilities in the formerly African schools could thereby be covered. Moves in this direction were made in 1994 and 1995, when it became illegal, under the new constitution, to deny access to schooling on the grounds of race. Parents and children have sought educational opportunities in schools where they would previously have been denied access. Many schools have responded with enthusiasm to the challenge, and have expanded their educational programmes and facilities to accommodate them (Government of South Africa 1995: 74).

On the other hand, it is unrealistic to suppose that equalization of pupil–teacher ratios throughout the whole school system could, or should, be the reform upon which all else depends. There are many government, and state-aided, schools which are situated in areas where sharply higher enrolments will prove impossible owing to residence patterns. Furthermore, many high-cost schools, with highly experienced and qualified teachers, and with well-endowed libraries and school resources, would continue to cost much more, per pupil, than the poorest schools, even with full equalization of pupil–teacher ratios. In any case, there will continue to be many parents or communities who wish to supplement school resources by making voluntary contributions to finance better teaching conditions for their children. Any legislated approach towards the equalization of these ratios, therefore, would fail.

We have shown that an alternative approach—initially equalizing, and ultimately making progressive, the distribution of per capita recurrent subsidies across all state schools—would be compatible with giving schools the option of raising additional monies from parental contributions. To accommodate the inevitable adjustment difficulties in the historically more advantaged schools, this would need to be phased in over a period of years, and would have the disadvantage of allowing a continuation of some elite schools within the state system. However, provided that the value of the subsidy for the poorest schools was set at a level that guaranteed a defensible level of school quality, many undesirable outcomes of differentiated systems could be avoided. Here, different objectives, to some extent, conflict. But there are grounds for optimism that South Africa, using a careful mix of efficiency and cost-shifting reforms, will be able to achieve reasonable equality of educational opportunity, even among the schools that prove less able to supplement state resources by funds raised from households or communities.

Most countries do not have the same opportunities as South Africa to improve school quality for the majority of pupils via redistribution. But the use of efficiency reforms to save resources and reduce costs is widely relevant. Close monitoring of the results of budgetary restructuring upon schooling outputs in South Africa should, therefore, provide highly instructive lessons for the application of efficiency reforms elsewhere.

References

African National Congress (ANC) 1994, *A Policy Framework for Education and Training*, (draft document), Education Department, February, (ANC, Johannesburg).

Arriagada, H. (1981), 'Determinants of Sixth Grade Student Achievement in Colombia', Education Department Paper, World Bank, Washington, DC.

Beebout, H. (1972), 'The Production Surface for Academic Achievement: An Economic Study of Malaysian Secondary Schools', Ph.D. Dissertation (University of Wisconsin, Madison).

Bowles, S., and Levin, H. (1968), 'The Determinants of Scholastic Achievement: An Appraisal of Some Recent Findings', *Journal of Human Resources*, 3(Winter): 3–24.

Bray, M. (1989), *Multiple-Shift Schooling: Design and Operation for Cost Effectiveness* (Commonwealth Secretariat, London).

—— with Lillis, K. (eds.) (1988), *Community Financing of Education: Issues and Policy Implications in Less Developed Countries* (Pergamon, Oxford).

Brown, B., and Saks, D. (1975), 'The Production and Distribution of Cognitive Skills within Schools', *Journal of Political Economy*, 83: 571–93.

Buckland, P., and Fielden, J. (1994), 'Public Expenditure on Education in South Africa, 1987/8 to 1991/2', mimeo (Centre for Education Policy Development, Johannesburg).

Central Statistical Services (CSS) (1992), *Census of Population, 1991*, Vol. 26 (Pretoria).

Colclough, C. (1990), 'Wage Flexibility in Sub-Saharan Africa: Evidence and Implications' in Standing and Tockman (1990: 211–32).

—— (1994), 'How Many Children Are Out of School?' mimeo, reproduced in Buckland and Fielden (1994: app. VI).

—— (1996), 'Education and the Market: Which Parts of the Neo-liberal Solution are Correct?' *World Development*, 24(4): 589–610.

—— with Lewin, K. (1993), *Educating All the Children: Strategies for Primary Schooling in the South* (Clarendon Press, Oxford).

—— and McCarthy, S. (1980), *The Political Economy of Botswana: A Study of Gro and Distribution* (Oxford University Press, Oxford).

Coleman, J., *et al.* (1966), *Equality of Educational Opportunity* (US Department of Health, Education and Welfare, Washington, DC).

Development Bank of Southern Africa (DBSA) (1993), *Public Expenditure on Education in South Africa 1987/8–1991/2* (DBSA, Pretoria).

Farrell, J., and Schiefelbein, E. (1974), 'Expanding the Scope of Educational Planning: The Experience of Chile', *Interchange* 5(2): 18–30.

Fuller, B. (1987), 'What School Factors Raise Achievement in the Third World?' *Review of Educational Research*, 57(3): 255–92.

Government of South Africa (1995), 'White Paper on Education and Training', *Government Gazette*, no. 16312, 15 March (Department of Education, Cape Town).

Gustafsson, I. (1987), *Schools and the Transformation of Work: A Comparative Study of Four Productive Work Programmes in Southern Africa* (Institute of International Education, University of Stockholm).

—— (1988), 'Work as Education: Perspectives on the Role of Work in Current Educational Reform in Zimbabwe', in Lauglo and Lillis (1988).

Hallak, J. (1972), *Financing and Educational Policy in Sri Lanka,* International Institute for Educational Planning (UNESCO, Paris).

Hanushek, E. (1986), 'The Economics of Schooling: Production and Efficiency in Public Schools', *Journal of Economic Literature*, 24: 1141–77.

—— (1987), 'Educational Production Functions', in Psacharopoulos (1987: 33–42).

Heyneman, S., and Loxley, W. (1983), 'The Effect of Primary School Quality on Academic Achievement across Twenty-Nine High and Low-Income Countries', *American Journal of Sociology*, 88: 1162–94.

Jimenez, E. (1987), *Pricing Policy in the Social Sectors: Cost Recovery for Education and Health in Developing Countries* (Johns Hopkins University Press for the World Bank, Baltimore).

Jolly, A. R. (1968), 'Employment, Wage Levels and Incentives', in International Institute for Educational Planning, *Manpower Aspects of Educational Planning: Problems for the Future* (UNESCO, Paris: 236–47).

Komba, D., and Temu, E. (1987), 'State of the Art Review of Education for Self-reliance Implementation', mimeo (Ministry of Education, Tanzania, and Foundation for Education with Production, Botswana).

Lauglo, J., and Lillis, K. (eds.) (1988), *Vocationalizing Education: An International Perspective* (Pergamon, Oxford).

Levin, H. (1976), 'Concepts of Economic Efficiency and Educational Production', in J. Froomkin, D. Jamison, and R. Radner (eds.), *Education as an Industry* (Ballinger, Cambridge, Mass.: 149–91).

Mingat, A., and Tan, J.-P. 1986, 'Expanding Education through User Charges: What Can be Achieved in Malawi and Other LDCs?' *Economics of Education Review*, 5(8): 273–86.

Mondon, P. and Thelot, C. (1989), 'Le Succès de l'école au Senegal', report to the Ministry of Education (Dakar, Senegal).

Murnane, R., and Nelson, R. (1984), 'Production and Innovation when Techniques are Tacit', *Journal of Economic Behaviour and Organization*, 5: 353–73.

National Educational Policy Investigation (NEPI) (1993), *Educational Planning, Systems and Structure* (Oxford University Press, Cape Town).

Perraton, H. (ed.) (1982), *Alternative Routes to Formal Education: Distance Teaching for School Equivalency* (Johns Hopkins University Press for the World Bank, Baltimore).

Postlethwaite, T., and Wiley, D. (1991), *Science Achievement in Twenty-Three Countries* (Pergamon, Oxford).

Psacharopoulos, G. (ed.) (1987), *Economics of Education: Research and Studies* (Pergamon, Oxford).

Simmons, J. (ed.) (1980), *The Education Dilemma: Policy Issues for Developing Countries in the 1980s* (Pergamon, Oxford).

—— and Alexander, L. (1980), 'Factors which Promote School Achievement in Developing Countries: A Review of the Research', in Simmons (1980: 77–95).

Sinclair, M., with Lillis, K. (1980), *School and Community in the Third World* (Croom Helm, London).

South African Reserve Bank (1993, 1995), *Quarterly Bulletin*, March.

Standing, G., and Tockman, V. (eds.) (1990), *Towards Social Adjustment* (ILO, Geneva).

Thorndike, R. (1973), *Reading Comprehension in Fifteen Countries* (Halstead Press, New York).

UNDP (1993), *Human Development Report 1993* (Oxford University Press, New York).

UNECA (1978), *A Survey of Economic and Social Conditions in Africa 1976–77*, Part 1 (UN, New York: 59–145).

UNESCO (1989), *Statistical Yearbook 1989* (UNESCO, Paris).

van Rensburg, P. (1974), *Report from Swaneng Hill* (Dag Hammarskjöld Foundation, Uppsala.)

World Bank (1974), *Education Sector Working Paper* (World Bank, Washington, DC).

—— (1986), *Financing Education in Developing Countries: An Exploration of Policy Options* (World Bank, Washington, DC).

—— (1988), *Education in Sub-Saharan Africa: Policies for Adjustment, Revitalisation and Expansion* (World Bank, Washington, DC).

PART VI

Fiscal and Governance Reforms

12

Fiscal Reform and the Extension of Basic Health and Education Coverage

ROBIN S. L. BURGESS

12.1. Introduction

Basic health and education are central to the development process. Good health and literacy have value in their own right and are key determinants of people's standard of living (see Sen 1987; Anand and Ravallion 1993; UNDP 1994). Expanding access can therefore have highly positive consequences in terms of social protection and the alleviation of poverty (World Bank 1990). Widespread provision of these basic services also helps to expand capabilities, improve skills and equalize opportunity sets across households. Thus, aside from their direct welfare consequences, basic health and education represent investments in human capital which are central to the process of economic growth (see Lucas 1988; Barro 1991; Stokey 1991). Healthy, literate populations are more able to take advantage of growth opportunities that arise. In the dynamic context, these basic services are increasingly seen to have a key role in the creation of 'virtuous cycles' of development whereby investments in basic health and education, through skill and product upgrading, lead to economic growth, which in turn generates additional resources for investments in human capital. Positive feedback loops of this type are seen by many analysts to underlie the creation of growth 'miracles' (Lucas 1993; World Bank 1993a).

Despite the centrality of these basic services to both welfare and economic growth, in the bulk of developing countries coverage is far from universal, and attainment—as proxied, for example, by infant mortality and literacy rates—is far below what is achieved in the developed nations. Low levels of attainment in terms of basic health and education are often associated with widespread poverty and stagnant growth. Many countries may be characterized as being caught in a low-level equilibrium, whereby limited investments in basic health and education imply that the capability of the population to learn new skills or engage in advanced production processes is limited, thereby contributing to low or negative rates of growth. Low economic growth coupled with high population growth may lead to net reductions in the resources available for future investments in human capital. This pattern of development, characterized by negative as opposed to positive feedbacks, has been widely observed in the developing world.

Widening access to health and education services may thus be seen as having a critical influence on the path of development in a given country. Lack of public finance usually stands out as a major constraint on extending such coverage. Even where aggregate resources are adequate, expanding access may be constrained by a limited commitment to provide it. Take-up of these services by households will also be influenced by such factors as the direct and opportunity costs that potential users face, household poverty, and the extent to which these services are valued within the household. If access to these basic services is to be widened, full account must be taken of financing and implementation constraints, the functioning of markets and institutions for providing these services, and the structure of incentives and preferences.[1]

This paper is about how fiscal reform can contribute to extending coverage of these basic services. The role of three sets of fiscal reforms—tax reform, expenditure reform, and decentralization—are examined in turn. Basic health is taken to refer to public (i.e. preventative) health interventions and essential clinical services, while basic education is taken to mean the primary span of schooling, which allows for at least the acquisition of basic literacy and numeracy.[2] The basic health and education package thus comprises goods and services that have strong public good characteristics and tend to be inadequately provided through private markets.[3] For a given level of expenditure, these interventions tend to have a relatively large impact on measures of health and education attainment.

The perception that public budgets cannot be expanded, combined with the observation of falling real levels of public resources for these services in some countries, has led to a focus on the potential for private financing, for example, through the imposition of user fees (see Jimenez 1987, 1994, and Chapters 2 and 3 above). Though appropriate in some circumstances and for particular types of intervention (in particular non-basic interventions), they should not be viewed as a panacea and cannot be relied upon to solve the financing problem or to ensure universal coverage of basic health and education.

Two assumptions underlie the prevalent view that (public) basic health and

---

[1] For an example of this approach, see Drèze and Saran (1993).

[2] The definition of the feasible or implementable basic health and education package will vary with the level of development of the country and the quantity of public finance that is available.

[3] These definitions of the basic health and education package should be made with reference to what is feasible through private markets (see Hammer 1993). Otherwise the case for public finance is unclear.

education budgets are of relatively constant size. First, limited administrative capacity and other constraints are taken to imply that overall tax capacity is fixed in most developing countries. Second, it is assumed that the allocation of revenue to different heads of expenditure is fixed by political and other considerations. In this paper we examine how both these (sets of) assumptions can be relaxed, through tax and expenditure reforms respectively, in order to expand the financing base available for basic health and education. Even with a fixed budget, measures that decentralize the finance and provision of basic health and education can help to increase the efficiency of public spending. It would therefore seem worthwhile to examine the contribution that direct fiscal reform, as opposed to the switch to private finance, can make in easing the financing constraint on basic health and education.

The paper thus has two core objectives. First, we wish to examine the role of tax and expenditure reform in increasing the overall size (in real terms) of the basic health and education budgets. Second, we wish to examine the extent to which measures such as decentralization can improve the efficiency of expenditure and revenue generation. The structure of the chapter is as follows.

Section 12.2 argues that taxation represents the only sustainable form of financing basic health and education in developing countries. Aid, debt, and inflation finance are not sustainable and may ultimately reduce financing capacity. Expansion of financing for these services is thus linked to the tax reform process where the overall objective is to raise the necessary revenue in the most efficient and least distortionary manner. In developing countries, both the theory of taxation and the structure of constraints imply that greater emphasis should be placed on indirect as opposed to direct taxes. In this context, taxes such as VAT can make significant contributions whereas systems that rely on the monitoring and extraction of personal contributions (e.g. formal social security systems) are unlikely to advance us much towards the goal of universal coverage.

Section 12.3 shows how expenditure reform is critical to achieving adequate public finance for basic health and education. Prioritization of basic health and education expenditures needs to take place both within health and education budgets and within the overall government budget. At the core of expenditure reform is a fundamental rethinking of the role of the state (see Stern 1991). Whereas some areas of state activity need to be downplayed (e.g. industrial production, defence), other areas may need to be given greater emphasis (e.g. basic health and education). This section examines some possible directions for expenditure reform that would have the net effect of increasing the overall size of the basic health and education budgets.

Section 12.4 examines whether efficiency gains are realizable through decentralization of provision and financing of basic health and education. Decentralization of provision represents one key mechanism by which accountability and hence commitment to these services can be improved.

Direct participation of the local community in the provision of these services will help widen access, strengthen sustainability, and encourage learning about the benefits of these services. Arguments relating to the decentralization of revenue are less strong as this involves significant losses in the scope for both redistribution and risk pooling.[4] Thus, although cost sharing at the local level can be helpful to the extent that it does not restrict access, as a means of easing the local budget constraint and strengthening accountability, it should not be seen as the dominant revenue source for financing basic health and education.

Section 12.5 concludes.

12.2. Tax Reform

Arguments presented in the Introduction to this volume would suggest that there is a significant role for government revenue in financing basic health and education services. Universal coverage of these services is unlikely to be achieved through the operation of private markets.[5] These services have been identified as being critical to welfare, productivity, and growth, yet in the bulk of developing countries they remain chronically underfunded. This has negative implications, in terms of both poor levels of health and education attainment, and poverty and growth.[6] The problem is that those with the greatest need for basic health and education are precisely those with the lowest ability to pay for them. This points to a role for the fiscal system in playing a redistributive role by raising adequate revenue to guarantee universal coverage of these basic services. This section examines how government revenue generation can be enhanced in order to expand aggregate basic health and education budgets and thus close these funding gaps.[7]

12.2.1. Properties of financing instruments

Before entering into a discussion of specific financing instruments, it is worthwhile to sketch the general requirements of tax instruments for financing basic health and education.

---

[4] With complete decentralization to a system of user fees, the scope for both these functions is negligible.

[5] Public interventions none the less need to be cognizant of how they affect incentives for private finance or provision.

[6] The gap between needs and available finance is much more pronounced in developing than in developed countries.

[7] How basic health and education services can receive greater priority, both within overall health and education budgets and within the total government budget, are considered under expenditure reform in S. 12.3 below.

Implementability

Large informal and agricultural sectors and weak administrative capability imply that the set of effective tax instruments is limited in developing countries (see Musgrave 1959; Hindrichs 1966). In contrast, economic activity in developed countries tends to be concentrated in the formal sector, which simplifies income measurement, tax enforcement and tax collection (see Burgess and Stern 1993: s. 3.1). This implies that taxes that require means-testing are likely to be less implementable in developing countries (Barr 1993*a*, *b*). Implementability must however be balanced against concerns of economic efficiency, and this may warn against excessive reliance on distortionary domestic taxes (e.g. taxes on inputs) or foreign trade taxes for financing basic health and education.

Stability

Aggregate demand for health and education is spread evenly across time, and systems that provide these services require a steady flow of finance in order to function effectively. The need for stability is particularly strong in the basic health and education sectors which are made up mainly of small projects with low start-up costs and high recurrent costs. Interruptions can be associated with high welfare costs. These problems are particularly severe in developing countries where highly imperfect capital markets imply that opportunities to borrow and hence to smooth finance over time are limited.[8] Revenue instruments that are unreliable or that provide finance only for limited periods of time should therefore not be selected. Stability is enhanced if beneficiaries value the services being provided and can exert influence on their provision being continued (e.g. through voting or public pressure).

Buoyancy

Tax instruments used to finance basic health and education should have the property that the resources they generate increase in line with economic growth. Buoyancy is also necessary to meet rising demands for basic health and education created by significant population growth in developing countries. Otherwise revenues generated will not match rising costs, with negative implications for quality and effectiveness. Linking basic health and education systems to marginal or non-buoyant sources of finance can lead to degradation of these systems over time. Attachment to marginal revenue sources may also be seen as the result of a low priority being attached to basic health and education expenditures in the budgeting process. Buoyant tax

---

[8] It is therefore necessary to look at both the mean and the variance of the revenue streams generated by alternative tax instruments.

instruments which are constantly freeing additional resources to be invested in basic health and education are also instrumental in strengthening positive feedback loops and generating 'virtuous' cycles of development. Basic health and education finance, the determination of living standards, and economic growth should therefore be viewed as interlinked processes. Considerations such as these can help to bring basic health and education finance to the core of the tax reform process and closer to the front of the government's list of policy priorities.

12.2.2. Centrality of taxation

The role of the public financing of basic health and education must always be assessed in relation to the changes it induces relative to the pre-reform status quo. The point here is that substituting a reasonably well functioning private sector is not as valuable as providing or financing services which a private sector cannot be expected to sustain (see Hammer 1993). Arguments presented in the Introduction to this volume suggest that basic health and education represent a set of goods and services that are likely to rely strongly on public finance to ensure sustainable provision. This does not imply that private markets do not have a role in finance or provision. Nearly all health and education systems in developing countries are mixed, but the point is that public finance is often most critical in guaranteeing access to these basic services in particular for the poor. In developing countries where markets for these key services are thin, only the government is in a position to provide a credible guarantee of universal access to basic health and education. The issue at the aggregate level then becomes one of what form this public finance should take. We can identify four possible sources of public finance: external aid, government revenue, borrowing, and printing money (see Burgess and Stern 1993: s. 2).[9]

Basic health and education are often targets of international aid. For domestic governments this source of finance is attractive, both because it is free (or subsidized), and because it removes a set of claims on meagre domestic tax resources. Recent cross-country macroeconomic evidence suggests that aid taken as a whole, though significant in scale,[10] has had insignificant effects on growth and welfare (see Mosley *et al.* 1987; Boone 1994*a*, *b*). Boone (1994*b*), for example, finds no significant impact of aid on improvements in

---

[9] Note that social security contributions, which represent a source of basic health and finance in some regions (e.g. Latin America), are included under taxation, which is a component of government revenue.

[10] Developing countries received on average 8.6% of GDP annually in official development assistance (i.e. aid) between 1981 and 1990 (Boone 1994*a*: 1).

infant mortality, primary schooling, or life expectancy.[11] Limited emphasis on productive investments and the channelling of aid to political elites and their supporters also may constrain the growth impact of aid in cross-country studies.[12] As Cassen *et al.* (1994) point out, the interpretation of these cross-country results is complicated by the fact that the regressions do not distinguish between consumption aid and aid intended for investment. In addition, Cassen *et al.* (1994) show that in particular countries aid has had a significant impact on growth and welfare.

This type of aggregate macroeconomic evidence cannot be taken as an argument against using external aid to finance basic social services *per se*. There are however other reasons why one should be wary of advocating foreign aid as a principal source of financing basic health and education in the developing nations. A central problem is that aid does not represent a stable source of finance. Levels of aid finance to specific basic health and education projects fluctuate widely depending on the (political) vagaries of Western donors. Resources released are also unlikely to increase in line with economic and population growth. This failure to satisfy stability and buoyancy criteria is particularly serious given that the bulk of costs in basic health and education projects are recurrent. It can also be argued that aid would be more effectively used to finance large capital (and foreign exchange)-intensive projects at the tertiary level (e.g. universities, hospitals), where start-up costs and technical demands are high and professional lessons more similar.[13]

The project focus of aid for basic health and education may also lead to limited emphasis being placed on building up domestic capacity in the medium to long run and on problems of co-ordination across different providers of basic health and education. Foreign funding can also reduce the extent to which the projects are perceived as a responsibility of the community in which they are located (see Section 12.4). Aid provided in a policy context in which there is limited commitment to continued provision of these services is thus likely to be ineffective.

Taken together, these micro and macro considerations suggest that aid should not be relied on as a principal source of finance for basic health and education programmes. Several types of reform may however help to improve the effectiveness of aid as an *additional* source of finance. First, there is a strong case for targeting a greater share of the aggregate available resources at productive areas of expenditure, such as basic health and education, where

[11] This result is true independent of the type of political regime in a given country, though Boone (1994b) interestingly does find that democratic/liberal political regimes have 30% lower infant mortality. This may be a consequence of the poor being more empowered under these regimes, which may induce governments to provide more basic services.

[12] Note that improvements in basic health and education indicators are possible, even if there is no additional spending in these areas, if aid increases the incomes of the poor and hence their ability to purchase these services.

[13] I am grateful to Christopher Colclough for pointing this out to me.

effects on both welfare and growth are proven. Second, provision of aid could be made contingent on the government implementing a coherent set of policies in the basic health and education sectors and this contingency can be enforced through the operation of a system of matched grants. Third, it can be argued that aid should be used to reform the organization of the state itself, in order to strengthen a commitment to basic health and education. Support of democratic regimes and the decentralization of provision to local government are two mechanisms that may be effective in making governments more accountable along these dimensions (see Section 12.4).

Borrowing, both domestic and foreign, represents another potential source of public finance. In developing countries, owing to distorted capital markets and repressed or undeveloped financial markets, borrowing is not 'equivalent' to taxation as a source of public finance for basic health and education. By definition, borrowing involves greater taxation, or reduced expenditure, in the future, and the evidence suggests that the costs of financing basic health and education through this mechanism are higher relative to taxing now. Compared with taxation, borrowing often carries additional costs in terms of generating inflation and crowding out private investment (see Burgess and Stern 1993: s. 2).

While with taxation government expenditure is constrained by the amount of tax revenue that can be generated in a given year, this is not the case with borrowing. For borrowing to represent an attractive financing source, the government must believe that the productivity of the loans along with the taxes generated will provide sufficient resources for the loan to be serviced and repaid in the future. This is particularly unlikely to be the case for quasi-public goods and services such as basic health and education, where the returns to investment are largely non-monetary. Excessive optimism in this respect can lead to serious problems. Governments with short time horizons, for example, will have an incentive to renege on their debt. If debt is used excessively, there will come a time when it will no longer be accepted and the government will have to resort to monetizing the debt with inflationary consequences (Sargent and Wallace 1981). Taxation therefore has an advantage over borrowing in terms of constraining and disciplining profligate governments.

Some governments have also turned to financing expenditure by printing money. The revenue potential of non-inflationary money finance is limited, accounting for only about 0.5 per cent of GDP in stable, low-inflation countries. However, when the rate of new money creation exceeds the increase in the demand for money, inflation results and this acts as a tax on the population by reducing the value of real money balances (Bailey 1956). The claims on resources through his mechanism can be significant, accounting for 4.0 and 6.2 per cent of GDP in Bolivia and Argentina respectively in 1980–5 (World Bank 1988). High inflation, however, has many disruptive and distortionary effects on economic functioning (Sachs 1989; Buiter 1990).

Collection lags and other factors also tend to imply that inflation will tend to have a negative impact on real tax revenues in less developed countries (Tanzi 1991). Further, the incidence of the inflation tax is likely to be regressive, as the poor tend to hold a larger proportion of their wealth as currency and are less able to change their portfolio in response to inflation (Gil Diaz 1987). Taken together, these factors preclude any serious consideration of the inflation tax as a significant method of public finance on basic health and education.

The central argument to emerge from this subsection is that in developing countries domestic taxation represents the only sustainable and viable means for financing government spending on basic health and education.[14] There are strong general equilibrium consequences connected with the choice of source of public finance. Failure to develop an effective system of tax finance, for example, can lead to reliance on alternative, inferior sources of finance such as debt and inflation finance. These methods are not only inferior to tax finance in terms of stability and buoyancy, but are also likely to have wider effects in terms of inducing macroeconomic instability and constraining growth. Dependence on these methods of finance thus will not only reduce the capacity of basic health and education systems to function but also will undermine the ability of the government to finance them.

12.2.3. Structure of taxation

The previous section has established that taxation should constitute the main revenue source for financing basic health and education services. Given the criteria outlined in Section 12.3.1, this subsection examines the structure of taxation in developing countries in an attempt to assess the relative role that different types of tax might play in financing basic health and education. I then go on to emphasize, in later sections on direct (Section 12.3.4) and indirect (Section 12.3.5) taxes, that, because of administrative and other constraints, the set of taxes that is appropriate for this purpose, in the sense of being implementable, stable, and buoyant, is different from that in developed economies. This analysis conveys the central point that financing methods which are commonplace in developed nations may perform badly in a developing country.

Examining the bottom two rows of Table 12.1 (or, equivalently, the top rows of Table 12.2), we see that there are marked differences between developing and industrial nations as regards tax structure. Developing countries obtain the bulk of their revenue from (i) domestic taxes on goods and services (5 per cent of GDP and 30 per cent of tax revenue—partly from taxes on sales and partly from excises), (ii) foreign trade taxes (5 per cent of GDP—mainly

---

14 See Burgess and Stern (1993: s. 2) for more detail on these arguments.

TABLE 12.1.   Income breakdown,

Income range (GNP per capita) ($)	Average GNP per capita ($)	Total tax	Income taxes				Domestic taxes	
			Total	Individual	Corporate	Other	Total	General sales, turnover, VAT
<360	239	14.02	3.46	1.36[a]	2.19[a]	0.19[a]	4.55	2.44
360–749	517	19.66	5.74	2.53[b]	2.92[b]	0.21[b]	4.74	2.30
750–1,619	1,127	18.62	5.98	2.18[c]	4.08[c]	0.30[c]	6.06	2.68
1,620–6,000	2,996	19.79	6.81	2.14	3.80	0.84	5.41	2.40
All developing	1,241	18.05	5.51	2.08[d]	3.29[d]	0.40[d]	5.21	2.46
>6,000 (indus-trial)	13,477	31.21	10.96	8.45	2.37	0.14	9.43	5.58

Notes: For each country, the breakdowns are unweighted averages over the three years closest to 1987 for which data were available. GNP per capita is for 1987, in 1987 dollars. Within the total of 82 developing countries, there are 20 countries in each of the lower brackets and 21 countries in each of the upper income brackets. There are 21 industrial countries with incomes above $6,000.

[a] excl. Maldives, Kenya, Pakistan, Myanmar.
[b] excl. Western Samoa.
[c] excl. Nicaragua, Peru, Jordan.
[d] excl. Jordan, Peru, Nicaragua, Western Samoa, Maldives, Kenya, Pakistan, Myanmar.

Source: Burgess and Stern (1993) using IMF Bureau of Statistics Data. These statistics were prepared by Christine Wu of the IMF Fiscal Affairs Department.

TABLE 12.2.   Regional breakdown

Region	Average GNP per capita ($)	Total tax	Income taxes				Domestic taxes	
			Total	Individual	Corporate	Other	Total	General sales, turnover, VAT
Industrial	13,477	31.21	10.96	8.45	2.37	0.14	9.43	5.58
Developing	1,241	18.05	5.51	2.08[a]	3.29[a]	0.40[a]	5.21	2.46
Africa	621	19.53	6.65	2.28[b]	4.13[b]	0.33[b]	4.85	2.96
Asia	743	14.84	4.46	2.37[c]	2.64[c]	0.09[c]	4.55	1.59
Europe	3,361	21.88	5.80	3.44	1.53	0.83	6.86	3.43
Middle East	2,339	14.73	4.83	0.47[d]	4.44[d]	0.45[d]	2.30	0.04
Western Hemisphere	1,581	18.16	4.84	1.63[e]	2.71[e]	0.64[e]	6.47	2.75

Notes: For each country the breakdowns are unweighted averages over the three years closest to 1987 fc which data were available. GNP per capita is for 1987, in 1987 dollars. Within the total of 82 developin countries, there are 31 countries in Africa, 16 in Asia, 6 in Europe, 6 in the Middle East, and 23 in th Western Hemisphere region. The total number of industrial countries is 21.

[a] excl. Jordan, Peru, Nicaragua, Western Samoa, Maldives, Kenya, Pakistan, Myanmar.
[b] excl. Kenya.
[c] excl. Western Samoa, Maldives, Pakistan, Myanmar.
[d] excl. Jordan.
[e] excl. Peru, Nicaragua.

Source: Burgess and Stern (1993) using IMF Bureau of Statistics data. These statistics were prepared b Christine Wu of the IMF Fiscal Affairs Department.

tax revenue by type (% of GDP)

Excises	Other	Foreign taxes				Social security	Wealth and property	Other
		Total	Import duties	Export duties	Other			
1.66	0.46	5.30	4.05	1.09	0.21	0.21	0.24	0.25
1.95	0.49	7.58	6.70	0.64	0.22	0.79	0.31	0.41
2.64	0.74	4.64	4.10	0.39	0.14	0.78	0.56	0.59
1.99	1.02	3.12	2.51	0.36	0.24	3.34	0.65	0.75
2.07	0.68	5.13	4.32	0.62	0.20	1.30	0.45	0.45
3.02	0.83	0.72	0.70	0.00	0.01	8.90	1.11	0.10

tax revenue by type of tax (% of GDP)

Excises	Other	Foreign taxes				Social security	Wealth and property	Other
		Total	Import duties	Export duties	Other			
.02	0.83	0.72	0.70	0.00	0.01	8.90	1.11	0.10
.07	0.68	5.13	4.32	0.62	0.20	1.30	0.45	0.45
.44	0.45	6.84	5.74	1.01	0.12	0.44	0.41	0.37
.23	0.72	5.46	4.82	0.48	0.15	0.04	0.16	0.16
.48	0.96	2.80	2.80	0.00	0.00	5.09	0.61	1.08
.58	0.67	4.16	4.11	0.04	0.01	1.21	0.71	1.52
.81	0.90	3.46	2.50	0.49	0.46	2.37	0.58	0.65

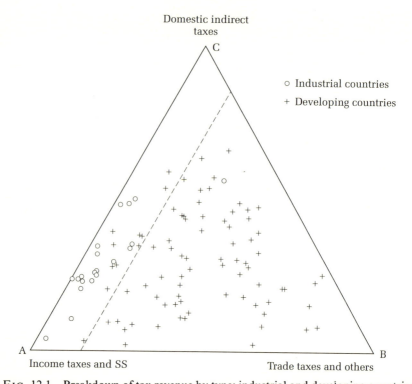

Fig. 12.1   Breakdown of tax revenue by type: industrial and developing countries
Note: The figure is constructed using the same IMF data used in Tables 12.1 and 12.2.
Source: Burgess and Stern (1993), using IMF Bureau of Statistics data. These statistics were prepared by Christine Wu of the IMF Fiscal Affairs Department.

import duties), and (iii) income taxes (6 per cent of GDP—mainly on corporations). In contrast, the three big sources of government revenue in industrial countries are (i) income taxes (11 per cent of GDP and 36 per cent of tax revenue—mainly on individuals), (ii) domestic taxes on goods and services (9 per cent of GDP and 28 per cent of tax revenue—mainly on sales), and (iii) social security contributions (9 per cent of GDP).

The different makeup of taxes in developing and industrial economies may be illustrated using the triangle diagram shown in Fig. 12.1. The points A, B, and C in the triangle represent 100 per cent of tax revenue from income and social security taxes, 100 per cent from trade and other taxes, and 100 per cent from domestic indirect taxes, respectively. A point on the line BC corresponds to a zero level of income and social security taxes, and similarly, the lines AC and AB represent the other axes. It can be seen that the industrialized countries cluster close to the AC axis and towards the direct tax corner (A), whereas the developing countries are spread out, with an average that is close to the centre of gravity of the triangle (i.e. where one-third of revenue comes from direct taxes, domestic indirect taxes, and foreign trade taxes respectively).

12.2.4. Direct taxes

Direct taxes, and in particular individual income taxes and social security contributions, dominate the tax structure in the developed economies (see Tables 12.1, 12.2; Fig. 12.1). These taxes may be less appropriate in the developing country setting, where problems of monitoring and means-testing are more pronounced, administrative capacity is more limited, and political opposition to these taxes is more effective. Choice of tax instruments for financing basic health and education must therefore be conditioned by a consideration of differences in the structure of constraints between developed and developing economies.

Looking at Tables 12.1 and 12.2 we see that income taxes from all sources account for 5.5 per cent of GDP and 28.9 per cent of total tax revenue for the developing country sample. This may be compared with industrial countries, where income taxes comprise 11.0 per cent of GDP and 35.8 per cent of tax revenue. Within these totals, corporate income taxes dominate in developing countries whereas individual income taxes dominate in developed countries. Corporations represent tax magnets in developing countries as they are large and visible and taxes can be levied directly at source. The scope for taxing corporations however is constrained by the fact that capital is increasingly mobile so that high marginal rates can act as a disincentive to investment and can lead to the flight of domestic capital.

Individual income taxes account for 2.1 (8.5) per cent of GDP and 10.6 (27.7) per cent of total tax revenue for the 82 developing (21 developed) countries examined. The constraints on raising revenue through this mechanism in developing countries are many and include problems of income measurement, administrative capability, low literacy, and poor accounting. An economic structure dominated by agriculture and small-scale (often unregistered) enterprises makes it difficult to trace, and hence tax, incomes (see Musgrave 1969; Goode 1984). As a result, revenue from this source in developing countries tends to accrue largely from taxes on the wages of employees in large public sector enterprises and private corporations to whom tax laws can be more easily applied. Collection from such a narrow base, often at high rates, creates resistance which is apparent in the experience of a number of countries (see Gillis 1989; Tanzi 1991). In industrial countries, wage and salary employment is more widespread and the capability to tax those outside this net (e.g. the self-employed) is greater, thus partly explaining the greater importance of individual income taxation in revenue which is revealed in the tables.

The importance of social security contributions in developing countries is also small, accounting for 1.3 per cent of GDP and 6.2 per cent of tax revenue. This is in sharp contrast to industrial countries, where they constitute one of the major sources of government revenue, contributing 5.9 per cent of GDP and 28.4 per cent of tax revenue. While this may partly reflect a low priority being attached to social security in developing countries, problems of extracting social security contributions are similar to those for individual income taxation. For this reason, coverage is often restricted to employees in the formal sector, leaving out most of those in the urban informal and rural sectors, while in industrial countries coverage is often close to universal (see Atkinson 1989; Ahmad *et al.* 1991; Burgess *et al.* 1993).[15]

The development of formal social security systems which has its roots in the rapid urbanization and industrialization during the late nineteenth and twentieth centuries, was seen as an efficient response to the identifiable contingencies of unemployment and retirement. While the broad objectives of social security remain essentially the same in developing and developed countries (i.e. to combat insecurity), the strategies that are relevant to these objectives and the nature of the risks being addressed may be quite different. For instance, the limitations of bureaucratic intervention, the paucity of resources, and the particular nature of incentive problems in poor countries may suggest the use of forms of intervention that have not been very prominent in the recent history of social security in developed countries: these might include basic health and education, public works programmes, food distribution systems, community-based support, and targeted pensions. The exact set of contingencies faced by individuals in developing countries is often different from that in industrial countries with, for example, a greater incidence of poverty and of health, education, and nutrition failures. Inter-generational concerns and the case for linking benefits and contributions are therefore weaker in developing countries.[16] Patterns of employment are also different from those applying in developed countries, and the informational and incentive problems connected with identifying needy individuals and financing social security tend to be more severe (see Ahmad *et al.* 1991; Burgess *et al.* 1993).

In strict contrast to many industrial nations, it would appear that formal social security systems in developing countries have only a limited role to play in financing basic social services. Midgley sums up the record of these measures in developing countries as follows:

---

[15] Given that the base of social security taxes in developing countries is largely wages, and that the share of wages in national income rises with per capita income, it is not surprising to find a strong positive correlation between the share of these taxes in GDP and log GNP per capita (see Burgess and Stern 1993).

[16] Effective management of social security funds also requires strong administrative capability, and the ability to spread risks across generations may be impaired by macroeconomic instability (e.g. high inflation).

Although the development of social security in the Third World during the post-war years has been impressive, these schemes have brought few, if any, benefits to ordinary people. They cater primarily for those who are already privileged by having secure jobs and steady incomes and exclude those whose needs for social security are the greatest. (Midgley 1984: ix)[17]

Evidence from Latin America, where these programmes have been most widespread (see Table 12.2) suggests that both contributions and benefits have been limited to a narrow group which is not the most needy (i.e. formal sector workers—see Mesa-Lago 1991). These individuals resist any attempts to extend benefits to more needy groups (i.e. those in the rural and informal sectors). Because those who benefit from these formal social security systems also tend to have the greatest political power, there has been a tendency to bid up the benefit levels to such an extent that in most countries benefits paid out exceed contributions with the residual having to be paid out of general taxation.[18] As a result, these systems do not fulfil the redistributive role that they play in the industrialized nations and their incidence tends to be regressive. Given these problems, there is a case to be made for delinking contributions from benefits and focusing instead on the generation of adequate revenue to fund basic health and education systems in the least distortionary manner possible (e.g. through broad-based indirect taxes).

In the industrial economies, both personal income and social security taxes are often viewed as key mechanisms for the redistribution of income (see Atkinson 1989). Their limited importance and regressive incidence in many developing economies implies that the scope for redistribution on the tax side of the budget is limited, thus partly eliminating the rationale for using redistributive direct taxes to finance basic health and education. Indeed, in developing countries the bulk of redistribution is done on the expenditure side of the budget, with widespread provision of basic health and education playing an important part in this process.[19] Limited implementability of personal income and social security taxes, combined with their limited redistributive power, implies that it may be wiser to focus on simple non-redistributive but implementable broad-based taxes (e.g. VAT) to fund basic health and education services. Development of a buoyant indirect tax base can also be supplemented by expansion of a direct tax base as administrative capability increases with economic development.[20]

[17] See also Atkinson and Hills (1991) for a discussion of the relevance and shortcomings of conventional social security measures for developing countries.
[18] The value of social security funds also tends to be eroded during high inflation episodes.
[19] On the expenditure side of the public budget, it appears that a range of basic social services, transfers, and safety nets are both more effective in reducing deprivation and better targeted towards the poor than formal social security measures and should therefore receive greater consideration given limited budgets (see Burgess *et al.* 1993).
[20] Failure to implement redistributive direct taxes also reflects a lack of government commitment and should be treated as a fixed constraint. In some countries tax reform has led to significant improvements in the contribution of direct taxes to overall revenue (see Burgess and Stern 1993: s. 6).

12.2.5. Indirect taxes

Domestic indirect taxes (i.e. VAT, sales taxes, excises) probably offer the greatest scope for generating additional public funds to finance basic health and education in developing countries. Whereas corporate income taxation has limited scope and individual income and social security taxes require sophisticated administration, domestic taxes on goods and services can be applied, or at least attempted, wherever markets for goods or services exist. In the developing country sample as a whole, domestic indirect taxes average 5.2 per cent of GDP and 30.4 per cent of tax revenue. This share of tax revenue is almost identical to that in industrial countries (29.3 per cent), though the share of GDP is lower.

The allocation of revenue between domestic sales taxes (2.5 per cent of GDP and 13.8 per cent of tax revenue) and excises (2.1 per cent of GDP and 12.6 per cent of tax revenue) is roughly equal for developing countries, while in industrial countries the contribution of sales taxes outweighs that of excises (see Tables 12.1 and 12.2). This partly reflects the administrative ease in developing countries of collecting revenue via excise systems.

Within sales taxes, the value added tax (VAT) stands out as the key vehicle for raising additional funds to finance basic health and education programmes. The introduction and successful operation of VAT systems have been heralded as 'the most significant event in the evolution of tax structure in the latter half of this century' (Cnossen 1991: 72). VAT systems have been introduced into over 30 developing countries, and further introductions, especially in Asia, Africa, and Eastern Europe, are planned. These systems have proved to be implementable in a wide range of settings, including in countries with low administrative capability.

There has been a movement over time away from foreign trade taxes, which represent important sources of revenue in developing countries (see Tables 12.1 and 12.2), and towards VAT and other forms of domestic indirect taxation. VAT systems have gradually replaced a range of other sales taxes which were often cascading and levied at multiple rates on different sets of goods.[21] Both these changes in tax structure are in the direction indicated by theory as being more efficient (see Burgess and Stern 1993: s. 6).

Because VAT is levied on value of sales minus purchases, tax neutrality is ensured in the sense that producers and users of a good in a production process face the same price for it. Thus, the inefficiencies associated with most other indirect tax instruments are avoided. In practice, the common price is

---

[21] Cascading occurs when taxes are added to each other as a product moves from production to final sale. With cascading, tax liabilities cumulate through the system and the effect on final prices is very hard to determine. They provide artificial incentives for vertical integration, and it is difficult to assess the tax content of exports or to decide the amount of tax to be imposed on imports (see Tait 1988; Burgess and Stern 1993: s. 3).

usually achieved by giving registered firms credit for tax paid on purchases against taxes paid on sales. This has the added benefit of creating a good audit trail. There is a built-in incentive to participate in the system in order to be able to claim for taxes paid on purchases (i.e. inputs). Tax neutrality in international trade is also ensured by applying a zero rate to exports (and allowing reclaim of tax paid on inputs) and by taxing imports equally with domestic products, thus providing no tax incentive to buy imported rather than domestically produced products and vice versa. VAT systems therefore have the attractive property that they do not impair efficient production and trade.

Nearly all categories of goods and service can be taxed using VAT, and the system typically extends through the retail stage (Cnossen 1991). Basic foodstuffs and medical articles may be exempted or taxed at a lower rate (while 'luxuries' are often taxed at a higher rate); however, overall coverage remains high. This differentiation introduces an element of redistribution into the system. Wide coverage implies that revenue stream generated by the VAT is relatively stable as there is limited scope to engage in substitution to evade the tax.

Because they cover a large fraction of the value added in a given economy, revenue from the VAT systems tend to increase in line with (or faster than) economic growth. This buoyancy contrasts with foreign trade taxes, which are highly sensitive to fluctuations in world prices, and with income taxes and social security contributions, which often decline as the size of the state sector is reduced. In Latin America, for example, the importance of VAT has been increasing over time, and now accounts for between 1 and 5 per cent of GDP for Uruguay, Peru, Mexico, Guatemala, Colombia, and Argentina, and for about 9 per cent of GDP in Chile. In nearly all developing countries where it has been introduced, its contribution to tax revenue has been increasing (see Tait 1988). It is also notable that VAT has been increasing in importance in the developed nations, despite the falling importance of domestic indirect taxes as a whole (Tait 1988). The VAT stands out as a tax instrument that is implementable, stable, and buoyant and therefore represents a good choice for the financing of basic health and education.

Excise taxes are almost as important as sales taxes in developing countries (see Tables 12.1 and 12.2). Excise goods typically have few producers and exhibit large sales volume, relatively inelastic demand, and easy observability. Three products—alcohol, tobacco, and petroleum—account for most excise revenue.[22] The fact that there are few producers (e.g. because of licence control) implies that close physical monitoring can be exercised over these goods. Thus, excises may be effectively levied on the basis of quantities (e.g. packets of tobacco, litres of alcohol) either leaving the factory or at the import stage. This simplifies measurement and collection, allows extensive coverage, and limits evasion through channels such as fraudulent invoices,

---

[22] Negative externalities provide an additional reason for singling out these goods.

understated business turnover, or spurious claims for exemption. Inelastic demand helps to contribute to the stability and buoyancy of revenue. Excises thus also stand out as an attractive source of tax finance for basic health and education. In general, excises should be restricted to a small set of goods, with the bulk of goods being taxed under a coherent and unified system of domestic indirect taxation (i.e. VAT), otherwise the system is likely to become unwieldy.

In the developing country context, domestic indirect taxes have clear advantages over direct taxes in terms of generating additional revenue in an efficient manner. There are fewer problems with monitoring and a larger fraction of value added can be reached through indirect as opposed to direct means. Domestic indirect taxes are less visible than direct taxes as they tend to be implicit as opposed to explicit, often being included in the prices of inter-mediate or final products. As these taxes are typically applied to the bulk of goods and services in the economy, they are also difficult to evade. Customers are often not as aware that they are paying indirect taxes and are therefore less likely to resist this form of taxation compared with, for example, personal income taxes or social security contributions. They also have the advantage that they are less painful as they entail a series of small payments spread out over time. In addition, domestic indirect taxes tend to have a wide incidence and are not concentrated on particular groups. This makes them less subject to political lobbying and capture. Behavioural responses to indirect taxes are less marked than for direct taxes. It can thus be argued that indirect taxes are more lump-sum in nature with positive implications for evasion. Given negative perceptions of taxation and the efficiency with which tax revenue is spent, low visibility and enforced compliance are attractive properties of instruments for financing basic health and education expenditures in develop-ing countries.

These taxes are not strictly progressive on the tax side but, since propor-tionally more of the tax revenue will be raised from better off people (who have higher commodity demands) while basic health and education expend-itures mainly benefit the poor, their overall incidence can be progressive. This is particularly so where the avoidance of direct taxation by the rich is widespread, as happens in many developing countries. Thus, though benefits are delinked from contributions, and though there is limited scope for redistribution via taxation alone, the fiscal system as a whole can none the less have strong redistributive and risk pooling characteristics.

12.3. Expenditure Reform

There can be little doubt that the chronic underfunding of basic health and education services reflects not only limited tax capacity but also a lack of commitment on the part of both central and local governments to fund these services and a failure of the public effectively to elicit such commitment.[23] The financing constraint for basic health and education is thus not exogenous but rather endogenous, given the political and institutional set-up of a given country. There is now a wide range of evidence to show that countries or regions of countries that have committed themselves to providing widespread access to basic health and education have attained strong improvements in living standards along these and other dimensions. Relevant evidence from the specific experiences of a number of countries (Drèze and Sen 1989, 1991, 1995) and from general inter-country comparisons (Anand and Ravallion 1993) suggest that widespread public provision of basic social services can be instrumental in transforming living standards even at an early stage of development when tax capacity is low. The point is that, to promote human development along these dimensions, what matters is not so much income per capita or taxable capacity, but rather the decision to devote large parts of the public expenditure budget to basic health and education services. As Drèze and Sen (1989) point out, the level of state commitment to these services is contingent on how effective action by the public is in eliciting this commitment. Issues of public pressure and expenditure reform are thus central to determining the fraction of the public budget devoted to these services.

In this section we examine mechanisms for expanding spending on basic health and education through reforms in the structure of expenditure. Expenditure reform thus represents the second dimension where there is potential to increase the aggregate size of the basic health and education budgets. Expenditure reform is fundamentally about rethinking the role of the state. With fiscal stringency increasing in many developing countries, difficult choices have to be made. Whereas there is excessive state activity in some areas (e.g. industrial production), there is too little activity in others (e.g. basic public goods). Significant improvements in welfare are possible without changing the overall size of the government budget.

Arguments outlined in the Introduction to this volume suggest that basic health and education are good candidates for expansion of government spending, and yet they generally represent small shares both of health and education budgets and of the government budget as a whole. Two dimensions of expenditure reform are considered: within the health and education sectors (Section 12.3.2) and in the government budget as a whole (Section 12.3.3). Section 12.3.4 examines the nature of the budget process and considers ways to prioritize basic health and education spending within the overall allocation. Issues connected to how public pressure can be used to elicit greater levels of basic health and education spending are treated in Section 12.4.

---

[23] There is evidence, for example, that in some countries spending on health and education have been falling as a share of total expenditure (Jimenez 1987, 1994; World Bank 1993*b*).

12.3.1. Rationalization of state activity

Expenditure reform involves a reconsideration of the appropriate nature and scale of government involvement in the economy. The view of the state as the dominant actor on the economic stage, and the large-scale expansion of state powers in the post-war period, were given theoretical backing by the theory of market failure (Stern 1991). During the 1980s there was a revision of this view, with a much greater emphasis on government failure (Krueger 1990). Given the efficiency of market exchanges, it was argued that economic agents should be allowed to make as many production and consumption decisions as possible.[24] Allowing government to make these decisions creates both information asymmetries and possibilities for rent-seeking leading to losses of efficiency. The revisionist view has led to widespread calls to decentralize a large number of economic functions to private markets which would then play the dominant role in allocating goods and services, with the state retaining a supervisory and regulatory function.[25] The optimality of decentralizing economic decison-making would point, for example, to moving the state out of industrial production.

Arguments relating to market failure, redistribution and poverty, basic rights, and externalities, however, still point fairly directly to a significant role for the state in particular areas, which include infrastructure and regulation, social protection, education, health, and the environment (see Burgess and Stern 1991, 1993, and the Introduction to this volume). Developing countries depart significantly from the fully competitive general equilibrium benchmark (see Colclough and Manor 1991: ch. 1). Problems of market failure are particularly prevalent in markets for basic health and education that are typically thin, incomplete, or missing. These are unlike normal private goods, in the sense that there are pervasive externalities associated with their provision which are not captured in private calculations of costs and benefits.[26] As a result, market prices may not represent an effective mechanism for allocating basic health and education (see Arrow 1963; Pauly 1986). Under these circumstances, only the government is in a position to provide a credible guarantee of universal access to basic health and education.

Even in the absence of market failures, government intervention is often justified on the grounds that market outcomes are unjust from a distribu-

---

[24] It should be kept in mind that the theory of efficiency or effectiveness of the market mechanism is based on the assumption of perfectly competitive markets in equilibrium. Developing economies, however, tend to be characterized by distorted markets.

[25] This section considers only the extent to which different economic functions should be decentralized from the state to private markets. Section 12.4 considers the role of decentralization of the state itself in improving the provision and finance of basic health and education services.

[26] This is less the case for non-basic interventions (e.g. hospitals, schools), which are more private in nature and where profit margins are larger.

tional point of view. The standard theory of welfare economics tells us that the most efficient way to redistribute is through lump-sum taxes and transfers. In practice, such taxes and transfers are impossible to implement, since they depend on the costless acquisition of private information which some of the individuals concerned have no incentive to reveal. Even less ambitious schemes of redistributing income and wealth through progressive taxation and transfers are often problematic, owing both to the ability of the rich to block or evade such measures and to the standard problems of identifying the poor. In view of these inherent limitations of lump-sum transfers and taxation, government expenditure can have an important redistributive role in developing countries. Basic health and education are central in this respect, as they help to equalize opportunity sets across households leading to a more egalitarian distribution of outcomes. Attempts to equalize human capital endowments are also of particular importance, given that other means of influencing the opportunity sets of poor households such as asset (e.g. land) redistribution are typically politically infeasible.

The argument then is that, while the state is doing too much in areas where it does not have a clear advantage over private markets (e.g. industrial production), it is doing too little in other areas where markets function poorly and where the consequences of such failure are severe. The guiding principle in the rationalization of state activity must be to increase social welfare, and widening the access to basic health and education can play an important role in this respect. What interventions are appropriate in a given country will depend both on the overall level of public finance and on what government is doing in other domains critical to the maintenance of living standards.[27] A system of cash transfers to the indigent or an insurance scheme for the elderly, for example, may partly obviate the need for basic health and education interventions.

I would also argue that there is a strong case to be made for universal as opposed to targeted provision of basic health and education. Despite an early emphasis on targeting as a means of easing the financing constraint (World Bank 1986; Jimenez 1987), a more pragmatic approach to targeting has arisen in recent years (see van de Walle and Nead 1994). This is partly due to growing realization that selection procedures are costly both in fiscal terms and also with respect to missing out deserving individuals.[28] As poverty and deprivations associated with inadequate access to basic health and education are not perfectly correlated, there are real problems with the choice of indicator as health and education outcomes often cannot be directly observed. Targeting makes more or less sense depending on the nature and distribution

---

[27] It is a standard principle of cost–benefit analysis that optimal policies in one part of the public sector can depend in a crucial way upon the government's 'control areas' in other areas (see Sen 1972; Drèze and Stern 1987).

[28] This is particularly the case in developing countries where problems associated with means testing are more severe.

of the condition being addressed. While we may want to target cash or in-kind transfers to the most needy during a famine, there is less of a case for focusing the benefits of public health or primary schooling on particular groups within the population. Also, though supply may be universal, the nature of demand for these services actually implies that benefits are in fact 'targeted' at specific groups such as mothers and school-age children. Moreover, leakages of basic health and education benefits tend to be very limited. In general, individuals cannot retrade allocations received from the government. Both these factors help to contain costs and reduce the force of arguments for targeting.

In addition, there are strong political economy reasons why access should be universal. If those with higher ability to pay perceive benefits from the programmes they will be more likely to be willing to pay for them through taxes or other means. Highly targeted programmes, where the better off perceive no benefit and yet provide the bulk of the costs will not receive the same level of support. Broadening provision leads to greater social cohesion in support of the basic health and education package.

There is an argument for public expenditure if the allocation of goods achieved under public provision and finance differs from the allocation that would pertain under private provision or finance (Besley 1988*a*). This is clearly the case for most elements in the basic health and education budget.[29] The issue then becomes one of how practically to guide these public expenditure decisions. Here we are on much weaker theoretical and empirical grounds than is the case with tax reform, where a set of consistent analytical tools and guidelines are available (see Newbery and Stern 1987). Whereas with tax reform there is a single shadow price of public funds, in the case of public expenditure shadow prices are likely to differ across sectors because different sectors are allocated different budgets. Questions of intra- and inter-sectoral expenditure reform are thus to some extent separable (Besley 1988*a*). This implies that the criteria by which aggregate revenue should be allocated across sectors are often unclear.[30] Methodologies to detect the pattern and determinants of demand for public services are much less developed than is the case for normal consumption goods.[31] Also, whereas tax reform is an inherently quantitative subject, expenditure reform, particularly within sectors, involves a large element of qualitative reform where judgement is needed on the appropriate mix of goods and services to be provided or financed. Which allocation is optimal also depends on the specification of the objective func-

---

[29] The public good characteristics of basic health and education make analysis of their allocation quite different from that for purely private consumer goods (see Ch. 1 above).

[30] The question of whether to allocate an additional dollar of revenue raised to telecommunications or health is a much more difficult question than asking whether tax X or tax Y should be preferred when raising this revenue.

[31] Household expenditure data which provide the key data resource in tax analysis have limited use, since many public services are free or subsidized and therefore are not fully reflected in household data.

tion of expenditure reform (e.g. health and education attainment, poverty reduction, welfare, or growth maximization).[32]

The simplest approach to expenditure reform which falls within normative public finance theory involves the calculation of benefit–cost ratios similar to those used in tax reform analysis (see Newbery and Stern 1987; Besley 1988a). Following Besley (1988a), benefit–cost ratios for publicly provided goods and services can be defined as:

$$\phi_j^h = \frac{\beta^h q_j^h(p, z_h, y_h)}{\sum_h \sum_i t_i x_{ij}^h - r_j}. \tag{1}$$

The numerator term gives the marginal social value or benefit of household h, increasing its consumption of publicly provided good or service z. Here β represents the social weight (the value in terms of social welfare) of a marginal increase in the income (y) of household h, and q is the shadow price of a unit of publicly provided good j to household h. The marginal cost of providing a further unit of the publicly provided good or service j to household h is given in the denominator and is obtained by differentiating the government budget constraint with respect to z. The first term refers to a change of household h's consumption of public good j on tax revenues, and the second term refers to the direct cost of providing the publicly provided good (r_j).

Optimal allocation of public expenditure requires that these benefit–cost ratios be equated across goods and households. This optimum is known as the command optimum (see Arrow 1971; Bruno 1976; Besley 1988a). If we consider the allocation of two goods j and k to household h, then it follows that the mix of j relative to k should be increased if $\phi_j^h > \phi_k^h$. Similarly, if we consider two households h and l, then more j should be given to household h than to l if $\phi_j^h > \phi_j^l$. The notion is that publicly provided goods and services with higher benefit–cost ratios should receive greater weight in the allocation of expenditure to households. Also, households that benefit most from public services should receive greater weight in the allocation process.

12.3.2. Intra-sectoral expenditure reform

Let us begin with the simpler case of thinking about expenditure reform within a given sector (i.e health or education). Basic health and education are characterized by having relatively higher benefit–cost ratios than their non-basic counterparts.[33] In this case, expenditure reform can be seen as a matter

---

[32] Maximization of one of these functions does not necessarily entail maximizing the others. See Hammer (1993) on how specification of different types of objective for the government in the health sector affect the choice of types of intervention.

[33] For a given cost, basic interventions have relatively higher impact on social welfare than their non-basic counterparts as might be proxied by infant mortality, life expectancy, or the level of poverty.

of equalizing benefit–cost ratios *within* a sector. Despite this, one tends to see health and education budgets in developing countries skewed towards non-basic interventions (e.g. hospital curative services, tertiary education) which benefit only a small fraction of the population. Given overall low levels of resources, the predominance of non-basic expenditure items in health and education budgets may be seen as a reflection of the dominance of the preferences of the ruling elite over those of the general population in spending policy. Elites that have adequate spending power to cover basic health and education needs will tend to favour public provision or finance of non-basic interventions. These are often large, costly projects (e.g. hospitals, universities) which end up absorbing large fractions of the health and education budgets. Involvement in higher levels of health and education provision also carries higher professional kudos, and this leads to a bias towards provision of non-basic services.[34]

Part of the problem here is that the information set of the poor concerning the spending priorities of the government may be very small. The idea that spending on non-essential, non-basic services involves an opportunity cost in terms of essential, basic services is often something that is poorly understood. In this situation the government can satisfy its own needs and those of its supporters behind a veil of ignorance. Measures that overcome these informational barriers and increase the transparency of decision-making can therefore lead to demands for greater finance or provision of basic services. A free press and free speech are important in this respect. Where universal access to basic health and education have become a central government commitment, the mass media and other methods have been used, for example, effectively to galvanize support for these measures.

To ensure access, the poor must have channels through which their preferences can be expressed. Representation of the poor in local and national political institutions is thus often critical in creating pressure to skew health and education expenditures towards basic services. One problem is that support for widespread provision of basic health and education is likely to be diffuse and less powerful than support for non-basic services, which tends to be concentrated in a powerful elite. Representation can also be improved by decentralizing government. Through this mechanism government is brought closer to the community and therefore can be made more accountable as regards fulfilling local needs for basic health and education (see Section 12.4).

The efficacy of public pressure is itself a function of achievement in basic health and education. Greater literacy and basic education, for example, can facilitate public discussion of health and education needs and encourage informed collective demands for basic health and education services leading to these items occupying a higher share in overall government health and education budgets. Higher levels of educational attainment are also likely to

---

[34] The fact that the non-basic services are often provided in cities may lead to an urban bias in health and education spending.

improve the utilization of available basic health and education services. Basic health and education may therefore be seen as tools for empowering the poor (see Drèze and Sen 1989, 1995).

So far, I have discussed expenditure reforms from the perspective of expanding the role of basic services in health and education budgets. Another dimension of intra-sectoral expenditure reform concerns the reduction of expenditures on non-basic services. Because these are typically large, centrally funded projects which are unlikely to fail for political reasons, non-basic health and education services typically face soft budget constraints relative to their basic counterparts. There is now a weight of evidence to suggest that this has led to these entities becoming inefficient. A major part of intra-sectoral reform must therefore concern itself with improving the cost efficiency of higher levels of health and education provision. There is a need to harden budget constraints, to decentralize financial responsibility, to introduce performance-linked incentives, and to allow firing and bankruptcy where necessary.[35] These types of reform parallel those for inefficient state industrial enterprises (see Aghion *et al.* 1994).[36]

In the command model publicly provided goods and services are assumed to be free, though this is not necessarily optimal (see Besley 1988*b*). Non-basic interventions which have weaker public good characteristics stand out as more attractive targets for the introduction of user fees than basic interventions.[37] Introduction of user fees at higher levels of provision (combined with targeted exemptions for those with low ability to pay) will both help to free up resources to widen access to basic health and education services, and bring benefit–cost ratios more closely in line. User fees can also be introduced in other public services where the case for subsidization is weaker than it is for higher health and education. In these ways, user fees can, in principle, serve an important redistributive function. In the command model outlined above, a positive charge (i.e. tax) on goods predominately consumed by the rich and a negative charge (i.e. subsidy) on goods predominately consumed by the poor are both optimal (Besley 1988*b*).

12.3.3. Inter-sectoral expenditure reform

The analysis of expenditure reform is complicated by the fact that government is divided into different spending divisions or ministries which face different budget constraints (see Tirole 1994). These different spending

[35] In the extreme, some higher levels of provision may be privatized.

[36] Financial responsibility must also be enforced in social security funds, which provide predominately non-basic services, to ensure that contributions cover expenditures.

[37] Aside from benefiting a smaller fraction of the population, ability to pay is higher and markets are thicker for higher levels of provision. The effects of a reduction of utilization caused by the introduction of user fees is less serious for higher levels of provision as consumers can fall back on basic services. The case for public finance of these services is therefore much weaker than for basic services.

units will face different shadow values of public funds, which makes it difficult to make judgements about the allocation of public funds across sectors.[38] For this reason, the command model is more useful in the analysis of intra-sectoral reform (see Section 12.3.2). One way around this problem is to examine the distribution of expenditures that would result if a single bene-volent social planner allocated the overall government budget on the basis of the benefit–cost ratios of individual expenditure items. In this hypothetical analysis, basic health or education are likely to stand out as attractive targets for public expenditure as social marginal benefit greatly exceeds social marginal cost where both are evaluated at shadow prices (Besley 1988*a*; Drèze and Stern 1987).[39] In contrast, transfers to non-performing parastatals or defence industries would not be favoured as targets for public expenditure under these criteria.[40]

In the bulk of developing countries, this type of analysis is likely to indicate that the structure of expenditure is far from any command optimum with a strong skew to non-productive expenditures. This gap between what is expected from the theory and the observed reality does not discredit the framework, but rather suggests that it be seen as a benchmark into which political economy and other constraints can be incorporated in an attempt to derive practicable rules for expenditure reform.

A drawback of the command model is that the demands of individual households are not taken into account. The assumption that the social planner knows *and* takes into account the preferences of households that underlie the model is unlikely to hold. As a result, some publicly provided goods and services will be in excess demand, leading to rationing and parallel markets. Other goods and services in excess supply will not be fully taken up.[41] Valuation by households will thus influence the manner in which alloca-tion translates into consumption.

High direct and opportunity costs for the poor may limit take-up of basic health and education. In other cases low take-up by the poor relates to limited information about the benefits of these services, resulting in low valuation.[42] The composition of expenditures thus tend to be skewed towards items that are actively valued and demanded by the non-poor (e.g. curative services, tertiary education). Widening access to basic services may reduce the take-up

[38] There are also serious problems associated with measurement of the shadow value of public funds in different sectors (Besley 1988*a*).

[39] This analysis is also likely to show that these expenditures be skewed towards poor households who are likely to have relatively high benefit–cost ratios for basic services.

[40] Inter-sectoral expenditure reform must therefore be guided by the rationalization of state activity as a whole (see S. 12.3.1).

[41] This may seem surprising if provision is free; however, there are costs associated with take-up (e.g. opportunity costs, travel time, and costs). In addition, there may be informational barriers relating to the benefits of take-up.

[42] Poor uneducated parents, for example, will be less likely to value education and hence to send their children to school.

costs faced by the poor, helping them to learn about the benefits of take-up and to exercise demand for these services.

Benefit–cost ratios also do not take any account of the degree of market incompleteness in a given area of expenditure. As Hammer (1993) and others have pointed out, government interventions which substitute for private provision are much less valuable than provision goods and services where the market is absent or thin. The allocation of public funds thus needs to capitalize on the comparative advantage of the state. Allowing private markets to satisfy demands for goods and services—for example at higher levels of provision, where the state has no comparative advantage—would therefore also lead to a more rational composition of expenditure. Market incompleteness in particular at lower levels of provision provides an added rationale for public funding of basic health and education.

The fundamental reason why the observed pattern of expenditures may differ significantly from the command optimum is because the allocation rules utilized by governments take into account a much wider set of criteria than consumer preferences and aggregate welfare. There has been a growing emphasis on how the preferences of those in government and their supporters figure strongly in expenditure decisions and differ significantly from those of large sections of the population (e.g. the poor). Given information asymmetries, governments may allocate expenditures in a manner that maximizes the rents accruing to them (Buchanan *et al.* 1980). The lack of consideration of political economy constraints thus represents a serious omission.

12.3.4. The budget process

In order to understand how political economy constraints affect the allocation of expenditures, one needs to understand the nature of the budget process in developing countries.[43] Chronic underfunding of basic health and education and of other pro-poor expenditures is as much a reflection of the low priority attached to these heads of expenditure in the budget process as it is a reflection of limited tax capacity.[44] Pro-poor expenditures are often determined as a residual after higher-priority budget demands have been met. With increasing fiscal stringency, the real amounts of funds being devoted to pro-poor expenditures may thus be falling, as has been observed in various countries (see Jimenez 1987). Priority within the budget is determined by the political power of the group or groups demanding particular types of expenditure. Though large in number, the poor may have limited political power and limited representation in the budget process.

[43] Within economics the process that determines the allocation of public resources is often treated as a black box.

[44] On education see Colclough with Lewin (1993: ch. 2) and on health see World Bank (1993*b*: ch. 3).

For these reasons, though basic health and education are valued more highly by the bulk of the population than a range of other expenditures (e.g. defence, subsidies to state-owned enterprises, hospitals, universities), they typically rank below these items in terms of magnitude of expenditure. The critical challenge as regards expenditure reform therefore concerns how the preferences of population and government as a whole can be brought more closely into line in order to raise the priority ranking of basic health and education within the overall composition of expenditure. Several sets of institutional reforms are relevant here.

Making the budget process transparent represents the first challenge, as it is often unclear how government revenue is being spent. Public budget information can be used by consumers or their representatives as the basis of lobbying for changes in the composition of expenditure. Opening channels of communication between the public and the government helps to increase the information available to the government concerning the preferences of consumers.[45] Representation and free media help to reduce problems of incomplete information in the allocation of public spending. Making the expansion of funding for and access to basic health and education a central and explicit objective within growth-oriented, social protection, tax, and adjustment policies represents a critical step in this respect.[46] This would involve bringing the expenditure needs of the ministries of health and education into the core of the ministry of finance budget process. At the same time the finance ministry would need to act as a check on the ambitions of other spending ministries (Tirole 1994).

Commitment to pro-poor expenditures, however, cannot be expected to emerge autonomously. The development of political institutions, at both the local and the central level, which allows the poor to exercise demand for public goods and services, is critical to enforcing provision by government.[47] Decentralization may also help to make governments more accountable in this respect (see Section 12.4). The expression of public demands through institutional reform also helps to ensure that pro-poor spending is continued, leading to the development of more sustainable systems of provision.

12.4. Decentralization

We have so far examined tax and expenditure reform issues connected with expanding the overall sizes of basic health and education budgets. In this

---

[45] Greater transparency may also increase the willingness of the public to fund publicly provided services through taxation (see Mulgan and Murray 1993).

[46] Note that it is possible to view basic and non-basic health and education as separate budgetary items. It is thus possible to assign a higher ranking to basic services while at the same time giving non-basic services a lower ranking.

[47] Democracy increases the probability that the preferences of the population as a whole will be expressed.

section I wish to delve below these macro resource issues to examine under what conditions decentralization can enhance the efficiency of provision and the financing of basic health and education services. This requires an analysis of how decentralization affects the structure of information and incentives, the valuation of these services, and the functioning of institutions and markets.

In a first-best world, the government would raise the necessary resources for basic health and education through lump-sum taxation and would allocate these resources in a manner that maximizes a Paretian social welfare function. In this world, where all information, power, and decision-making can be incorporated into one centre, the centralization of the provision (and financing) of basic health and education services is optimal. This optimality of centralization may not hold when there are informational asymmetries between different levels of government or when there are transaction costs associated with processing and transmitting information.

In a second-best world, where lump-sum taxation is infeasible, where information is imperfect, and where power is shared between different levels of government, decentralization can relax the basic health and education financing constraint through two distinct channels. First, decentralization of expenditure responsibility may improve the efficiency of provision, leading to greater impact for a given level of basic health or education expenditure. Second, decentralization of revenue generation may in some areas be more efficient, and may therefore create additional revenue for basic health and education services. The basic argument is that efficiency gains are realizable as lower levels of government have a comparative advantage as regards implementation and financing basic health and education *vis-à-vis* higher levels of government. Decentralization can therefore contribute to achieving the objective of providing universal access to basic health and education.[48]

Although there is a literature which points to the optimality of decentralizing economic activity to private markets, these arguments are less strong in the case of quasi-public goods such as basic health and education, where the market mechanism provides an inadequate basis for (efficient) provision and utilization (see Section 12.3 and Chapter 1 above).[49] Thus, though we have established a clear role for the state in the financing and provision of these goods, we are less clear on the relative merits of centralized and decentralized forms of government in achieving these functions.

---

[48] In any organization (e.g. a health or education system) both information and authority are to some extent decentralized in the sense that different agents have different information and make decisions that affect both provision and utilization of basic health and education services (Haniotis 1993). In this context it is not so much the extent but rather the form of decentralization that is important, in terms of how it affects the structure of incentives and the functioning of institutions.

[49] Indeed, it is the optimality of decentralizing major areas of economic activity that has led to a rethinking of the role of the state and fundamental reforms in the structure of government expenditure (see S. 12.3).

Governments may be modelled as organizations, and it is possible to draw on recent developments in the theory of the firm to examine how decentralization and local implementation can both improve the efficiency of provision *and* ease the financing constraint (see Grossman and Hart 1986; Cremer *et al.* 1993). Inclusion of information on these types of models makes it possible to look at how decentralization affects the incentives both of government to provide these services and of consumers to utilize them. Within this framework, we can examine where the power to make expenditure decisions and raise revenue should reside. Experience over the last few decades has made it clear that citizens cannot take it for granted that politicians and bureaucrats will act in their interest, and that constitutions or contracts cannot be written to ensure that they do (see Section 12.3). The allocation of power implied by the nature and extent of decentralization affects the incentives of government to act in the interests of citizens.

12.4.1. Decentralization of provision

Decentralization of provision can be used to capitalize on informational advantages at the local level regarding preferences. Basic health and education needs and implementation constraints will vary across localities. Better information on these factors and on preferences at the local level implies that decentralized provision may serve local needs more exactly. Problems such as moral hazard and adverse selection are also much less pronounced when numbers are small than when they are large, and this can help to improve the efficiency of provision. The critical issue, however, is not just the availability of information but rather whether there is an incentive to utilize this information.

There is no *a priori* reason to believe that local government is more well meaning than central government.[50] What matters is whether channels exist to force politicians to act in the interest of the majority of citizens as regards the provision of basic health and education. Explicit contracts to enforce this cannot be written, so the only way to provide politicians with the right incentives is to give voters the right to eject them. It can be argued that households are likely to be more able to influence decisions that affect their welfare when government is decentralized than when it is centralized. Local governments have to be more responsive to preferences of coalitions of local households than central governments, as their political survival is more dependent on satisfying local needs. Households or groups of households will thus tend to be more pivotal in determining the outcomes of political decisions at the local as opposed to central level (Cremer *et al.* 1993). This interaction leads to greater accountability at the local government level with

[50] Corruption can be just as prevalent at subnational levels as it is at the national level.

respect to satisfying demands for basic health and education.[51] Decentralization may therefore act as a potent force in bringing the mapping of preferences of the government and general population more closely into alignment. Though a degree of decentralization does seem advisable, this raises questions as to what should be the optimal size of the jurisdiction implementing health and education services.

Decentralization is likely to be successful in this respect only if local government is democratic. If the institutions of government are undemocratic and are controlled by a rich elite, then the mapping of preferences for basic health and education between the local government and population may be very weak, and it may be better for central government directly to provide these services.[52] Local government is more sensitive to local needs, but it is the local needs as they are perceived by the political system, and in the absence of democratic institutions these may be the needs of a powerful minority (Cremer *et al.* 1993). The success of decentralization depends on the ability of groups that are likely to benefit from basic health and education policies (i.e. the poor) to organize and influence public policy. Grass-roots organizations and other NGOs can be critical in providing conduits through which public pressure can be expressed.

Decentralization is often associated with a greater emphasis on the geographical dispersion of clinics and schools. Deconcentration of the health and education sectors through decentralization can increase take-up by the poor through two mechanisms. First, greater proximity reduces the direct and opportunity costs associated with taking up these services.[53] Second, deconcentration can help households to learn about the benefits of these services, leading to greater valuation and demand. Under a geographically dispersed system of schools and clinics, poor households are more likely to observe the benefits of provision.[54] Changing the valuation of basic health and education by poor parents who may have never personally experienced their benefits represents a central challenge, as it is these individuals who decide whether their male or female children should attend schools or visit clinics.[55]

---

[51] What weakens the accountability of central government is not the fact that localities will require different policies but rather that localities which are differently satisfied with the policies they receive have less ability to express their dissatisfaction.

[52] Within India, considerations such as these would suggest that decentralization may work well in Kerala, where village councils and other organs of local government function well, but not in Uttar Pradesh, where such institutions are either non-existent or are controlled by the land-owning elite (see Drèze and Sen 1995).

[53] Even where provision is free, costs of access, including the opportunity costs of time and travel costs, can be considerable, in particular for poor people living in remote rural areas.

[54] The benefits of basic health and education are often least transparent to those who need them most (i.e. the poor).

[55] Learning in this situation often proceeds by example: a mother witnessing or hearing about the beneficial effect of oral rehydration therapy (ORT) on the diarrhoeal condition of the child of a neighbour is more likely to have her children attend the clinic.

Poor health and education outcomes (e.g. high infant mortality rate, low literacy) are often themselves the result of inadequate demand as opposed to failures in targeting. In any case, access does not guarantee take-up. Nevertheless, universal provision combined with coercive measures (e.g. mandatory attendance) will have a better chance of increasing the valuation of and hence the demand for basic health and education than targeted provision. This also suggests that the availability and benefits of these services need to be widely publicized to ensure that eligible individuals are not excluded. Directly involving the local population in the provision of basic health and education can help in this respect.

Local participation associated with decentralization may also enhance the sustainability of projects. Through this mechanism, demands on central administrative capacity, which represent a critical constraint on widening access, are reduced. If decision-making is localized, there is also likely to be a greater sense of the project belonging to the community. Locals involved in the administration of basic health and education projects learn valuable skills and are more likely to stay with the project.[56] They are also likely to be more accountable, so that, for example, absenteeism by teachers or health workers is less likely to be countenanced in a community-based school or clinic than in its centrally provided equivalent. Cost participation, for example in the form of contributing labour to build the school or clinic, will also strengthen accountability.[57] Provision is also likely to be more effective if it is in the hands of groups of local individuals who directly value basic health and education and whose incentives are compatible with those of the national policy-maker.[58] Women's groups, for example, have been an important force in widening access to basic health services in sub-Saharan Africa. In the dynamic context, local providers are likely to have greater latitude to experiment with different methods of delivery than a central agency. Successful policies generated by this process of experimentation may then be incorporated into national health and education guidelines.

Central government is likely to continue to play an important financing, regulatory, and co-ordinating role in a decentralized system of provision. If central government maintains a primary financing role, then its redistributive and risk-pooling roles are not impaired under a decentralized system of provision. Central finance can be made contingent on local government

[56] Poor local health workers or teachers are likely to be much more effective in communicating the benefits of health and education to members of their community and in organizing support for these measures than are middle-class non-locals.

[57] Aid-financed projects have often been seen as being particularly unsustainable, both because of their undependable source of finance and because they were seen to belong to foreigners.

[58] To ensure provision of high-quality services, attention must be paid to monetary incentives (i.e. salaries) for clinic workers or teachers. Neglect of these considerations can greatly reduce the impact of local health and education expenditures. For example, there may be a negative correlation between quality of teaching and number of repeat years; thus, raising teachers' salaries could lead to a reduction in total costs.

meeting performance criteria, thus strengthening incentives for downstream suppliers to provide basic health and education services. Where costs are shared, matching grants can be used to achieve a similar function. Although the degree of co-ordination that is achievable will decline as provision becomes more decentralized, central government will none the less have a role in setting and updating national health and education guidelines (e.g. national curricula) and in training teachers and clinic workers.[59] In many cases central government will also play a role in regulating the costs of services and of critical inputs (e.g. drugs, school materials). Because of the size of its resource base, central government often stands out as the only level of government that can credibly guarantee universal access to basic health and education. Perception of this right can then filter down until it becomes 'locked' into the political system so that basic health provision is demanded and political survival at the local and central levels may, to some extent, depend on supply.

12.4.2. Decentralization of revenue generation

The failure of central revenue to meet basic health and education financing needs has led to calls to decentralize revenue generation. Decentralization here is taken to mean the devolution of basic health and financing to lower levels of government.[60] A range of tax and non-tax measures can be employed by local governments to fulfil this objective. It has to be kept in mind that arguments for revenue-raising as between different tiers of government are competitive: raising revenue at one level reduces that available to another. For this reason, decentralization is justified only if we can demonstrate that lower levels of government have a comparative advantage in terms of raising revenue, or if locally raised revenue is used more efficiently. On balance, arguments for decentralization of revenue generation are much less convincing than arguments for decentralization of provision.

One clear problem is that there is a smaller toolbox to choose from at the local as opposed to the central level. There can be no assumption that taxes that are implementable at the local level are optimal in terms of financing basic health and education. Some taxes (e.g. foreign trade taxes) are unavailable, while others (e.g. VAT) typically need to be co-ordinated and controlled by the centre. The local tax base may thus be inadequate with respect to providing universal access to basic health and education.

Dependence on local tax bases also reduces the risk pooling capacity of government. Indeed, in risky agricultural environments it may be optimal to

[59] Note that the incentive to provide training is lower for local governments, because trained individuals may leave the local jurisdiction.

[60] At the extreme, decentralization of revenue generation implies that costs of provision are passed directly to the consumer through user fees (see Jimenez 1987, 1994, and Chs. 2 and 3 above).

depend on non-local taxes. The presence of covariate risk (e.g. drought) in these environments may imply that local tax yields are lowest when the demand for basic health and education is greatest. Non-local taxes provide a more steady and dependable stream of revenue and are more robust against local income fluctuations. Central finance of basic health and education thus helps to guard against failures in local risk-sharing institutions (e.g. village councils) which cannot fully insure against covariate risk (see Besley 1994).

Decentralizing revenue generation also limits the redistributive scope of government action. The scope for redistribution on both the tax and expenditure sides of the budgets will be constrained by the size of the local budget, and thus will be extremely limited in poor regions. In a decentralized system of finance, the scope to equalize opportunity sets across households by providing widespread access to basic health and education will be much more limited than under a centralized system of finance. This failure is serious given that the bulk of redistribution in developing countries is achieved through the expenditure side of the budget. In the extreme, where responsibility for financing basic health and education is decentralized to households through the introduction of user fees, all scope for redistribution and risk-pooling will have been lost. In this system there will be full earmarking of funds but no redistribution.[61]

If responsibility for financing basic health and education is left completely to the discretion of the local government, strong regional differences in commitment to funding these services are likely to emerge. These problems are compounded where local governments are undemocratic or controlled by elites that do not value basic health and education, in which case scant attention may be given to these issues in large regions of a country.[62] With complete decentralization, the power to use central finance as an incentive to provide these services at the local level is also lost.

Human capital investments also create strong externalities which cannot be internalized by local governments, as people, having benefited from the investments, can move outside their jurisdiction. This problem is compounded by the fact that human capital investments may act as an incentive to leave. (For example, peasants who receive basic education and health may perceive benefits in leaving for cities.) The inability to internalize these externalities at the local level may imply that local government finance of basic health and education may fall below socially optimal levels. Central government, on the

---

[61] There can be no redistribution in a system of user fees unless fees (e.g. on non-basic services) are used to cross-subsidize basic services.

[62] This point can be illustrated using the example of India (see Drèze and Sen 1995). Since the 1947 Constitution, which granted responsibility for basic health and education to the states, there has been wide variation in attainment measures, depending on the degree of commitment of different state governments to these areas of public action. For example, in 1991 life expectancy ranged from about 54 in the worst performing state (Madhya Pradesh) to 72 in Kerala, and female/male 7+ literacy rates ranged from 20/55% (Rajasthan) to 86/94% (Kerala) (Drèze and Sen 1995: 47).

other hand, can do so,[63] and therefore may be willing to devote greater tax effort to basic health and education.

Differences in tax capacity, and in commitment to funding these services, are likely to imply that the (per capita) level of finance for basic health and education is likely to vary strongly across local jurisdictions. This pattern of variation will tend to be more marked than under centralized finance, where equalization of finance and provision are the governing principles. Capability of or commitment to funding these services will also tend to vary inversely with the need for provision, with poorer regions being worst off. Because the overall resource base is both unstable and uncertain, local government— unlike central government—may not have the power to guarantee provision. The objective of universal access to basic health and education may therefore be more difficult to achieve under decentralized, than under centralized finance.

Despite these problems, there are a few factors which might argue for a degree of decentralization in revenue generation. A paucity of resources at the central level may also dictate a degree of local cost participation.[64] If local government has an informational advantage over central government, then it may be able to collect taxes with less effort. Nevertheless, it should, in principle, be possible for central government to enter into a tax contract with local agents in order to capitalize on this informational advantage (see Cremer *et al.* 1993).[65] Furthermore, at the local level the connection between tax contributions and benefits is clear, and as a result people may be more willing to pay local taxes than central taxes. This argument is strengthened where local governments are more accountable than central governments. Cost participation can also enhance the sense of the basic health or education project belonging to the village (see Section 12.4.1).

12.5. Conclusions

This paper has examined how fiscal reform can contribute to extending coverage of basic health and education. The role of three sets of fiscal reforms—tax reform, expenditure reform, and decentralization—have been identified. Under tax and expenditure reform, we questioned the fixed budget assumption and examined routes through which budgets for basic health and education could be expanded. Under decentralization, we examined the

---

63 Unless individuals leave the country.

64 This may take the form of e.g. using some local taxes to partially fund basic health and education as well as introducing user fees for non-essential services.

65 This factor also has to be balanced against the fact that opportunities for collusion between the taxpayer and tax collector may be more prevalent at the local government level, particularly where local government is controlled by representatives of individuals who would benefit strongly from tax evasion (e.g. rich landowners).

extent to which this mechanism could improve the efficiency of basic health and education expenditures and revenue generation.

Fiscal reforms need to be designed in the light of the required properties of revenue instruments to finance basic health and education programmes. These include implementability, stability, and buoyancy. Using this framework, we argued that there is no viable, long-term alternative to taxation as a means of financing basic health and education services. Aid, debt, and inflation finance are not sustainable alternatives. The exact choice of tax instruments must be sensitive to the nature of the constraints that affect revenue generation in developing countries. Empirical evidence on the structure of taxation in developing and industrial economies was used to identify the most promising tax instruments for generating revenue for basic health and education. The appropriate sets of instruments differ strongly between developing and industrial economies. Contributory social security schemes, for example, are unlikely to represent a significant source of additional funding in most developing countries. Our main conclusion here is that the bulk of additional basic health and education finance should come from broad-based domestic indirect taxes (e.g. VAT). Direct taxes are less suitable, both because of difficulties of implementation and because of their limited scope for achieving redistribution.

With certain qualifications, the financing problem reduces to raising the necessary tax revenue in the least distortionary and most effective manner possible. Reform of health and education financing in developing economies is thus intimately linked to the principles and process of tax reform. To be successful, it is critical that an expansion of funding for basic health and education services be seen as a central and explicit objective of tax reform. Limited tax capacity, however, is not the only constraint on achieving adequate funding. I have argued that expenditure priorities are critically important, and have considered how the share of total revenue devoted to basic health and education could be increased. Expenditure reform is, fundamentally, about rethinking the role of the state. With increasing fiscal stringency in many developing countries, difficult choices have to be made. Whereas there is excessive state activity in some areas (e.g. industrial production), there is too little activity in others (e.g. basic health and education). Two dimensions of expenditure reform were considered: within the health and education sectors, and within the government budget as a whole. I argued that limited government commitment to these expenditures constitutes the main constraint on extending coverage. Such commitment is not exogenously determined but rather is a function of the extent to which the public values and demands the provision of education and health services. Significant improvements in social welfare are possible through changes in the composition of public budgets without changing the size of the aggregate budget.

Finally, there are strong arguments in favour of decentralizing provision where local governments are committed and accountable, but arguments for the decentralization of revenue generation are less convincing. At most, decentralization of revenue generation should be partial, given the advantages of central government in terms of redistribution, risk-pooling, and the stability of revenue. Decentralized provision combined with centralized finance would seem to represent the best broad solution. In general, and in most countries, it will be more promising to investigate the contribution that direct fiscal reform, as opposed to a switch to private finance, can make in easing the financing constraint on the provision of basic health and education services.

References

Aghion, P., Blanchard, O., and Burgess, R. S. L. (1994). 'The Behaviour of State Firms in Eastern Europe: Pre-Privatisation', *European Economic Review*, 37: 1327–49.

Ahmad, S. E., Drèze, J. P., Hills, J., and Sen, A. K. (eds.) (1991). *Social Security in Developing Countries* (Oxford: Clarendon Press).

Anand, S. and Ravallion, M. (1993). 'Human Development in Poor Countries', *Journal of Economic Perspectives*, 7(1): 133–50.

Arrow, K. J. (1963). 'Uncertainty and the Welfare Economics of Medical Care', *American Economic Review*, 53(5): 941–84.

——(1971). 'Equality in Public Expenditure', *Quarterly Journal of Economics*, 85: 409–15.

Atkinson, A. B. (1989). *Poverty and Social Security* (Brighton: Harvester Wheatsheaf).

——and Hills, J. (1991). 'Social Security in Developed Countries: Are There Lessons for Developing Countries?' in Ahmad *et al.* (1991).

Bailey, M. J. (1956). 'The Welfare Costs of Inflationary Finance', *Journal of Political Economy*, 64: 93–100.

Barr, N. (1993*a*). 'Safety Nets for the Rural Poor', mimeo, London School of Economics.

——(1993*b*). 'On the Design of Social Safety Nets', mimeo, London School of Economics.

Barro, R. J. (1991). 'Economic Growth in a Cross Section of Countries', *Quarterly Journal of Economics*, 106: 407–44.

Besley, T. (1988*a*). 'Reforming Public Expenditures: Some Methodological Issues', mimeo, Princeton University.

——(1988*b*). 'Welfare Improving User Fees for Publicly Provided Private Goods', Nuffield College Discussion Papers in Economics no. 32.

——(1994). 'Savings, Credit and Insurance', forthcoming in J. Behrman and T. N. Srinivasan (eds.), *Handbook of Development Economics*, iii (Amsterdam: North-Holland).

Boone, P. (1994*a*). 'The Impact of Foreign Aid on Savings and Growth', mimeo, London School of Economics.

Boone, P. (1994*b*). 'Politics and the Effectiveness of Foreign Aid', mimeo, London School of Economics.

Bruno, M. (1976). 'Equality, Complementarity and the Incidence of Public Expenditure', *Journal of Public Economics*, 35: 495–507.

Buchanan, J. M., Tollison, R. D., and Tullock, G. (eds.) (1980). *Towards a Theory of the Rent-Seeking Society* (College Station, Texas: Texas A&M University Press).

Buiter, W. H. (1990). *Principles of Budgetary and Financial Policy* (Brighton: Harvester Wheatsheaf).

Burgess, R. S. L. and Stern, N. H. (1991). 'Social Security in Developing Countries: What, Why, Who and How?', in Ahmad *et al.* (1991).

——— (1993). 'Taxation and Development', *Journal of Economic Literature*, 31: 762–830.

—— Drèze, J. P., Ferriera, F., Hussain, A., and Thomas, J. J. (1993). 'Social Protection and Structural Adjustment', mimeo, STICERD, London School of Economics.

Cassen, R. and Associates (1994). *Does Aid Work?* (Oxford: Clarendon Press).

Colclough, C. with Lewin, K. M. (1993). *Educating All the Children* (Oxford: Clarendon Press).

—— and Manor, J. (eds.) (1991). *States or Markets? Neo-liberalism and the Development Policy Debate* (Oxford: Clarendon Press).

Cnossen, S. (1991). 'Design of the Value Added Tax: Lessons from Experience' in J. Khalizadeh-Shirazi and A. Shah (eds.), *Tax Policy in Developing Countries* (Washington, DC: World Bank).

Cremer, J., Estache, A., and Seabright, A. (1993). 'The Decentralisation of Public Services: Lessons from the Theory of the Firm', mimeo, World Bank, Washington, DC.

Drèze, J. and Saran, M. (1993). 'Primary Education and Economic Development in China and India: Overview and Two Case Studies', DERP Working Paper no. 47, STICERD, London School of Economics.

—— and Sen, A. K (1989). *Hunger and Public Action* (Oxford: Clarendon Press).

——— (1991). *The Political Economy of Hunger* (Oxford: Clarendon Press).

——— (1995). *Economic Development and Social Opportunity* (Oxford: Clarendon Press).

—— and Stern, N. H. (1987). 'The Theory of Cost–Benefit Analysis', in A. Auerbach and M. Feldstein (eds.), *Handbook of Public Economics* (Amsterdam: North-Holland).

Gil Díaz, F. (1987). 'Some Lessons from Mexico's Tax Reform', in Newbery and Stern (1987).

Gillis, M. (1989). *Tax Reform in Developing Countries* (Durham, NC: Duke University Press).

Goode, R. (1984). *Government Finance in Developing Countries* (Washington, DC: Brookings Institution).

Grossman, S. and Hart, O. (1986). 'The Costs and Benefits of Ownership: A Theory of Vertical and Lateral Integration', *Journal of Political Economy*, 94(4): 691–719.

Hammer, J. S. (1993). 'Prices and Protocols in Public Health Care', Policy Research Working Paper WPS 1131, World Bank, Washington, DC.

Haniotis, T. (1993). 'Fiscal Federalism and Decentralisation', mimeo, STICERD, London School of Economics.

Hindrichs, H. (1966). 'A General Theory of Tax Structure Change during Economic Development', Harvard Law School International Tax Programme.

Jimenez, E. (1987). *Pricing Policy in the Social Sectors: Cost Recovery for Education and Health in Developing Countries* (Baltimore: Johns Hopkins University Press).

—— (1994). 'Human and Physical Infrastructure: Public Investment and Pricing Policies in Developing Countries', Policy Research Working Paper no. 1281, World Bank, Washington, DC.

Krueger, A. O. (1990). 'Government Failures in Development', *Journal of Economic Perspectives*, 4: 9–24.

Lucas, R. E. (1988). 'On the Mechanics of Economic Development', *Journal of Monetary Economics*, 22: 3–42.

—— (1993). 'Making a Miracle', *Econometrica*, 61: 251–72.

Mesa-Lago, C. (1991). 'Social Security and Prospects for Equity in Latin America', World Bank Discussion Paper no. 140, World Bank, Washington, DC.

Midgley, J. (1984). *Social Security, Inequality and the Third World* (Chichester, John Wiley).

Mosley, P., Huson, J., and Horrell, S. (1987). 'Aid, the Public Sector and the Market in Less Developed Countries', *Economic Journal,* 97: 616–41.

Mulgan, G. and Murray, R. (1993). *Reconnecting Taxation* (London: Demos).

Musgrave, R. A. (1959). *The Theory of Public Finance* (New York: McGraw-Hill).

—— (1969). *Fiscal Systems* (New Haven: Yale University Press).

Newbery, D. M. G. and Stern, N. H. (eds.) (1987). *The Theory of Taxation for Developing Countries* (New York: Oxford University Press).

Pauly, M. V. (1986). 'Taxation, Health Insurance and Market Failure in the Medical Economy', *Journal of Economic Literature*, 24: 629–75.

Sachs, J. D. (ed.) (1989). *Developing Country Debt and Economic Performance*, i–iii (Chicago: University of Chicago Press).

Samuelson, P. (1954). 'The Pure Theory of Public Expenditure', *Review of Economics and Statistics*, 36: 387–9.

Sargent, T. J. and Wallace, N. (1981). 'Some Unpleasant Monetarist Arithmetic', *Federal Bank of Minneapolis Quarterly Review*, 5(3): 15–41.

Sen, A. K. (1972). 'Control Areas and Accounting Practices: An Approach to Economic Evaluation', *Economic Journal*, 82: 486–501.

—— (1987). *The Standard of Living* (Cambridge: Cambridge University Press).

Stern, N. H. (1991). 'Public Policy and the Economics of Development', *European Economic Review*, 35: 241–71.

Stokey, N. (1991). 'Human Capital, Product Quality and Growth', *Quarterly Journal of Economics*, 106: 587–616.

Tait, A. A. (1988). *Value Added Tax: International Practice and Problems* (Washington, DC: IMF)

Tanzi, V. (1987). 'Quantitative Characteristics of the Tax Systems of Developing Countries', in Newbery and Stern (1987).

—— (1991). *Public Finance in Developing Countries* (Aldershot: Edward Elgar).

Tirole, J. (1994). *The Internal Organization of Government* (Oxford: Clarendon Press).

UNDP (1994). *Human Development Report* (Oxford: Oxford University Press).

van de Walle, D. and Nead, K. (eds.) (1994). *Public Spending and the Poor*, World Bank, Washington, DC.

World Bank (1986). *Poverty and Hunger* (Washington, DC: World Bank).

World Bank (1988). *World Development Report 1988* (New York: Oxford University Press).

World Bank (1990). *World Development Report 1990* (New York: Oxford University Press).

—— (1993*a*). *The East Asian Miracle* (New York: Oxford University Press).

—— (1993*b*). *World Development Report 1993* (New York: Oxford University Press).

13

Swimming against the Tide: Strategies for Improving Equity in Health

NANCY BIRDSALL AND ROBERT HECHT

13.1. Introduction

A major objective of developing country governments and of donor agencies, stated repeatedly in their policy documents and speeches, is achieving greater equity in health. Chile's constitution, for example, states that the government has an obligation to 'protect free and egalitarian access to actions that promote, protect, restore health and rehabilitate the health status of individuals' (Chile, 1992). The World Health Organisation's most recent report on implementation of 'Health for All by the Year 2000' concludes by advocating a new policy framework for 'ensuring equity in health through more effective inter-sectoral health promotion and protection; and pursuing equality in access to primary health care . . .' (WHO, 1992).

This concern for achieving greater equity in health is based largely on the view, now widely held in most societies, that everyone should have access to basic health care independently of their ability to pay for it.[1] Put another way, the tolerance level for inequality in health is lower in most societies than the tolerance level for inequality in income. It is probably lower than the tolerance level for inequalities in education, too, since differences in health are so much more, literally, a matter of life and death.

But the reality in virtually every society is far removed from this objective: the poor die earlier and are ill more often. In this chapter, we aim to show that this cruel reality is not very surprising: it is the predictable outcome of the usual alignment of economic and political forces, which like a powerful ocean current constrains the extent to which public resources can and will go to the poor. Awareness of this powerful current should not, however, be a cause for

---

[1] It may also stem, of course, from the growing recognition that better health care can accelerate economic growth by improving productivity at work and learning in school, and can help reduce poverty directly and indirectly. In this paper, we start from the premise that there is also an independent political and social objective of achieving equity.

pessimism and inaction. On the contrary, awareness is the only sensible starting point for designing and implementing realistic policies and programmes to swim against the tide.

The first issue we face is the measure of equity itself. There is little agreement on how to measure equity—whether by actual health outcomes across different groups, by utilization of services, or by access itself—and there are currently few data for any of these measures, within or across countries. We argue that the simplest and most useful measures of equity from a policy-making point of view are access to services, and the cost of publicly financed services consumed by different income groups; these measures are conservative, in that they generally register less inequality than do indicators of health outcomes (Section 13.2). We then review what little evidence there is within countries on equity using these measures (Section 13.3); and discuss why public policies in health (as well as in education) usually favour the wealthy at the expense of the poor (Section 13.4). We close (Section 13.5) with an analysis of the cases of certain countries that have achieved a more equitable distribution of public resources for health, and identify some lessons for reform strategies elsewhere.

13.2. Measuring Equity in Health

For most policy-makers, and for the general public, 'improving equity' means working towards greater equality in health outcomes or status among all the individuals in a country, regardless of the income group to which they belong. Such equality is far from being a reality in developing countries today—on the contrary, health status differs dramatically according to income level. In Indonesia, India, and Kenya child mortality is higher in states or provinces with larger proportions of poor people. Within cities, there are large differences in child survival between rich and poor neighbourhoods (see Fig. 13.1). In Madurai, the second largest city in India's Tamil Nadu State, children in the poorest households were more than twice as likely to suffer from serious physical or mental disabilities as children from slightly better-off households. In Porto Alegre, Brazil, child mortality in poor households in 1980 was twice the level for wealthier families.

Differences in health outcomes across income groups, however, are likely to exaggerate differences in inputs of public resources to health across income groups. Health outcomes are in fact 'produced' by households, using a combination of inputs, including benefits of public health services but also housing, food and nutrition, sanitation practices, exercise, smoking and other habits, and so on. Many of these inputs are in turn related to the education of household members; many are accidental inputs to health in that other objectives may largely govern their use or lack of use. For many reasons, high-income households are likely to 'produce' more and better health than low-income households, since their members tend to be better educated and

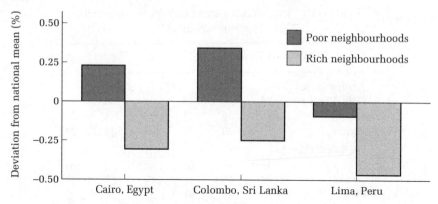

FIG. 13.1   Child mortality in rich and poor neighbourhoods in selected
metropolitan areas, late 1980s

Note: Child mortality indices for each neighbourhood are calculated by dividing the observed number of deaths among children of women in the sampled households of a neighbourhood by the expected number (given the distribution of women by the length of time they have been bearing children and the national average child mortality levels at each duration of childbearing). Percentage deviations from the national average are obtained by subtracting 1 from a neighbourhood's index and multiplying the result by 100. Neighbourhoods in each city were ranked according to the proportion of houses with concrete floors. Poor neighbourhoods were the lowest 25 per cent in the rankings; rich neighbourhoods were the top 25 per cent.

Source: World Bank (1993*a*: 40).

their higher incomes can purchase more food and better water and sanitation.[2] In high-income countries in some periods, the very rich, able to overfeed themselves into obesity and to smoke more, may have suffered some health disadvantages. Today, however, with more widespread understanding of how health is maintained, the rich virtually everywhere combine more education and more income with better access to information about the causes of good health to ensure better health outcomes than the poor enjoy—and this would be true even if there were no systematic differences across income groups in access to health services *per se*. Indeed, in a few countries the rich may not rely on public services at all, instead purchasing medical services directly from private providers. In these countries, even if all public resources for health were spent entirely on the poor, the rich could still end up with better health outcomes.

If the problem with measuring differences by health outcome is that many other factors affect outcomes besides health services, why not measure outcomes once individuals are sick? Do individuals with the same health problems fare systematically differently depending on their income? Again, there is strong evidence of major gaps between rich and poor in developing countries in treatment for identical health conditions. In rural parts of Côte d'Ivoire, Ghana, and Peru, individuals in rich and poor households have

---

[2] Behrman and Deolikar (1988) present an economic model that incorporates the household production of health.

TABLE 13.1   Percentages seeking care for illness or injury,
by income quintiles

	1	2	3	4	5	all
Rural quintiles						
Côte d'Ivoire	23	35	49	39	44	36
Ghana	26	39	41	46	46	41
Peru	20	20	30	34	39	29
Urban quintiles						
Côte d'Ivoire	49	58	63	65	64	60
Ghana	40	46	55	58	59	52
Peru	35	44	48	53	57	48

Source: Baker and van der Gaag (1993: 384).

TABLE 13.2   Vaccination coverage of children under 5 in Peru, by
mother's education, 1984 (%)

	None	Some primary	Complete primary	Secondary	Higher
National total	16.2	26.7	42.2	55.8	65.3
Urban	34.4	43.5	50.2	58.5	65.5
Rural	11.8	15.1	26.8	36.0	61.0

Source: Musgrove (1986: 325–35).

roughly equal chances of being ill at any given time; but as shown in Table 13.1, of those who fall ill, individuals in wealthy families are about twice as likely to obtain care. In rural Peru in 1984, children in families in which the mother had secondary or university education (with education status closely correlated with income) were between three and six times more likely to be vaccinated than in families in which the mother had no education (see Table 13.2).

These measures are also, unfortunately, likely to underestimate true differences across income groups in access to health care. Even for a given sickness, the poor are less likely to acknowledge that they are sick; and when sickness is acknowledged, the poor are still less likely to use available services than the rich.[3] The tendency of the poor to minimize sickness (or of the rich to

---

[3] Baker and van der Gaag (1992) report systematic differences in the extent to which different income groups report sickness, using data from household surveys in several different countries. Though not new, their finding of the same pattern in different countries is convincing. It is also well-known that women are systematically less likely to report themselves sick than are men—another apparent instance of differences across groups.

exaggerate it) is generally assumed to reflect different expectations of what is normal and of the efficacy of individual actions. The tendency of the poor to utilize available services less, even when sickness is acknowledged, is not surprising since the use of services, even if the services themselves are free, usually involves other costs, e.g. time lost from work and transportation. In short, for reasons that have nothing to do with health services, the poor are less able to 'produce' good health outcomes, and are less likely to utilize health services that are available to them.

These two realities lead to two conclusions. First, differences in health outcomes across income groups exaggerate differences in policy 'effort' by an amount that is unknown and changes over time. Therefore measures of equality in terms of public resources, to be comparable over time or across countries, must be restricted to simple measures of public expenditures per person or of physical access, independent of demand. Such measures also have the advantage of being relatively conservative; i.e., they minimize inequality. Second, it is clear that equality in health outcomes requires much higher public spending on the poor per person than on the rich.

This second point has interesting implications for policy. For example, the 1993 *World Development Report* (World Bank 1993*a*) places substantial emphasis on the point that many factors outside the health sector, especially household income and education, influence health outcomes.[4] At the same time, the *Report* concludes that countries can greatly improve health outcomes by making available a minimum package of highly cost-effective public health and clinical services—the costs of which are not presumed to vary at all across households within countries or across countries (except for differences in supply costs). The estimated costs ($12 in low-income and $22 in middle-income countries) are underestimates to the extent they are based on average costs of current supply, and fail to take into account the additional costs of generating demand and subsidizing utilization by poor households.

In the remainder of this chapter, however, we focus on the first point: comparable measures of health equity across countries, and the implications of this more conservative measure of equity for policy.

13.3. Evidence of Inequity:
Public Expenditures and Physical Access

The increase in household surveys in the last two decades in developing countries provides a rich new source of systematic data on differences in physical access to health services for different income groups. These data tell the same story virtually everywhere: access to basic health care is unequal, with the poor having much less access to simple, cost-effective services. Data

---

[4] Ch. 2 of the report is entirely devoted to this point (World Bank 1993*a*: 37–51).

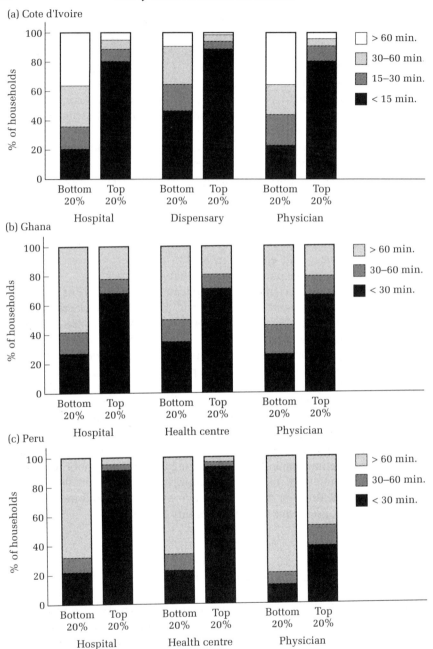

FIG. 13.2   Travel times to various types of health centre in three developing
countries (Nationally based expenditure deciles)
(*a*) Côte d'Ivoire   (*b*) Ghana   (*c*) Peru

Source: authors' calculations, based on World Bank Living Standards Survey data.

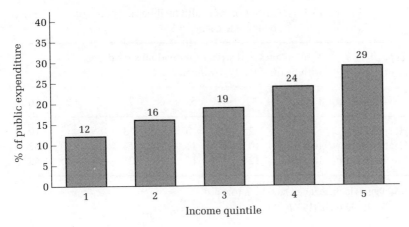

FIG. 13.3   Public spending for health in Indonesia, 1990
Source: World Bank (1993*b*: 33).

gathered through the World Bank's Living Standards Measurement Survey project (LSMS) show this result for Côte d'Ivoire, Ghana, and Peru (see Fig. 13.2). The differences between rich and poor are most dramatic in Peru, where nearly two-thirds of low-income families have to travel for more than an hour to reach a primary care provider; by contrast, more than 95 per cent of wealthy households are located less than half an hour from their primary provider. In Côte d'Ivoire the disparities are also striking. Even in Ghana, where primary care centres are more widely distributed throughout the country, about half of the poor are more than an hour from such facilities, compared with less than 20 per cent of the better-off.

Data on public expenditures can also provide a good measure of health equity. Early studies by Meerman on Malaysia (1979) and Selowsky on Colombia (1979) showed how household survey data on utilization of services and household expenditures on services could be used to study the incidence of public expenditures on health and other public programmes by income group. While these studies discuss the role of demand in the utilization of services across income groups, estimations of public subsidies nevertheless are based on utilization of services, a measure that is highly sensitive to differing levels of demand.

Recent data from Indonesia show a highly skewed distribution of public monies in 1990: the bottom 20 per cent of households received only 12 per cent of public spending for health, while the top fifth obtained nearly 30 per cent of public expenditures (see Fig. 13.3) (World Bank 1993*b*). As with the earlier studies, however, these results reflect in part differences across income groups in the demand for and use of publicly financed services.

A result from a 1991 national household survey in Indonesia (Table 13.3) is more revealing: families in the top income deciles reside on average in areas

TABLE 13.3	Distribution of health facilities in Indonesia
by income decile, 1986[a]

Type of health facility	% of villages in district of individual's residence with health facility, by income decile									
	1	2	3	4	5	6	7	8	9	10
Hospital	2	2	2	2	3	3	3	5	7	10
Health centre	10	10	10	11	11	11	14	16	23	32
Private doctor	10	11	12	14	15	18	21	26	35	48

[a] All figures in these tables have been rounded.
Source: World Bank (1993*b*: 18).

where the density of primary care centres and private doctors is around three
to five times greater on average than in areas inhabited by the poor. During
the 1980s the Government of Indonesia had made a major effort to reduce
even greater earlier inequities by building more health centres and health
posts in low-income areas of the country. As a result, the share of the poor
falling ill in rural Java who used modern health providers (doctor, hospital,
primary care centre, polyclinic, paramedic) rose from 47 per cent in 1978 to
55 per cent a decade later. However, possibly because of the factors affecting
health production in the household, and demand for health services, the gap
between rich and poor remained large: the share of those from wealthy rural
households falling ill who used modern providers was nearly 73 per cent in
1987. And for Indonesia as a whole, individuals in the highest rural income
decile made more than twice as many annual visits to modern providers as
those living in the lowest decile (3.00 versus 1.41), including one and a half
times as many visits to a primary health centre (1.17 versus 0.77) (van de
Walle 1992).

Comprehensive national data on the incidence of government spending by
income groups is scarce. Two datasets that are available (Costa Rica and
Malaysia) show government spending that favours the poor, but the more
common pattern is of bias towards the wealthy:

1. In South Africa, public subsidies to the wealthiest 15 per cent of families
   covered by private health insurance, in the form of tax relief, in 1990
   amounted to nearly a fifth of all public spending for health—without
   counting direct government expenditures for the wealthy (Broomberg
   1992).
2. In Zambia, more than 20 per cent of the Ministry of Health budget in
   the late 1980s went to a single teaching hospital serving the population
   of the capital city, whose inhabitants had incomes far above the national
   average.

3. In the Northwest Frontier Province of Pakistan, nearly 27 per cent of the provincial health budget for 1991–2 was earmarked for two teaching hospitals (Smithson, 1993).
4. In Brazil in the mid-1980s, nearly 80 per cent of all public spending for health was devoted to largely curative, high-cost hospital care concentrated in urban areas and especially in the affluent southern part of the country. Households in the top income quintile received about 38 per cent of public subsidies for health (World Bank 1988).
5. In Peru in 1984, the Lima health region consumed nearly 47 per cent of the government's budget for patient-related care, even though the relatively affluent capital region had only 32 per cent of the country's population (Musgrove, 1986).
6. In many Latin American countries, ministry of health spending appears to be fairly progressive because only the poor use subsidized government health centres and hospitals. But when this distributional pattern is combined with the large public subsidies to social-security-based health care for the middle classes, total government expenditure for health is again weighted strongly towards the better-off (Mesa-Lago 1991).

Recent analysis of data collected from household surveys in rural Kenya (Dayton and Demery 1994) tells a story similar to the one from Indonesia (see Fig. 13.4). Overall, the distribution of public subsidies to health care is regressive: even within rural areas, the bottom quintile receives only 14 per cent of the total health subsidy, compared with 24 per cent for the top rural quintile. The average subsidy for households in the bottom 10 per cent of rural income is less than half the subsidy for households in the top rural decile. This skewed pattern is the result of significantly higher use by the upper-income rural households of hospital-based services, for which the unit

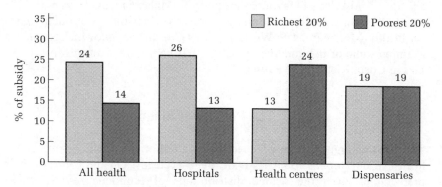

FIG. 13.4 Share of health subsidy targeted to the poor, rural Kenya, 1993 financial year
Source: Dayton and Demery (1994: 17).

subsidy is also much greater than for clinic or dispensary-based care. By contrast, the distribution of government health subsidies through the lower-level facilities (health centres and dispensaries) shows a more progressive pattern. The incidence of health centre subsidies, for example, is estimated to be 24 per cent for the bottom rural quintile and 13 per cent for the top rural quintile.

Data indicating disproportionately large hospital expenditures in major cities do not necessarily signify inequity, for two reasons. First, most such expenditures potentially benefit all parts of the population, including the rural poor who can in principle travel to exploit hospital care when their medical needs require it. Second, most of the most cost-effective health programmes that government can finance do not require hospital stays. Once all these cost-effective programmes are fully available to the entire population, they may reasonably take up only a small portion of overall public spending—and the remainder of such spending, for critical referral care, may reasonably occur in urban hospitals and with high unit costs could constitute a large portion of total spending. However, wherever the most basic services are not fully accessible to the rural poor—as is the case in Kenya, Pakistan, and Peru—a high proportion of public resources going to urban hospitals should suggest a problem of inequity. Coupled with other information of the type reported above, indicating lower demand and utilization of all kinds of public health services among the poor, and much worse health outcomes among the poor, the data on heavy concentrations of public spending on urban hospitals at the least amount to a strong warning signal of inequity.

As mentioned above, data from Costa Rica and Malaysia show a different pattern—one of public expenditures favouring the poor. In Costa Rica in 1986, 28 per cent of government health spending accrued to the poorest fifth of households, while just 11 per cent went to the wealthiest quintile (World Bank 1990). Even when these shares are adjusted for the fact that the average poor household had more members than the average wealthy family, public spending for health still favoured the poor. In Malaysia, data from both 1978 and 1990 show a similar continuing progressive distribution of public funds for health (Meerman 1979; World Bank 1992*a*). In the following section, we examine some of the underlying factors that help to explain this 'pro-poor' bias in Costa Rica and Malaysia.

13.4. The Politics of Inequity[5]

The predominant pattern of unequal distribution of public resources for health in developing countries is no mere accident. On the contrary, it is predictable, given the related distributions of economic resources and political power in these countries. The explanation for this inequity can be

---

[5] The discussion in this section is from Birdsall and James (1993).

understood in the context of public choice theory, which provides a positive model of what the government will do, under the assumption that the chief agents act to maximize individual utility rather than social welfare.[6] According to the theory, politicians and bureaucrats seek not to optimize economic efficiency but rather to maximize their own chances of getting re-elected and staying employed; similarly, individuals use governments to maximize their own income by creating and protecting market positions and capturing publicly financed services and transfers.

Politicians and political parties have some discretionary power because of barriers to entry and because they are in a position to shape as well as respond to people's tastes and preferences. At the same time, they must act in a way that deters threats from potential competitors, and this limits the scope of their monopoly power. Where democracy does not exist in developing countries, a similar process can occur with even fewer political checks on the use of government resources to benefit the already powerful.

The allocation of resources resulting from public choice politics is often inefficient, for several reasons. First, in a setting of imperfect information, people may not know the degree and direction of redistribution going on. If well-defined groups know they are 'losers', they are more likely to mobilize and foment opposition to existing policies; therefore the 'gainers' benefit from perpetuating a 'veil of ignorance'. Second, the real costs of publicly produced goods may be above minimal levels, because government imposes costs of bureaucracy and red-tape, often lacks competitive pressures for internal efficiency, and uses distortionary tax financing. Third, the diversion of entrepreneurial energies towards extracting a surplus from public agencies rather than towards productivity-enhancing market activities can impede private sector efficiency and growth.

This is not to say that there will be no redistribution to poorer groups under public choice theory. The extremes of poverty and socioeconomic immobility may raise fears of crime or revolution which will ultimately hurt the rich; historically, the provision of basic education, employment, or medical insurance have been ways of combating these problems. Also, since there are more poor people than rich, the desire to constrain the popularity of opposition political groups in a democracy leads to some redistribution to lower-income groups on grounds of expediency.

The social services sectors, including health and education, are arenas in which many of these forces play themselves out, as they involve a variety of quasi-public goods with different mixes of public and private benefits. The fact that health and education services generate social as well as private benefits, and their frequent designation as 'merit' goods, provide justification for government intervention along welfare theory lines. Yet once this

---

[6] This 'public choice' approach (see Buchanan *et al.* 1980) is sometimes referred to as 'new political economy' (NPE).

intervention begins, ostensibly to correct for market failures and to benefit
poor consumers, it is often seized by producer groups and the allocation of
resources diverted to a more private service mix that predominantly benefits
the rich. While rhetoric stresses the importance of avoiding price-rationing in
order to preserve access for the poor and thereby garner their political
support, alternative rationing mechanisms emerge, such as proximity to hospitals, knowledge of how to use the health system, and selection tests for
admission to free public universities which are equally income-biased.

Three politically influential groups often work actively to protect the flow
of government funds towards health services that benefit them directly, and
resist efforts to reallocate public resources for health to the poor. First,
government officials and politicians stand to gain from construction projects
for large hospitals. These major civil works are highly visible and popular,
often seen by the general public as evidence of government commitment to
medical care. At the local level, they are seen as evidence of the commitment
of local politicians to local needs, and often of the ability of these politicians
to command central resources for local programmes. Those seeking re-
election will point to new hospitals as among their major accomplishments.
High-ranking civil servants also benefit disproportionately from access to free
medical services in these major hospital facilities. At the extreme, many
developing countries allow senior officials and their families to obtain
sophisticated medical care abroad, in Europe or North America, at
government expense. Such medical 'evacuations' may even have a line in the
ministry of health budget.

Second, various middle-income consumer groups object strongly to any
erosion of their public subsidies for health services. These groups include professionals from the private sector and labour organizations. British colonial
policies in Ghana and Zambia, for example, dictated that public hospitals in
Accra and Lusaka, respectively, should provide free or heavily subsidized
medical care to the colonial elites. Once established, it has been extremely
difficult for policy-makers in those countries to shift this demand for medical
care to private hospitals or to charge full costs to the wealthy for care in the
government teaching hospitals. Labour unions seek to protect public subsidies in the middle-income countries of Latin America, where governments
extend financial support to social security-based health care through some
combination of tax relief, public contributions to insurance premiums, and
direct budgetary transfers to social security agencies (Mesa-Lago 1991). This
social-security-based care benefits only those in the formal sector.[7]

Third, the health workers and their respective labour organizations themselves are a major source of resistance to change. A shift in public funding to

[7] Several countries in Latin America, including Costa Rica (discussed below) and Brazil, have
recently extended some forms of social-security-based care, such as emergency hospital services,
to all, in an effort to eliminate at least the most glaring forms of a two-tier system. Colombia is
currently studying this option.

basic care would require that doctors and nurses be redeployed from large urban-based hospitals to smaller peripheral facilities in poor urban neighbourhoods and rural areas. Living and working conditions in these may well be more difficult than in the central hospitals; it is thus not surprising that health workers oppose these changes. Similarly, a reallocation of government spending for health would reduce the demand for publicly financed services from medical specialists. The specialists, through their professional associations, can be vocal and influential lobbyists for continued spending on sophisticated equipment (such as diagnostic imaging machines) and hospital facilities. As Hausmann (1993) points out in the case of Venezuela, '[Public sector] budgets have become an entitlement of producers, not the purchase of a service on behalf of consumers . . . Centralisation breeds unionisation and the consequence is a bilateral monopoly in which the government is bound to be the weaker member and will compromise the future to get over the present.'

For the above pattern of public subsidies to dominate, it is not necessary that all politicians and officials pursue only their own individual interests, nor that service providers and middle-class consumers have complete control of public revenue and expenditure patterns.[8] It is only necessary that these tendencies occur widely enough and often enough to minimize countervailing efforts to reach the poor—that is, to prevent what we have referred to above as 'swimming against the tide'.

The more equal the overall distribution of income, and the stronger the political voice of the poor, the easier it should be to design and implement pro-poor programmes. And indeed, as discussed below, pro-poor bias has and can emerge, particularly in countries with relatively low income inequality, or political systems that rely on the bottom third of the income distribution to maintain political legitimacy. Malaysia and Costa Rica, discussed below, as well as Sri Lanka, Korea, and the Indian state of Kerala, are examples of economies with relatively low income inequality and histories of broad-based social programmes to reach the poor. Communist countries, including China and Cuba, are examples of economies in which the political legitimacy of the ruling party has relied heavily on support of the working and peasant classes. Taiwan, Korea, Hong Kong, Singapore, Thailand, and Malaysia are other examples of countries in which political leaders, in the face of external and internal communist threats in the post-war period, have employed a variety of mechanisms to ensure that urban workers and the rural poor have shared in economic growth. These mechanisms included public housing programmes (Hong Kong and Singapore), extensive investment in rural infrastructure (Indonesia and Thailand), land reform (Korea and Taiwan), and heavy

---

[8] Toye (1991), e.g., in a lengthy discussion of the NPE, argues that many leaders have demonstrated powerful social consciences, and that the idea of the state as embodying common social goals has and will continue to affect resource allocation patterns.

emphasis on universal access to basic health services and primary education.[9] In all these countries of East Asia, the political situation required some swimming against the tide. These as well as other examples discussed below demonstrate that the public choice view of the world need not and does not always dominate.

13.5. Strategies for Reform

Faced with these powerful forces that maintain an inequitable distribution of public resources for health, some countries such as Costa Rica, Malaysia, and Zimbabwe have nevertheless achieved greater equity. How have they done so? We argue below that certain kinds of macroeconomic policies and political arrangements are important in determining a country's successful equity orientation in the health sector. We then point to the specific strategies and policy and programme instruments that some developing countries have adopted to enhance equity in health.

13.5.1. Macroeconomic and political determinants

One factor seems clear: the countries that have been most successful in achieving equity have experienced moderate to high economic growth rates, and have been able to tap that expanding resource base to improve health care for the population as a whole, including the poor. Such a 'shared growth' policy stance ensures that all segments of the population, including the poorest segments, benefit from and are able to participate in their country's economic growth. While growth does not automatically lead to a redistribution of basic public services, it is extremely difficult to achieve such a redistribution without it. Ghana, Peru, and Zambia are examples of countries that suffered from stagnating or even declining national income in the 1970s and 1980s. During this period, government spending for health was severely constrained. There was no incremental public funding for health that might have been allocated to primary care for the poor.

By contrast, Costa Rica's economy grew at an average of nearly 6 per cent a year in the 1970s and by 3 per cent in the 1980s. Malaysia did even better, growing at an average of 7 per cent a year during the two decades. Zimbabwe grew by 6 per cent annually in the first half of the 1980s, when the government's redistributive efforts in health were most vigorously pursued (World Bank 1992b). Other countries that made strong advances in improving equity in health, such as Chile, China, and Korea, have also been among the fastest growing economies in the developing world.

[9] For a discussion of this approach to 'shared growth' in East Asia, see World Bank (1993c). For the implications of income inequality, see Birdsall *et al.* (1994).

As mentioned in the previous section, political dynamics have been a key factor in those developing countries that have moved strongly towards, or struggled to maintain, equity in health. These pro-poor political forces take different forms, including the post-independence drive to redress earlier discrimination, as in Zimbabwe, and the search for legitimacy by a modernizing authoritarian regime, as in Korea (and Chile, too). In Malaysia, the government's consistently progressive approach to health was prompted by its objective of assisting the relatively disadvantaged ethnic majority and maintaining its important political base in the country's rural areas, where lower-income households are concentrated.

In Zimbabwe, the main impetus for change was national independence and majority democratic rule, starting in 1980. The newly independent government recognized that its political support came from low-income rural households that had previously been disenfranchized. Members of these rural households had joined the guerrilla movements that had fought against the previous regime. The new government sought to reward its supporters, and to redress earlier imbalances favouring the urban middle class, by investing heavily in the rehabilitation and construction of over 500 health centres, in the training of thousands of nurses to staff these facilities, and in basic programmes of immunization, antenatal care, and infectious disease control. There was a concomitant decision to place a moratorium on new investments in the central hospitals, which had benefited mainly the urban populations and especially the country's white minority.

At the same time that these governments shifted health spending towards the poor, they explicitly sought to preserve existing high-quality health services for middle and upper-income groups, thus maintaining broad political support for their reform efforts. In Zimbabwe, the two highest-quality tertiary care hospitals, in Harare and Bulawayo, respectively, received generous operating budgets from the government during the 1980s, even though new capital spending was severely restricted. At the end of the decade, the two hospitals still accounted for over 10 per cent of the Ministry of Health budget. In Costa Rica and Malaysia, middle-class families continued to have access to well funded health care in public facilities, even as coverage was extended to poor households. And the wealthy enjoyed the choice of opting out of the public system and utilizing private health care with its associated amenities—services financed privately with private insurance and/or out-of-pocket payments, and not with public funds.

13.5.2. Instruments for promoting equity

In this political environment favourable to more equitable access to health services and to more equitable distribution of public resources for health, the pro-equity governments have used several instruments to achieve this objective. First, at the same time that the wealthy were encouraged to shift much

of their consumption of health services to the private sector, these governments have sought consciously to reduce, eliminate, or altogether avoid
public subsidies to private financing and delivery of health care to the better-
off. These subsidies can take many 'hidden' forms, including government
budget transfers to social-security-based insurance and tax deductions on
employer and employer contributions to insurance schemes. In Zimbabwe,
the government has gradually reduced large subsidies to the better-off by
cutting down their deductions from income tax for premiums paid to private
health insurance. In Costa Rica, the wealthy must contribute to the social-
security-based health fund, even if they are served by private doctors and
hospitals.

Second, pro-poor governments have targeted public spending towards
health interventions and facilities serving primarily, but not exclusively, the
poor. Zimbabwe's focus on rural health facilities and district hospitals is a
good example of this type of targeting using simple geographical criteria.
Costa Rica's emphasis on basic primary and preventive care—immunizations, control of diarrhoeal disease, safe childbirth services—in the 1970s also
effectively targeted the poor, who suffered greater disease burden from
vaccine-preventable illnesses, diarrhoea, and childbirth complications than
did the rich. At the same time, these primary and preventive services also
benefited the middle class and the wealthy, thus helping to maintain political
support for these initiatives.

Third, at least in the case of middle-income countries, equitable access and
public spending for health have been pursued through the effective universalization of health insurance. In Costa Rica, for example, the democratically
elected government decided in the early 1980s to expand the social-security-
based health system to the entire population. This meant covering the 20 per
cent of Costa Ricans who had not previously been covered, and especially the
poor. Such a decision required the government to subsidize health services for
the poor, since their employment-based contributions to the social security
fund would not be large enough to meet the cost of services for them. At the
same time, ministry of health and social security hospitals were unified, and
all Costa Ricans became eligible for care in the same public hospitals,
managed by the social security agency.

Improved equity in health through the universalization of insurance was
also the course followed by Korea during the 1980s. In less than ten years, the
Korean government created a comprehensive national health insurance
system from scratch, forging together several hundred regional and industry-
based social insurance funds (modelled on the German 'sickness funds'). To
achieve truly universal coverage, the government chose to subsidize the
insurance funds for the roughly 8 per cent of the population that is disabled
or indigent (Yang 1991).

Chile has also pursued greater equity in health in recent years by establishing a single national health fund (FONASA), into which both payroll

deductions for social insurance and a general revenue subsidy for health care are deposited. All Chileans are eligible for health care financed from the FONASA, whether in the form of payment vouchers to private service providers or capitated and diagnostic-related payments to public sector providers. In this way, Chile has managed to reach the roughly 15 per cent of the population that until recently was not covered by social insurance (Chile 1992).

The successful experience of these reforming countries reveals several important lessons for other developing countries: the need for sustained economic growth to underpin policies for reallocation of public financing, the crucial political conditions that allow for fuller and more equal participation by all segments of the population, and the use of a gradual approach in which services for the wealthy and middle-class are not undercut, even when the share of public spending for these groups is declining.

These examples of successful countries also show that maintaining a more egalitarian health system is a constant struggle to 'swim against the tide'. There are always interests that would skew essential health services and public funds for health away from the poor. In Costa Rica and Zimbabwe, for example, pressures from government doctors to concentrate in the main tertiary hospitals in the largest cities and to acquire complex diagnostic equipment have been only partially resisted.

China is a good example of a country where the tide has been so strong in recent years that important egalitarian features of the health system have been eroded. In the 1960s and 1970s, China experienced one of the most dramatic advances in health of any developing country: child mortality, for example, declined from 210 to 85 per 1,000 live births between 1960 and 1975. Much of this progress was due to broad-based provision of public health services in the areas of insect vector control, immunization, improved hygiene, and family planning (Jamison 1985), backed by well-targeted public spending. At the same time, China's unique rural health insurance system, which covered about 500 million persons in the 1970s, guaranteed adequate funding for basic clinical services (e.g. treatment of tuberculosis and respiratory infections and safe pregnancy and delivery care) throughout the country. As an unfortunate consequence of China's economic liberalization programme of the past decade, government funding for public health has declined and the rural insurance system has now largely disintegrated (see Chapter 9 above). A recent study (World Bank 1992c) suggests that these new health policies have made the distribution of government spending for health in China more unequal and may be contributing to an increased incidence of easily treatable diseases such as tuberculosis.

The experience of the few reforming countries and of the much larger number of countries that have not yet shifted the balance of public resources for health towards low-income groups also points to the many serious obstacles to equity-oriented reforms. Politically influential groups that stand to lose from a change in the status quo will block changes. Achieving lasting reforms requires a combination of political enfranchisement, skilful coalition-building and negotiations, and enlightened leadership.

The generation and dissemination of information—for example on differences in health status, service utilization, total health spending, and government expenditures among different income groups in a given country—can be a crucial element in achieving reforms that improve equity. Policy-relevant information becomes an especially powerful force for change in societies with democratic political institutions, a broadly educated population, and a diverse and critical press. Under these circumstances, the analysis of health spending levels and patterns across geographical and income groupings can be a potent tool in the hands of reformers, and can be used to counteract the efforts of others (e.g. politicians in power, elite civil servants, professional associations) to obtain a disproportionate share of public resources for health. This has been the case in Chile and in some OECD countries such as the Netherlands, where equity-enhancing health reforms are currently taking place.

The international community can play a catalytic role in this process of change, by providing information and extending financing to soften the transitional costs of reform. External development agencies have stimulated information dissemination and debate on equity issues in health through their sponsorship of sectoral studies and policy seminars. Recent donor-supported studies of government spending for the social sectors in countries as geographically diverse as Indonesia, Kenya, and Uruguay are helping to shape the health policy debate in each of these countries. When these studies are embedded within broader country 'public expenditure reviews' that analyse both the incidence of taxation and spending, as in Argentina and the Philippines, they further enrich the debate.

Financial backing from development institutions has also facilitated and strengthened equity-oriented health reforms. In Costa Rica, the Inter-American Development Bank and the World Bank have financed improvements in the Ministry of Health and the social insurance agency that are designed to sustain the country's long-standing emphasis on primary care for all population groups, including the poor, and to ensure that all workers contribute their stipulated share of social insurance costs. In Zimbabwe, a coalition of European bilateral donors and the World Bank have helped to finance a substantial share of public investments in community and clinic-based services for poor rural groups. These international institutions and others should continue to support public policies and programmes for improved equity in the health sector in developing countries. However, the impetus for sustained reform will have to continue to come mainly from within the developing countries themselves.

References

Baker, J. L. and van der Gaag, J. (1993). 'Equity in Health Care and Health Care Financing: Evidence from Five Developing Countries', in E. van Doorslaer, A. Wagstaff, and F. Rutten (eds.), *Equity in the Finance and Delivery of Health Care: An International Perspective*. Oxford: Oxford University Press.

Behrman, J. and Deolikar, A. B. (1988). 'Health and Nutrition', in H. Chenery and T. N. Srinivasan (eds.), *Handbook of Development Economics*, i: 631–711, North Holland, Amsterdam.

Birdsall, N. (1993). 'Pragmatism, Robin Hood, and Other Themes: Good Government and Social Well-Being in Developing Countries', in L. C. Chen, A. Kleinman, and N. C. P. Ware (eds.), *Health and Social Science in International Perspective*. Harvard University Press, Cambridge, Mass.

—— and James, E. (1993), 'Efficiency and Equity in Social Spending: How and Why Governments Misbehave', in M. Lipton and J. van der Gaag (eds.), *Including the Poor*. New York: Oxford University Press.

—— Ross, D., and Sabot, R. (1994). 'Inequality and Growth Reconsidered'. Paper for the Annual Meetings of the American Economics Association, Boston, 3–4 January 1994.

Broomberg, J. (1992), 'Aspects of Health Care Financing in South Africa', unpublished paper.

Buchanan, J. M., Tollison, R. D., and Tullock, G. (1980), *Towards a Rent-Seeking Society*, College Station: Texas A & M University Press.

Chile, Government of (1992). *Health Care Situation and Health Care in Chile*. Santiago: Ministry of Health.

Dayton, J. and Demery, L. (1994). *Public Health Expenditure and the Rural Poor in Kenya*. Washington, DC: World Bank.

Hausmann, R. (1993). 'Sustaining Reform: What Role for Social Policy?' in C. Bradford Jr (ed.), *Redefining the State in Latin America*. Paris: OECD.

Jamison, D. (1985). 'China's Health Care System: Policies, Organisation, Inputs, and Finance'. In S. B. Halstead, J. A. Walsh, and K. S. Warren (eds.), *Good Health at Low Cost*. New York: Rockefeller Foundation.

Meerman, J. P. (1979). *Public Expenditure in Malaysia: Who Benefits and Why*. New York: Oxford University Press.

Mesa-Lago, C. 1991. 'Social Security and Prospects for Equity in Latin America'. World Bank Discussion Paper no. 140. Washington, DC: World Bank.

Musgrove, P. (1986). 'The Measurement of Equity in Health'. *World Health Statistics Quarterly*, 39: 325–35.

Rosero-Bixby, L. (1985). 'Infant Mortality Decline in Costa Rica'. In S. B. Halstead, J. A. Walsh, and K. S. Warren (eds.), *Good Health at Low Cost*. New York: Rockefeller Foundation.

Selowsky, M. (1979). *Who Benefits from Government Expenditure? A Case Study of Colombia*, World Bank Research Publication. New York: Oxford University Press.

Smithson, P. (1993). *Public Sector Health Financing and Sustainability in Pakistan*. London: Save the Children Fund (UK).

Toye, J. (1991), 'Is There a New Political Economy of Development?' in C. Colclough and J. Manor (eds.), *States or Markets? Neo-Liberalism and the Development Policy Debate*. Oxford: Clarendon Press, pp. 321–38.

van de Walle, D. (1992). 'The Distribution of the Benefits from Social Services in Indonesia, 1978–87'. World Bank Working Paper no. 871, Washington, DC.

World Bank (1984). *China: The Health Sector*, World Bank Country Study no. 4664–CH. Washington, DC: World Bank

—— (1988). *Brazil: Public Spending on Social Programs: Issues and Options*, Report no. 7086–BR. Washington, DC: World Bank.

—— (1990). *Costa Rica: Public Sector Social Spending*, Report no. 8519–CR. Washington, DC: World Bank.

—— (1992a). *Malaysia: Fiscal Reform for Stable Growth*, Report no. 10120. Washington, DC: World Bank.

—— (1992b). *Zimbabwe: Financing Health Services*, Report no. 8100–ZIM. Washington, DC: World Bank.

—— (1992c). *China: Long-Term Issues and Options in the Health Transition*, Report no. 11269. Washington, DC: World Bank.

—— (1993a). *Investing in Health: The 1993 World Development Report*. New York: Oxford University Press.

—— (1993b). *Indonesia: Public Expenditures, Prices, and the Poor*, Report no. 11293–IND. Washington, DC: World Bank.

—— (1993c). *The East Asian Economic Miracle: Economic Growth and Public Policy*. New York: Oxford University Press.

World Health Organisation (1992). *Implementation of the Global Strategy for Health for All by the Year 2000: Second Evaluation*. Geneva: WHO.

Yang, B.-M. (1991). 'Health Insurance in Korea: Opportunities and Challenges'. *Health Policy and Planning*, 6(2): 119–29.

Index

Pauly, M. V. 109, 233, 326
payroll tax for cost recovery in education
79–80
Peachey, D. K. 115
Péano, S. 190
Perraton, H. 287
Peru:
  cost recovery: in education 70; in health
  52
  health: equity in services 349–50; expenditure 8, 355, 360; hospital expenditure
  356; travel times to health centres 352–3;
  vaccinations 350
  VAT in 323
Phijaisanit, W. 100
Philippines:
  education: cost recovery in 73; differences
  between private and public 138; returns
  to, declining 69
  health: equity in 364; expenditure 7
Postlethwaite, T. 289
poverty:
  and equity in health services 348–9, 357;
  targeted spending 362
  and expenditure reform 330
  in rural China 227
Prescott, N. 224
Preston, R. 192, 200
Price, M. 265
private education:
  achievement differences with public education 129–38; in developed countries
  129–31; in developing countries 131–3;
  multi-level models of 134–7
  cost effectiveness, *see* cost effectiveness
  enrolment, Indonesia 171, 173
  financing 166–8
  unit costs of 137–8
private health care 93–123
  allocative efficiency in 98–9
  and consumer choice 97–8; evidence of
  107–8
  efficiency in 95–6; evidence of 100–3; and
  market failure 101–3; and public care,
  comparisons 100–1
  equity in 96–7; evidence of 103–5
  externalities in 98
  government influence on 108–13; market
  structure 108–10; regulation framework
  110–12; socioeconomic conditions
  112–13
  government regulation 113–18; evidence
  116–17; strategy 114–16
  quality of 95–6; evidence of 100–3
  resources in 97; evidence of 105–7
  technical efficiency in 98–9
privatization of health care 103–5, 106
production function in education 276–9
Propper, C. 118

Psacharopoulos, G. 64, 65, 76, 131, 152, 200
public choice theory and equity in health services 357
public education:
  achievement differences with private education 129–38; in developed countries
  129–31; in developing countries 131–3;
  multi-level models of 134–7
  cost effectiveness, *see* cost effectiveness
  financing 166–8
  Indonesia: distance to school 170–1; enrolment 171–2; family expenditure on
  175–6; subsidies 177, 178
  unit costs of 137–8
public expenditure:
  and cost recovery in health services 39–40
  and equity in health services 351–6
public financing of health and education
  21–4
public sector health services, efficiency of
  245–74
  bureaucratic approaches 251–9; and
  decentralization 251; drugs, use of 257;
  financing changes 254; management
  improvements 255–8; and NGOs 253;
  planning procedures 255; policy
  improvements 254–5; privatization of
  tertiary facilities 252–3; reorganization
  of ministries 252; staffing 256–7; structural changes 251–3
  cost effectiveness of 247, 248
  inefficiencies in 249–50
  market approaches 259–70; competition:
  providers 262–4, purchasing 260–2;
  contracting 263–4; contracting systems
  268–70; managing contracts 266–7; and
  market structure 265–6; success, conditions for 264–8; transaction costs 260
  operating efficiency 247
  technical efficiency 247
Purohit, B. C. 248

quality:
  of community education 193–5
  of private health care 95–6; comparisons
  with public care 101; evidence of 100–3
  in public sector health services 258

racial communities 186, 197
Rai, V. 248
Rasmusson, R. 194, 200
Raudenbush, S. W. 140
Ravallion, M. 307, 325
regulation of private health care 113–18
  evidence 116–17
  government influence on 110–12
  strategy 114–16
resource use in private health care 97
  evidence of 105–7